— *POWER* —

MANCHESTER
UNIVERSITY PRESS

— *POWER* —
A philosophical analysis

second edition

PETER MORRISS

Manchester University Press

Manchester and New York

distributed exclusively in the USA by Palgrave

First edition published 1987 by Manchester University Press

This edition published 2002 by
Manchester University Press
Oxford Road, Manchester M13 9NR, UK
and Room 400, 175 Fifth Avenue, New York, NY 10010, USA
www.manchesteruniversitypress.co.uk

Distributed exclusively in the USA by
Palgrave, 175 Fifth Avenue, New York,
NY 10010, USA

Distributed exclusively in Canada by
UBC Press, University of British Columbia, 2029 West Mall, Vancouver, BC,
Canada V6T 1Z2

British Library Cataloguing-in-Publication Data
A catalogue record for this book is available from the British Library

Library of Congress Cataloging-in-Publication Data applied for

ISBN 0 7190 5996 8 *paperback*

This edition first published 2002

10 09 08 07 06 05 04 03 02   10 9 8 7 6 5 4 3 2 1

Typeset in Times
by Best-set Typesetter Ltd., Hong Kong
Printed in Great Britain
by Biddles Ltd, Guildford and King's Lynn

The not distinguishing where things should be distinguished,
and the not confounding where things should be confounded,
is the cause of all the mistakes in the world.

JOHN SELDEN

Contents

Figures and tables

FIGURES

TABLES

Acknowledgements

Many people have helped me during the years that I have been working on this topic. The most crucial were those friends who gave me support when I felt that the task was beyond me or was not worth doing at all. A formal acknowledgement to them would be an inappropriate way of expressing my feelings: my personal thanks should be delivered personally. But my many intellectual debts can, and should, be mentioned here.

Brian Barry and Michael Freeman first stimulated my interest in power when I was an undergraduate. Later, when I worked on the subject for a PhD, I was supervised first by Geraint Parry and then Hillel Steiner; it was under their guidance that this work grew from a few unconnected ideas into a book-length piece with an argument of its own.

Brian Barry, Joe Femia, Michael Freeman, Norman Geras, Alvin Goldman and Geraint Parry commented most helpfully on earlier versions of parts of this book. Many others, particularly my contemporaries at Manchester University, also helped in various ways to form my ideas.

Geoff Cupit, Bob Goodin, Ted Honderich, Michael Laver, Steven Lukes, David Miller, Alan Ryan and Hugh Ward all read an earlier – and very different – draft of this book in its entirety, and very kindly sent me their comments. It is in part because of these comments (and those from anonymous readers for various publishers) that this version is so different from the previous one. They, of course, bear no responsibility for the use I have made of their suggestions; nor do they necessarily agree with a word I say.

I am indebted to Peter James for his thorough copy-editing, and also for suggesting changes which considerably shortened this book.

Hillel Steiner not only read and commented on the previous book-length version, but also discussed my many preliminary drafts with me at length. I am deeply grateful for all the trouble that he has taken, and for the great help that he has been to me.

P. M.

Acknowledgements for the
second edition

Since writing the first edition of this book, I have moved to the Department of Political Science and Sociology at University College Galway (now renamed NUI, Galway). I am very glad to have found such a congenial home, and I am most grateful for the help of my new colleagues. I must single out the Head of Department (Chris Curtin) and also Mick Donnelly, Ricca Edmondson, Mark Haugaard, Donal Igoe, and Tony Varley.

Others who have provided intellectual assistance since the first edition include Brian Barry, Sven Berg, Keith Dowding, Marc Kilgour, Jack Nagel, and Joanna Price. Stephen Buckle, Geoff Cupit, Mark Haugaard, Moshé Machover, and Niall Ó Cíosáin have read sections of the Introduction, and saved me from many errors. That they have not saved me from more is my fault and not theirs. Moshé Machover has been particularly helpful in helping me to improve my understanding of voting power.

I am also grateful to Ray Offord for his thorough proofreading and copy-editing of the entire work, which, for technical reasons, had to be freshly typeset for this edition. Many minor improvements have been introduced as a result of his suggestions.

I am sad to have to say that my cat, who kept me company throughout most of my time working on *Power*, and who made an appearance on pp. 74–5, did not long survive the book's publication. She never did turn into a dog.

Introduction to the second edition

The first edition of *Power* was completed at the very end of 1985, by which time, I will confess, my interest in the topic of power was all but exhausted. Seeing the book through the press took another two years, which killed off what little enthusiasm I had left. So when the book finally emerged, I was happy to walk away from the topic, and I made no systematic attempt to keep up with the subsequent literature. I had said all I had to say, and left the book to speak for itself.

So producing this new edition has meant returning to look at 'power' after some fifteen years away from the subject. I first reread the book (and reviews), to see how much of it I can still stand by. To my genuine surprise, there is virtually nothing of substance that I wish to retract. Whilst the arguments could always be expressed differently, I have decided to leave the text unaltered apart from correcting a few typographical mistakes and updating some of the references. I remain worryingly unrepentant about the main theses; even fifteen years away from the topic has not made me wise enough to see the errors that are undoubtedly there.[1]

The next task was to search out, and read, the literature on the topic that has appeared since 1985. The searching part was surprisingly difficult, for whilst there are now many computerized databases that did not exist when I first did a literature search in the 1970s, they are all-but worthless: when one types in 'power' one is likely to get several hundreds of thousands of references, all but a handful of which will be quite irrelevant. I have tried various ways of doing a comprehensive search, but I am sure that I have missed a number of important recent works.

My search did show clearly, however, that there are now many different, and quite separate, subdisciplines that all claim to consider power but which pay no attention to each other – even, one might say, treat other approaches with contempt. Some of these subdisciplines are defined by their intellectual pedigree (for example the extensive recent literature in postmodernism, or that on bargaining theory). Others are characterized by their subject-matter, so that there are very broad fields of research (such as sociological theory, or international relations) that claim to put the concept of power at the centre of the subject.[2] This fragmentation into self-contained intellectual areas is perhaps just a reflection of our times, but it is brought out more starkly when they all use the same term, and yet use it in an amazing variety of different ways. I have neither the competence nor the interest to try to explore more than a handful of these attempts to describe 'power'. Perhaps a great work of synthesis is possible, and would tell us much; but this is not it.

The diversity of interests of those who write on power should perhaps be borne in mind when considering some (but by no means all) of the explicit criticisms made of arguments in this book. Some reviewers (not mentioned here) have been annoyed, and consequently dismissive, when I completely ignored their own areas of interest. But others, usually those who have engaged most closely with my efforts, have sometimes made the opposite mistake, and taken me to be doing more than I am doing. They have paid me the compliment of assuming that I must be interested in what they are interested in, and then criticized my arguments as inadequate ways of addressing their concerns. Such critics miss their mark, because they misunderstand what the arguments here are arguments *about*. It is therefore necessary sometimes to bear in mind the necessarily limited range of issues and approaches that I address.

Whilst my initial reaction to the recent literature was of its unhealthy fragmentation, I eventually uncovered a number of excellent, and provocative, discussions of power, which are discussed below. I have also found it encouraging that some of the main claims of the earlier part of the book – which were radical when I first made them – seem now to have become almost the orthodoxy. One such is the importance of avoiding what I call the vehicle and exercise fallacies (see Chapter 3). Several writers have followed me in abhorring one or both of these;[3] nobody (to my knowledge) has tried to argue that these are not fallacious; yet (as we shall see) that has not stopped people still committing these fallacies. It is now also probably the dominant view that power is best thought of as a capacity or disposition of some sort,[4] and that 'power-to' is more basic than 'power-over'.[5]

However, I now wish to add a sort of caveat to this last point: I do not think (and never did think) that the notion of 'power-over' can be removed entirely from our discourse; my point is rather to object to those who try to rephrase all talk of 'power-to' into a form of 'power-over'. Now that it is less important to fight this battle, I would give more space to discussing 'power-over'. I would do so all the more because recently Philip Pettit has developed a very strong argument about the importance of 'power-over' in our normative framework, in his book *Republicanism* (Pettit, 1997). This is of particular relevance to what I here call the context of social evaluation. When I introduce this context on pp. 40–1, I stress that power can enter in two ways: "we can be interested either in the extent to which citizens have the power to satisfy their own ends, or in the extent to which one person is subject to the power of another" (p. 40). This latter I characterize as a concern with being dominated or enslaved, but I say very little more about it. I now think that this silence is a mistake.

Pettit succeeds, I think, in articulating a sort of grievance; one which he thinks recent political theory has tended to overlook.

> The grievance I have in mind is that of having to live at the mercy of another, having to live in a manner that leaves you vulnerable to some ill that the other is in a position arbitrarily to impose; and this, in particular, when each of you is in a position to see that you are dominated by the other. . . . It is the grievance expressed by the wife who finds herself in a position where her husband can beat her at will, and without any possibility of redress; by the employee who dare not raise a complaint against an employer, and who is vulnerable to any of a range of abuses, some petty, some serious, that the employer may choose to perpetrate . . . .. (Pettit, 1997: pp. 4–5)

Pettit contrasts this emphasis with mainstream liberalism, which has not been particularly concerned (he thinks) with non-domination as such: for these liberals "there is nothing inherently oppressive about some people having dominating power over others, provided that they do not exercise that power and are not likely to exercise it" (Pettit, 1997: p. 9). Pettit's republican, by contrast, *is* very worried about such domination. For even when the power is *not* exercised, "the power-victim acts in the relevant area by the leave, explicit or implicit, of the power-bearer; it means that they live at the mercy of that person, that they are in a position of a dependant or debtor or something of the kind" (Pettit, 1997: p. 63; see also pp. 123–4). And a society in which some (many) people live at the mercy of others is a shameful one.

It is still deplorable when people are powerless (when they lack the power to do essential things), as I will illustrate below (sections II.ii and II.iii); but it is also deplorable when people are dominated. To investigate how extensive is this domination – to discover who is in the power of others – requires a concept of 'power-over' that is not reducible to 'power-to'. When we are evaluating societies, therefore, we must deploy both concepts of power.

I—CONCEPTS AND WORDS

As a further preliminary, I want to add to a few remarks I make in the final chapter (Chapter 25), about how to approach understanding concepts.

I must confess to being deplorably monolingual; I have little knowledge of languages other than English. Therefore, in this book, I draw only on English usage and interests. This is not a stunning defect: the book is, after all, written in English, and draws on a very extensive English-language literature. But it might be thought that I hold a sort of Victorian imperialist attitude to English: that it is such a peculiarly perfect language that we can, by examining it, uncover general truths. (A view perhaps best encapsulated in the alleged American fundamentalist assertion that English must be the best language, otherwise God would not have written the Bible in it.) I lay myself open to this charge all the more by my reliance on, and praise of, the *Oxford English Dictionary*, which has come under fire of late as an exemplar of precisely this Victorian linguistic nationalism (see Willinsky, 1994). I admit to being sometimes tempted by this error (if only because English is the only language in which I can think) but I do strive not to succumb to it.

More philosophically, there are an infinite number of ways of creating conceptual schemes and, in any one language, only a finite number of words. All languages, then, lack words for many of the possible concepts we could want to use. Further, it seems that different languages prioritize slightly different sets of concepts, presumably reflecting the interests or approaches of different linguistic communities. Exactly *why* languages include words for the concepts that they do seems to me to be a fascinating and, as far as I am aware, underexplored intellectual area. I cannot attempt to go into it here, of course. But what I am leading up to is the (surely uncontentious) claim that the word which is nearest to 'power' in languages other than English (and which is usually translated as 'power') might not encapsulate exactly the same set of concepts as the English word 'power' does. This is often explicitly recognized by translators: thus Weber's well-known definition of power starts, in the standard English translation, " 'power' (*Macht*) is . . ." (Weber, 1920: p. 152), precisely to indicate that 'power' is not (necessarily) an exact translation of '*Macht*'.

So what I say here about power is meant to be true only of 'power' in English (and any *exact* translations into other languages that might exist) and not of words in other languages that are close to 'power'. I had supposed that that would not really need saying, but it seems that it does.

One straightforward example of this mistake is made by Valeri Ledyaev, in an otherwise very thorough discussion of power (in which, it must be said, he mainly agrees with my analysis). Ledyaev has a passage in which he is arguing against my contention that 'power-to' is more central than 'power-over'. Amongst other arguments, he has the following: that in other languages "power" is more likely to be associated with *control over somebody*. For example, in Russian the term "power" [*vlast*] is usually used for the description of someone's ability to control (dominate, compel, influence) *others*, "power" is imagined as something that is "over" us, that limits our freedom, creates obstacles, etc. In the examples cited by Morriss [on pp. 32–3], Russians would prefer to use other terms . . .. (Ledyaev, 1997: p. 95)

I find this (truly) fascinating, but the last sentence (and my insertion of the Russian word '*vlast*') shows that it is hardly a counter-argument to my claim. If I am right about (the English word) 'power', then it is sometimes closer to these other Russian terms than it is to '*vlast*'. Clearly something resembling a complete analysis of power must include an extensive consideration of how the concepts represented by *vlast* (and Ledyaev's other Russian terms) work; and also *Macht* and many others. This would be a gargantuan task for any multi-lingual scholar, and (I think) a worthwhile one. As I have admitted, it is well outside my competence. But I don't think the existence of words in other languages that represent different sets of concepts undermines anything I say here about the concepts that *are* represented by the (English) word 'power'.

I want to use these ideas to look very briefly at Foucault. Some people have found it strange that a book on power should contain no mention at all of Foucault's writings; others might think that whilst I could get away with that gap in the original edition written in the early 1980s, this new introduction must have to look at his work in some detail. Anyone who thinks like that will be disappointed. There is a very simple reason for my avoidance of Foucault: I do not think he is writing about power at all, and I think this can be shown very easily. Certainly, several of Foucault's less sycophantic commentators have complained that his use of language is distorted.[6] But my main complaint here is not against Foucault himself, but against his translators into English.

Many years ago Raymond Aron wrote a well-known article, in which he pointed out that "French has two words to translate . . . 'power': '*pouvoir*' and '*puissance*'" (Aron, 1964: p. 255). These words, whilst both derived from a common Latin root, have, as one would expect, different uses.

'*Pouvoir*' . . . "merely denotes the action", whilst '*puissance*' . . . designates "something lasting and permanent". One has the *puissance* to do something, and one exercises the *pouvoir* to do it. It is for this reason that we talk of the *puissance* of a machine, and not its *pouvoir*. This distinction would therefore be roughly that between potential and act.[7]

Aron goes on to say that '*puissance*' is closer than '*pouvoir*' to the English 'power', precisely because it denotes a capacity and not just an action (Aron, 1964: p. 257).[8]

Foucault writes almost entirely about *pouvoir*, and uses '*puissance*' rarely, if at all. That, of course, is his privilege; and he undoubtedly says some interesting things about *pouvoir* (though I would disagree with many of them). But the English-language literature on "Foucault on power" seems to quite overlook this distinction between *pouvoir* and *puissance* and just translates '*pouvoir*', seemingly unproblematically, as 'power'. This often produces nonsense, which Foucault's followers then solemnly declare is some extraordinary new insight. Thus – to cite an example virtually at random – Foucault is translated into English as writing "power exists only when it is put into action" (Foucault, 1982b: p. 219). In this English translation this is just a crude example of the exercise fallacy (see pp. 14–17). However in French, according to Aron, this would certainly be true as written (about *pouvoir*), although quite false about *puissance*.[9] Hence I claim that the widespread belief that Foucault has anything to say about power (i.e. *puissance*, or something quite close to it) is simply based on a lax translation.

Having illustrated some of the complexities of taking a multi-lingual approach, I now want to turn back to English usage. In the remainder of this Introduction I will look at some recent writings, and consider how they bear on some of the claims I make in this book.

II—THE THREE CONTEXTS REVISITED

Early on in this book I ask, and attempt to answer, the question *why* we might want a concept of power. When I wrote the first edition, I thought that it was most surprising that no one else seemed to have wondered about this (p. 36); I am therefore encouraged that, whilst the book was going through the publication process, two others writers were also asking the same question. Since then it seems to have become almost obligatory.[10] I am further encouraged that most of the answers produced are along the same lines as the three contexts which I isolate in Chapter 6.

But some recent discussions have convinced me that notions of power are even more widespread than I used to think. I want to start by looking at the rather different work of two authors – Stephen Buckle and Amartya Sen – who *use* (rather than analyse) concepts of power, in ways that I do not explicitly mention in Chapter 6. Neither author – alas! – was aware of my book; yet I think both show rather well the importance of the approach adopted here, and also that there are some points on which I should amend my own analysis. And both show how central the concept of power is to our most important concerns.

II.i—Buckle on potential

Stephen Buckle has provided a very careful analysis of the nature of potentiality arguments, as used in discussions of the permissibility of abortion or of experimentation on human embryos.[11] The potentiality arguments in question go something like this. It is agreed that it is (in general) impermissible to kill adult human beings (leaving aside special cases, such as killing in self-defence or in a just war). The reason it is so impermissible must be that adult human beings have some quality, the possession of which makes killing them wrong: call this quality 'moral standing'. If it is by virtue of their moral standing that it is wrong to kill adult human beings, then it is also wrong to kill any other beings that have the same moral standing; conversely it is not wrong, in this way, to kill any other beings that lack this moral standing. Now it is very difficult to pin down exactly what this moral standing is, and the basis on which we can assert that it exists; but most think that it, whatever it is, must derive from a property that adult humans possess and (say) flies do not. Hence something like 'life' will not do: humans and flies share this property. Neither will a notion of 'human life' do, for this simply begs the question. If we reject unobservable theological entities such as immortal souls, the main candidates offered are something like a sophisticated consciousness, a sense of a self existing over time, or having a moral sense. For our purposes here it does not matter which such property we choose, for it is clear that embryos do not possess any of the main candidates. (Foetuses younger than eight weeks have no brain at all, and therefore must have a *less* developed consciousness than a fly.) If we try to ground the moral standing of an entity in some existing property that it has, then embryos clearly lack moral standing.

Those who reject this conclusion – and who have no wish to resort to mumbo-jumbo about unobservable souls – therefore have to resort to a potentiality argument. For it is clearly the case that a mature, adult, fly and a human embryo differ in one respect that is in the latter's favour: the embryo has the potentiality to develop into an adult human being (with moral standing), the fly does not. Hence the appeal of the potentiality argument. However, it has usually been thought of as suffering from a grave drawback, which is that we invariably treat things by the properties that they *have*, not the properties that they have the potential to acquire. As the argument goes, an acorn clearly has the potential to develop into a fine oak tree, but you cannot obtain a tree-preservation order on an acorn. Or a child of six has the potential to become an adult of eighteen, but must wait until actually becoming eighteen before being given the vote. And so on. So why should potentialities matter when it comes to determining moral standing? Is not the use of the potentiality argument simply a sign of desperation by those who wish to give embryos a status higher than that they deserve?

This is the background to Buckle's article. But Buckle argues that those who want to advance a potentiality argument could state it more carefully. For

> despite the dilemma just pointed out, the capacity to develop morally significant characteristics is indeed morally significant. . . . It could be argued that it is precisely capacities, in particular the capacities of individuals, which *are* morally significant; that moral behaviour is a matter of respecting the capacities of other beings.
>
> Briefly, . . . respect is due to an existing being because it possesses the capacity or power to develop into a being which is worthy of respect in its own right; and respect is due to such a being because it is *the very same being* as the later being into which it develops. (Buckle, 1988: p. 230; or Buckle, 1990: pp. 92–3)

If the potentiality argument is to work, then, what is involved is not, as both advocates and critics of the potentiality argument have too often thought, potentiality as a mere prediction about the future (that is, as a possibility or a probability) but potentiality as a currently existing power. In so far as it is a currently existing power – "the power possessed by an entity to undergo changes which are changes to itself, that is, to undergo growth or, better still, *development*" (Buckle, 1988: p. 233; or Buckle, 1990: p. 95) – then it is a morally relevant characteristic that is indeed possessed by a human embryo (and not by a fly). And in so far as it is a power, then the analysis of this book applies to it (or so, of course, I claim).

I want to suggest that applying the analysis of this book to Buckle's interpretation of the potentiality argument shows that it does have force, but a weaker force than most advocates would like. Buckle is certainly correct that most of the criteria of moral standing that have been offered refer to capacities or powers. Thus someone who is asleep does not lose her moral standing: her higher mental powers still give her higher moral standing than a fly, even though the (awake, active) fly might actually be *doing* rather more.[12] So when we have to decide on an entity's moral standing, we must do so on the basis of whether it possesses the relevant powers (whatever these are judged to be). The potentiality argument is, in this, no different from the standard approach to moral standing. It therefore cannot be quickly dismissed as erroneous in form.

But things look less promising if we examine more closely the sort of powers that are involved. We should notice, first, that the embryo's power to develop is not what I call a two-way power (pp. 24–5) or truly human power: it is not something that the embryo can exercise at will. It is a latent power (see pp. 57–9) that becomes an actual power if appropriate things are done to, or for, the embryo.[13] This latent power is, moreover, what I call a 'mere' disposition or a natural power (pp. 24–5, 27–8). It is thus somewhat too quick to say that we look at the embryo's powers when assessing its moral standing, just as we look at the adult human's powers: as I am at pains to stress throughout this book, there are many different sorts of powers, and what can be correctly said of one sort of power may not be appropriate to say of another sort. The sorts of powers that give moral standing are more likely to be 'two-way' powers than latent natural powers,[14] so some further argument is needed to establish that these latent powers are sufficient to establish moral standing.

Even if this further argument is not forthcoming, this in itself does not destroy the potentiality argument. I say, briefly, on pp. 103–4 (and explore in more detail below in section II.ii) that we often consider that we are under a moral imperative to develop (suitable) powers of others; there is no reason why such a moral imperative should not apply as much to developing the powers of embryos as of children and adults. But this would usually be taken as a much weaker moral requirement: what is normally called 'common morality' draws a sharp distinction between failing to actualize a latent power when we could do so (on the one hand) and *killing* someone (on the other); the former obligation is taken as much weaker.[15] If this gradation in moral arguments is accepted, then the potentiality argument might succeed in extending the desired *scope* of moral standing to embryos, but not the desired *strength* of that moral standing.

Let us next look more closely at the embryo's latent powers. Since they are 'mere' dispositions, my analysis of dispositions should apply here. In particular, crucial to the analysis of a disposition is what I call the *descriptive conditional* (pp. 61–2, 83–5): the circumstances in which the power can operate (or, in this case, the latent power can become an actual power). The embryo will develop and acquire the appropriate powers for moral standing if it is in certain conditions; it will not so develop in other conditions. When I discuss this on pp. 84–5, I say that the conditions appropriate for generic powers (the sort at issue here)[16] are some "set of *standard* conditions, and it is a matter of *convention* what is to count as standard" (p. 85). The first half of this quotation applies here; but I think the second cannot.

Buckle and I agree that what are to count as the relevant standard conditions is not an empirical question: we are not talking here about possibility or probability, so the potentiality argument is immune to statistical points about (say) the prevalence of spontaneous miscarriages. What matters is not what *will* happen to this embryo (or is likely to happen to it) if it is not interfered with; what matters is what its powers are in standard conditions.[17] Even if it has a very small chance of finding itself in circumstances that will allow it to develop fully, this does not diminish its current powers, and hence its moral standing. It is therefore also quite irrelevant to this argument whether the embryo is cosily ensconced in a woman's womb (and therefore could expect in the natural course of events to grow into a healthy baby), or is in a petri dish and about to be washed down the sink. The life-chances of the latter are much worse; but the moral standing of the two cannot differ (assuming that they are at the same stage of development).[18] In short what matters here are the embryo's abilities, not its ablenesses, to use my vocabulary (see Chapter 11).

But it would seem that in this sort of case we cannot say that what are to count as standard conditions is simply a matter of convention (as I do say on pp. 84–5). The *moral* status of someone must depend on something with a better moral grounding than that. Buckle states his proposal for the appropriate descriptive condition as follows: "An entity . . . has the power to become X . . . if it will become X . . . given circumstances *conducive to the operation*" of the factors that will lead it to become X.[19] That is almost to say that the entity has the power to become X if there are *any* circumstances in which it will become X.

Almost, but not quite: there are limitations. A (notorious) example in the literature is Michael Tooley's kitten example (Tooley, 1972: pp. 86–8, or Tooley, 1983: pp. 191–3) which runs as follows. You have a kitten which would naturally grow into an adult cat; such an adult cat would lack (let us agree, for the sake of argument) the properties that give moral standing. But if you inject this kitten with a magic chemical, it will grow into a cat with human levels of consciousness; that is to say, it *will* have the properties that give moral standing. Therefore this kitten (as yet not injected) has the potential to gain moral standing; therefore, via the potentiality argument, it now *has* moral standing. So, provided we have a suitable magic chemical, virtually everything will have moral standing.[20]

Buckle rejects this argument (he considers a similar one at Buckle, 1988: p. 253 n. 25) because the injection would *change* the powers of the kitten rather than realize them. Hence in the explanation of what I call the descriptive conditional, quoted above (text to n. 19), he includes a qualifying clause (which I omitted when I quoted the passage in the text) of "it will become X in virtue of the operation or expression of properties of its own" (Buckle, 1988: p. 247; or Buckle, 1990: p. 106).

So Buckle suggests that the appropriate descriptive conditional is to allow an entity moral standing if there are *any* circumstances at all in which it can acquire the appropriate powers, with the proviso that the powers acquired must be the realization of already-existing latent powers, rather than being new powers provided from outside.[21] For the purposes of assessing moral standing, this generosity might be appropriate, although it does require further argument.

In conclusion, Buckle has used a power-analysis of the potentiality argument to make it much stronger than it has been hitherto. However, I think that a careful analysis of the powers involved show the argument, even when thus strengthened, to be weaker than its advocates would like. For the purposes of this book, I hope to have shown that power is even more significant than I had thought, for we need a well-developed analysis of the concept of power in order to get to grips with issues as important as the morality of abortion and experimentation on human embryos. I think that the analysis in this book can do the job, but it does need to be suitably amended.

II.ii—Amartya Sen on capabilities

Amartya Sen's interests seem at first glance to be very different from Buckle's, but there is a connection, in that both are concerned with *development*: Buckle in the development of the embryo (as quoted above, p. xix), Sen in what is usually called developmental economics. Unlike Buckle, Sen does not explicitly talk of power as central to his concerns, so I need to sketch his approach briefly to justify my claim that he is, indeed, talking about power.[22]

Sen started by thinking about poverty, and the attempts to overcome it that can be called international development. Reflecting on this, he thought that we need some normative account of what this 'development' should be. The economists tend to equate development with increase in per capita Gross National Product, which is hopeless.[23] Sen then turned to proposals current philosophers have to offer, and rejected them all (for reasons I need not go into here). So he had to set to and produce his own account of what international development should seek to advance. However, if we remove the emphasis on "international development", we have here nothing less than the question of what political action should be about: what should we collectively be aiming to do? Sen's answer is in terms of two key ideas: functionings and capabilities.

'Functionings' are states of a person that can be accepted as desirable, such as being adequately nourished and having good health.[24] But Sen then says that knowledge of 'functionings' is not enough. Sen often uses the example that we should not look merely at whether a person has enough food: food is, of course, essential for adequate functioning, but we draw a very different normative lesson about those who are starving because they choose to starve themselves (for instance, as part of a religious purification ritual, or as IRA hunger-strikers) than we do about those unable to get hold of any food.[25] That is to say, it is often less important what goods people actually have than what goods they are able to have.[26] The aim of development policy (and public policy in general) is to ensure that people are in positions such that they can get whatever is necessary for a satisfactory life; not that they actually do get these things, should their wishes be to the contrary. We must, in short, include an assessment of people's capabilities (or, as I would say, their powers). As Sen put it: "the object of public action can be seen to be the enhancement of the capability of people to undertake valuable and valued 'doings and beings'" (Drèze and Sen, 1989: p. 12).

What Sen means here by 'capability' is simply an ability or a power; indeed, he explicitly defines 'capability' as an ability.[27] However, he rarely uses the word 'power' as an alternative to 'capability'.[28] One simple reason why talking of 'powers' or 'abilities' would better suit Sen's purpose is that 'capability' does not actually mean what he seems to think it does. The *OED* defines 'capability' as "an undeveloped faculty or property; a condition capable of being turned to use" and cites a biography of Capability Brown as explaining that he "got his nickname from his habit of saying the grounds which he was asked to lay out had *capabilities*".[29] That is to say, a capability is what I call a *latent* ability (pp. 57–9), and it is clear that this is not what Sen is intending: by 'capabilities' Sen means fully-fledged abilities. That this does create a significant ambiguity can be seen in his discussion of whether (what I call) latent abilities should count as capabilities:

> To avoid confusion, it should also be noted that the term 'basic capabilities' [by which Sen means "the ability to satisfy certain crucially important functionings up to certain minimally adequate levels"] is sometimes used in a quite different sense ... , e.g. as a person's *potential* capabilities that *could* be developed, whether or not they are actually realized (this is the sense in which the term is used, for example, by Martha Nussbaum). (Sen, 1993: p. 41 n. 32)

It seems to me that Martha Nussbaum's use is the more natural one, and that the confusion could have been avoided had Sen talked of 'abilities' (or 'powers') rather than 'capabilities'.

A capability is, then, an ability; or rather it is, in my language, an able-ness (see Chapter 11). When I introduce my distinction between an ability and an ableness, I use a (supposedly) humorous example, contrasting the masticatory ability of the poor to eat expensive food (an ability that does exist) with their lack of ableness to eat such food (because they cannot obtain it) (p. 81). Sen's writings on famines show that this distinction is not humorous at all: it is (literally) deadly serious.[30]

Sen is, then, focusing on a power (in the sense of ableness), and putting the ableness to function adequately at the core of development theory. I think that he is right to do so: it is a natural (and very valuable) extension of some of my brief remarks on the context of social evaluation (see, for instance, pp. 147–8).

That we are interested in similar things can also be seen by noting that we have similar conceptual problems to deal with; and (I am pleased to note) we often deal with them in very similar ways. One such is the problem of aggregating someone's powers to do different things. I discuss this in Chapter 12, and consider that sometimes we may be well advised not to try to aggregate (see, e.g., p. 89). Sen's conclusions are similar:

> The overall ranking of living standard is only one way of seeing this evaluation. Sometimes the assessment of particular components of the standard of living may be of no less interest. If it turns out that there has been an improvement in, say, the standard of nourishment but a decline in the standard of being sheltered, that itself may be an interesting enough assessment, even when we are unable to decide whether 'altogether' this indicates an improvement or a deterioration. The passion for aggregation makes good sense in many contexts, but it can be futile or pointless in others. Indeed, the primary view of the living standard . . . is in terms of a collection of functionings and capabilities, with the overall ranking being the secondary view. The secondary view does have its uses, but it has no monopoly of usefulness. When we hear of variety, we need not invariably reach for our aggregator. (Sen, 1987: p. 33)

Sometimes, as Sen and I both suggest, we can reach agreement in the ranking, and one outcome may dominate another. When this does not happen, it is not a major drawback: we cannot aggregate, so we do not.

> There is nothing particularly embarrassing in not being able to compare every pair of life styles in terms of living standard. The ambiguities in evaluation . . . may require us to be silent on some comparisons while being articulate on others. There is no great failure in the inability to babble. (Sen, 1987: p. 33)

This is a conclusion which I heartily endorse.

Further, in this book I describe something which I call 'passive power', and insist on its importance (see pp. 99–102); this is perhaps the one point that has been most often criticized.[31] I am therefore pleased that exactly the same idea has been used by Jerry Cohen in a discussion of Sen. Cohen thinks that Sen has made major advances, but that his emphasis on capabilities is a mistake, for it leads Sen to emphasize "what a person *can* get, as opposed to (just) what he *does*" (Cohen, 1993: p. 10). Cohen believes that at the back of his mind "Sen intends capability to have an athletic character. He associates it with the Marxist idea of a person fulfilling his potential through activity, which is to be contrasted with the idea of a person finding his *summum bonum* in passive consumption."[32] Yet Cohen thinks that we must include such "passive consumption", and that Sen himself often wants to include this. Cohen considers one of Sen's main concerns: the capability to get food.

> The main good thing that food does for people is that it nourishes them. Typically, of course, people become nourished by nourishing or feeding themselves, by exercising the capability of nourishing themselves which ownership of food confers on them. But the fact that food gives a person the capability to nourish himself is not the same fact as (and is usually less important than) the fact that it enables him to be nourished. To say that food enables him to be nourished is to say that it makes it possible for him to be nourished. That he characteristically actualizes the possibility himself is a further (and usually less important) fact. When, moreover, we ask how well nourished a person is, we are not asking how well he has nourished himself, even though the answer to the two questions will usually be the same; and we are usually primarily interested in the answer to the first question. (Cohen, 1993: p. 20; see, further, pp. 20–5)

As an alternative example, Cohen mentions the vital importance of not suffering from the widespread diseases associated with poverty. Sen (rightly) includes such things in his lists of 'functionings', but Cohen points out that "being free from malaria is not something that one *does*" (Cohen, 1993: p. 21; my emphasis). In other words, Cohen is here saying that when we consider well-being we must look not only at what a person *can* get for herself, but also what she *does* get (even if she can do nothing about getting it – as when she is indeed free from malaria, but not because of anything *she* could do or has done about it). This is exactly what I say about the importance of passive power on pp. 99–102.

So Sen is arguing that what international development should be about is developing latent powers and, particularly, increasing people's ableness (including passive ableness) to function in certain desirable ways.

II.iii—Empowerment

Both Buckle and Sen, then, stress the importance of *latent* powers, which is an area that I somewhat neglect in this book. Latent powers may be of importance in their own right (in that they might give rise to moral standing); they are certainly important in that we do better if (appropriate) latent powers become actual powers. This is usually described nowadays as the importance of *empowerment* as a political goal.

Of the three contexts that I describe in Chapter 6, within which we talk of power, empowerment falls within what I call the *evaluative* context, provided the scope of that context is somewhat expanded. Introducing the evaluative context, I say that when we evaluate social systems (or the performance of governments) "we are often very concerned about the distribution – and the extent – of power within a society" (p. 40). I still think that this is correct, but it is too limited. Sen's work, and the more general concern with empowerment, has reminded me of something I should never have forgotten: that we should not only be interested in the (rather passive) exercise of evaluating societies, but also in the more active endeavour of trying to intervene in order to improve them.[33]

But, despite the term 'empowerment' being currently fashionable, very little of the literature that I have read has bothered to include any discussion of exactly *what* the power is that empowerment should produce. It does seem clear that at issue here is the ability (usually of hitherto marginalized groups) to achieve, obtain, or do things.[34] As Allen puts it, "in the empowerment theoretical view, power is a capacity or creative ability that individuals have *to do* something. . . . This conception sees power as the capacity or ability to pursue certain life projects."[35] This must presumably involve the realization of some of the individuals' latent powers; it seems that those who are satisfactorily empowered now have the power to do a range of (important) things, and that that is seen as a good thing. This is clearly quite compatible with the notion of power that I develop in this book. However, I think that the demand for empowerment would be more persuasive if it included a more rigorous examination of the sort of power that was thought desirable, in particular taking into account the sorts of distinctions I discuss in this book. Sen's work (and the literature on it) provides an excellent start at this.

So far I have amended my discussion in Chapter 6 of the relevant contexts within which we talk of power in two ways: first, I now think that latent powers may well have moral significance in their own right; and, secondly, I want to widen the scope of the context of social evaluation by including both a desire for empowerment and (see p. xiv) a concern to avoid domination.

II.iv—Ted Benton, and the realist approach to power

I now turn to consider a suggestion that there is a further context within which we talk of power, which I should consider in this book. This has been claimed by Ted Benton, who writes:

> To develop one of Morriss's own examples [see pp. 43–4]: suppose someone drops a cup and it breaks. To say of this cup 'It was fragile' is to do more than simply identify the breakage as an instance of the disposition of the cup to break on impact. It is, rather, to indicate that the breakage had more to do with the nature (materials, structure, physical state etc.) of the cup than the scale of the impact (an ordinary cup would have survived such a blow). Of course, the attribution can perfectly sensibly be made without a knowledge of *which* properties of the cup determine its disposition to break under such minor impacts – Morriss is right to see this as a matter for empirical determination – but that this is the *direction in which to look* is part of the content of the attribution.
>
> Power-attributions can thus function as explanation-sketches, or perhaps as 'explanation-indicators' . . .. (Benton, 1988: p. 492; I have corrected the spelling of my name.)

Benton therefore thinks that there is a further context in which concepts of power are at work: that of providing explanation-indicators.

Benton is here following Rom Harré, who in a series of articles and books in the 1970s developed (what he called) a *realist* approach to power and dispositionals. I consider, and dismiss (very quickly), a similar view on p. 18, where I label it "the vehicle fallacy" (see also pp. 83–4). I still think that the view is mistaken, but I think that it deserves a closer look, for it does indeed raise issues of importance.

The key idea of the realist approach is that a dispositional is not *merely* a (Humean) report of a constant conjunction of events; it is a reference to something *real* underlying this constant conjunction. Without such a reference (explicit or implied) the assertion of a dispositional is empty. Harré, indeed, went slightly further than this:

> the proper analysis of the ascription of a power to a thing or material (and, with some qualifications, also to a person) is this:
>
> X has the power to A = if X is subject to stimuli or conditions of an appropriate kind, then X will do A, *in virtue of its intrinsic nature*.
>
> . . . In ascribing powers to people 'can' must be substituted for 'will' . . .. (Harré, 1970: p. 85)

Further, "to ascribe a power is to assert a specific behavioural hypothetical together with an unspecified categorical referring to the nature or constitution of the thing or material concerned" (Harré, 1970: p. 90) – which is just a less elegant way of saying what Benton said about explanation-indicators.[36]

Are Benton and Harré right? I think it might help to understand the claim being made here if we look at a somewhat similar argument that has been made in the philosophical literature on dispositions, originally by C. B. Martin. Martin starts his argument (surely correctly) as follows:

> Dispositions have duration and they can change. A piece of glass can be fragile for an hour and cease to be fragile for an hour. This change of disposition can be arranged by a change of temperature.

Having reminded us of this fact about glass (and about dispositions), he then constructs his argument:

> Someone says, 'I shall make the glass cease to be fragile, but whenever anything happens to it that would make it break if it were fragile, I shall *make* it fragile again. So it will break whenever anything happens that breaks fragile glass – because it will *become* fragile on those occasions. At all other times I shall make it cease to be fragile.' If the individual is taken seriously, then in creating the piece of glass and attaching the label reading 'Fragile, handle with care', the word 'fragile' may be crossed out but the phrase 'handle with care' retained.[37]

It follows that if the glass exists now (as you read this), and nothing is happening now to the glass that would make it break (if it were fragile), then it is true to say that the glass is currently not fragile; but it is *also* true to say that *if* the glass was to be dropped it would break (because Martin's "someone" would quickly make it fragile as it dropped). Martin calls this a "finkish dispositional", and concludes from it that the standard counterfactual analysis of 'fragile' (namely "something is fragile if and only if were the object to be dropped, it would break") cannot be correct: this object is currently *not* fragile, and yet if it were dropped it *would* break. This refusal to describe the object as fragile (even though it is true that if it were dropped it would break) has been widely followed.[38]

So Martin (and others) describe the object as at present not fragile, even though it will indeed break whenever it is dropped, because its breaking requires an intervention by this mysterious "someone". This would seem to accord well with the views of Harré and Benton: to say that the cup is fragile (says Benton) is to point to something *about the cup* that makes it break, not about some mysterious intervener.

But I am not convinced. Or, to be more accurate, I think the correct approach is that sometimes we must take one view and sometimes the other. I also think that this difference in perspective can be important.

Consider, again, Martin's glass example: as his gloss implies, if you're running a haulage firm you'd do better to treat the glass as fragile than as not fragile. The *Oxford English Dictionary*'s first definition of 'fragile' is "liable to break or be broken", and this *does* seem to be true of Martin's glass. But Martin could well reply that the *OED*'s *second* definition of fragile is "brittle" and (ex hypothesi) the glass is not brittle. So this example seems to cut one of our ordinary everyday concepts down the middle. Of course, these two meanings of the term usually cohere so well together because Martin's example is fantastical: we do not need to distinguish (in ordinary language) between something being brittle and breaking when dropped, because Martin's mysterious intervener does not exist. Nevertheless, if he *did* exist, what would we say?

I think it would depend on who "we" were. A scientist would probably be more interested in the properties of the object, and fascinated at the way the properties changed. But in labelling the glass for a haulage company, you would be more interested in the practical question of making sure that they did not drop the object entrusted to their care; whether it broke when dropped because it was permanently fragile or because Martin's story applied would not matter overmuch to you. And I suspect that if someone sold you some of Martin's amazing glass, and assured you when she did so that it was not at all fragile, you would be understandably aggrieved when you discovered that it broke when you dropped it; you might even consider that you would have a good case in the courts when you found out that the seller had known all along that it was certain to do just that. For the main reason we have a word such as 'fragile' (in everyday language, if not in science) is to help us know how to handle things.

So far so far-fetched. But this distinction *does* matter. That it does can be seen from Buckle's discussion of the potentiality argument, in the previous section. What I called Tooley's kitten example (see p. xxi) is rather similar to Martin's finkish dispositional: the kitten has the power if (and only if) some mysterious intervener injects it. Buckle's interpretation of this scenario is similar to Martin's: he calls this a *change* in the kitten's powers, not a realization of them. And Buckle also says (plausibly) that such a change in powers, externally produced, does not 'count' as one of the kitten's powers. It follows that *in this instance* we must adopt Martin's analysis: we must look at the 'intrinsic properties' of the kitten, and ignore what can be brought about by external interveners.[39]

But we would be wrong to conclude that we always want to take this approach, particularly when considering social power. If we did, a person's power would have to be some intrinsic property of that person. That that would be a mistake has been put strongly by Barry Barnes: "the powerful agent possesses power in a sense, but the power he possesses resides in the social context and outside its possessor. . . . [Our talk of someone 'possessing' power tends to mislead us into thinking that] dominant figures are 'powerful', as if jugs of power have been poured down their throats."[40] Clearly this is not the case. So if a person's social power is a property of the intrinsic nature of anything, it would seem to be the intrinsic nature of that society. And this is what 'realist' social scientists, such as J. C. Isaac, have indeed claimed:

> Social science should be similarly concerned with the ascription of powers to social agents, and with the explanatory reference of these powers to agents' intrinsic natures. By the intrinsic natures of social agents I mean not their unique characteristics as individuals, but their social identities as participants in enduring, socially structured relationships. Theories of power, then, should be conceived as interpretative models . . . about the social structures which shape human action and distribute the capacities to act among social agents.[41]

It seems, then, that in so far as we are indeed interested in social power, we are interested in what people can do *that in some way flows from the structure of that society*.

If Benton is right, and ascriptions of powers can serve as 'explanation-indicators', then it seems that they do not carry the indication on their face: *some* ascriptions of powers are indicating the structure of the powerful object or person; but others are indicating the social structure, which acts somewhat like Martin's mysterious intervener. Yet others seem to lack such indicators completely. For instance, it has been well known since (at least) Weber that a leader's political power can sometimes rest on a bureaucratic structure, but that it also, in other times and other places, might depend on a leader's charismatic personality. It may be that each of two leaders has the power to do the same specific thing, but the explanations of their powers could be very different: the power of one would derive from the social structure, whilst the other's would come from the leader's personality.

If this example is not compelling, consider another: one which has been rather over-worked in the literature. If I have the power to get my students to read *Leviathan*, this could possibly be because my description of the book makes it sound so exciting that students rush straight from my lecture to read it (which would indicate that my power is some personal property of mine), or it could be because the students know that if they don't read it they will fail an exam (which points to the social structures within which students and lecturers operate).[42]

When Isaac discusses this example, he ignores the former possibility: he is being 'realist' in a different sense (in the sense used in International Relations, in which only force and threats gets anyone to do anything):

> My instructions to my class to read Machiavelli [a significant choice!—PM], and their obeying of these instructions, presuppose a set of shared concepts (teacher/ student, homework/grades) and norms (regarding school, the value of learning, the value of good grades). . . .
>
> Social power must be understood relationally. By relationally, I do not mean, as in empiricism, in terms of contingent behavioral regularities, but rather in terms of the *real* underlying social relations that structure behavioral interaction. The relation between teacher and student, for example, is not a contingent relation between two parties who happen to encounter one another. It is a historically enduring relation, the nature of which is precisely that teachers have students and vice versa; it is the nature of these social identities to be in relation to one another. And, as such, it is their nature to possess certain powers, powers that simply cannot be conceived as contingent regularities between the behaviors of teacher and student. (Isaac, 1987a: pp. 77 and 79)

Well, actually, not necessarily: this is not a description of any university I recognize. In my experience, bad students take this line: they do what they do only when there is a structural, coercive, relationship. But for good students, the relationship with their teachers *is* contingent, in the sense that some teachers can get them to do more (and, moreover, do it willingly and enthusiastically).

It is clear that Isaac has a particular *theory* about power in social structures like universities, and he is reading his theory back into his description. He *wants* power to reside in a social structure, and so he asserts that it *must* so reside. This may (or may not) be true of universities in general, or Isaac's in particular, but it is certainly not a truth (or an indicator) that can be simply read off the face of the ascription of a certain power to a certain lecturer. Isaac's power to get his students to read Machiavelli *may* indicate their respective positions in a structure of social relations; but it may equally indicate his charismatic personality or excellent teaching skills. Thus, to return to Benton, I think that, just as he and I agree that the cup's fragility can be established without a knowledge of *which* properties of the cup determine its disposition to break, so its fragility can be established without even knowing whether it is a property of the *cup* at all (rather than, perhaps, Martin's mysterious intervener).

In conclusion, sometimes the location of the power can be crucial (as with Buckle's potentiality argument), but sometimes not (as with a haulage firm carrying Martin's glass); and, in any case, the ascription of the power need not allude to it. I therefore want to deny Benton's claim that power-attributions can function as explanation-indicators: the likely explanation is not contained in the (mere) attribution of a specific power, but is a product of some theory – though often the theory is so obvious that we do not notice that it is there.[43]

Having set the scene in this section with an account of a couple of uses of concepts of power, and a defence of my three contexts, I will now turn to consider some explicit criticisms of my analysis of concepts of power in Part II of the book.

III—ABLENESS REVISITED

The writers who have given greatest attention to the general arguments in this book are Brian Barry and Keith Dowding; I owe it to them to give their views some consideration.[44] Both are in sympathy with much of what I have to say, and indeed their general tone is kind and complimentary. But it is, I take it, in the nature of Introductions to second editions that they have to deal with *criticisms* of the first edition, and pass lightly over any praise that might have been offered. In this section, then, I will respond only to these critical passages, at the risk of creating an incorrect impression in the mind of any reader who may be unaware of the large areas of agreement between Barry, Dowding, and myself.

Barry and Dowding seem to me to have little quarrel with what I say about power-as-ability; the differences arise when I get on to power-as-ableness.[45] Between them, they seem to have four, related, criticisms, which I will discuss in order: that my approach to power errs in ignoring the centrality of overcoming resistance; that the notion of ableness is in itself dubious; that I misunderstand the relation between power and luck (included here is the claim that my idea of passive power is mistaken); and that I overlook the significance of resources. I hope to rebut these criticisms; but I will also try to be more positive, and use this opportunity to develop some new ideas.

III.i—Power and resistance

Barry is unhappy with some of my analysis, because he thinks there is a necessary connection between power and the ability to *overcome resistance*.

In his review, he rewrites some of the things I say to include this connection; but I want to resist such rewriting.

Barry states his view, bluntly, as follows:

> We must . . . insist that there is more to (social) power than being able to do what you choose to do. Your having power entails that you have the ability to overcome resistance or opposition and by this means achieve an outcome different from the one that would have occurred in the absence of your intervention.[46]

So, for Barry, there is a necessary connection between power and resistance: if there is no resistance to overcome, there can be no power. As Barry rightly points out (Barry, 1988a: pp. 310–14), this assumption creates all sorts of problems for my notion of power as ableness. He does concede that my notion of ableness is an important one (Barry, 1988a: p. 317); but he claims that whatever ableness is, it is not a power.

Why Barry would conclude this can be brought out by thinking about God. God, it is claimed, is omnipotent. Now suppose Barry is right that one cannot have power if there is no resistance to overcome. Then, according to my concept of power-as-ableness, if none of us resists God's will, He (or she or it, according to your taste) is powerless. But certainly God, who is, after all, omnipotent, cannot be rendered powerless by any choices by us mere mortals: such a suggestion is hubris on a cosmic scale. Note here that the problem cannot be sidestepped by saying that God *could* overcome any resistance we offered, and therefore His power stands. The whole point of ableness, as Barry and I agree, is that we are concerned solely with the *actual* resistance that is offered.[47] So, if Barry is right, I must be committed to the unorthodox theological position that if no resistance is, in fact, offered to God, then God is rendered powerless.[48]

So either ableness is not a power, or the connection between power and resistance has to be abandoned. When Barry discusses a somewhat similar argument (at Barry, 1988a: p. 313), he is sufficiently convinced of the association of power and resistance to see this as a problem with the notion of power-as-ableness; but I am sufficiently convinced of the necessity of having a concept of power-as-ableness to see this as a problem with the association of power and resistance. For I think that adopting Barry's position on resistance has the following highly counter-intuitive result. It is common ground between us that we can describe as 'power' your ableness to overcome my slight resistance (Barry, 1988a: p. 311). Barry also seems to accept that, as my resistance to you decreases, your overall power-as-ableness increases, because (as I say in a passage on p. 88 which Barry quotes), you then have more resources left over, and so can achieve more. So as my actual resistance gradually decreases, your power-as-ableness gets larger and larger until, when my resistance falls from negligible to nothing – poof, your power suddenly vanishes. I fail to see how creating a concept that behaves in this way is helpful.[49]

I think it might be instructive to consider why Barry makes his identification of power with overcoming opposition. Barry comes to 'power' from bargaining theory.[50] When one starts from a bargaining approach, one doubtless tends to think of power as necessarily involving (at least) two parties, who bargain with each other: power would then consist in being able to achieve one's ends by getting someone else to do something, and that is indeed where Barry started in his (1976).

I do not take this approach. I think of power as involving an actor (or group) and something like the rest of the world, which provides the environment in which (s)he acts.[51] Particularly, in Part II I am concerned with explicating the concept of 'power to', and take the actions of others as just part of the background conditions. As part of my distaste for the notion of 'power over', I say next to nothing about how my concepts would work when people are involved in trying to change each other's behaviour.

Given Barry's rather different preoccupations, it is perhaps not surprising if he reads my account of power through the lens of bargaining power. As a consequence, even when he is ostensibly accepting my emphasis on 'power to', he finds it impossible to let go of 'power over'. So he says that "I have power as ableness . . . in relation to you if I can overcome your actual resistance to what I want you to do" (Barry, 1988a: p. 311); that is, my power resides in being able to get you to do something you would not otherwise have done. This is simply Dahl's original definition of 'power over',[52] which I am at pains to reject early on in the book (see Chapters 2 and 5).

So this identification of power with overcoming opposition collapses the concept of 'power to' into that of 'power over'. This is a loss. Since our powers to do even things that do *not* involve overcoming opposition are (sadly) limited, it is of interest to us to know what they are; they cannot be dismissed as non-existent by definitional fiat. As the discussion of Sen on famines should have made clear, it is very important to ask who has the power to avoid starvation, precisely because many lack this power. That some lack this power does not (necessarily) mean that those who do not lack it must have to overcome some resistance when exercising it. It is, then, crucial to retain the possibility of a wide concept of power, that covers being able to do things irrespective of whether that would involve overcoming any resistance.

I readily concede that what is usually thought of as 'political power' (and, maybe, 'social power') is less broad than the account of power I develop here, and it may be that interesting things can be said about these (more constrained) sorts of power that my broader approach obscures (and which are not covered by my brief remarks on pp. 45–6). But I remain insistent that the mundane powers of which Sen writes are of the first importance politically. A regime that cares nothing for the basic well-being of its population, or is quite inadequate at providing such well-being, should be condemned, and (if possible) overthrown in favour of a regime that could do better, if such exists. This concern is political if anything is. As I have argued, to express this demand adequately requires an appropriately constructed concept of power.

III.ii—The ableness of 'the Maverick Justice'
Although Barry has the doubts just discussed about my concept of ableness, he does think that there are reasons for keeping the concept in our vocabulary. He concedes that "in the context of committees and legislatures it does seem quite natural to talk of power in a way that is clearly power as ableness" (Barry, 1988a: p. 312), and gives the following illustrative example.

> If we look at the US Supreme Court, it is manifest that, knowing only the voting rule for decisions of the Court, we must say that each Justice has an equal amount of power. This is power as ability: each Justice has an a priori equal chance of being able by his vote to bring about the outcome he favours. But now suppose that there are two blocs of four Justices which take opposite sides on every question that comes before the Court. We shall, I suspect, feel little reluctance in saying that the remaining Justice, who sometimes votes with one bloc and sometimes with the other, has more power than his brethren. We may, indeed, say that he has all the power since he is always in a position to ensure by his vote that the outcome will be the one that he favours. Clearly, this is power as ableness, since it depends on the distribution of preferences among the Justices.[53]

Keith Dowding has used Barry's example to disagree with both of us (Dowding, 1991: pp. 59–63; 1996: pp. 48–52). If I understand Dowding's argument correctly, he thinks that the individual justice (whom he calls a Maverick Justice, or MJ for short) has no more power than any other Justice, in any sense of 'power' that is useful. This seems to me to be simply wrong. The errors are a mixture of the elementary and the instructive. I think that it is worth exploring them; doing so will deepen our understanding of 'power'.

The elementary error is misunderstanding how we counterfactualize when considering ableness; if Dowding (who has read this book closely) misunderstands this, I should probably state at greater length what is involved. Dowding's view is that

> MJ only appears to have more power because she happens to have been denoted in the example as MJ; that is, she has a different preference structure from the others. Her different preference structure does not, in fact, give her greater power over the results since the two blocs have their *reasons* for voting together and she has her *reasons* for voting as she does. She only appears more powerful because the preferences of the other two blocs are taken as given but hers is not.[54]

But this last sentence is just wrong. When investigating the power-as-ableness of an actor,[55] we take the actions of all other actors as fixed, and examine the outcomes that can be brought about by the actor whose power is being investigated.[56] We determine MJ's power by asking how all the other Justices would have voted; we discover the answer is 4–4; and we therefore conclude that she can always win the vote.

We now turn to the power of a member of one of the blocs; let us call him BJ. Since we are considering the power of BJ, not MJ, we need to ask how all the Justices other than BJ (not other than MJ, this time) would have voted; from the information that Barry gives in setting up the example we only know that "sometimes" the answer is 4–4 (when MJ votes with the other three members of BJ's bloc) and "sometimes" it is 3–5 (when MJ votes with the other bloc); and we therefore conclude that BJ is only sometimes able to win the vote.[57] MJ therefore does have more power than any BJ.

We can see that this must be the case if we use the rather distasteful rule-of-thumb that I borrowed from an earlier article by Brian Barry (see p. 37): if we bribe MJ, we will be certain that we will always get the outcome we want, whilst the same cannot be said of bribing any other Justice. However, it is certainly the case that MJ's extra power is, as Barry says, "fragile" and "evanescent", since it depends on the votes of the others being precisely equal – which is something beyond her control, and liable to change over time (Barry, 1988a: pp. 312–13). She does not have the second-order power of ensuring this power: ex hypothesi, she can't appoint Justices to the Court to ensure the 4–4 balance is maintained as Justices retire. Neither does she have any part in determining the views of the other Justices; if one of them deserts his bloc for the other one, her power is wiped out; and there is (ex hypothesi, again) nothing she can do about that. Her power would be greater if she *could* somehow keep them divided 4–4; but she can't. So her power is less than she would ideally want it to be. But she still has more power, as things stand, than the other Justices. You'd want to bribe her – to repeat – in preference to any of the others.

That is Dowding's elementary mistake; his others are more interesting. He proceeds to say that MJ is not any more powerful than any of the other Justices, but she is *lucky*. So let us look at this contrast between luck and power.

III.iii—Ableness and luck

I suggest that the relationship between power and luck, which has exercised both Dowding and Barry, is complicated, and that it is important to work it out carefully.

First, we need to distinguish between two ways that luck might be considered relevant. When Barry introduced this idea (in Barry, 1980b) he defined luck, simply, as getting what one wants without actually doing anything. Applied to voting, this means getting your desired outcome even if you abstain – that is, don't vote at all (Barry, 1980b: p. 285). Call this Barry-luck. Dowding also sometimes seems to use 'luck' in this way.[58]

But in the discussion of the Justices, Dowding would seem to be extending the idea of luck, or using it in a different way. Clearly MJ doesn't win by abstaining; she has to do something, namely vote. Yet it is true that we could well call MJ lucky: she's lucky that she's in a position to be always decisive. This is 'luck' in a more common-or-garden sense, but it is not Barry-luck;[59] so let us call it Dowding-luck. Dowding-luck involves having a lot of ableness but little ability; that is, your ableness is high because the environment turns out to be particularly favourable to you (due to circumstances beyond your control). If you win the Olympic discus event because, fortuitously, a strong gust of wind springs up just as you throw, and carries your discus that extra few centimetres, that is winning by luck; but it is Dowding-luck, not Barry-luck (for you still have to throw the discus).

So MJ has Dowding-luck, but not Barry-luck. She would have Barry-luck if she could always rely on a majority of the other eight Justices to vote her way; but, ex hypothesi, she cannot do that, and has actually to turn up and vote in order to win.

So is Dowding-luck incompatible with power-as-ableness? It would seem clearly not. MJ does have the power to get her preferred motions passed, as long as the circumstances described in the example remain. Two things could be said of her. The first is that her power may disappear when circumstances change; but there is nothing odd or problematic in that. (Martin said just the same about standard glass, as quoted on p. xxviii.) Secondly, she is lucky that she has this power; it is fortuitous. It is not within her power to bring it about. Neither is it, say, some property of the social structure, such that she is appointed to represent a small group intermediate between two large, and balanced, groups. In *that* case her pivotal position would not be luck; it would follow from the social structure. But in this example it is due to luck. She has power-as-ableness; but it is good luck that suitable circumstances happen to arise that allows her to have this power. So we can agree with Barry that MJ is powerful, *and* agree with Dowding that she is lucky, provided that we are careful about what we are saying. Where Dowding goes wrong is in thinking that luck (in his sense) and power are incompatible.

But, most interestingly, Dowding goes on to say more about luck. He says that it may be, as it were, no accident that someone is lucky. This Dowding calls – in an admittedly oxymoronic phrase – *systematic* luck. "[Systematic] luck . . . is non-random but rather may be predicted methodically. . . . Systematic luck . . . attaches to individuals in certain positions in society, and it attaches to them *because* they hold those positions in society . . ." (Dowding, 1991: pp. 137–8).[60] For this reason I think it would be better if we talked of systematic (or perhaps 'systemic') *bias*, instead of luck. This removes the oxymoron, and also any residual hint that these favourable outcomes are due merely to a fortuitous chance.

Some idea of what Dowding means by systematic luck can be obtained by supposing that you are a member of some social group which is completely excluded from political power (say, the clergy); all decisions are taken by the members of another closed group – say, aristocrats – who have all the power.[61] But it so happens that when the aristocrats make decisions (in what they perceive as their own self-interest) their decisions invariably benefit the clergy. You are then (in Dowding's terms) systematically lucky. To be clear, this good fortune is not because you clergy somehow persuade the aristocrats that they will burn in hell if they do not humour you: that would be power. It is simply that your interests are sufficiently similar to the aristocrats' interests for you generally to do rather well out of their decisions.

Dowding uses this idea to suggest that if studies show that political decisions are invariably highly advantageous to business, but yet the business interests seem to be able to do very little to influence political decisions, the business group is not powerful but systematically lucky. Many elitist studies have claimed that those who clearly do very well out of the system must therefore have power, but have failed to produce evidence for this claim. Dowding suggests that we do not need to use conceptual or methodological sleights of hand, such as postulating unobservable non-decisions or hypothesizing further faces or dimensions of power: if there is no evidence that those who did well were powerful, then they probably were just (sys-tematically) lucky. Even so, this might be enough for the critique that some elitists have made: they might just want to go on to ask why something is not done to ensure that luck is (systematically) spread around somewhat more evenly.

If this idea of systematic luck makes sense (and I think it does) it might make more understandable my notion of 'passive power' (see Chapter 13), which Barry (along with most commentators) has criticized (Barry, 1988a: pp. 314–17).[62]

Barry allows that, for some purposes, we *do* need to include the idea that I call 'passive power';[63] nevertheless, he thinks it is a mistake (and mis-leading) to label it as a sort of power. Barry's point does get some support from the fact that my usage has certainly misled Barry. Hence he writes that:

> . . . to move to the most significant issue that is implicated, when we find a pattern of privilege in a society we should surely wish to treat it as an empirical ques-tion how far this state of affairs arises as the result of the exercise of power by the beneficiaries. But if we equate power and success, the empirical gap is closed and it becomes a logical truth that the beneficiaries are powerful.[64]

But I don't close the empirical gap. It certainly is a logical truth that the right sort of beneficiary has passive power; but this still leaves it as an empir-ical question how far this state of affairs arises as the result of the exercise of power by the beneficiaries. Indeed, the passive power *cannot* be the cause of the privilege since, by definition, one cannot "exercise" passive power. It would certainly be a mistake to assert that since A has passive power (or systematic luck, or benefits from systemic bias) she *must* therefore have active power; but I am careful (I hope) not to assert this. In short, the claim that someone has passive power says nothing at all about how this state of affairs has arisen. In this, indeed, the notion of passive power is no differ-ent from active power: as we have seen in the discussion of MJ, Barry accepts that the statement that someone has active power says nothing at all about whether this power arises by the power-holder's exercise of power, or by circumstances beyond the power-holder's control. Whether a power exists, and how it arose, are simply two very different questions.

Having removed this misunderstanding, I turn to what I take to be Barry's main argument:

> There are, I believe, very good reasons for resisting the proposal that 'power' should be extended so as to include cases where desired outcomes occur with no intervention. For we surely want, in looking at people who do well under some

set of arrangements, to distinguish between those who do well by exercising power and those who are the passive beneficiaries of the activities of others. . . . (Barry, 1988a: p. 315)

I must admit that I am not sure how to respond to these claims of what "we surely want" (or wish) to do. I think many writers are interested in different things from Barry, and therefore they want to make their distinctions in different places.

Passive power has its main role in the context of social evaluation. We have already seen how useful Cohen found the idea of passive power, in an analogous context (p. xxv). When Cohen was considering the capability to be adequately nourished, what *he* was interested in was not who could feed themselves (which would seem to be Barry's concern), but to single out those who are doomed to be ill-nourished: those who are not well-nourished (as things stand) and yet cannot nourish themselves. That is, those who lack *both* active *and* passive power. Or consider Cohen's other example, of illness. As Hugh Ward has reminded us, there is a social patterning to illness. "There are social structures which relate diseases to particular occupations: certain poor peasants to stunted development; workers in the nuclear industry to cancer of the prostate; coalminers to black-lung" (Ward, 1987: p. 603). Other, more fortunate, individuals are free of these afflictions. Whether they are free of them because they can do something to ward them off, or whether they are free of them because they are fortunate enough never have to face these diseases, is not here an important distinction. (See also pp. 147–51.)

This has been well put by C. Wright Mills. In *The Sociological Imagination* Mills invites us to

> . . . consider unemployment. When, in a city of 100,000, only one man is unem-
> ployed, that is his personal trouble, and for its relief we properly look to the char-
> acter of the man, his skills, and his immediate opportunities. But when in a nation
> of 50 million employees, 15 million . . . are unemployed, that is an issue, and we
> may not hope to find its solution within the range of opportunities open to any
> one individual. The very structure of opportunities has collapsed. Both the
> correct statement of the problem and the range of possible solutions require us
> to consider the economic and political institutions of the society, and not merely
> the personal situation and character of a scatter of individuals. (Mills, 1959: p. 9)

The point, as I take it, of the sociological approach to power is that society has structures that are the product of human action although not (neces-sarily) of human design;[65] that these structures might significantly benefit some rather than others; that if they do, we want to know about it. Further (as I say when discussing Sen on p. xxvi) when we know about it, we can (and should) do something about it.[66]

This is the truth contained in the realist approach of those like Isaac (discussed earlier on pp. xxx–xxxi). When we are evaluating (or seeking to improve) societies we need to investigate what flows from the structures of these societies.[67] Unlike the other two contexts that I consider (in Chapter 6), we are here not looking at individuals' powers for their *own* sake, but for what this can tell us about the society.

This has been one of the main concerns of those who have been interested in power in this context. They have been interested because they want to examine how social structures distribute life-chances amongst people. Most such distribution involves allocating resources (widely conceived) such that people have to act to get desired goods: that is, structures create a distribution of active power. But systemic bias also gives some people the desired goods (such as freedom from certain diseases) directly, without these fortunate people having to act at all. If we only look at the distribution of active power we get an incomplete view of the impact of the social structures or biases. Often one person can get something if (and only if) she struggles long and hard to get it; another gets it for free; whilst a third cannot get it however hard he strives. In such a case, whilst the first person clearly has some power, it is not useful, in this context, to lump the last two together as lacking power. We must therefore include a consideration of (what I call) passive power. Whether we actually *call* this 'passive power' or not seems to me quite irrelevant. My label is helpful in that it points to the reasons many writers have wanted to look at power in the first place; but if you'd rather call it something else then please do. Just don't ignore it.

III.iv—Resources and opportunities

Let us return to Dowding's claim that Barry's Maverick Justice lacks power (see p. xxxv). One argument that he offers for this conclusion is that MJ would indeed be powerful if she *realized* her crucial position between the two groups. Once she realized it, she could use it as a resource, and start bargaining with one or both of the other blocs.[68] This is what small parties or crucial independents do in hung parliaments: they bargain like fury, and thereby get more than their numbers would lead one to expect. *That*, says Dowding, is power; on the other hand, a crucial voter who is too stupid (or principled?) to recognize that fact and just turns up and votes, has no more power than any other voter.

Dowding's account of the power of small parties is, of course, correct. But because an independent would have power in one way does not mean that she cannot also have power in another way. Dowding is here concentrating exclusively on power as bargaining advantage (sensibly so, since his chapter is titled 'Political Power and Bargaining Theory'). This is an example of the general tendency that I alluded to at the beginning of this Introduction (p. xiii): Dowding is doing something that I do not touch on in this book,[69] and thereby, arguably, giving us a deeper understanding of power. However he then makes the further move that I have complained about: he seems to claim that power by bargaining is the only sort that matters (or, perhaps, the most important), and that therefore what I do say, since it does not mention this, must be wrong. It is not wrong (although it is perhaps incomplete).

Dowding offers the following argument for claiming that, if MJ doesn't use her pivotal position for bargaining, she cannot have any more power than the others: "what she brings to each occasion of voting is her one vote, which is the same as what the other eight Justices bring. . . . [P]ower . . . reduces to the resources of the actor and, in these examples, a vote is all the resources each voter has" (Dowding, 1991: p. 61). That all voters have the same resources is obviously true (in a sense); and yet this truth hides an important falsehood, which is revealed if we look more closely at what a resource is.

Towards the beginning of the chapter I call "Resources" (Chapter 19), I say that we cannot observe resources directly, for "whilst we may be able to observe the *thing* that is the resource . . . we can only determine *that* it is a resource on the basis of [a] theory" connecting resources to power (pp. 138–9). I then go on, somewhat unusually for me, to look at resources in interpersonal relations: whatever you have is only a resource if other people treat it as such. Thus you can only use your money to bribe people if people will accept bribes; if they won't, your money is simply not a resource. In general, therefore, it is true that resources can be said to be what gives people power; but it is not true that we can simply use someone's resources as a measure of their power; and it is not even true that we can *identify* something *as* a resource without some knowledge of how others will react to it. It may be the case, for instance, that I am rich and you are poor, and that neither of us has any other discernible resources; but if it happens to be the case that (for any reason, or none) some official will accept a bribe from you of £5 (which you have), but will not accept any bribe within my wealth from me, then you have more power-as-ableness than I do. Even more obviously, if we are dealing with *different* officials, and mine is completely incorruptible whilst yours is, shall we say, persuadable, then your little money gives you more power than my riches.[70]

I hope it should be clear from this that we cannot 'read off' someone's power from knowledge of their resources; to think that we can is to commit the vehicle fallacy (see pp. 14–15, 18–19). It is not at all paradoxical to say that I have more than you of something that is usually a resource, yet you have more power.[71]

This is perhaps most obvious in interpersonal relations, yet it applies to votes as well. To return to Dowding's discussion of Barry's example, it is true that BJ and MJ have the same number of votes, and therefore, in a sense, the same resources (it being accepted in this part of the discussion that we are simply ignoring any *other* resources they might have, such as being able to bribe, coerce, or seduce another Justice to change their vote). But we have seen that the same resource in different situations can give rise to greatly differing amounts of power; and the two Justices *do* face greatly different situations (as laid out in Barry's account of the hypothetical example): MJ faces a situation which is certain to be split 4–4, whilst BJ faces a situation that might be 4–4 and might be 3–5. This is analogous to you facing a bribable official whilst I face an incorruptible one.

This argument should not cause much surprise, because the knowledge that the *value* of a resource can change even though the resource stays the same is very well known in voting theory, even when we are considering ability rather than ableness. Consider a simple three-person committee, consisting of you, Ann, and Ben, with one vote each, and two votes out of the three required to win a vote. It can hardly be denied that (in the absence of other information) you, Ann, and Ben each have the same amount of voting power. Now suppose that Ben somehow transfers his vote to Ann, so that Ann now has two votes out of the three. Now Ann has all the power, since whichever way she votes she must win; you have no (active) power, since however you vote you can always be outvoted by Ann.[72] Yet you still have one vote: whilst your resources would seem to have remained exactly constant, your power has evaporated.[73]

So, in the Justices example, there is no problem in accepting Dowding's premises that "a vote is all the resources each voter has" (Dowding, 1991: p. 61) and that "the Maverick Justice only has one vote just like the others" (Dowding, 1996: pp. 49–50) whilst denying his conclusion that the Maverick Justice necessarily has the same amount of power as each of the other Justices. For whilst Dowding is correct to say that one's power *depends* on one's resources, he is *not* correct to say that "power . . . *reduces to* the resources of the actor" (Dowding, 1991: p. 61; my emphasis). The relationship between resources and power is far more complicated than that.

I therefore want to claim that far from power being *reducible to* the resources of an actor, we cannot tell whether what the person has *is* a resource until we know what the effect of using it will be. In this a resource is somewhat similar to an opportunity, which I discuss very briefly elsewhere in the book: in a footnote, I say that "an opportunity is not *distinct* from [an] ability: what is an opportunity for someone depends on the nature of his abilities" (pp. 247–8, n. 2; see this note for supportive examples). Yet it is pervasive to think of an opportunity, like a resource, as somehow "given", quite distinct from someone's ability to use it. This mistake seems to me to infect much of the discussion of equality of opportunity.

Rawls expresses the popular view of the principle (which he calls the liberal interpretation) as well as anyone:

> Assuming that there is a distribution of natural assets, those who are at the same level of talent and ability, and have the same willingness to use them, would have the same prospects of success regardless of their initial place in the social system. (Rawls, 1971: p. 73)

The liberal interpretation of the principle of equality of opportunity (which Rawls goes on to reject as not far-reaching enough) is introduced to distinguish it from the more restrictive interpretation as a career open to talents, which requires only "a formal equality of opportunity in that all have at least the same legal rights of access to all advantaged social positions" (Rawls, 1971: p. 72).[74]

But it is misleading to label either interpretation as *equality* of opportunity. Giving people with different abilities the same legal rights is precisely to give them *different* opportunities (see the examples in pp. 247–8, n. 2), just as giving people in different situations the same resource may be to give them different powers. Equally, Rawls's liberal interpretation is designed precisely to give people of lesser abilities *less* opportunity to succeed. If everybody really did have equal opportunities, then those with the greatest willingness, *irrespective of their abilities*, would have the greatest success.

This confusion is of obvious value to defenders of the status quo. For if a system existed that *did* give equality of opportunity (*real* equality – everybody's opportunities were indeed equal), and you failed to be successful, it would be because you were not willing to make, or not interested in making, the most of your abilities. It would be entirely *your* fault that you were not a success, since you did not avail yourself, as others did, of the opportunities given equally to each of you. Such an attitude of self-criticism in response to failure is bound to carry over, to a certain extent, to a situation falsely, but widely, thought of as providing equal opportunities.

That this confusion is not a figment of my imagination is shown neatly by the following passage in a lecture given by Kingman Brewster –

who was in a position to know better than anyone how the phrase 'equality of opportunity' was usually used.[75] "Equality of opportunity," Brewster said, assures that

> even if there is not room at the top for everyone, the paths to the top are open on the basis of merit. Perhaps the best we can hope for is to have those who end up at the bottom feel that "I had my chance and I muffed it". (Brewster, 1983: p. 30)

But this is clearly a non sequitur: those without merit who end up at the bottom haven't had a chance to muff.[76]

Hence it is quite mistaken to talk of either equal opportunities or equal resources, as if opportunities or resources could be located, and then equalized, without reference to the abilities and circumstances of the actors concerned. Something only becomes an opportunity or a resource for some actor (to obtain some given end) when it enables her to obtain that end. I hope that we can see from this how important it is to understand the correct (and complicated) relationship between resources, opportunities, and powers.

So to conclude this section, I hope to have shown that the notion of power-as-ableness is important, and that my analysis of it, when properly interpreted, can resist the criticisms made by Barry and Dowding.

IV—INDICES OF VOTING POWER

Since the first edition of this book was published, there has probably been more work done in the area of mathematical voting power than in all other areas put together. Unfortunately, the quality of this work has all too often been extremely poor: the lament with which I start Part IV (see p. 154) is as true now as when I first wrote it. If anything, the quality has tended to decline: it seems as if, as simple mistakes get published, more writers are emboldened to follow these mistakes. The latest nonsense is that several reputable authors have seen fit to declare (with apparently straight faces) that you can have two votes and I can have ten votes, and yet you can somehow have more power than I do.[77]

However, not all is gloom in this field. Recently an excellent book has been published on voting power (Felsenthal and Machover, 1998); if this book gets the attention it deserves then, at the very least, far fewer authors will rush into print to utter complete nonsense. I am relieved that my own attempts in Part IV of this book stand up quite well to Felsenthal and

Machover's analysis, but I think that some of my conclusions can now be put more strongly and coherently. I would therefore like to sketch here what Felsenthal and Machover do in their book, and the impact it has on what I say in Part IV.

IV.i—Measures of power as ability

The first point to make is that Felsenthal and Machover are *only* concerned with measures of a priori power: that is to say, in my terminology, of ability.[78] Within this notion of power as ability, Felsenthal and Machover distinguish two viewpoints – which they call the *policy-seeking* and *office-seeking* viewpoints – "corresponding to ... two motivations of voting behaviour".[79] These two viewpoints Felsenthal and Machover call (somewhat inelegantly) I-power and P-power, respectively. They are defined as follows:

> From [the] policy-seeking viewpoint, a member's voting power is the degree to which that member's vote is able to *influence* the outcome of a division: whether the bill in question will pass or fail. We shall refer to this notion of voting power as *I-power*.
>
> From the rival, office-seeking, viewpoint on voting, ... the real and ultimate outcome is the distribution of a fixed purse – the prize of power – among the victors. From this viewpoint, a member's voting power ... is to be measured by that member's expected or estimated share in the fixed purse. We shall refer to this notion of voting power as *P-power*.[80]

Felsenthal and Machover then show, very persuasively, that the correct measure of I-power is the Penrose index.[81] In particular, they give detailed mathematical support to the contention in this book that when, as a voter, you have to consider the desirability of different voting rules, you should seek to maximize your *absolute* power (as measured by the Penrose index) and not your power *relative* to other voters (as measured by the Banzhaf or Shapley–Shubik indices). If your power to achieve your ends goes up, then you are better off; and this remains true even if the power of others to obtain their ends goes up even more (so that your relative power goes down). When we are considering I-power, then, Felsenthal and Machover consider that we should use the Penrose index, as argued here (in Chapter 22 and pp. 184–6).

But many still feel unhappy if their relative power goes down, even if their absolute power goes up. Two reasons for this have been offered. One (suggested to me independently in correspondence by two people – one North American and the other European) is that Americans are peculiarly obsessed with procedural equality, to the exclusion of most other values.

My (somewhat scathing) dismissal of relative power on pp. 185–6 may then be seen as my European bias. As the American constitutional system of checks and balances suggests, maybe to an American it really is better if nobody can do anything in the political sphere, so long as they are equally not able to do anything. I leave this suggestion to specialists in transatlantic cultural differences.

The other reason for preferring a relative measure is that one is not interested in I-power, but in P-power. Since P-power concerns, by definition, your share of a *fixed* amount (the 'spoils of victory'), relative measures are here appropriate: what one person gains another necessarily loses.[82] The measure of P-power is, then, very different from that of I-power.

Felsenthal and Machover think that probably the best measure of P-power is the Shapley–Shubik index, although they are somewhat hesitant about reaching that conclusion (see their 1988: chs 6 and 7, particularly pp. 266–77). In my view they are wrong to be hesitant: the Shapley–Shubik index is the appropriate one. My reasoning relies on my conjecture that the Shapley–Shubik index provides a measure of the worth of an actor to an outside briber (see pp. 162–5 and 223–8). Felsenthal and Machover have proved this conjecture.[83] This estimate of the worth to an outside briber is simpler and clearer than the office-seeking postulate, and would seem clearly to measure the same thing. The Shapley–Shubik index is therefore appropriate as a measure of P-power, for similar reasons to those I express on pp. 162–5 and 168.

IV.ii—Creating power: the square-root rules
In Chapter 24 I look at the question of how we should allocate votes if we want to bring about certain desirable distributions of power, particularly in two-tier voting systems (see p. 187). I start with a very brief allusion to a series of redistricting court cases involving Banzhaf, for the purposes of which he invented his index (see pp. 184–5). Felsenthal and Machover (1998: ch. 4) give a very much fuller account of these cases, which were far more complicated and messy than I had ever imagined. I recommend their discussion.

I then look at (what I call) the 'failed solution' of the square-root rule. In fact, as Felsenthal and Machover show very neatly (see their 1998: pp. 63–79; and 1999), there are *two*, quite different, square-root rules; I mention them both, but I certainly do not distinguish them with the clarity that I should do. When I talk about 'the' square-root rule (pp. 186–9), I refer to setting the *votes* of delegates proportional to the square-roots of the size of their constituencies, and I say that adopting this would achieve two – apparently different – objectives. The first is that this maximizes the probability of producing the decision of the majority of the whole electorate; the second is that it maximizes the sum total of Penrose-power of the whole electorate. Felsenthal and Machover, who call this the *second* square-root rule, and attribute it to me, prove the second of these conjectures, and also a result somewhat similar to my first conjecture.[84]

The other square-root rule (which I allude to somewhat in passing on p. 229, and which Felsenthal and Machover attribute to Penrose) requires the *powers* – not votes – of the delegates to be proportional to the square-root of the size of their constituencies. When this can be done – and it certainly cannot always be done – the citizens' individual voting powers would be equal.[85] As I have said above, I am fairly scathing about the wish to seek simply to *equalize* power: I think we should be more concerned to *maximize* power.[86] Felsenthal and Machover also think that we should bear in mind both maximization and equalization. Their discussion of how we might be able to take both of these aims into account is along similar lines to, and almost as messy as, my own attempt on pp. 192–7.[87]

But Felsenthal and Machover, in an important new development, have recently argued that the two square-root rules can usually both be satisfied simultaneously. For they have looked at what happens with weighted voting when the number of voters gets large. When there are only a *few* voters, voting power and voting weights tend to be very different, as my examples throughout Part IV show (see, for instance, pp. 157–60). But it seems that as the number of voters becomes relatively large, then "their voting powers tend to become more and more nearly proportional to their weights".[88] So that if a voter has (say) 3 per cent of the votes, she will have (approximately) 3 per cent of the power.

What this means is that in large bodies (such as the United Nations, or an enlarged EU of 28 countries) we can (nearly) satisfy both square-root rules simultaneously, by setting the weight of the vote of a state's representative proportional to the square root of its electorate (or, if desired, its population). This satisfies *my* square-root rule directly (because the votes of a state's representative are set proportional to the square-root of the state's electorate); it also (nearly) satisfies Penrose's square-root rule *indirectly*, because the relative *powers* of the states' representatives are then (nearly) proportional to the square-root of their respective electorates. So it does seem that if we set the weight of each delegate (or representative) proportional to the square-root of the electorate in their constituency, then we do, at the same time, *both* maximize *and* (nearly) equalize the constituents' powers.

It has long been a problem how we should set the weights in bodies of representatives from unequal-sized constituencies. We now know how we must do it for most such bodies that are of medium-to-large size: we should allocate to each representative a number of votes proportional to the square-root of the number of voters in their constituency. It is to be hoped that those who design such two-tier voting systems will take this result very seriously indeed.

In conclusion, much still remains to be done in clarifying the measures of voting power, but whatever is done must be built on Felsenthal and Machover's foundations.

V—CONCLUSION

In this Introduction I have chosen to look at a few topics in some depth. There are many more that need to be addressed, both to defend what I say here, and (particularly) to extend it into other areas. But time, space, my abilities, and your patience are all limited. There is little more that I can do here to introduce you to this book, except to ask you to read it sympathetically and then feel free to show me how it might be done much better.

—1—
Prologue

'Power' is a word that is used often, by all of us, both in our everyday lives – in conversations in the pub – and in academic discussions. The number of books with the word in their titles is large, to say the least; more still attempt to tell us the truth about power in general or in some particular locality. Yet, in spite of this, we find it very difficult to say exactly what we mean by 'power'. We all have an intuitive understanding of the term, which is (usually) perfectly sufficient for pub conversations. But the rapidly growing mountain of literature on the concept of power indicates that this under-standing is not considered adequate for academic discourse.

The meaning of the word 'power' seems like a will-o'-the-wisp: it tends to dissolve entirely whenever we look at it closely. We are sure that we meant *something* by the word, and have a vague idea what it is: but this understanding tends to fade away upon examination, until 'power' seems nothing more than "a giant glob of oily ambiguity" (Dahl, 1957b: p. 1056). Part of the import of my argument in this work is that we usually talk more sense in the pub than in the seminar: those who have spent longest puzzling over the meaning of the term seem to make least sense of it in their writings.

Quite early on in my perusal of the literature I came to the conclusion that our academic emperors wear very little in the way of clothes. However, my intention is not to spend too much time supporting this view; stripping away the arguments of others is not a totally satisfying occupation, and gives rise to the often justified suspicion that one is pointing to the nakedness of others as a means of drawing attention away from one's own. I shall be attempting to put forward constructive, as well as destructive, proposals; much critical argument on the views of others, originally intended for incorporation, has been discarded.

Also abandoned is a review of the literature to date; such a review, if not grotesquely superficial, would leave me no space to state my own case.

What I have tried to do is present my account of 'power' in as coherent a fashion as I can manage. Sometimes I have felt that my account is made clearer by stating how it differs from that of some other writer; and I have then done so. On other occasions I have tried to strengthen my account by showing *why* it differs from that of another. I therefore certainly do refer to the works of others; but I do not attempt a systematic survey.[1]

Perhaps one of the dangers of an enterprise such as mine is that people will think that I am just stating the obvious. However, I take courage from the knowledge that the little boy in the Andersen fairy story was also just stating the obvious – but something so obvious that nobody had believed it before.

Before we can start constructing an account of power we need to know what sort of thing we are dealing with: we must decide just *what* it is that we are trying to analyse. And we must decide, as well, how we go about deciding *that*. Most writers in the social sciences pay far too little attention to these preliminary problems, with the result that they go rushing off in the wrong direction, pursuing the wrong quarry. When they eventually catch it, they may claim to have caught the beast they sought; but how do they know, if they didn't know what they were looking for? Worse still; having caught *something*, our hunters try to persuade us that that was indeed what they were looking for all along, and what we wanted them to catch for us.

It is unfortunately all too tempting to embark on the search straight away; tempting for writer and reader alike. Nevertheless, I am afraid that I shall try to proceed more slowly and circumspectly. For my disagreements with the many writers on power that have preceded me lie not so much in the analysis they provide as in what it is they choose to analyse. I think that power is a totally different animal from the ones that have been caught up till now. And to justify this claim I need to say a few words on the methodology of the identification of concepts.

One approach is to attempt to argue to the meaning of a term from examples of what 'we' would or would not say. I think that this is misguided. Sometimes what 'we' would – and do – say is confused, inconsistent, unjustifiable, or empty of content. Philosophically acute discourse should not reflect these vices. The study of the way that people use language and words is a reputable and worthwhile discipline in its own right: but philology is not philosophy.

For although I claim that ordinary men and women frequently know more than academics about the meanings of 'power', I think it is merely contingent – and lamentable – that this is so; and the main object of my exercise is to make it no longer so. (I expect that whatever impact this book has, it will be greater in academic than non-academic circles.) I thus hold no philosophical brief for ordinary language. Philosophers *ought* to use language more precisely than non-philosophers: that is what we are in business to do. If an engineer is supposed to be good at constructing bridges, philosophers should be able to claim some competence at constructing arguments. Both engineers and philosophers should be better able than others to use the tools of their trade; and the tools of the philosopher's peculiar trade involve language. So I am not endeavouring to explicate ordinary usage; I am attempting to improve on it.

But neither is the object of the philosophical enterprise simply stipulating definitions. Arriving at a definition of a term does not necessarily produce greater clarity; indeed, if the definition appears purely arbitrary it can often engender needless disputes. Stipulating a definition out of thin air and for no justifiable reason can never be an adequate philosophical move. Ordinary language must, therefore, be our starting point. Austin's formulation of 'ordinary language philosophy' (if not his practice of it) seems to me the correct guide:

> Certainly, then, ordinary language is *not* the last word: in principle it can everywhere be supplemented and improved upon and superseded. Only remember, it *is* the *first* word. (Austin, 1956b: p. 185)

But *why* is ordinary language the first word? Simply, I think, that if we want to sort out and clarify what people mean by 'power' we have to make sure that we are talking about what they are talking about. People use the word 'power' a great deal, so it is obviously thought to represent something important. It would be perverse in the extreme to write a book on 'power' that bears no relationship to whatever it is that people think they are talking about when they talk of power. The first task, then, must be to get some preliminary idea of what is usually understood by the word 'power'; this is accomplished in Part I.

Part I starts with the relevant entries in the *Oxford English Dictionary*, for in so far as there is an authoritative source of ordinary English, the *OED* is it. But the dictionary, whilst pointing us in the right direction (as I hope to show), cannot solve all our problems. We need something far more developed and detailed than the definitions a dictionary can provide. And to this end we need to ask other questions; questions such as: "What do we want the term to do?", "Why do we feel the need for it?", and "Why is it so prevalent in our language?". I am not asserting that the meaning of a word is discovered in its use – far from it – but that we can examine different interpretations of a word intelligently only if we know to what use the word is to be put.

In this spirit, I am not trying to produce just a *definition* of 'power', but to advance towards the solution of problems involving the term. A term such as 'power' is a shorthand for previously understood ideas; such short-hand terms are obviously useful unless and until it is unclear, or contentious, how they work as a shorthand. The solution to this lack of clarity is not to abandon the term, but to ask what the reasons for developing such a short-hand term were (and are). Reasons (plural): for one frequent problem is that people with different concerns will discuss slightly different things, to which they may well attach the same label. Part of the job of the philo-sopher is to point this out, and prevent this from creating confusions. I start this task in Chapter 6.

By attending to ordinary usage we can discover which concepts are the ones employed when we talk about power, and why we use these concepts. We can then look at these concepts in detail and see how we can improve on our unreflective linguistic habits. This provides the subject-matter for Part II.

Once we have clarified our concepts we can consider what evidence we would require to make ascriptions of power, and how we might set about obtaining this evidence. This is done in Part III. Part IV extends the analy-sis of Part II by showing how – given certain assumptions – we can create numerical indices of power.

I must stress that I consider it essential to proceed this way round, and work out carefully the exact nature of our concepts before we seek to use them in empirical investigation or manipulate them mathematically. I hope to show that we can refine our concepts of power sufficiently to use them fruitfully; and, conversely, that it is disastrous to talk of power without first engaging in an analytical exercise of some complexity.

This, highly abbreviated, is the philosophical thesis I wish to illustrate. I hope to show that we can make sense even of terms like 'power' if we approach them in the right way; and I hope to indicate what this way is. Thus, whilst almost all of this book considers power and problems that arise when thinking about it, at the back of all this is a position of deeper significance.

Perhaps, though, I may be permitted to add a brief autobiographical note. I did not first embrace a philosophical position, and then apply it. As long-suffering colleagues – who read draft chapters long since entirely discarded – will know, my approach changed slowly as I puzzled over 'power'. Initially, I attempted to develop criteria of meaning from the writings of logical positivists, and sought to fit 'power' into a formalized language expressible in symbolic logic. It was quite a while before I abandoned this tack. It was through the practice of making sense out of 'power' that I came to the theory of how it might be done. In particular, it was through a slow realization of how others were *not* making sense, and why they were not, that I came to my approach to the problem.

I say this to try to dispel any thoughts that I fell under the spell of some philosophical system and then simply applied it – and that you can therefore ignore my application if you hold to different philosophical views. That is why I put the discussion of my general views on how to understand concepts at the end, as an Epilogue, and not at the beginning. I would like what I say about 'power' to be considered on its merits as an attempt to solve the problem of understanding and analysing what we mean by this difficult term. If I fail it is because I do not say anything useful at this level. What I am trying to do is make sense of 'power', and it is on this that I wish to be judged. If I have achieved any success in this, then I may also be indirectly saying something worthwhile about philosophy.

—PART I—
What power is
and what power is not

—2—
Power and influence contrasted

In this Part, I shall be concerned with explicating ordinary usage and with understanding the reasons why our language is as it is. It is true that we cannot discover the purpose of a word just by looking it up in a dictionary. But we can gain an insight into the point of a word by contrasting it with near-synonyms, particularly near-synonyms that cannot be substituted for it without either changing the sense or – as often happens – changing sense into nonsense. We must be sensitive to the nuances of language. (My thinking here has been confirmed and much improved by Fowler's *Modern English Usage*, which I stumbled across when writing the final version of this book. Fowler should be essential reading for anyone trying to philosophize about language and concepts.)

I start this Part by contrasting the near-synonyms 'power' and 'influence'. My approach here is thus the complete opposite of that adopted by the early and influential behaviouralists, who cavalierly collapsed terms such as 'power', 'influence', 'control' and 'coercion' into one category, and then endeavoured to find the one definition that 'lay behind' all of these terms.[1] This single-minded, and simple-minded, attitude to concepts has had disastrously stultifying results over the last fifty years or so. I hope to show how much more fruitful it is to take note of the considerable differences between 'power' and 'influence', rather than deliberately to overlook them. For 'power' and 'influence' are not interchangeable; there are good conceptual reasons for this; and clarity demands that we do not blur these conceptual distinctions.

I shall start with three different sorts of evidence about the words 'power' and 'influence': their grammar, their derivations, and their current meanings as given by a dictionary.

The most obvious fact about the words is that 'influence' is both a noun and a verb, whilst 'power' is primarily a noun. (The verb 'to power' does exist, meaning "to provide power" or "empower". It is certainly common to form verbs from nouns in this way – for instance 'to house' – but the verb only has meaning through the noun, as it were. 'To influence', on the other hand, does not mean "to provide influence"; it counts as a verb in its own right.) This grammatical difference between 'influence' and 'power' is not something to be shrugged off as a peculiarity of the English language (as Dahl tries to do in Dahl, 1957a: p. 80), for it may turn out that 'power' refers to something that cannot be expressed by a verb. Verbs describe happenings, actions, events, occurrences and the like; but 'power', I shall suggest, is in an entirely different logical category. It would indeed be odd if 'power' and 'influence' were synonyms, and yet one of them had a verb form that the other lacked; the oddity would disappear if they were not synonyms after all.

A second difference between the two words is shown by their derivations. 'Power' came from the Latin *potere*, which meant "to be able". 'Influence', however, derived from the Latin *influere*, "to flow in", and referred to an astrological belief that a substance emanated from the stars and flowed into people in the sublunary world, changing their behaviour or at least affecting them in some way. Hence 'under the influence', and also 'influenza'.

So 'power' and 'influence' started out in their linguistic life as expressions of completely different ideas: for being able and being affected by occult fluids are not exactly similar. But the meanings of words change, and maybe 'power' and 'influence' are now indistinguishable. That this is not the case is easily shown by looking at the entries in the *Oxford English Dictionary*, which is the most authoritative source of current linguistic usage. The *OED* confirms the suspicion that the meanings of the words have changed so that there is now a considerable amount of overlap, but demonstrates conclusively that there also remain several differences. The best way of showing the range of meanings of the words is by quoting all the non-obsolete entries in the *OED*.

Influence (noun)
2. (Specifically in Astrology) The supposed flowing or streaming from the stars or heavens of an etherial fluid acting upon the character and destiny of men, and affecting sublunary things generally. In later times gradually viewed less literally, as an exercise of power or 'virtue', or of an occult force, and in late use chiefly a poetical or humorous reflex of earlier notions.
  b. (transferred sense) The exercise of personal power by human beings, figured as something of the same nature as astral influence. (Now only poetic.)

4. The exertion of action of which the operation is unseen or insensible (or perceptible only in its effects), by one person or thing upon another; the action thus exercised.

5. The capacity or faculty of producing effects by insensible or invisible means, without the employment of material force, or the exercise of formal authority; ascendancy of a person or social group; moral power over or with a person; ascendancy, sway, control, or authority, not formally or overtly expressed.

6. A thing (or person) that exercises action or power of a non-material or unexpressed kind.

Influence (verb)

1. (transitive) To exert influence upon, to affect by influence.

    a. To affect the mind or action of; to move or induce by influence; sometimes especially to move by improper or undue influence.

    b. To affect the condition of, to have an effect on.

Power (noun)

1. Ability to do or effect something or anything, or to act upon a person or thing.

2. Ability to act or affect something strongly; physical or mental strength; might; vigour, energy; force of character; telling force, effect.

    b. Political or national strength.

3. Of inanimate things: Active property; capacity of producing some effect; the active principle of a herb, etc.

4. Possession of control or command over others; dominion, rule; government, domination, sway, command; control, influence, authority. Often followed by *over*.

    b. Authority given or committed; hence, sometimes, liberty or permission to act.

    d. Personal or social ascendancy, influence.

    e. Political ascendancy or influence in the government of a country or state.

5. Legal ability, capacity, or authority to act; especially delegated authority; authorization, commission, faculty; specifically legal authority vested in a person or persons in a particular capacity.

6. One who or that which is possessed of or exercises power, influence, or government; an influential or governing person, body or thing; in early use, one in authority, a ruler, governor.

    b. In late use, a state or nation regarded from the point of view of its international authority or influence.[2]

That there is an overlap, an area of synonymity, is clear: we only have to compare Influence₅ with Power₄ to see that. But that there is not complete synonymity should also be clear.

Indeed, a closer analysis reveals (at least) six different ideas present in these definitions of the two words: two of these ideas are common to both words, a further two are restricted to 'influence', and the remaining two are restricted to 'power'. The range of senses can be most clearly shown, I think, by starting with the senses that 'influence' alone has, moving into the area of overlap, and ending by looking at the senses peculiar to 'power'. I shall make free use of the awe-inspiring scholarship of the *OED*'s editors by using their illustrative examples.

1. 'Influence' as a verb describes an event in which something is affected in a certain manner: "the Pope influences all the Powers and all the Princes of Europe [on this matter]". This is the sense closest to the original derivation: altering by imperceptible means.

We can start to understand the nuances of this verb by considering how the illustrative sentence is altered if various possible alternatives are substituted for 'influences'. First, 'powers' is not even a possible alternative, since the verb form cannot be used in this context. Second, 'causes' would make the sentence grammatically correct but meaningless: the Pope causes the Princes – to do *what* on this matter? So 'cause' and 'influence' are not synonyms: the former requires a description of an event as its object, whilst 'influence' takes as object the thing or person affected. Nevertheless, 'influence' and 'cause' are clearly related: when the Pope influences the Princes he causes *something* to happen. Third, 'affects' could be substituted for 'influences', though with a loss of meaning. Influencing is a *specific* form of affecting, to be contrasted, for instance, with bribing or coercing. Since we are now less impressed with the power of occult forces, we tend to mean by 'influencing' any process in which someone's views or ideas are altered by some non-obvious mechanism, such as rational argument or an ill-understood working of the psyche.

It follows from this that anything could be the subject of the verb 'influence': a person, a thing, or an abstract quality like an idea. Similarly, anything can be the object of the verb that is capable of being affected in the appropriate way. To influence, then, is to affect in some hidden, unclear or unknown way.

2. 'Influence' is also the noun describing an act of influencing, as in Influence$_4$: "the land tax would ... have comparatively little influence in preventing or retarding improvements".

3. It is perhaps a natural step to move from Influence$_4$ to Influence$_5$: from an influence as an *action* that influences, to an influence as a *capacity* to influence. Hence "this position gave him a vast amount of influence which he continued to use for his own advantage". Here 'power' *can* be substituted for 'influence', with only a slight change in nuance; indeed,

the *OED* gives an almost identical example under Power$_{4e}$ – "they employed the power which they possessed in the state for the purpose of making their king mighty and honoured".

4. The move from Influence$_5$ to Influence$_6$ (and Power$_4$ to Power$_6$) is another understandable one: 'an Influence' is extended to describe the person (or thing) that has influence or that influences. Thus: "He was an influence in the Dominion Legislature". Again the *OED* provides a parallel example for 'power': "Bell was a power in the house in Upper Parchment Street".

5. Whilst Influence$_5$ is control that is "not formally or overtly expressed", power has no such limitation; Power$_5$ refers specifically to control that *is* formally or overtly expressed: *de jure* power. "He was careful not to assume any of those powers which the Constitution had placed in other hands" has no counterpart for 'influence', precisely because constitutions do not allocate influences: there is no such thing as *de jure* influence.[3]

6. Whilst the operation of influence is invisible, no such limitation is placed on the operation of power; hence a power is *any* capacity to produce effects, whatever the method of production. Power$_1$ is no more than a description of a (any) dispositional property. "They were ready to afford any information in their power" means nothing more specific than that they would provide any information they could. This sense of 'power' – the "ability to . . . effect . . . anything" – is not an idea that can be expressed using 'influence'; we have now left that word far behind.

It would seem from this survey that 'power' and 'influence' do overlap; but that at their cores are very different ideas, and that therefore neither is a subcategory of the other or can be replaced by it.

The first difference between 'power' and 'influence' that I want to draw attention to is that 'power' always refers to a *capacity* to do things, whilst 'influence' sometimes (and typically) does not. Thus *all* the definitions of 'power' refer to the ability to do something or the possession of control (or the person possessing such an ability); there is no meaning of 'power' comparable to Influence$_4$. This is brought out clearly in Influence$_2$ and Influence$_6$, which both refer to influence as an *exercise* of power, but not as the *possession* of power.

Indeed, this difference is so obvious that even those who claim that 'power' and 'influence' are synonyms recognize it, subconsciously, even when their 'official' analysis denies it. For instance, two of the definitions that Dahl offered of the allegedly identical 'power' and 'influence' were:

> My intuitive idea of power, then, is something like this: A *has power* over B to the extent that he *can* get B to do something that B would not otherwise do. (Dahl, 1957a: p. 80; my emphases)

> Our common-sense notion, then, goes something like this: A *influences* B to the extent that he *gets* B to do something that B would not otherwise do. (Dahl, 1963: p. 40; my emphases)

It is a great pity that Dahl did not draw from these different definitions the conclusion that power might be a dispositional form of influence – for even though that would not have been quite right, it would at least have moved the discussion in the right direction.

Dahl also sometimes uses 'power' in the pure dispositional sense – the one at the furthest extreme from 'influence':

> When one says that the President has more *power to influence* foreign policy than I have, then I think one means that the President *can cause* behaviour in the State Department or Congress or in Germany or elsewhere that I *cannot* cause. (Dahl, 1965; p. 93; my emphases)

Quite so; but it is *influence* here that carries the causal weight, whilst *power* is simply a stand-in for 'can': the sentence has the same meaning as "the President can influence foreign policy more than I can". And, of course, if 'power' and 'influence' *are* synonyms, then the phrase 'power to influence' becomes nonsense.

It is easy to find other examples that amply support Hannah Pitkin's complaint that "the social scientist who purports to use 'power' and 'influence' interchangeably does not really do so. He has simply abdicated from the task of noticing the patterns in accord with which he uses now one term, now the other" (Pitkin, 1972: pp. 277–8). Dahl himself *uses* language quite acutely; it is when he tries to write about it that his acuteness evaporates.[4]

'Power', then, I claim, is always a concept referring to an ability, capacity or dispositional property. Since this claim underlies everything in this book, perhaps a brief account of dispositional concepts would not be inappropriate at this point. In the next chapter I shall describe them, stress their importance, and look quickly at how to treat them – and how not to treat them. By the end of this slight detour I hope that any unease you may feel at my description of 'power' as a dispositional concept will have disappeared.

—3—
Dispositional concepts

3.1—DISPOSITIONALS INTRODUCED

In both everyday language and scientific discourse constant reference is made to events and happenings: things that, put crudely, we can observe. We look to see whether it is raining, whether the window is open, or if the litmus paper is turning red. But this is not all we talk about; we constantly find it necessary to 'go behind' the changing flux of events, by referring to relatively unchanging underlying conditions, called the dispositional properties of the world.

A standard dispositional term, such as 'soluble', is different from a term like 'dissolving' which describes an event, since to state that a sugar lump is soluble in water is not to describe any episode, occurrence or event, but is to describe a property of the object. So dispositional concepts do different work from episodic ones in our conceptual vocabulary: episodic concepts report happenings or events, whilst dispositionals refer to relatively enduring capacities of objects. We must always make sure that we do not confuse these two quite different ideas.

We can understand the nature of dispositional concepts better by exposing two fallacies often committed in interpreting them. These involve confusing the existence of a disposition with its *exercise*, on the one hand, and its *vehicle*, on the other. These fallacies have been well summarized by Kenny:

> Consider the capacity of whisky to intoxicate. The possession of this capacity is clearly distinct from its exercise: the whisky possesses the capacity while it is standing harmlessly in the bottle, but it only begins to exercise it after being imbibed. The vehicle of this capacity to intoxicate is the alcohol that the whisky contains: it is the ingredient in virtue of which the whisky has the power to intoxicate. The vehicle of a power need not be a substantial ingredient like alcohol which can be physically separated from the possessor of the

power.. . . The connection between the power and its vehicle may be a necessary or a contingent one. It is a contingent matter, discovered by experiment, that alcohol is the vehicle of intoxication; but it is a conceptual truth that a round peg has the power to fit into a round hole.

Throughout the history of philosophy there has been a tendency for philosophers – especially scientifically-minded philosophers – to attempt to reduce potentialities to actualities. But there have been two different forms of reductionism, often combined and often confused, depending on whether the attempt was to reduce a power to its exercise or to its vehicle. Hume when he said that the distinction between a power and its exercise was wholly frivolous wanted to reduce powers to their exercises. Descartes when he attempted to identify all the powers of bodies with their geometrical properties wanted to reduce powers to their vehicles. (Kenny, 1975: p. 10. See also his ch. VII)

The former fallacy – reducing a power to its exercise – has been more prevalent in political science, perhaps mainly because operationalism (an extreme form of this fallacy) has had no little influence on the thinking of recent political scientists. I shall discuss this fallacy first, and then the vehicle fallacy.

3.2—THE EXERCISE FALLACY

The exercise fallacy is the claim that the power to do something is nothing more than the doing of it: that talking of your *having* power is simply a metaphysically illegitimate way of saying that you are *exercising* that power. This view is present in Hobbes and Hume, and was revived during the post-war behavioural revolution by social scientists impressed by pre-war positivism. A typical expression of this view is Dahl's: "for the assertion 'C has power over R', one can substitute the assertion, 'C's behavior causes R's behavior' ".[1]

But that there is a difference between a disposition and its exercise was noticed by Aristotle over two thousand years ago, so one might have hoped that it would not still be regularly overlooked. Yet it is, and there seem to be two reasons why many recent social scientists have refused to recognize the dispositional nature of power: either they have adopted a mistaken view of science or they have striven too hard to avoid falling into the other trap and committing the vehicle fallacy.

The reliance on a hopelessly oversimplified view of science is well demonstrated by Nelson Polsby's claim that:

the assertion that any group "potentially" could exercise significant, or decisive, or any influence in community affairs is not easy to discuss in a scientific manner. How can one tell, after all, whether or not an actor is powerful unless some sequence of events, competently observed, attests to his power? If these events take place, then the power of the actor is not "potential" but actual. If these events do not occur, then what grounds have we to suppose that the actor is powerful? There appear to be no scientific grounds for such a supposition. . . . [It is] impossible to confirm or disprove *in principle*. (Polsby, 1963/1980: pp. 60, 68)

Unfortunately for Polsby's argument, all philosophers of science have accepted for many years that all sciences are chock-full of statements that are impossible to confirm or disprove in principle, and that these sciences are none the worse for that. Indeed, science would disappear altogether if such statements were dismissed as meaningless. For compare Polsby's passage with the following:

How can one tell, after all, whether or not a sugar lump is soluble unless some sequence of events, competently observed, attests to its solubility? If these events take place, then the solubility of the sugar lump is not "potential" but actual [i.e., presumably, the sugar lump dissolves]. If these events do not occur, then what grounds have we to suppose that the sugar lump is soluble?

The answer, of course, is innumerable observations of sugar lumps, together with well-confirmed low-level generalizations about them.

As well as being confused about science, Polsby's logic is confused. It is, of course, true that one cannot tell whether an actor is powerful unless *some* set of observations "attests to" his power. But there is no reason whatsoever why these observations should be of the actualization of that power. When I go to a zoo, I can see that a lion is powerful enough to eat me up by observing its jaws, teeth and muscles, and combining these observations with my general knowledge of animals' masticatory performances. If I am still in doubt, I can observe what the lion does to a hunk of meat, and induce. Not even the most dogmatic positivist would declare that he couldn't know if the lion could eat him up until it had actually done so.

But dispositions do go beyond the evidence of our senses – and beyond the possible evidence of our senses. Whilst actualities can be observed, potentialities cannot be; we can therefore never *observe* a disposition, but only manifestations of it. Therefore it is incoherent to apply an operationalist approach to evidence to dispositional terms. Operationalism demands that the only terms that can be used are those which refer to direct or indirect observations, but this is simply not what dispositional concepts are concerned with. Gilbert Ryle, in his discussion of dispositions in *The Concept of Mind*, is particularly concerned to nail this fallacy, and open up a space for dispositions.

> Naturally, the addicts of the superstition that all true indicative sentences either describe existents or report occurrences will demand that sentences such as 'this wire conducts electricity', or 'John Doe knows French', shall be construed as conveying factual information of the same type as that conveyed by 'this wire is conducting electricity' and 'John Doe is speaking French'. How could the statements be true unless there were something now going on, even though going on, unfortunately, behind the scenes? Yet they have to agree that we do often know that a wire conducts electricity and that individuals know French, without having first discovered any undiscoverable goings on. (Ryle, 1949: p. 124)

Indeed, dispositions can remain forever unmanifested: a fragile cup remains fragile throughout its existence, even if it never breaks; a sample of sulphuric acid has the power to dissolve zinc, even though none is ever put into it; the Congress has the power to pass bills vetoed by the President (by passing them with a two-thirds majority), even if the President vetoes no bills. So a dispositional property can exist and yet never give rise to anything that actually occurs. A sentence about a dispositional property, as we shall see, often refers to a hypothetical event – and hypothetical events are by definition unobservable.

An operationalist approach to power thus solves the problem at a stroke – but the stroke is that of a guillotine. For a consistent radical operationalism demands that we no longer talk about powers; that is, it 'solves' the problem by killing it.

This would be a loss. Whilst it is possible to devise a vocabulary which does not contain dispositional concepts, it would be a very impoverished one. For the world viewed through this linguistic framework would contain only a series of more or less unrelated events or happenings. A. J. Ayer has said how in his younger, more harshly positivist, days he lost a favourite fountain pen, and tried to persuade himself that all that had happened was the cessation of a stream of favourable sensations, rather than the disappearance of an *object*. Even at that time, when his ontology did not admit anything as far removed from sense-data as ordinary objects, he was not convinced by his description of what had happened – and rightly so. For if we ignore its dispositional properties, the world must appear just a buzzing, bewildering confusion of haphazard events: indeed it is unlikely that anybody could view the world in that way for very long without going mad.

3.3—THE VEHICLE FALLACY

Unlike the exercise fallacy, the vehicle fallacy tends to be committed by philosophers rather than by political scientists. Quine, for example, advances a realist interpretation of dispositions, considering that when we say that something is soluble at a given time, we are intruding a "stabilizing factor" of

> a theory of subvisible structure. What we have seen dissolve in water had, according to the theory, a structure suited to dissolving; and when now we speak of some new dry sugar lump as soluble, we may be considered merely to be saying that it, whether destined for water or not, is similarly structured. (Quine, 1960: p. 223)

But there is no reason why dispositionals should refer to "subvisible structures". They may; but we can talk perfectly sensibly about the dispositional properties of an object without bothering our heads about its structure, visible or otherwise. For, as Stanley Benn has commented, "the power to extinguish a flame is possessed alike by a bucket of water, a cold wind, or a quantity of pyrene foam, each possessing the same power by virtue of quite different [structural] properties" (Benn, 1972: pp. 191–2). To ask *why* a substance has a property (by virtue of *what*?) is different from, and not necessary for, asserting that it *does* have this property.

When we come to consider the dispositional properties of *people* it becomes obvious that talk of 'subvisible structure' is simply no help at all. It is either false or empty to claim that someone who can speak French has a different subvisible structure from someone who cannot.

3.4—CONCLUSION

One obvious way to start studying power is by cataloguing the actors' resources. Doubtless some sociologists who have tried this have carelessly claimed or implied that resources themselves were power, thus falling into the vehicle fallacy. On the other hand, part of the reason why behaviouralists have refused to infer power from resources has been a laudable desire to avoid this fallacy (see, e.g., Dahl, 1984: pp. 21–2). Wealth is not political power, they have said, since, whilst some people use their wealth to collect politicians, others can only collect paintings. Even position in a formal hierarchy is not, in itself, power: the President may be too incompetent to use the resources of office, or the *real* power may lie elsewhere. How can we know where the power is, then, unless we see it exercised?

But there is a big difference between committing the vehicle fallacy by *identifying* power with the resources that give rise to it and acknowledging that resources can be useful *evidence* in reaching assessments of power. Using such evidence is not easy, but that it is certainly possible I try to show in Chapter 19. All I am concerned to argue here is that there is, logically, a third alternative, so that we need not identify power with its exercise in order to avoid identifying it with resources.

So power, as a dispositional concept, is neither a *thing* (a resource or vehicle) nor an *event* (an exercise of power): it is a *capacity*. And dispositional concepts are perfectly respectable ones that we do not need to replace by concepts of some other sort. On the contrary we clearly need such dispositional concepts in our conceptual vocabulary. We need not feel ashamed that 'power' is such a dispositional concept.

—4—
Power as a dispositional concept

I hope that I have now established that a power is a disposition of some sort. In this chapter I will expand on the significance of this, and examine further exactly what the dispositional nature of power is.

4.1—POWER AND ITS EXERCISE

When power is *exercised*, something happens: for instance, the United States overthrows the government in Grenada. Such an event could be described in many different ways, of course – you may prefer talking about the liberation of Grenada from communist tyranny, perhaps. But in this section I want to contrast two possible types of description of this event: the description of the event as the overthrow of a government or the liberation of a country, on the one hand, and the description of the same event as the United States *exercising its power* to overthrow a government or liberate a country. I shall suggest that the fact that we can rephrase many descriptions of events into statements about the exercise of power has led many social scientists (and philosophers) to misunderstand the significance of power, and to think that we are interested in the acts that people do *because* they are exercises of power, and not simply because they are acts of a certain sort.

A good example of what can happen if one doesn't exercise care is the following gaffe made by Quentin Gibson. Gibson refers to Stanley Benn's (Benn, 1967: p. 426) example

> of the careless smoker who constantly causes fires but never achieves anything he intends. Such a person, says Benn, could not be called powerful. But this, it seems to me, is to misjudge normal usage. The man is clearly able to cause fires, whether he actually intends to or not, and *it is precisely in this that the regrettable power of such people lies*. (Gibson, 1971: p. 103; my emphasis)

But this is just wrong. What is regrettable about careless smokers is not that they are *able* to cause fires, but that they *do* cause fires. It is not the *power* to cause fires that we regret in this case since you also have this power and no one regrets *that* – unless, of course, you are a careless smoker or a pyromaniac. We are typically interested simply in who *does* set fire to things.

A similar mistake vitiates the analysis of power that William Connolly provides in his chapter on Power and Responsibility in *The Terms of Political Discourse* (Connolly, 1974/1983: ch. 3). Most commentators have concentrated on exposing weaknesses in the way Connolly talks about responsibility,[1] but have not noticed that Connolly is not really talking about power at all in this chapter, despite his frequent use of the word. Instead, Connolly has fallen into the trap of thinking that because something can be *described* as an exercise of power we must be interested in it *as* an exercise of power. It is instructive to see how he makes this mistake.

Connolly draws up a "paradigm" of power which "briefly stated" is that "A exercises power over B when he is responsible for some X that increases the costs, risks, or difficulties to B in promoting B's desires or in recogniz-ing or promoting B's interests or obligations" (pp. 102–3). But Connolly recognizes that the locution '*having* power' is "basic" (p. 101), and so he recasts his paradigm so that someone *has* power, but does not exercise it, "when he could, but does not, limit B in the ways specified" (p. 103). This is Connolly's definition, or paradigm, of "A *has* power over B".

What Connolly completely overlooks is that this move destroys the main thesis of his chapter, which is "that there is a particularly intimate connect-ion between alleging that A has power over B and concluding that A is properly held responsible to some degree for B's conduct or situation" (p. 95). For if A could, *but does not*, "limit" B in some way, then there is nothing in B's conduct or situation for which A can be held responsible: ex hypo-thesi, A has *not* contributed to the situation that B faces. It is only when A *does* act that he can be held responsible for the act's consequences. So it is not *power* that Connolly tries to link with responsibility, but various sorts of *acts*.[2]

What Connolly is doing in his chapter, then, is discussing which types of action are always permissible (persuasion is one such, he thinks), and which types of action have a "moral presumption" against them (p. 95). This is certainly a very important subject, and one which involves our whole moral outlook on personal interaction – but it does not refer to power, and it only obscures the issue to include 'power' in it. When it comes to holding people morally responsible – praising and blaming them – it is invariably their actions (and omissions) that we look at, not their powers. One is not censured for having the *power* to start forest fires or the *power* to coerce people to do one's bidding, but only for actually doing such things. When discussing the rightness or wrongness of someone's actions, we require a morally appropriate vocabulary for describing these actions, and a set of moral beliefs for judging them; we do not require a redrawn concept of power.[3]

The message of this section is that, whilst many events can be described as an exercise of power, we should only use the vocabulary of power if we are interested specifically in the *capacity* for producing events of this sort, and not if we are just interested in the events themselves.

4.2—HABITUAL AND CONDITIONAL DISPOSITIONS

But the capacity for producing events may mean two different things, for there are two different sorts of disposition. This distinction is of considerable importance for understanding 'power', and yet it has not received the attention due to it.

We can understand this distinction by analysing the following passage by Gilbert Ryle, in which he describes dispositional properties.

> To possess a dispositional property is not to be in a particular state, or to undergo a particular change; it is to be bound or liable to be in a particular state, or to undergo a particular change, when a particular condition is realised. The same is true about specifically human dispositions such as qualities of character. My being an habitual smoker does not entail that I am at this or that moment smoking; it is my permanent proneness to smoke when I am not eating, sleeping, lecturing or attending funerals, and have not quite recently been smoking. (Ryle, 1949: p. 43)

But that someone is a smoker is a different sort of property from a standard dispositional one such as a sugar lump being soluble – for the latter involves *conditionals* whilst the former does not. To say that a sugar lump is soluble is to say that *if* it were to be placed in water, it would dissolve. The conditional clause here states an activating condition: a circumstance necessary for the dispositional property to be actualized. But to say that Samantha is a smoker does not mean that, if the present conditions were different from what they are, she would be smoking; rather it is to assert that in a relatively short amount of time from now she will be smoking, and that a relatively short amount of time ago she was smoking (barring the sort of exceptions that Ryle mentions). And *these* are straightforward future and past indicative sentences, without conditional elements.

Attempts at introducing sensible conditionals all fail. Thus we can try, as a translation of "Samantha is a smoker", "if Samantha experienced the relevant sort of cravings for a smoke now, she would smoke". This differentiates between the smoker and the person who, giving up, successfully fights against her occasional desires for a smoke; but a true non-smoker never experiences these cravings, and whether she should succumb to them if she did is not the relevant issue. Thus to distinguish the smoker from the non-smoker we have to add to the conditional some such codicil as "and Samantha frequently experiences such cravings" – which is a straightforward descriptive statement. One could, I suppose, try some such formula as "if it were two hours later than it is now, Samantha would have smoked in the last two hours", or "if Samantha had not smoked in the last two hours, she would be smoking now", but these seem unnecessarily tortuous. Ryle's comment about the smoker's "permanent proneness" to smoke seems little help indeed – and it is precisely such sorts of account that Ryle is attacking in *The Concept of Mind*.

It is worth noting that my suggested analysis of "Samantha smokes" would be different if, for some reason, cigarettes were in short supply: *then* the dispositional term 'smoker' *could* be used conditionally, meaning "if Samantha could have obtained some cigarettes today, she would have smoked them". This could well occur to someone who smokes dope – if cannabis becomes unusually difficult to obtain, we would still say of someone that she smokes it even if she hasn't touched the stuff for months because she has been unable to get hold of any.

I will call this the distinction between habitual dispositions and true or conditional dispositions. We would recognize, I think, that it is a distinction we draw in ordinary language, particularly if we change the example from smoking to drinking (alcohol). A habitual drinker is one who drinks regularly (and frequently) regardless of circumstances; we normally want to distinguish such a person from one who drinks only in certain circumstances (e.g. a 'social' drinker); and differentiate the latter from a person who is teetotal. The habits of the habitual drinker and of the teetotaller will accurately be described by a suitable non-conditional sentence, whilst the moderate or occasional drinker will require some suitable conditional to describe his drinking.

I think we can now see why treating influence as a special sort of power (as do, for instance, Partridge [1963] and Oppenheim [1981]) immediately gives rise to odd consequences. We readily talk of the influence of Cézanne on painting or Joyce on literature (Partridge's examples: p. 111);

hence, if influence is a sort of power, a less specific way of saying much the same thing would be to talk of the *power* of Cézanne on (over?) painting. But we rarely attribute powers to people after they are dead.

It is my feeling that 'influence', used in its capacity sense, refers to a habitual disposition, whilst 'power' most usually indicates a conditional disposition. To say that someone is an influence is of a similar logical form to saying that someone is a smoker: it is to say that they *do* influence (smoke), and not just once but often. The episodes of influencing take place so frequently that, rather than enumerating them, we roll them all together and talk of the person's influence extending continuously over time. This is the sense in which we talk of the influence of Cézanne on painting.

A power, however, is a disposition that may or may not be activated: TNT is explosive because it explodes *when the conditions are right*, not because it explodes frequently. A person is powerful if she can do things *when she wants to* – not only if she does do things frequently. From this it is fairly clear why the dead have no powers of this sort: whilst they can still influence, they do not have a disposition to influence that they can activate.

This is why we do not say that someone had influence, or was influential, but never bothered to influence anyone; we do say that people have power, or are powerful, but do not bother to use it. An influence, then, is a capacity in the sense of a continuing influence; not a capacity in the sense of a potential influence. If we want to describe someone as having the capacity to influence in this latter sense, we have to say that they have the *power* to influence.

4.3—DISPOSITIONAL PROPERTIES AND ABILITIES

In this section I shall consider the logic of *our* dispositional properties – that is, of human powers. Let us start by returning to Aristotle,

who drew a sharp distinction between rational powers, such as the ability to speak Greek, and natural powers like the power of fire to burn. If all the necessary conditions for the exercise of a natural power were present, then, he maintained, the power was necessarily exercised: put the wood, appropriately dry, on the fire, and the fire will burn it; there are no two ways about it. Rational powers, however, are essentially, he argued, two-way powers, powers which can be exercised at will: a rational agent, presented with all the necessary external conditions for exercising a power, may choose not to do so. (Kenny, 1975: pp. 52–3, citing Aristotle, c. 330 BC: Theta 1046a–1048a)

But this distinction is not quite correct; for, as Kenny points out, "Aristotle was surely wrong to identify rational powers and two-way powers. If someone speaks a language I know in my hearing it isn't in my power not to understand it" (Kenny, 1975: p. 53).

It seems, then, that people have ordinary dispositional powers and also powers which can be exercised at will, and that these two are very different. I shall call the latter *abilities*. The difference between a human ability and a mere disposition is that the ability involves, in some way, an act of will, a choice or a decision. Abilities refer not to things which happen to us, but to things which we do.[4] So abilities are conditional dispositional properties that depend on the actor activating them: one of the necessary conditions for exercising an ability is that the actor must choose to do so.

4.4—POWER AND INTENTION

Whilst many writers have defined power as the ability to affect people in accordance with one's intentions,[5] some have denied any connection at all between power and intentions. Those who have resisted the suggestion that 'power' makes some reference to the intentions of the power-holder have advanced three sorts of arguments against it. The first 'argument' is that intention is such a difficult concept that we are better off without it.[6] This is not worth the trouble of taking seriously: if it turns out that an analysis of 'power' requires us to include intentions, then we have to make the best of it. I hope to show, in any case, that we can cope with all the terrors that the concept of intention can produce for us.

The second sort of argument consists of producing examples that are allegedly self-evident examples of power but which contain no intentional element. The trouble with this method is that most such examples are clearly cases of influence, not power, and often are even described as such. The plausibility of these examples depends on the prior identification of 'influence' and 'power', which is, of course, something I am at pains to deny. Hence Oppenheim invites us to "take the pollsters who predicted that Truman would lose the presidential election of 1948, and thereby quite unintentionally *influenced* voters – to disconfirm that prediction. Did they not *exercise power* over voters who voted for Truman because of these polls?" (Oppenheim, 1981: pp. 44–5; my emphases). Oppenheim has many more such examples, all equally unconvincing. "We are inclined to regard", he says, people who prevent others from doing things, without intending to do so, as "thereby acquiring power" over them – for instance, "the winner in an athletic competition has power over the losers" (p. 45). Conceptual arguments that rely on ordinary usage are, by themselves, never convincing – but they are even less convincing when they so clearly get ordinary usage wrong.

Connolly and Lukes adopt a rather more sophisticated version of this approach. They have already defined an exercise of power as an action (or failure to act) for which the actor is responsible and which adversely affects someone in some way, and they then point out, rightly, that we can all adversely affect people without intending to do so, and we can then even (sometimes) be held morally responsible for adversely affecting them.[7] According to their definitions, we have thereby exercised power unintentionally. But all this only follows, of course, if we accept the link between responsibility and power that Lukes and Connolly claimed – and I have already shown that the arguments for this link fail to hold because of the confusion between power and its exercise (see above, pp. 21–2). The examples they offer, then, will fail to convince a disbeliever that power can be exercised unintentionally.

The third, and most interesting, way of trying to separate power from intention has been suggested by Quentin Gibson.[8] Gibson considers that "intentions are irrelevant", for

> to insist on intentionality has one extremely odd result. It prevents us, at one stroke, from attributing power to inanimate things. That a stormy sea has the power to wreck a ship or an engine the power to turn the wheels is surely something which no one should feel hesitant about maintaining. It may be said that this is anthropomorphism, and that in the literal sense only people have power. But this would be to confuse the origin of the concept with its nature. It may well be that in earlier and more animistic days, power, like causal efficacy, was attributable only to human or other spiritual agencies with wills. But generalization of the concept has taken place long since, certainly by the time of Hobbes and Locke. The move from human power to horse power, and from horse power to engine power is a matter of history. (Gibson, 1971: pp. 103–4)

What Gibson here is missing is that the 'move' from human power to engine power is not a generalization, but a change in meaning. When we assert that a stormy sea has the power to wreck a ship, what we are referring to is either a dispositional property, pure and simple (Power$_1$), or Power$_2$ ("the ability to . . . affect something strongly; vigour, energy"). The word 'power' is undoubtedly used in both these senses. But when we talk about, for instance, the Prime Minister's power to dissolve Parliament,[9] it is quite clear that neither of these senses is being employed. For whilst "the sulphuric acid has the power to dissolve zinc" means (more or less) that if zinc is placed in sulphuric acid it will dissolve, the corresponding power of the British Prime Minister is to dissolve Parliament *when she wants to*.

Gibson's argument fails, then, because he does not realize that 'power' can refer to a variety of different dispositional properties, each of which may have a slightly different logic. Intentions are *sometimes* irrelevant to an actor's powers, but Gibson's examples do not show that intentions are *always* irrelevant. Intentions are usually not relevant when we are considering powers that are not abilities; but an intention is usually part of the definition of any power that is an ability – for abilities are things we can do *when we want*.[10]

To explore further the nature of this distinction, I would like to consider an interesting passage of Danto's in which he discusses sexual impotence. It seems that, if Danto is right, our use of 'impotence' in this context is in accord with the sense of power as a mere dispositional, and not as an ability.

Danto starts with a passage from Hume: "We are not able to move all the organs of the body with like authority, though we cannot assign any reason besides experience, for so remarkable a difference between one and the other." He then quotes St Augustine, who agreed with Hume that:

> We *could* have been framed with our authority differently seated: 'God could easily have made us with all our members subjected to the will', he [Augustine] writes, adding the possibility which obviously haunted him as a man, as we might recall from the *Confessions*, 'even those which *now* are moved by lust'. I italicize the word 'now', which occurs twice in this passage. For it was Augustine's curious view that Adam, in paradise, indeed was so framed that he could perform what I have termed basic actions with his sexual organ, and hence achieve the sexual act immune from the contaminations of sin. . . .
>
> I am not at all certain that it is a merely contingent matter that voluntary erection lies outside the boundaries of direct action. For curiously enough, a man who were able to erect at will might in fact be impotent in the received sense, which is an incapacity for genuine sexual *response*; where *response* implies precisely the absence of that order of control Augustine supposes our first parent to have exemplified. A man who had direct control, or who was obliged to exercise direct control, would be a man without *feeling*, erection being the common *expression* of male sexual feeling. And it is in some measure a logical truth that if erection were an action it would not be an expression, and the entire meaning of sexuality would be altered were tumescence something over which we had 'authority'. (Danto, 1973: pp. 116–17)[11]

It would seem, then, that the power which those who are impotent lack is a power in the purely dispositional sense of the term, and not the ability sense. For if erection (in the appropriate situations) is not an *action*, then we cannot have (or lack) the ability to perform it. Erection as a response is like the knee-jerk reflex or laughing: something that happens to our bodies rather than something we do. Danto's discussion of such responses, how they differ from actions done at will, and how important they are in our social lives, is, I think, very well done, and could form the basis of some important work. If Danto is right, then, it seems that our natural powers, which we do not exercise at will, are very important to us in our social interactions.

And these natural powers are very different from our abilities. The lesson to be drawn from this discussion is that we must not confuse abilities with natural powers, and think that because they are both powers they must have an identical analysis. There is a crucial difference here, which Gibson overlooked.

If Gibson's argument fails, he is nevertheless quite right to suggest that power is not influence with some added intentions. The difference between power and influence runs deeper than this. I shall argue in the next chapter that most accounts of 'power' are defective because they have been modelled too closely on 'influence'.

—5—
Power and influence: the differences concluded

5.1—AFFECTING AND EFFECTING

The most common account of 'power' in the social science literature is one that involves somehow *affecting* others. Hence Steven Lukes claims as (almost) uncontroversial that "the absolutely basic common core to, or primitive notion lying behind, all talk of power is the notion that A in some way affects B" (Lukes, 1974: p. 26).[1] And this "primitive notion" certainly does lie behind almost all recent analyses of power.

Yet several writers have pointed out that simply *affecting* someone is not what we understand by power. For if it were, then the victim who incautiously displays a well-filled wallet would exercise power over the thief who robs him (Wormuth, 1967: p. 817); a person who overturned their car and burdened the insurance company with the bill would, likewise, have thereby exercised power (Young, 1978: p. 643); and so would the bankrupt financier whose fall ruined thousands of people who had invested their savings with him (Benn, 1967: p. 426).

I want to suggest that we cannot get rid of these anomalies by putting restrictions on the sorts of affecting that are to 'count' as an exercise of power, as Lukes and others want to do. The error runs deeper: 'power' is not concerned at all with affecting, though 'influence' is. 'Power' is concerned with *effecting*, which is a very different idea.

To *affect* something is to alter it or impinge on it in some way (*any* way); to *effect* something is to bring about or accomplish it. For example, "a single glass of brandy may affect [i.e. alter for better or worse the prospects of] his recovery" is very different from "a single glass of brandy may effect [i.e. bring about] his recovery".[2]

It follows from this difference in meaning that the verbs 'affect' and 'effect' take different objects: you can affect something if you can alter it in some way; you can effect something if you can accomplish it. Hence you can affect, but not effect, a person; and you can effect, but not affect, a state of affairs that does not now exist.

The subjects of the verbs sometimes differ as well. Only beings that are in some (perhaps metaphorical) sense conscious and active can effect anything because only these beings can bring about or accomplish something; whilst a much wider range of entities can affect. Hence books and ideas can affect but not effect, and so can famous but dead people, like Cézanne.

I hope that by now 'affects' is beginning to look very similar to 'influences', and 'effects' rather like 'exercises power'. This is not surprising since, if you glance back at the definitions given on pp. 9–10, you will see that 'influence' is defined as *affecting* (in a certain way), whilst 'power' is usually defined as the ability to *effect*. The examples given in the second paragraph of this section seem so clearly not to be examples of power precisely because no effecting is going on in them: those who affect others without effecting anything are rightly seen not as powerful but merely as nuisances. Benn's bankrupt financier had a certain amount of power *before* his fall, which he lost when his empire collapsed; although his fall possibly affected people more drastically than any of his previous actions, he did not thereby exercise power.

To affect something (or somebody) but not effect (accomplish) anything seems, then, not to be an exercise of power.

5.2—POWER WITHOUT AFFECTING

I have suggested that simply affecting something or somebody is not an exercise of power unless the actor thereby effects something, and that, correspondingly, the capacity to affect is not power unless the capacity to effect is also present. I now want to go one step further, and argue that someone may be powerful when they have the capacity to *effect* something even when they cannot *affect* anything.

Let us look a bit closer at the idea that power involves the capacity to affect an existing state of affairs (or person). Here is an example (an adaptation of one of Alvin Goldman's). You have a rain-making machine. On clear sunny days (all clear sunny days, and only clear sunny days) you can crank up your machine, and within six hours a gentle drizzle will be falling from the heavens. It never fails. Sometimes, of course, it would have rained anyway, and then you can't take much credit for the rain (you don't make it rain any harder); but often it would not have rained, and then you have made it rain. You have the power to make rain (on clear sunny days). But do you have the power to make rain on all clear sunny days *including* those when it would have rained anyway; or only on those clear sunny days when it would *not* have rained? It would seem that when it would have rained anyway you are impotent to do anything about the weather with your rain-making machine (you don't have a rain-*preventing* machine): your machine can make no difference at all. So, since it rains whatever you do, you don't have any powers or abilities with respect to the issue of whether it rains or not on these necessarily rainy occasions.

This is, more or less, how Goldman argues.[3] I think he is wrong to do so. I think that one can have the power or ability to do something even if it would have been brought about in any case. It is true that, on days when it would have rained, your machine cannot affect the weather: it rains whether or not you set your machine to work. If it is power to affect the weather that we are interested in, then Goldman's approach is the right one: you lack this power on rainy days. But you *do* still have the power *to ensure rain*. Your power (or your machine's power) to produce rain does not somehow disappear when rain-clouds are gathering unseen beyond the horizon. Your machine ensures that you can have rain whenever you want it: that you do indeed have the power to produce rain.

At this point we need to ask exactly what it is that we want to know. I have assumed that we are interested in whether your machine can ensure that it will rain whenever you set it going, and this seems to me a not unreasonable interpretation. (That is what a gardener, for instance, would want to know when wondering whether to buy your machine.) But we might be interested, I suppose, in whether your machine could *make* it rain (perhaps on a given occasion), and by this mean that the rain must be created by the machine rather than by any other means. If this is what we want to know, then we are inquiring whether the machine can both effect rain *and* affect the weather, and your machine, which cannot do both of these if the weather would have been wet anyway, must be judged powerless. So the power to *make* rain, unlike the power to *ensure* rain, requires both effecting and affecting.[4]

From this it should be clear that it is crucial to specify very carefully the exact power which we are interested in. Goldman goes wrong, I think, in choosing to analyse the cumbersome formulation "power with respect to the issue of whether or not it rains" and not the more straightforward (and informative) "power to make (it) rain" or "power to ensure rain". This seems difficult to defend: doctors and would-be assassins both have power with respect to the issue of whether we live or die, yet the power to prevent a chronically ill person dying is one that we usually wish to distinguish from the power to kill a healthy person.

Clearly, if the phrase we are trying to analyse is "power with respect to an issue", then we will be led to an account of power that involves affecting and not effecting; for one can *affect* whether or not it rains, whilst one cannot *effect* whether or not it rains. Yet, as I have suggested, it is more likely than not that it is the power to effect rain that really interests us. If so we must look at power to effect *outcomes* (states of affairs) and not power over *issues*.[5] It is, therefore, very important which phrase, containing the word 'power', we choose to employ. This will be the topic of the next section.

5.3—POWER-TO OR POWER-OVER?

"A has power" is incomplete: it tells us that A has *some* dispositional property or capacity or ability, but it does not say *which*. Since all objects, of whatever sort, have dispositional properties, "A has power" is a singularly unhelpful utterance. We clearly need to specify the power in some way. This has been widely recognized in the literature, and most writers have felt that, in the social sciences, we must immediately go on to specify *over whom* A has power. For instance:

> I do not "have power – period". I have (perhaps) power over my students wrt [the author's abbreviation for "with respect to"] their reading *Leviathan*. Such expressions are elliptical. (Oppenheim, 1981: p. 6)

Thus Oppenheim's chosen definiendum is "P has power over R wrt his not doing X" (p. 21), and any statement about power that doesn't specify the person that the power is over – and 'with respect to' which of their actions – is considered by Oppenheim to be incomplete.

This move is a mistake, and we can now see why so many people have been led to make it. If 'power' is thought of as involving affecting, then a full statement of the power must state what is affected. When we are concerned with *social* power, it is natural to suppose that a *person* (rather than a thing) must be affected by the power. The only way that the English language allows 'power' to be followed by a word for a person is by talking of the power being *over* the person. Ergo, it seems, all social power becomes power over someone.

Now anyone with an ear for language, or knowledge of English usage, would find this conclusion very odd. It is far more common to say that someone has the power *to do something* than it is to say that they have power *over someone*.[6] We readily contrast the Prime Minister's power to dissolve Parliament with the American President's lack of such power; we talk (as even Dahl does) of the President having more power to influence foreign policy than we do; we lament that we do not have the power to paint our council house the colour of our choice, or we rejoice that we do have the power to make our views known to our elected representatives – and, periodically, the power to dismiss them. None of these powers can be expressed adequately using 'power over'; these are all powers to obtain some specified *outcome*, and whilst affecting others *may* be the desired outcome (I paint my council house crimson to annoy the neighbours), it is more likely not to be.

Further, when we do say that A has power over a person B – or that B is in A's power – we do so when A can get B to do a large number of things, not just one. A blackmailer has power over his victim if there is a wide range of things that the victim will do readily rather than have his guilty secret revealed; we would say that a Congressperson who owes another a favour is within her power if the latter can call in this debt at a time and in a manner of her own choosing.[7] So the locution 'power over' has a specific use of its own; it is not the general, and certainly not the main, way we talk of power.

This emphasis on power as affecting others has had serious repercussions, which have stemmed from the loose way that 'power over' has been used. Mostly the phrase 'A has power over B' was meant in a wide sense, to mean that B is the object of A's power (that is, B is the person *through* whom A attains his ends, or who is affected *by* A attaining his ends). But the more natural reading of the phrase is the much narrower one that the sub-ordination of B is the *objective* of A's power.[8] Concentration on 'power over' has had the deplorable tendency of emphasizing this latter sort of power, so that Dahl, Lukes and many others have defined power in terms of someone's ability to affect others in various nasty ways. But our ability to kick others around (or to harm their interests, or get them to do things they don't want to do) can scarcely encompass *everything* we understand as power in social contexts.[9] Frequently we value power simply because it enables us to do things we want to do: to have more control over our own lives.

This distortion has, I think, had worse results than just causing academic confusion: it has had pernicious political consequences. The reception of the slogan "Black Power" is a case in point. "Black Power" encapsulated a platform aimed at giving blacks the power to run their own lives; it represented a demand for autonomy. The originators of the movement never intended the slogan to imply that black people should have disproportionate power *over* non-blacks – should somehow dominate them.[10] Indeed, one strand of the movement sought to eliminate as much contact between white and black people as it could: it advocated setting up black enclaves which were as self-governing as possible. White supremacists, however, by equating power-to with power-over, were able to portray the legitimate demands of black people for equality as equivalent to a desire for black domination. It is regrettable that reputable, and liberal, academics, by considering power over others as the only sort of power, may have unwittingly encouraged such distortions.

How, then, have social scientists defended their near exclusive emphasis on power *over* people? I think it is fair to say that this really crucial decision has never been adequately considered in the literature: either the matter is ignored entirely; or (spurious) considerations of ordinary language are adduced; or the author simply declares that power to do things is not what he is interested in.[11] The one argument that has been tried is the claim that talking about power *to* do things "cannot bring out what seems to me the important distinguishing feature of *social* power; namely, that it refers to an interaction relation, a relationship between some action y of P and some possible *action* x of R" (Oppenheim, 1981: p. 31). Or, from a more self-consciously radical perspective, the locution 'power to' "indicates a 'capacity', a 'facility', an 'ability', not a relationship. Accordingly, the conflictual aspect of power – the fact [*sic*] that it is exercised *over* people – disappears altogether from view" (Lukes, 1974: p. 31).

But this talk of power as a relationship is not particularly enlightening. As Hannah Pitkin points out: "one may . . . 'have' a 'relationship', but always 'with' someone else. . . . And one does not 'exercise' a 'relationship' at all. What the social scientists mean by calling power relational, if I understand them, is that the phenomena of power go on among people" (Pitkin, 1972: p. 276). If we are interested in the "conflictual aspect" of power, we can very easily look at someone's power *to* kick others around, or their power *to* win conflicts. Everything that needs to be said about power can be said using the idea of the capacity to effect outcomes – unless we are mesmerized by a desire to get the notion of *affecting* into 'power' at all costs.

There is a further dubious aspect to Lukes's argument, since what he seems to be doing is cramming into his chosen *concept* of power claims which ought to be considered as empirical. Thus even if Lukes is correct, and if it *is* a fact that power is always exercised over people, this is not a reason for defining power so that it can *only* be exercised over people. If conflict is indeed omnipresent within society, then a neutral definition will surely discover it.[12]

It may be worth noting that no empirical researcher has taken such a limited attitude to power in their research. Even Dahl, whose conceptual writings stress repeatedly that power is exercised over someone, forgets this in his empirical work, in which he equates a person's power with their success in matters of key importance (Dahl, 1961: p. 333).

5.4—CONCLUSION

Oppenheim's definiendum is so contorted and clumsy because of his misunderstanding of our use of 'power': he wants to use the word 'power'; he wants to use a notion of power as affecting; and he wants the thing affected to be a person. But these three desires do not fit naturally together. If I want to say that I have the power to get my students to read *Leviathan*, I can say just that; I don't have to say that I have power over my students with respect to their reading *Leviathan*; nor is it natural to do so. Oppenheim, Goldman and many others are pushed into the position of talking about power "with respect to" someone's action, or "with respect to" some issue, because of their reliance on the model of power as a form of affecting.[13] But, as I have already suggested, it is both more natural and more informative to fill out the content of our powers by describing the outcomes that we are capable of effecting. This is invariably what we do say (when we are not captivated by an erroneous theory), and it enables us to say what we want to say neatly and accurately.

In the next chapter I shall look somewhat more closely at what sorts of things we *do* want to say when we use this concept of power.

—6—
Why we need concepts of power

So far I have been making conceptual distinctions; suggesting that ordinary language reflects and employs these distinctions; and defending their propriety. But I need to do more than just that. Philosophy is full of distinctions which are defended in the most brilliantly subtle way – but which are pointless. I now need to show that the concept of the ability to effect outcomes allows us to say important things that cannot be said without such a concept. And, what is more, that these things are the sort of things we talk about when we use the word 'power'.

But why *do* we use 'power'? What jobs do we want concepts of power to do? It strikes me as amazing that we can search the now voluminous literature on 'power' without finding a remotely systematic consideration of how the term fits into our vocabulary. Neither those who have concluded that 'power' is too ambiguous or unclear to be useful, nor those who claim that it represents an idea of central importance, have given any thought to the question of the uses for which we require the term.

Now it may be thought that we can study power (or anything else) for any reason at all, or none – that it is quite acceptable to study power just because one finds it interesting, as some people collect matchbox tops. But this is both unhelpful and implausible. Power is not something that one *finds* at all:

> concepts like 'power' . . . are not real 'things', although they are intended to point to some significant aspect about . . . things. They represent, instead, an added element, something created by the . . . theorist. Their function is to render . . . facts significant, either for purposes of analysis, criticism, or justification, or a combination of all three. (Wolin, 1960: p. 5)[1]

Concepts that render facts significant must render them significant *for something*; there must be a purpose behind studying something like power. What, then, is the purpose?

I shall suggest that there are several different purposes: we employ 'power' – in its peculiarly human uses – in several distinct contexts, in each of which we mean something different when we talk of power. These contexts can be found clearly referred to in the literature, but hitherto each writer on the subject has concentrated on just one context, ignored all others, and claimed that his chosen context was *the* context. Thus a lot of needless argument has taken place, which can be avoided by recognizing the plurality of contexts in which 'power' operates.

We talk of power in at least three contexts – practical, moral and evaluative – and I shall discuss them in turn. I believe that these three are the only contexts. In section 6.4 I go some way towards supporting this assertion by rejecting three other contexts which have been suggested; and in Appendix 1, which considers the view that *all* concepts of power are redundant, I arrive at the same three contexts. But I would not be troubled if you succeeded in demonstrating the existence of a fourth context; it is the *plurality* of contexts on which I want to insist.

6.1—THE PRACTICAL CONTEXT

Brian Barry has remarked that, whatever one thinks about the concept of power, the powerful people in any society must include those whom the CIA would want to bribe (Barry, 1974: p. 189, or 1976: p. 222). CIA operatives are practical people, interested in power for the practical reason that they want to bring certain things about. And even if the things the CIA want to bring about may not be to your taste, you are very much like them in that you, too, want to bring things about from time to time.

For this you want to know your powers: you want to know what things you can bring about, and what you can't. If you know that you can't do something, then you will either not try to do it (thus saving yourself a lot of bother) or you will endeavour to alter things so that you *can* do it. If you think (wrongly) that you cannot do something, then you may miss out on welcome opportunities.

Knowing your powers is, therefore, important to you. But so is knowing the powers of others, and for two different sorts of reasons: you may want to get them to do things *for* you, or you may want to make sure that you don't run the risk of them doing unwelcome things *to* you. Taking the first of these first, if you are wondering whether to ask someone to do you a favour, you want to know (amongst other things) whether she *can* do what you'd like her to do. If you are paying (or bribing) her, you want to make sure you are not wasting your money. When she says that for

$10,000 she'll make sure that the arms contract is given to an American firm, you want to know if she can deliver. We make decisions of this sort, on a more mundane level, all the time.

But we also need to know about powers when we engage in what I call counterfactual practical reasoning. For instance, one of the powers of sulphuric acid is that it burns flesh; knowing this, and not wanting your hand burnt, you don't put your hand into the acid. The acid's power remains unexercised; but it is still important that you know about it, since it is only this knowledge that prevents you putting your hand into the acid and getting it burnt. Similarly, if you tease that dog it will have your hand off; but a toothless old hound that couldn't do you any damage can be teased mercilessly, should you so wish. And before you antagonize a person it would be wise to pause for a moment and consider what harm she could do you should she really turn nasty – people who publish satirical cartoons of their monarch survive longer in Britain than in Saudi Arabia.[2]

In short, the sort of concept that is being used in practical contexts is clearly the capacity to effect outcomes.

6.2—THE MORAL CONTEXT

The second context in which we use concepts of power is the moral one of blaming, excusing and allocating responsibility. Here

> when we say that someone has power or is powerful we are . . . *assigning responsibility* to a human agent or agency for bringing (or failing to bring) about certain outcomes that impinge upon the interests of other human beings. (Ball, 1976: p. 249)

I have already mentioned that both Lukes and Connolly are mainly interested (they say) in assigning responsibility, and I have argued that they fail to connect responsibility with any concept recognizable as power (see section 4.1). So how *does* 'power' get into this moral context? I suggest that it is relevant in two different ways.

First, you are not usually considered responsible for something if you didn't do it. We are rarely happy attributing responsibility vicariously, particularly moral (rather than legal) responsibility; so, if some catastrophe occurs, you are morally blameless if you did not do it. And you can prove that you did not do it by showing that you were incapable of doing it – that doing it lay outside your powers. All claims involving alibis contain such an implicit reference to lack of power. It is a defence to prove that you were 350 miles away from the bank at the time it was robbed, only because we know that you are not able to rob banks across that sort of distance: moving banknotes at a distance is just not one of your powers.

The second, and more important, connection between power and responsibility was well, if sternly, stated by Lord Salisbury: "Those who have the absolute power of preventing lamentable events and, knowing what is taking place, refuse to exercise that power, are responsible for what happens."[3]

As I argued earlier when discussing Connolly, we are blamed for our acts (and omissions), not for having power. But it is a defence to a charge such as Lord Salisbury's that you *did not* have the power of which he spoke: that you were, in fact, powerless to prevent the lamentable events. If you can show this then you escape censure, for you could not refuse (or even fail) to exercise a power that you didn't have.

In other words, you can fail to do something for two broad reasons: *disinclination* and *inability*.[4] You are only blameworthy if your failure is for the first of these two reasons. This principle, usually called the principle that 'ought' implies 'can', is almost universally held in our culture: it states that one cannot be under an obligation to do something one cannot do. So if someone wishes to censure you for your failure to prevent a lamentable event, they have to demonstrate that you had the power to prevent it – and you may well try to claim that you were powerless, for you are blameworthy only if it can be demonstrated that you had the relevant power. But it is important to keep clear that you are not being blamed *for* having the power. There is nothing whatsoever wrong with having the power to prevent lamentable events – indeed, the more people there are with this power the better. What is wrong is having the power and refusing to use it.

The connection between power and responsibility is, then, essentially negative: you can deny all responsibility by demonstrating lack of power. You can do this, as in the alibi example, by proving that you couldn't have *done* the crime. Or you can do this by showing that you couldn't have *prevented* the catastrophe. In either case, power is a necessary (but not sufficient) condition for blame: if you didn't have the power, you are blameless.[5]

It is clear from this discussion, I hope, that 'power' is here being used in the sense of the power to bring about certain outcomes. In the alibi case, the power referred to must be the power to *effect* something – the bank has been robbed; the question is, could you have done it? In the other case – in which we want to know if you had the power of preventing a lamentable event – effecting and affecting might seem to overlap. The disaster occurred: could you have prevented it? Preventing the disaster would, clearly, have affected it; but nothing is gained, and much lost, by asking merely whether you could have affected the disaster, rather than whether you could have prevented it.

So, in this context, power as the ability to effect something is the concept we need.

6.3—THE EVALUATIVE CONTEXT

We also use the concept of power when we evaluate social systems; when we judge them. We are often very concerned about the distribution – and extent – of power within a society, and we often praise (and condemn) societies if they (fail to) meet our expectations. It is within this third context that most recent academic discussion of power has taken place: the main reason that pluralists took issue with Wright Mills's *The Power Elite* was that they did not feel that America fell that far short of realistic democratic expectations. Regrettably, however, this context has been given less emphasis in the literature on the *concept* of power.

This evaluative context is the most complicated of the three, if only because the range of things that people can value is so great. It is impossible here to write a treatise on the different things people can value in societies, but two broad perspectives involving power may be discerned: we can be interested either in the extent to which citizens have the power to satisfy their own ends, or in the extent to which one person is subject to the power of another. It is frequently unclear which is meant at any one time, but these two categories need to be kept analytically distinct. Thus most of us praise autonomy – that an individual can make his own decisions and act on them – but often we are less clear than we should be with what we are contrasting this. One possible contrast is a Hobbesian state of nature: individuals cannot make meaningful decisions because they have so little control over their environment: life, even without the interference of other humans, is solitary, poor and short. Here people are unable to do much because they are subject to the force of a nature over which they have virtually no control.

As people band together, and co-operate to achieve their goals, each comes to have more control over his own life: his power is increased with the help of others. But, simultaneously, other people start having some control over him. This process can lead to the alternative horror with which to contrast an ideal, autonomous life: that in which one is enslaved.

So we can judge societies either by the extent to which they give their citizens freedom from the power of others, or by the extent to which citizens have the power to meet their own needs or wants. To be impotent is to lack a power; to be dominated is to be subject to the power of another; these are not the same and need not be found together.

Being able to obtain your desired ends is obviously a valuable thing; the more you have this power the better. Societies can be condemned if such power is stifled or its development is hindered. It is clear from the moving opening sentences of *The Power Elite* (Mills, 1956) that one of Mills's main themes is the lack of power of ordinary American men and women, which he contrasts both with the great power of his power elite and with the great potential of the richest-ever nation. By 'power' here he clearly means the power to be effective, to shape and control one's own life: power to do things. Power, that is, as the capacity to effect.[6]

It is important to keep clear the difference between this context and the previous one: a difference that, it seems to me, Lukes and Connolly overlook. When we censure *people*, and consider them morally responsible for the occurrence of a disaster, we usually feel that they had to intend that the disaster should come about, or at least that they foresaw it: to attach responsibility to someone we have to inquire into his state of mind or, as lawyers say, his *mens rea*. But when we censure a *set of social arrangements*, all that needs to be shown is that it, rather than the sufferers themselves, is responsible for the sufferings that people have within that society. One does not need to establish that the harm is intended or foreseen by anybody; it is enough that the harm is unnecessary. A social set-up is bad, and should be criticized, if there is a better one available or if it could be improved. Whether anybody intends the harm, or benefits from the harm, is irrelevant.

Lukes and Connolly, as radicals, want to emphasize the plight of the powerless and thus to persuade people of the evils of contemporary capitalism. But they fail to achieve their aim, because they mistake their target. They think that what is wrong if you are powerless is that you are thereby in someone else's power, and that that someone else must be responsible for your powerlessness if you are to have a valid complaint. Both of these assumptions are wrong, as I have argued. What is wrong with being powerless is that you *are* powerless – that is, lacking in power. And if people are powerless because they live in a certain sort of society – that is, they would have more power if the social arrangements were changed – then that, itself, is a condemnation of that society. A radical critique of a society requires us to evaluate *that society*, not distribute praise or blame to *people*. The two are very different procedures, and must be sharply distinguished.

6.4—SOME OTHER CONTEXTS REJECTED

The practical, moral and evaluative contexts are, I think, the three main ones in which we are interested in power. But since we are interested in power, we are also interested in theorizing *about* power, and for both practical and evaluative reasons.

Many books have been written over the centuries giving advice to rulers on how to keep and increase their power, although Machiavelli's *The Prince* is the only one that gets read nowadays. It is also not surprising, given the great interest people have had in obtaining power, that people have tried to construct theories about where power lies in different societies. Many massive tomes have been written on this topic, though hardly any are worth taking seriously. What is relevant here is that the *concept* of power used in all these works is the concept appropriate to practical matters, which I have suggested is the power to effect.

More interesting, though no more conclusive, has been the theoretical work motivated by evaluative concerns. To evaluate something like a set of social arrangements requires a theoretical exercise of some complexity. As I have suggested in the last section, critics of a society have to show that things in it are bad and could be better. There are two possible empirical responses to this: the straightforward one that things are *not* that bad; and the more complex one that things, whilst bad, could be no better.[7] If the critic is complaining about the extent or distribution of powerlessness, the latter response would be that that's just the way it is – nothing can be done about it. The argument then veers off into a dispute between different theories of what the society could be like.

This is one theme in the arguments that took place between pluralists and so-called "elitists". The elitist case, as put forward by people like Wright Mills and Peter Bachrach, was, in a nutshell, that power in America was in the hands of a few, and not widely distributed as democratic pretensions would require. The pluralist response was, in part, that democratic ideals were unattainable, and that the distribution of power in America was (apart from the South) not that far away from the best that could realistically be achieved. That raises the question, of course, of what *could* realistically be achieved. The answers offered to this question are not what I am concerned with in this book. All that I want to show is that the concept of power that is being used in these theoretical works must be identical to that being used by the society's critics, if the impossibility-claim is indeed to refute the criticism. And so we see that theoretical work on power takes place firmly within the practical or evaluative contexts; there is no separate theoretical use of power.[8]

But is not 'power' also a crucial term in producing a (scientific) explanation of social and political phenomena?[9] I think it is not. To see why, let us consider very briefly what science does. It proceeds by making theories; and this theory-building "can be said to serve two main purposes. One is to *predict* the occurrences of events or outcomes of experiments, and thus to anticipate new facts. The other is to *explain*, or to make intelligible facts which have already been recorded" (von Wright, 1971: p. 1). Yet ever since Molière it has been recognized that referring to a person's power (or, indeed, an object's dispositional properties) is not providing much of an explanation: referring to opium's dormitive powers tells us no more than that opium induces drowsiness. But whilst we cannot use dispositional properties such as opium's soporific properties to *explain* the lethargy of the takers, we *can* use this property to *predict* the effects of opium on its users. This has puzzled people, because it has become widely accepted – since Hempel, if no earlier – that the logic of science is such that there is no difference between an explanation of an event that has taken place and a prediction of an event that is yet to occur. Yet here we have an asymmetry.

To see how this occurs, let us consider an everyday example. If we drop a cup and it shatters, and we search for an explanation of this event, we are not usually satisfied by a response that one of the cup's dispositional properties was fragility. We *know* that the cup was fragile; we can infer that without difficulty by watching it break. To point to the fragility of the cup is merely to assert that its breaking upon hitting the floor was not an accident or in any way unusual. This, it is true, advances us a small step along the road to an adequate explanation of the occurrence, but only a small and (usually) an insignificant one. We want to know either why the cup was dropped, or exactly why that sort of cup is particularly fragile: the evidence for its fragility is staring us in the eyes, littered all over the floor. To say it is fragile is to say that it breaks when hit like that; but we *know* it breaks when hit like that. An adequate explanation must do more than repeat what needs to be explained.

Similarly, subsuming an event under a covering law doesn't furnish an explanation in von Wright's sense of rendering known facts intelligible. If we are wondering why we keep seeing black ravens, our puzzlement at their blackness is not removed when we are told that ravens are always black. (We might then give up our hunt for white ravens; but this is using the 'covering law' to *predict* the absence of white ravens, not *explain* the blackness of those we have seen.) If we want to know *why* the ravens we have seen are black, it is no answer to tell us *that* ravens are black. Similarly, if we desire an explanation of the dropped cup's breaking, we don't usually provide one by saying that it was fragile – that it would always break when dropped. Dispositional statements *summarize* observations; they don't *explain* them.

However, let us suppose that we had not dropped the cup, but are playing with it somewhat carelessly; somebody tells us to be careful, because the cup is fragile. Now, *not* having just seen the cup shatter, this is a new and useful bit of information for us, and we can now ensure that the cup is not broken.

So all dispositional statements are handy summaries of an object's properties – useful for prediction but not providing explanations. And the same goes for statements of abilities and powers. It is somewhat ironic that the post-war interest in the social sciences in providing a rigorous analysis of 'power' is largely a product of the behavioural revolution, and one of the main tenets of the behavioural movement has been that the study of society should be reconstructed along the lines of the natural sciences in order to produce an explanatory science of politics. Since the term 'power' is obviously important in social science, it was seen as playing a crucial explanatory role. Yet this is the one role that concepts of power do *not* play in the natural sciences.[10]

It has sometimes been suggested that 'power' is the subject matter of the discipline of political science. Can my analysis cope with this claim? I think not; but I think the suggestion, as it stands, is stupid.

Let us first note how easy it is to be led astray. Dahl, as is well known, holds to the familiar idea that the subject-matter of political science is human relationships involving power, and he also believes that power is simply a causal concept. With more logic than common sense he deduces from these two premises that the "notion of power [is] rather peculiar as a central concept in political science: Does any other field of empirical investigation take *cause itself* . . . as an object of study?"[11] It is hardly credible that anybody can take this question seriously, even if it is meant rhetorically. No empirical field of study can study cause *itself*. Philosophers can 'study' cause, in the sense of investigating the meaning and/or the logic of the notion; but 'cause' is a part of the technical vocabulary of *any* empirical science, not an object of empirical study.

Neither would the study of power as the ability to effect make much sense as a discipline: one's powers are far too varied for even the most systematic synthesist to say anything general about them. We must remember Alistair MacIntyre's cautionary tale of the man

> who aspired to be the author of the general theory of holes. [When MacIntyre read this as a paper he had to point out, since his audience contained many sociologists, that "holes" was spelt here without a w.] When asked "What kind of hole – holes dug by children in the sand for amusement, holes dug by gardeners to plant lettuce seedlings, tank traps, holes made by road-makers?" he would reply indignantly that he wished for a *general* theory that would explain all of these. (MacIntyre, 1971: p. 260)

A general theory of power is as far-fetched as a general theory of holes – or of wholes.

So power is not the subject-matter of the discipline of politics, from which it follows that political power is a subcategory of power: the adjective is not redundant. Distinguishing between political power and other sorts of power is not something I consider particularly important, and often it is downright obfuscatory (sometimes deliberately so, I suspect). Nevertheless, a work on power should say something about what we understand by political power, and so I shall briefly do so here. Since I consider this topic not very important I shall state, but not defend, my views.

We can distinguish political power from other sorts of power in two different ways. I shall describe the wider sense first.

Your powers include your ability to effect things directly, by yourself. But they also include indirect power, mediated through others, in which they obtain the end for you. Such mediators act as power transformers, transforming the power to do something into the power to do something else. Individuals are not the only such mediators: social organizations of many sorts exist which can help you to attain your ends. The state is perhaps the most visible and pervasive such social organization.

Such power-transformers are important to you, since the way they work determines the powers you have – and they can work in many different ways. You are likely, therefore, to want to have the power to determine how they *do* work. It is this, rather instrumental, power that is political power: it is the power to determine how, through a process of collective decision-making, our individual powers are transformed from the power to do one set of things into the power to do another set.

Power-transformers can augment or limit your individual powers. Which they do – and which the best sort of transformer is – is a subject that political theorists have argued over since Plato, and probably before. The possibility for transforming people's powers is quite awesome, which is, I take it, why a recent writer has referred to the "perils and splendours" and "the moral queasiness" of power (Dunn, 1979: p. 112).

The power to determine how power is transformed is the wide sense of political power. The narrow sense is formal power, as written down in constitutions and discussed by constitutional lawyers; the sort of power that you exceed when you act ultra vires – beyond your powers. Power in this sense is a form of legal right.

Legal powers of this sort, when recognized and enforced, are clearly important – in part because of their apparent fragility. Powers can be affixed or removed by the stroke of a pen. We all recognize that some people have more abilities than others, that sometimes this is deserved and sometimes not, but that in the short term it is very difficult to do anything about it. Not so with power: power can be seized or lost overnight. When a tyrant goes into exile, he goes with all his abilities intact, but powerless. It is this arbitrary nature of formal power – arbitrary in the sense that it is not given in nature but is created by us, and could be created differently – which gives it its importance.

6.5—CONCLUSION

In this chapter I have argued (as I do further in Appendix 1) that the notion of power as the ability to effect is one that is important to us in (at least) three different contexts – practical, moral and evaluative – and for several different reasons. We require ability concepts when trying to answer the following questions:

Practical	(a) What can I do?
	(b) What can you do for me?
	(c) What can you do to me?
Moral	(a) Could you have done it (e.g. a crime)?
	(b) Could you have prevented it (e.g. a disaster)?
Evaluative	How good is the distribution and amount of power here?

So not only does this sense of 'power' fit with ordinary language, but it is one for which we have a vital need. It is worth taking it seriously, and going to some trouble to analyse it carefully. This I shall do in Part II.

—PART II—

The concepts of power

—7—
The family of ability concepts: introduction

I argued in Part I that there are good reasons for conceptualizing 'power' as a sort of ability: the basic idea is that your powers are capacities to do things when you choose. In Part II I look in much greater detail at abilities. I shall try to demonstrate that there are many slightly different ability-concepts, and that we need to distinguish them carefully. We could say that there is a *family* of ability-concepts, rather than just one concept of ability, though the family is more a group of related adults than parents and off-spring. I shall introduce you to the members of the family in Chapters 8, 11 and 13. Interwoven between these chapters are ones that defend and apply my approach.

My analysis of ability is not universally accepted, and so it needs some defence. I cannot defend it, however, before embarking on it, since part of my case is that critics have failed to make the important distinctions that I draw in Chapter 8. The defence of my general analysis thus has to wait until Chapters 9 and 10, and in these chapters I also try to develop my basic analysis further. You might like to be told now that these are the most philo-sophical bits of the book and are intended mainly for readers who might already have philosophical doubts about my approach. Non-philosophers who find themselves not worried overmuch about the way I am proceed-ing may wish to skip these chapters, or save them for later.

In Chapters 12, 14 and 15 I try to demonstrate the worth of my analysis by showing how it allows us to cope (in my view, rather well) with the different things we want to do with our concepts of power.

In this chapter, though, I provide some necessary background for all this by first drawing a preliminary distinction within abilities.

7.1—GENERIC AND TIME-SPECIFIC ABILITIES

Several writers on power – most notably Alvin Goldman – have analysed the power or ability to do something *at some specified time*. Others have concentrated on power as a *generic* (and therefore, in a sense, timeless) capacity.[1] I shall suggest that which standpoint we adopt is not arbitrary: sometimes we are interested in time-specific abilities (as I shall call them here); sometimes in generic abilities; and it is a mistake to employ one sort when the other is required.

We therefore need to consider both sorts of ability, but – books being the linear things they are – one sort must be discussed before the other. Throughout Chapters 8 and 9 I shall be concerned mainly with generic abilities (and "ability" is to be read as "generic ability"); in Chapter 11 I shall consider the special features of time-specific abilities. Such a presentational decision needs little justification: if it succeeds in making things clearer, that is justification enough; if it doesn't then no justifications will compensate.

Generic abilities, of course, and as we shall see, come and go, sometimes at clearly marked times. If you learn to speak a language you acquire the generic ability to do so: you didn't have it two years ago, whilst you do have it now. Nevertheless it is a *generic* ability when it is an ability at all: your ability to speak English *now* is exactly the same ability as your ability to speak English five minutes, or five months, or five years ago. Ordinary dispositionals are always generic in this way: water has the power to dissolve sugar generally, not just at certain specified times. We do not need to append time-suffixes to ordinary dispositional claims – not even when talking about the powers of unique objects rather than classes of objects.

To forestall misunderstandings, I should perhaps mention that even generic abilities sometimes contain a reference to time, since there are many things that I cannot do instantaneously but can do if given sufficient time. I can learn Greek or read the complete plays of Shakespeare, but I cannot do either in an afternoon. Similarly, sulphuric acid can dissolve zinc, but it cannot dissolve a cube six feet high in a second. In a complete description of a generic ability there will be a mention of the time it takes the actor to perform the action in question – some people *can* read Shakespeare's plays in an afternoon. This reference to the time it takes to do something (present in all dispositional descriptions) must not be confused with the quite different reference to the time *at which* someone can do something.[2]

In my analysis of ability I shall start out from a consideration of abilities as no more (and no less) than a certain sort of disposition: I shall look first at what makes an ability a *special* sort of disposition, and then at how abilities can *differ* from dispositions altogether. The peculiarities of time-specific abilities come in the latter category, and so they will be considered later.

First, though, I shall look briefly in the next section at what *actions* are. Actions are important in the analysis of ability, since an ability is usually either the capacity to perform some action or the capacity to obtain some good by performing an action. It is through understanding how actions can be analysed that we can start thinking about abilities.

7.2—BASIC ACTIONS

I can raise my arm. When I do, my arm rises because of the contraction and expansion of certain muscles: this is the cause, in a sense, of my arm rising. But, as a matter of psychological fact, I do not know how to contract and expand these muscles *except* by raising my arm – or (maybe) causing it to rise by, for example, lifting it with my other hand. When I decide to exercise these muscles, I do so by raising and lowering my arm. Now it may be empirically possible to tie my arm down, and exercise the muscles without moving the arm – or somehow to develop independent control of the muscles. But the chain must end somewhere. There must be bodily actions which we do, and when asked how we do them can only reply "I don't know, I just do them".

A *basic action* is the end of such a chain. Basic actions are actions "of which it would not be true to say that they are performed by doing something else", or that "we do but not *through* any distinct thing which we also do".[3] It does not make sense to say of basic actions that I tried to do one, but did the wrong thing.

I am not sure how we analyse basic actions and distinguish them from the identical pieces of mere bodily behaviour. But since we all know, at least for ourselves, the difference between arms rising and being raised, I can take it as philosophically primitive and not requiring analysis. We don't need philosophers to tell us how we know a nervous tic from a wink. Further, since our ability to do basic actions is so far removed from my main concerns, I need not puzzle over intricacies which can be relied upon to come out in the wash.

Most basic actions can be done non-basically if we wish: I can raise my arm as a basic action, but I can also raise it by lifting it with my other hand. Thus, whilst every action must involve one basic action (or more), it does not follow that any actions are such that they can *only* be basic. When I talk about a person's basic-act repertoire it must be understood as containing all those acts which *might* be performed basically – not those which must be performed basically if at all. (Whether any such acts exist appears to me to be very doubtful.)

All actions are built up in some way from our basic-act repertoire; more complicated actions are either a series of basic actions performed sequentially, or are level-generated from basic actions.[4] The idea of a basic action will prove helpful in the next chapters in describing different sorts of ability: the task to which I now turn.

—8—
The family of ability concepts I: epistemic, non-epistemic and latent abilities

8.1—EPISTEMIC AND NON-EPISTEMIC ABILITIES

What abilities do you have? We could start by noting that you have a very large number of basic actions at your disposal, and an even larger number of strings of basic actions; depending on which you choose you could end up doing any one of a large range of different things. We *could* say that all those things you could do are things that you have the ability to do.

But if you want to do something specific you must choose which of your available strings of basic actions to do, and this requires some knowledge on your part: you must choose correctly. Sometimes you won't know which to choose; or you might think you know, but be wrong. So you might choose the wrong string of actions, and so not succeed in doing what you wanted to do. There is another sense of 'ability' in which consistent failures of this kind demonstrate lack of ability, even though actions are available to you that would succeed.

Ability in this latter sense is an *epistemic ability*, since we are here interested in, and taking into account, the actor's knowledge; ability in the sense used in the last-but-one paragraph I shall call *non-epistemic ability*.[1] We say both "He's so incompetent that he's unable to do it" and "He's able to do it all right, but too incompetent to manage it". These statements do not contradict each other; they simply use epistemic and non-epistemic senses of ability.

So there are two different ways in which I can be unable to bring about a chosen goal: I may lack the basic acts, or may lack the necessary competence. Thus I cannot put the shot more than a few feet, because I do not possess the basic acts necessary to propel the object very far – and even if I were to study the techniques of shot-putting intensively, I would still not be able to improve much unless I took steps to increase my strength. Neither can I do *The Times* crossword puzzle, but this is not because I don't possess the strength to fill in the letters: it is, of course, because I lack the required knowledge, training, skills or whatever.

Philosophers writing about action have worried a lot about how we describe, and distinguish between, actions: for instance, does what a person *does* include the unintended (perhaps unforeseen) consequences of their bodily actions? Thus if I want to keep the person who lives in the flat downstairs awake at night, I can do this quite successfully by playing loud music on my stereo: we would say that what I am *doing* is keeping my neighbour awake, and the means to this is playing music. However, it could also be that all I want to do is listen to loud music, and that this has the consequence of keeping others awake. Is, in this case, what I am *doing* keeping them awake, or is this merely a *consequence* of what I am doing? Am I doing two things at once and, if so, am I performing two different actions or one action with two descriptions?

In general, neither answer seems more correct than the other; but we can now see that when we are specifically considering abilities the problem disappears. If non-epistemic abilities are our concern, then all the consequences of actions count, for actions are available to the actor that bring these things about. If we are considering epistemic abilities, then we restrict our attention to those actions (and their consequences) that the actor knows how to do or bring about.

Your *non-epistemic* abilities, therefore, include all the basic actions you can do, all the actions made up from, and level-generated by, these actions, and all the consequences of these actions that will occur in the time allowed. Your *epistemic* abilities include all your basic actions, and all your actions, and the consequences of them, that you know how to do or bring about. In neither case do we want to distinguish between an action and its consequences; nor need we bother whether the same event with two descriptions (such as my playing loud music *and* keeping the neighbours awake) is one action or two.[2]

Having distinguished between epistemic and non-epistemic ability, I want to make a further distinction within the notion of epistemic ability.

You have the epistemic ability to do something if you know how to do it and possess the required basic actions. But you may still fail to do it when you try if you also think, wrongly, that you can do it some other way, and that is the way you choose. You *could* do it in a long and laborious manner; but you're too impatient for that (let's suppose), you try to cut some corners or do it on the cheap, and you consistently fail. You *still* have the epistemic ability to do it; but you do not succeed when you try.

By contrast, there are things that you *can* do in the full sense that you *do* do them whenever you choose to. Such abilities I shall call *effective* epistemic abilities.[3]

To summarize this section, we have the following three categories of ability:

A has the *non-epistemic ability* to do X if there exists W (a string of A's basic actions) such that if A does W then X results.

A has the *epistemic ability* to do X if there exists W (a string of A's basic actions) such that if A does W then X results; and A knows that if she does W then X results.

A has the *effective epistemic ability* to do X if there exists W (a string of A's basic actions) such that if A does W then X results; A knows that if she does W then X results; and A would do W if she wanted to do X.

8.2—THE EPISTEMIC/NON-EPISTEMIC DISTINCTION APPLIED

To show the importance of the difference between epistemic and non-epistemic power, I shall in this section show how the three senses of 'ability' from the last section have to be kept distinct when we look at the various uses of 'power' from Chapter 6. On each occasion, we must be careful to choose the correct sense; and all three senses have a use.

In practical contexts we may have to use *effective epistemic* power or *non-epistemic* power. When the CIA are interested in the power of the people they might bribe, they are interested in effective epistemic power: they want to know whether someone will succeed when they try. The CIA will not waste money bribing people who are too incompetent to obtain the outcomes desired. They want results.

But when we are interested in power for the practical reason that we want to work out what people might do to us, it is non-epistemic power that we are concerned with. We want to know not only what people can do to us deliberately, but what they might do accidentally. If you worry about the existence of nuclear weapons, for instance, you will be worried about the consequences of their going off by mistake as well as their being fired deliberately. If we want to know what might happen to us, we need to keep our eyes open for disasters nobody intends – for they are just as disastrous. An ant in a jungle needs to watch out for elephants as well as ant-eaters.

When our concern with power is moral, we have to use *non-epistemic* or *epistemic* power, depending on our exact purpose. When you invoke your impotence as part of an alibi (you couldn't have done it, because . . .), it is again non-epistemic power that is at issue. You are saying that you couldn't *possibly* have done it; that nothing you can do could have brought it about. You can't run this sort of defence by showing that you lack the appropriate skill – that your shooting is so bad that you invariably miss at 100 yards. You have to show that *whatever* you did you would not have shot him. The question "Are you able to hit someone at 100 yards?" has a different meaning when asked by your counsel at your trial or by someone recruiting for a hit-squad. If you hit every hundred shots or so, you must answer your counsel in the affirmative and the recruiter in the negative.

When the excuse is the second one – that you could not intervene to prevent the disaster – then the appropriate sense is the middle, epistemic one: that there was nothing *that you knew of* that you could do. This is worth looking at at some length.

Using the non-epistemic sense is far too harsh, since it would mean that you are under an obligation to know how to accomplish everything that you might conceivably do. To see this, suppose that you are in a building that you don't know well and that has just caught fire. Unknown to you there is a fire extinguisher in a cupboard in one of the rooms; if you found this extinguisher you could put the fire out. Yet you would be right to say that, not knowing about the fire extinguisher, you were powerless to prevent the blaze – and hence cannot be blamed for not preventing it. To rule out this plea is to demand that you should have known of the fire extinguisher, and this seems an unfairly severe demand to make: some knowledge just is not the sort of thing that we can require people to have. It *may* be that you should have known about the fire extinguisher on this occasion (perhaps it was pointed out to you last time you visited the building; or you are the Fire Safety Officer for this site) – but that is a separate obligation. Sometimes people are under an obligation to know certain things, and sometimes not; these obligations need to be carefully stated. The principle 'ought implies can' does not imply that as a matter of logic you are under an obligation to know how to do everything that you could possibly do.

So showing that you did not know how to prevent the fire is sufficient to prove that you *could not* have prevented the fire – though it may merely lead to the accusation that you *should* have known how to prevent the fire. But this is a different obligation from the original one to prevent the fire – and one which itself has to adhere to the principle of 'ought implies can'.

Yet the principle 'ought implies can' requires the epistemic sense of power, not the *effective* epistemic sense. The difference arises if you think there are two ways of putting out the fire (you could smother it with your coat, or go hunting for a fire extinguisher, say) and you choose the one that is ineffective. Your course of action may have been very reasonable – it is an excellent coat, too good to waste; and large buildings usually have fire extinguishers somewhere – but you cannot escape responsibility on the grounds that you *could not* put out the fire. For of course you *could*, and you knew it – although it would have cost you your coat. But the *cost* to you of preventing the disaster is not relevant to whether you *can* prevent it. As the cost to you of putting out the fire rises from the loss of a coat to the loss of a limb to the almost certain loss of your life, we become increasingly ready to pardon you for not intervening – but not because you become increasingly powerless to intervene. In this context the cost, or sacrifice, to you of doing something is a separate issue from your power to do it. If the cost is too high you may well be considered blameless even though you allowed a disaster to occur; but this is because failing to intervene is *reasonable*, not because it is *unavoidable*. Your defence would not be based on the principle 'ought implies can' (and its corollary, that if you cannot do something you cannot be under an obligation to do it) but would depend on a completely different (and usually weaker) argument based on what it is reasonable to expect people to suffer when carrying out this sort of obligation. Since this latter defence leaves room for disagreement about what is a reasonable cost, while the former leaves no room for argument at all, we can appreciate the motive to claim that a large cost renders you unable. Nevertheless, these two arguments *are* different: the amount of sacrifice involved is often a perfectly acceptable reason for failing to intervene, but it is a *different* reason from being (literally) powerless to intervene (or not knowing how to intervene).

I have thus shown, in this section, that we employ all three variants of power – non-epistemic, epistemic and effective epistemic – and that we employ each for a different job. It hardly needs saying, I hope, that when we have a job in mind for 'power' we should choose the sense appropriate for our purpose.

8.3—LATENT ABILITIES

So far in this chapter I have assumed that our basic-act repertoires and our abilities are fixed and unchangeable. But this is, of course, not the case: we can all add to our act repertoires and knowledge in many ways, thereby making us able to do things we cannot now do. Such abilities can be said to be *latent*, in that they are not now present but can be obtained. Most of our current abilities were once only latent: the ability to read, for example.

Both epistemic and non-epistemic abilities may be latent: when I acquire new knowledge and skills I may convert a non-epistemic ability into an epistemic one, whilst when I increase my range of basic actions I gain non-epistemic abilities. In this sense I have the epistemic ability to do *The Times* crossword, even though I don't know how to at the moment, in a way that a chimpanzee or an imbecile does not; all three of us could fill in the letters, but only I could learn how to work them out. I also can be a better (though certainly not a champion) shot-putter, if I were to take that Mr Universe Body-Building Course.

We can see from Philip Agee's book describing the workings of the CIA that they consider people with latent power well worth bribing (see Agee, 1975). In order to plan for the future, the CIA maintain a large number of contacts which are of no immediate use, but which may yield fruit later on. Often agents are planted in the opposition parties and the trade unions in the hope that they will be able to manoeuvre themselves into positions of power. This power is latent in that it cannot be used right now – these people have to do certain things (or certain things have to happen to them) before they have power itself.

Whilst we do sometimes refer to abilities in this latent sense simply as an ability, strictly speaking we have here an iterated modality: a latent ability is an ability to acquire an ability. The ability to acquire the ability to do X is not the same as the ability to do X: the distinction between a present and a potential ability is an important one. Being able to *speak* Greek is a different ability from being able to *learn* Greek.

Since a latent ability is an ability to do something (this something being acquiring an ability), there can be effective epistemic, epistemic and non-epistemic latent abilities. I only have the effective epistemic ability to learn Greek if I would choose an appropriate method of learning it. (This example is not as far-fetched as it might seem: a friend of mine who wanted to learn German obtained a labouring job in Germany to this end, only to discover that he was working such long hours that he didn't have time to talk to anybody except his workmates – who were all Turkish.)

There is, at least in principle, the possibility of an infinite chain of abilities: one can have the ability to acquire the ability to acquire the ability
to . . .. I doubt, though, whether we usually want to look beyond second-
order abilities.

Indeed, when we consider time-specific abilities the distinction between
a latent ability and a present ability collapses; the distinction only holds for
generic abilities. When we are interested in your ability to bring something
about at (or by) some specified future time t, then the iterated modalities
of latent abilities collapse into an ordinary ability. You are (now) able to
do X (at t) if you are able to do everything required for doing X at t. There
may well be a number of intermediary steps you have to take, even abilities that need to be acquired, but as long as you can take the appropriate
steps at the appropriate times you have the ability to do X at t. Hence I am
able (now) to deliver a series of lectures on power in Greek in two years'
time if I can learn Greek well enough in that time; I am as able to do so as
I would be if I could now speak Greek. When I accept the invitation by
saying that I can do it, the nature of the chain of actions involved is
irrelevant: I can do it only by doing other things first, but I can still do it –
assuming, that is, that I *can* learn Greek in two years.[4]

When iterated abilities collapse in this way they do so according to the
principle that the strength of the chain is its weakest link. That is to say, if
you have the epistemic ability to acquire the non-epistemic ability to do X,
this reduces to the *non*-epistemic ability to do X: for to say that you know
how to get yourself into a position in which you have actions available to
you to do X at t is the same as saying simply that you have actions available to you to do X at t. Similarly the non-epistemic ability to acquire the
epistemic ability to do X implies simply the non-epistemic ability to do it.
The final, single ability is always non-epistemic if anywhere along the line
there is a non-epistemic ability.

To summarize this section. A latent ability is the ability to acquire an ability: it is a second-order ability. Both this higher-order ability and the
lower-order ability contained in it may be of any of the three sorts discussed in section 8.1: one could have an epistemic ability to acquire a non-
epistemic ability (I know how to increase my range of basic actions by
developing my muscles), a non-epistemic ability to acquire an epistemic
ability (there are many skills I could somehow possess, but I don't know
how to go about acquiring them), and so on through the nine possible
combinations. But the latent ability is only distinct from a present ability
when generic abilities are under consideration; the distinction disappears
when the lower-order ability is time-specific: the ability to acquire the

ability to do X at t becomes simply the ability to do X at t, with the resulting ability taking the weakest epistemic value that occurs in the chain.

A final warning: we must be careful not to confuse the potentiality present with all power (power being a capacity that needs to be exercised by the actor) with the quite different sort of potentiality present in latent power (the power being potential in the sense of not yet existing). The power of a ruler is there even though it may not be being used at the moment; the power of the heir-apparent is not yet there – it is latent.

Now that some members of the ability-family have been introduced and distinguished, we can investigate the nature of abilities further, with less danger of making the mistake of assuming that an analysis that is appropriate (or inappropriate) for one member of the family must therefore be appropriate (or inappropriate) for all members.

—9—
The ifs and cans of abilities

Philosophers have lavished much attention on the questions whether 'can' is "constitutionally iffy" (Austin, 1956a: p. 205) and, if it is, how it is. I think that we are now in a position to answer these questions, and that doing so will deepen our understanding of 'ability'. I should point out at once that I shall be considering *only* the 'can' of ability (and also of 'mere' dispositions), and not any of the other uses of 'can'. We do use 'can' in many other ways (for instance, to indicate mere possibility, as in "that statement could have been false"); these uses fall outside my concerns.[1] I do not, therefore, attempt a complete account of 'can'; but what I do do here is sufficient to throw doubt on many such accounts.

Austin introduced the "problem of ifs and cans" as follows:

> There are *two* quite distinct and incompatible views that may be put forward concerning *if*s and *can*s, which are fatally easy to confuse with each other. One view is that wherever we have *can* or *could have* as our main verb, an *if*-clause must always be understood or supplied, if it is not actually present, in order to complete the sense of the sentence. The other view is that the meaning of 'can' or 'could have' can be more clearly reproduced by *some other verb* (notably 'shall' or 'should have') with an *if*-clause appended to *it*. The first view is that an *if* is required to *complete* a *can*-sentence: the second view is that an *if* is required in the *analysis* of a *can*-sentence. (Austin, 1956a: p. 214)

In addition to these two views, it has been argued that *neither* 'if' is appropriate, at least for the 'can' of ability (e.g. Ayers, 1968: ch. 7). I want to argue the thesis that Austin is wrong in claiming that the two views are incompatible, for I maintain that they are in fact both correct. Or, to be more circumspect, 'ifs' are related to 'cans' in many different ways, two of which are captured by Austin's distinction: *some* 'ifs' complete 'can'-sentences; *others* are part of the analysis; and it is to over-look the complexity of the conditional aspects of ability to try to force *all* 'ifs' into the one category or the other.

9.1—CONDITIONAL CLAUSES AND DISPOSITIONAL PROPERTIES

Let us start by looking again at straightforward conditional dispositionals, such as the power of water to dissolve sugar. This is a *conditional* disposi-tional (and not a habitual one) because its analysis contains a conditional clause: this dispositional is only manifested if there is some sugar in the water to *be* dissolved. At all other times this power, whilst still present *as a power*, remains unmanifested. I shall call this conditional the '*if of mani-festation*': it is part of the *analysis* of the dispositional property, and not required to complete the description of that property. It is not correct to say that the *power* is present (only) if there is sugar in the water; the power is present at all times but is only brought into use, as it were, when there is sugar in the water.

But water does not dissolve sugar in all conceivable circumstances – it does not, for instance, if the water is already saturated with sugar or is very cold, or if the sugar has been heated and caramelized. If we wish to describe more fully the power of water to dissolve sugar we can append a long list of conditions to the statement of the power: water has the power to dissolve sugar if the water is not very cold and if the sugar has not been caramelized and if . . .. Now these conditions are certainly not part of the *analysis* of the statement "water can dissolve sugar"; rather they are necessary to make the statement more accurate. Water's power to dissolve sugar is not unlimited, and these conditionals state the limitations on, or scope of, that power. Since they serve to describe the dispositional property, let us call these conditionals '*ifs of description*' or *descriptive conditionals*. 'Ifs of description' are, of course, the 'ifs' Austin had in mind when saying that some believe that 'ifs' are needed to *complete* 'can'-sentences.

Finally, we should remember that there are ordinary (as it were) 'ifs' that can crop up in this connection: for example, "if that's sugar, the water can dissolve it". These 'ifs' neither analyse nor complete the dispositional claim: instead they *utilize* it, or take it as given. They will not concern us here.

Since abilities are a (type of) disposition, 'ifs' occur in ability-claims in both the ways just introduced. An '*if of manifestation*' could be "If there were a book here, I would read it", which is an 'if' of the same sort as "If there were some sugar here, the water would dissolve it".[2] My ability to read is present but unused when there is nothing to read within my visual field. An '*if of description*' could be "I can read if there is sufficient light" or "If this were in less microscopic print, I could read it". That is to say, whilst I *can* read, I cannot *always* read *everything* – just as water cannot always dissolve sugar. We could, should we wish, append any number of conditional clauses to define my reading further.[3]

9.2—THE ACT CONDITIONAL AND THE CHOICE CONDITIONAL

The sort of examples just given cause little trouble: the difficulties occur with those conditionals that are peculiar to abilities.

As a start, let us remind ourselves that an ability, by definition, involves the power to do something, or bring something about, by means of an *action*. It follows from this that the manifestation of an ability must be brought about by an action: an ability is a disposition which if activated by the actor produces the required outcome. I shall henceforth refer to this conditional as the *act conditional*. The act conditional is a sort of manifestation conditional and, as such, is part of the *analysis* of the ability. Every ability, when fully analysed, must have some act conditional.

Two points are worth noting here. The first is that, since the conditional "if A does W, then X results" is present in the definition of all three sub-categories of ability distinguished in section 8.1 (that is, non-epistemic, epistemic and effective epistemic), an act conditional is *always* present in the analysis of an ability. Secondly, this act conditional does *not* refer to the content of the ability itself (it refers to W, not X). This, far from being odd,[4] is a commonplace of manifestation conditionals. It is *dissolving sugar* that water has the power to do, yet manifestation conditionals make no reference to that – they refer to the sugar being in the water; it is then up to the water to do the dissolving.

Now it is definitive of an action that the actor be choosing, wanting or trying to do something: if no choosing, wanting or trying is occurring, then the person is not *acting*. The act conditional "if A does W then X results" implies that A's doing W is voluntary – is a product of her choice.

But for *effective epistemic* ability we need a further conditional that specifies exactly what the actor must choose. We want to know if A would succeed in doing X if she chose, wanted and tried to do X,[5] and we are not interested in whether she would succeed (by accident) if she tried to do something else. This ability, then, specifies that A would do X if she wanted to do X. I shall call this conditional the *choice conditional*.

To summarize: a full analysis of any ability-claim will include at least one ordinary manifestation conditional *and* an act conditional. A full analysis of an effective epistemic ability claim will also include an explicit choice conditional. Most of the problems with ifs and cans occur with choice conditionals, so I will look at them in more detail in the next section.

9.3—"IF I CHOOSE"

Since choice conditionals are used in the *analysis* of 'can' statements, they are not usually *appended* to such statements. This has led some philosophers to claim that "I can if I choose", if it means anything, is an inaccurate way of saying "I can": that "if I choose" can *never* be meaningfully tacked on to "I can".

This conclusion is false in two quite different ways: there are situations in which a choice conditional can legitimately and meaningfully be appended to a 'can' statement; and there are uses of "if I choose" in which it does not play the role of a choice conditional, but of a descriptive conditional or, indeed, of another sort of conditional altogether. I shall demonstrate these claims by giving five illustrations of legitimate uses of the sentence "I can if I choose": in the first three "if I choose" is a choice conditional; in the fourth it is a descriptive conditional; and in the fifth it is something else entirely.

Firstly, "I can if I choose" can occur in the analysis of a *latent* ability. Here "if I choose" is a genuine choice conditional, though the sentence is always of the form "I can do X if I choose to do W". I have the latent ability to speak Greek; that is, I could speak Greek if I chose to learn it – I can if I choose to. Just as the analysis of an ability involves a manifestation conditional of the form "if A chose to do W, X would occur", so the analysis of a latent ability involves a manifestation conditional of the form "if A chose to do W, A's ability to do X would occur" – that is, "A could do X if she chose to do W".

Secondly, we sometimes add "if I choose to" to "I can" to signify that the 'can' is the 'can' of ability, and not a (mere) disposition. Thus "I can cry if I choose to (cry)" can be read not as "I can cry, if I choose to" but as "I can cry-if-I-choose-to" – that is to say, I can cry at will.[6] Most of us cannot cry-at-will, but some can (for instance, actors); and if you are being auditioned for a part that requires you to burst into tears at just the right time, it is the *ability* to cry that is being sought, and this is captured by asking you if you can cry if you choose to.

Thirdly, we often colloquially say "I could have, if I had chosen/

wanted" as an emphatic way of saying "I could have" – to emphasize that
it is only my choosing that prevents me doing it. Thus "I could have had
you killed, dismissed, transferred . . . if I had wanted". "If I had wanted"
here is, I think, part of the *analysis* of the ability (a genuine choice conditional), but a part that the speaker wants to stress. This sentence is an
abbreviation of "I could have had you killed (etc.) . . . and I would have
done if I had wanted".[7]

But, fourthly, "if I had wanted" can also be a descriptive 'if'. Consider a
non-athletic fugitive from the secret police who, victim of necessity, leaps
from one rooftop to another to avoid capture, even though he can never
again repeat this feat, never again having the same motivation.[8] The
most plausible reading of this situation is that the fear, by producing large
quantities of adrenalin, *gives* the fugitive non-epistemic abilities that he
does not have without this fear. That is, we can say that he can leap across
rooftops "if he wanted to *enough*", where he can *only* "want to enough" in
moments of grave danger, externally produced. Wanting to do it "enough"
is, that is, not something within his control; it is a consequence of his environment; and it is *only* if he wants it enough that he has the ability to do
it. The ability is contingent on external circumstances causing him to want
it enough, just as water's power to dissolve sugar is contingent on it being
warm enough. Hence, "I could, if I wanted to (enough)" (said, perhaps, with
a sigh) is using the conditional to qualify or describe the ability, implying
that the appropriate sort of wanting is beyond my control; "I could if I
wanted to" (said, perhaps, aggressively) is likely to be the colloquial use of
the last paragraph, implying exactly the opposite: that it is solely up to me
whether or not I do it.[9]

Finally, in "I can if I choose to" the "can" is often not a 'can' of ability at
all; it might, for instance, be the 'can' of permission. Then "I can if I choose
to" means "I am not under an obligation not to" or, perhaps (as an *assertion* of a permission), "I don't consider myself under an obligation not to".
Hence in "It's my party; I can cry if I want to" the chanteuse is not claiming the ability to cry-at-will as one of her party tricks, but is asserting her
freedom from the obligation to refrain from crying. Not all uses of 'can' –
even in "I can if I choose" – refer to abilities.

The upshot of all this is that the 'can' of ability is indeed "constitutionally iffy", and far more so than Austin realized: abilities make reference to conditionals both in their analysis and in their description; both
sorts of conditionals can be of the form "if A chose, wanted, tried . . .";
and at least one of the conditionals in the *analysis* of abilities *must* be of
this form, either implicitly (the act conditional) or explicitly (the choice
conditional).

There is, so far as I know, only one serious argument that has been advanced against the position I have developed here; but it *is* a serious one.[10] I shall try to meet it by modifying, and deepening, my analysis, rather than by abandoning it. The argument objects to my last claim in the previous paragraph – that the analysis of an ability *requires* a choice conditional – and it is the subject of the next section.

9.4—CHISHOLM'S ARGUMENT AGAINST THE CONDITIONAL ANALYSIS OF ABILITY

Chisholm's argument is directed against an analysis very like mine: one that claims that in saying "He could have arranged things this morning so that he could be in Boston now" we are saying something like "There are certain things such that, if this morning he had undertaken (chosen, willed, tried, set out) to bring it about that those things would occur, then he would be in Boston now". But this formula fails to capture the required meaning, Chisholm argues, since:

> There would seem to be things consistent with the 'if' statement that are not consistent with our 'could' statement. If this is true, the 'could' statement cannot have the same meaning as the 'if' statement. Consider, for example, those things which are such that, if this morning our agent had undertaken (chosen, willed, tried, set out) to bring them about, then he would be in Boston now. And let us suppose (i) that he *could not* have undertaken (chosen, willed, tried, set out) to bring any of these things about and (ii) that he would be in Boston now only if he *had* undertaken (chosen, willed, tried, set out) to bring them about. These suppositions are consistent with saying that he *would* be in Boston now *if* he had undertaken those things but they are not consistent with saying that he *could* then have arranged things so that he would be in Boston now. (Chisholm, 1976: p. 57)

This argument holds against my proposed analysis of epistemic ability (and effective epistemic ability), which is wrong as it stands. However, Chisholm fails to demolish a conditional analysis of *non-epistemic* ability, simply because those "things" that the agent could not have undertaken would be excluded anyway in my conditional analysis. This is because the "things" are, on my analysis, strings of basic actions, and it is part of the definition of a basic action that the agent *can* do it, and do it by undertaking (choosing, etc.) to do it. There is no *other* way of doing a basic action than by choosing (etc.) to do it. So if the "things" are basic actions, the agent must have been able to choose to do them. W was defined (on p. 54 above) as that string of A's basic actions such that, if A does W, then X results. There may well be *no* such string of basic actions, in which case A lacks the ability to do X. But if there *is* such a string, then A must be able to do it, and able to choose to do it. For otherwise it wouldn't be a string of A's basic actions.

But Chisholm's argument does hold for epistemic abilities. His reasoning, which is sound, is that we treat abilities slightly differently from other dispositionals: we ask more of actors than we do of objects. With objects we don't expect them to activate their own powers; with actors we do (in part). I have said that ability-statements include two sorts of manifestation conditionals: ordinary ones ("if there were a book here, I would read it") and choice conditionals. Ordinary manifestation conditionals are (at least in part) a property of the environment,[11] but the choice conditional is entirely activated by the *agent*. Hence, whilst the impossibility of the fulfilment of an ordinary manifestation conditional allows me to say "I could have done it, if circumstances had been different", we cannot say this if the choice conditional cannot be fulfilled. Wants are not circumstances: if it is up to me to activate the choice conditional then my ability to do this becomes part of the ability claim itself. We therefore need to amend the analysis of both the epistemic abilities by adding the clause "and A *can* choose (etc.) to do X".

But does this not simply land us with an infinite regress? If the 'can' in this new clause is the 'can' of ability, the analysis of "A has the ability to do X" will include "A has the ability to choose to do X", which in turn will include "A has the ability to choose to choose to do X", and so on.

One possible answer might be that choosing is not an action, and so a different analysis of the ability to choose would apply; but I do not want to restrict my analysis to any narrow interpretation of actions, and I do not want to provide an analysis of choosing, trying and so on that tries to prove they are not actions in the relevant sense. I shall also accept that the 'can' of the new clause is the 'can' of ability. So I must admit that there is, logically, an infinite regress here.

But it is not a vicious infinite regress; we can easily cut it off. There are very few ways that anybody could *lack* the ability to choose to do X, and we can simply list them. I shall do so in the next section.

9.5—INABILITY TO CHOOSE

Everybody – at least every agent – is able to choose to bring things about in general;[12] so if A cannot choose to do *X*, there must be (for A) something peculiar about X.

One uncontentious peculiarity arises from the logical impossibility of choosing or wanting anything one is completely unaware of – that one lacks the concept for. Time-travellers from the Stone Age who find themselves in a modern house could not choose or want to turn on the light, because they would have no conception of electricity. Of course they might flip the switch, and thus turn the light on, but this would be, to them, a totally unexpected consequence; when they tried to flip the switch they were definitely *not* trying to turn on the light.

Whilst you could feel warm without having the concept of warmth in your vocabulary, you could not *want* to feel warm (nor believe or know that you were warm, for that matter). And if you could not want to turn on the light, you would lack the effective epistemic ability to turn on the light. When considering someone's epistemic abilities we cannot suppose she has more knowledge than she has. So if she has not enough knowledge to be able to want or choose to do something, she lacks the effective epistemic ability to do it.

Lack of knowledge of the concept of X would in any case rule out the epistemic ability to do X, for the actor cannot know that acts W result in X if she has no knowledge whatsoever of X. Sentences involving knowledge and belief (and other mental elements such as choosing, wanting and trying) are *referentially opaque*; that is, if A knows X (or knows how to do X), then it is X *under that description* that A knows (or knows how to do), and we cannot substitute a term with the same reference as X without changing the meaning, and possibly the truth-value, of the sentence. You probably know that the capital of Honduras is in Honduras; you may not know that Tegucigalpa is in Honduras; yet Tegucigalpa *is* the capital of Honduras.[13] Thus we cannot substitute terms with the same reference in knowledge-sentences. It follows that someone cannot have the epistemic ability to do X if she has no knowledge whatsoever of X, through lacking the concept of X – however great her knowledge is of some X' that has the same reference as X.[14]

It also follows – this time from the referential opacity of choosing and trying – that someone only has the effective epistemic ability to do X if she can do it when she tries to do it *under that description*. An example. You are a superb cook; you have a natural flair for it. Particularly excellent are your soufflés which are, everyone agrees, the best in town. You are persuaded to enter the town's annual cookery competition since, this year, the dish everyone is required to make is a soufflé. Normally you try to make a *good* soufflé; in the competition you have to make the *best*. Rather than trust to your natural flair, you weigh all the ingredients out carefully and try to follow accurately the recipe you learnt years ago. The result is – literally – a flop. You can, it seems, make the best soufflés in town – but only when you don't *try* to make the best soufflés in town. Such examples are, of course, not unfamiliar.

A second set of limitations on our abilities to choose is provided by psychological phenomena such as phobias and manias. If agoraphobia and kleptomania really do exist, then those people who suffer from them just *cannot* go into open spaces or refrain from stealing. The block is mental, rather than physical, but this does not make it any less of a block.

What is meant here is that it is somehow *impossible* for the actor to choose a certain end, or to do anything meaningful about putting her choice into operation.[15] What the exact nature of this impossibility may be I do not know, nor do I have to say. For elucidating the nature of phobias and the like is a matter for psychologists and psychoanalysts, not for philosophical disputation. It is no more necessary for me to say here how we may know that someone is unable to choose something (or carry this choice out) than it is necessary to enter into a discussion of how we know that someone who is paralysed cannot move a limb. If we are prepared to accept this latter as unproblematic, then I think we can also accept the former.

We can thus provide an answer, however apparently question-begging, to Quentin Gibson's quandary: "Should we accept the policeman's statement to his psychiatrist that an impulse to stand quietly and watch the traffic jam deprived him of all power to give the signals?" (Gibson, 1971: p. 109). If the "impulse" is part of some phobia, such that we conclude that he *could* not choose to give the signals, then we must concur with his view that he lost the ability. The answer to the question, therefore, is that we should accept the policeman's statement if his psychiatrist does.

A third way in which one may be unable to *try*, if not unable to *choose*, to do something involves *weakness of will*. Weakness of will can be accepted as a limitation on abilities if it is really beyond the actor's control. Some people have relatively weak bodies, and this lack of strength is a restriction on their abilities; so is ignorance, or simple-mindedness. Other people are weak-willed, and this lack of will is equally a limitation on their abilities, and one which restricts the number of things they can achieve. We cannot, as a philosophical principle, decree that all such limitations on the will can be dismissed, while analogous limitations on the body are not.[16] It is no doubt more difficult to observe somebody trying and failing to (say) give up smoking or refrain from stealing than it is to see someone shoving against a door but failing to open it; but this does not mean that the former failure is incomprehensible. The actor really does try, but the will breaks (or the attention wanders) and he finds himself overriding his (genuine) long-term wants for his short-term desires. It is not that he did not try hard enough; it is that *however* hard he tried he would have cracked at some point. None of our minds are perfect, and it seems significant that we talk of will-power and power of concentration, as well as bodily powers. This may be partly metaphorical, but it does bring out that we think that our powers to will or concentrate are not limitless.

Here we are back with psychic states akin to phobias and other forms of compulsive behaviour. Most people who fail to do things do not fail in this way: they succumb through lack of effort. But some people doubtless fail to do some things because they literally could not try to do them. Nowadays we do not believe that all failures are due to lack of effort; we believe in non-rational factors governing at least some choices, and that these factors are sometimes both beyond our conscious control and too strong to override. To know whether this is what is happening we need the psychiatrist again.[17]

I claim that these three categories – lack of the relevant concept, phobias, and weakness of will – exhaust the ways in which one can be unable to choose or want or try to do something. If this claim is true, we can replace the clause "A can choose to do X", which I added to my analysis of epistemic ability on p. 66, by "and A possesses the concept of X, and does not suffer either from a phobia or from weakness of will sufficient to prevent her from choosing, wanting and trying to do X". If this change is made, we see that the infinite regress alluded to at the end of the last section disappears.

I cannot *prove* that these three categories exhaust the possibilities, but I know of no others; there seems to be only one further candidate for inclusion, and we must reject it. This candidate is well presented as follows:

> Most of us cannot try to undertake certain things we find abhorrent – killing our friends or our families. At least, we cannot undertake these things without having some reason or motive *for* undertaking them. When such a reason or motive is lacking, the undertaking will not be within our power. (Chisholm, 1976: p. 57)

There is a short answer to arguments of this sort, which has been given by Kenny. What those who argue like Chisholm seem to to be saying, in short, is that:

> 'He cannot' must mean 'given his . . . desires, he cannot'; i.e. the doing of this is incompatible with his . . . desires. But of course to say that a man cannot do

something because he is prevented by his desires is just to say that he can do it, but won't because he doesn't want to. (Kenny, 1975: p. 105)

This unwillingness may be very reasonable and laudable, but it doesn't turn an unwillingness into an inability: "taking a vow of chastity [is not] like submitting to sterilization; a nun does not lose her power [to have children] when she takes her vows, nor regain what she has lost when she breaks them" (Benn, 1972: p. 198).

Even if there is *no* conceivable reason, motive or inducement that would make you choose to do something, this does not mean you are *unable* to choose to do it – it just means you will not choose it. If you fail to rescue a child drowning in a paddling pool, you cannot argue that you were *unable* to rescue her because you find getting your clothes wet abhorrent. However true this may be, for your defence of inability to be acceptable you need to demonstrate far more than abhorrence – you need to demonstrate some phobia that really *does* make you unable to wade into paddling pools.

9.6—SUMMARY

In this chapter I have tried to do several things. I have argued that ability-sentences are "constitutionally iffy" in that conditional clauses are used *both* to complete descriptions of an ability *and* as part of the analysis of an ability. On rare occasions the special conditional "if I choose/want/try" can be used as part of the description of an ability; on *all* occasions such a conditional must be part of the analysis of an ability-sentence.[18] In defending my conditional analysis against a strong counter-argument, I have deepened the analysis of abilities by investigating the ability to choose and isolating three rather complex ways people sometimes lack abilities. I have, finally, rejected a fourth possible limitation on our ability to choose or want something – our unwillingness to do things we find utterly repugnant – which is often offered as really rendering us unable to do things.

But there is another way of arguing against my conditional analysis of ability, which is that it simply replaces one problem with a more difficult one. For conditionals, themselves, are not straightforward. I therefore have to defend myself against the justifiable outburst that "It is really a scandal that people should count it a philosophical advance to adopt a programme of analysing ostensible categoricals into unfulfilled conditionals" (Geach, 1960: p. 7). In the next chapter I shall show that we can cope with unfulfilled (and other) conditionals.

—10—
How to interpret
conditional sentences

In the last chapter I argued that a full analysis of an ability-claim will involve several different conditional components. In this chapter I shall consider conditional sentences in more detail. It might be thought that all that we need to do to find a definitive account of conditionals is to look the term up in the index of some suitable philosophical textbook. Unfortunately, the philosophers are not that obliging: there is no consensus on the correct approach.[1]

In this chapter I shall state the account of counterfactual conditionals that I favour; develop it a little; and show how we can use it to make sense of the conditionals that arise in this book. I shall here neither defend this account against its critics[2] nor try to construct a general account of conditionals; I think both can be done but they remain tasks for another occasion.

10.1—THE SUPPOSITIONIST ACCOUNT OF CONDITIONALS

As Geach pointed out, the trouble with conditionals arises with unfulfilled and counterfactual conditionals – those for which the antecedent is not true. All the main conditionals that occur in the analysis of abilities are unfulfilled ones: your ability to do something means that you do it if you want to or if you do the appropriate basic actions, and if certain manifestation conditions are met. And your ability is present whether or not these conditions *do*, as a matter of fact, occur: you are able to do it *if* you want to, not only *when you do* want to (and similarly for the other conditions). So I need to provide some method of coping with such unfulfilled conditionals.

The approach that I want to advocate is a form of the 'suppositionist' approach to conditionals. This views a conditional as an assertion of something (the conditional's consequent) within the scope of the supposition that the conditional's antecedent is true.[3] That is, asserting a conditional is playing a (more or less) sophisticated game of "let's pretend". When someone says "If Hitler had invaded England in 1940, he would have won the war", he is saying "Let's pretend Hitler had invaded England in 1940; then, surely, he would have won the war". When we play "let's pretend" seriously we use our imagination, but not in an uncontrolled way. We don't permit absolutely anything. There are rules.

The rules are roughly the following. We first assume that whatever we are pretending to be true is true. That may well give us an inconsistent set of beliefs. If our beliefs are not inconsistent then there is no problem; but if they are inconsistent we then fiddle with our existing beliefs – altering some, rejecting others – until consistency is restored and the intruding new belief accommodated. We then look at our set of consistent beliefs and pretend-beliefs, and see what they tell us about the counterfactual's consequent. Having pretended that Hitler invaded England, do our beliefs and pretend-beliefs lead us to assert that he would have won the war or not won it? If the former, we consider the counterfactual to be justifiable or assertable; if the latter, we do not. (We might also not want to be so definite, and, if our pretend-beliefs are compatible with either outcome, conclude that he might have won or might not.)

This – simplified – is Nicholas Rescher's account of belief-contravening hypotheses (as he calls them), which we can take here as being the same as unfulfilled and counterfactual conditionals.[4] I shall now discuss one of Rescher's examples, showing how his analysis is no more than "let's pretend", but also showing how he manages to draw some very important insights from this game.

Suppose we know the following (and no more, just to keep matters simple):

1. Tigers are felines;
2. Tigers are not canines;
3. No felines are canines;

and let us entertain the belief-contravening supposition that

4. Tigers are canines.

Now we cannot consistently believe (1–4), and since (ex hypothesi) we must believe (4) we must abandon (2). But (1,3,4) still form an inconsistent set, so we must abandon *either* (1) *or* (3), leaving both (1,4) and (3,4) as possible consistent pairs. But we have no reason for choosing one pair rather than the other, so we don't know whether supposing that tigers are canines would lead us to conclude that tigers aren't felines or that some felines are also canines.

Rescher asserts that this situation is completely general: all suppositions are *necessarily ambiguous*.[5] For any belief-contravening hypothesis will conflict with other beliefs, which will have to be altered to maintain consistency, and this alteration can be done in a number of different ways. Saying "let's pretend tigers are canines" tells us *that* we have to alter some of our other beliefs; but it doesn't tell us *how* to do this. And if we are not told how, we just do not know what to do. Quine's famous pair of conditionals,

(VB1) If Verdi and Berlioz were compatriots, Berlioz would be Italian;
(VB2) If Verdi and Berlioz were compatriots, Verdi would be French;

are a problem for just this reason. Clearly, if one of these is true then the other must be false but, by their symmetry, it would seem impossible to find any reason for asserting one without this reason also forcing us to assert the other (Quine, 1952: p. 15).

So a counterfactual sentence, taken by itself, is ambiguous. The ambiguity arises, to repeat, because the counterfactual asserts that we are to pretend things are different from the way we know they are ("If Verdi and Berlioz were compatriots"), and then asserts a conclusion ("they would be Italian") that follows if, and only if, we pretend things are different in some specific way, where the counterfactual itself is completely silent about whether this is the right way of pretending things are different. It is this silence about exactly how we are to carry out the pretending that leads to the ambiguity of counterfactualization.

10.2—RESCHER'S PROBLEM OF AMBIGUITY RESOLVED

The problem of ambiguity arises because we are not provided with any clues that could help us choose between the two alternatives; lacking these, no choice can be made. But philosophical examples (such as Quine's) are usually ripped from their context, and so many helpful clues are lost; the problem of the ambiguity of counterfactuals recedes when we look at the context in which the counterfactual is asserted. And it disappears altogether when we consider counterfactuals from the point of view of the people asserting them.

Any counterfactual sentence should be asserted in such a way that it is clear which beliefs are to be retained and which can be abandoned –

which possible world or worlds it refers to, to use currently fashionable terminology.[6] Any counterfactual where this is not stated, implied or clear from the context is not a meaningful sentence: it is as meaningless as my saying "There's a crab-apple tree over there" when sitting in the middle of an orchard and not pointing or looking in any particular direction, so that you don't know what is meant by "over there". Strictly speaking, the particular rules to be used for rejecting and retaining beliefs are as much part of the counterfactual as pointing is part of the crab-apple sentence; asserting a counterfactual without having in mind a particular possible world (or set of worlds), or specific method for choosing between beliefs, would be like claiming that there is a crab-apple tree "over there" without having any particular direction in mind.

So when *we* want to assert a counterfactual the solution is simple: we must make very sure that we know exactly what we mean. If we are careful, we can remove ambiguity in the counterfactuals we use.

But the ambiguity of counterfactuals does seem a real problem when we consider the counterfactuals that *others* have asserted: for just what did they have in mind? We have to try to resolve the problem by using the clues provided by the context in which the counterfactual was uttered and the point the speaker was trying to make. And there are also two general reasons why most counterfactuals escape the problem of ambiguity, as I shall now try to show.

"Let's pretend" can be an amusing children's parlour-game because one can pretend anything ("Alice once had really frightened her old nurse by shouting suddenly in her ear 'Nurse! Do let's pretend that I'm a hungry hyaena, and you're a bone!'"). When we play it seriously, however, there are limits. These start to emerge when we consider some far-fetched conditionals, for instance:

(C1) If/When my cat is hungry, it meows;
(C2) If/When my cat is a dog, it barks;
(C3) If/When my cat is a dog, it meows.

Now (C1) is obviously a straightforward dispositional property of my cat (or possibly an ability of it): it has the property, or characteristic, of meowing when hungry. (C2) is, however, not a property of my cat, and never could become one. And this difference between (C1) and (C2) is not merely because there are several instances of (C1) and none at all of (C2): (C1) could be a property of my cat even though it has never yet been hungry (because I always leave food out for it, for instance). It is not merely that as a matter of contingent fact (C2) is unfulfilled; it is that we consider it nonsense to think that (C2) could be fulfilled – for cats just do not become dogs on occasions. Yet the putative property of my cat – of barking-when-a-dog – is of exactly the same *logical* form as its actual property of meowing-when-hungry.[7] So the fact (I assert that it *is* a fact) that we do not allow the former amongst my cat's powers has nothing to do with the logical characterization of the claim. It has, though, everything to do with our knowledge of how the world (particularly the feline world) works, and our purposes in asserting animals' powers.

Notice that Rescher's Problem is often more significant for our *actual* beliefs than for *hypothetical* beliefs. For when we *do* have a set of logically conflicting beliefs we do have to decide between them, and how we should decide cannot be expressed in a mechanical manner: we have to choose. None of the rules on offer – for instance that one observed disconfirming instance refutes a theory – is sensible in all circumstances. Thus if I did see my cat turn into a dog, wag its tail, bark and then turn into a cat again, I should almost certainly conclude that I was hallucinating. If ten of us saw it, then it is an open question whether to think we had been possessed by some sort of mass hysteria, witnessed a very clever illusion, or that a cat *had* turned into a dog for a while. But in the counterfactual case the question need not be asked. If I ponder "Suppose I saw my cat turn into a dog . . .", then I could continue "then I would have been hallucinating" or "then someone would have put a spell on it" – or I could continue the sentence in many other ways. But the most sensible course to take is almost certainly to refuse to consider the question unless we actually *do* see the cat turn into a dog.

So I want to suggest that, even though it is probable that we would prefer (C2) to (C3), we would never assert either – except as a rather stupid joke. The reason rests on our usual beliefs that cats remain cats and do not turn into dogs, and that there seems no point in pretending otherwise. Faced with the choice between (C2) and (C3), we can sensibly say "Cats don't become dogs", and refuse to consider the matter further. There are, then, counterfactuals we can dismiss because the antecedent is so absurd that, in the context, the counterfactual has no point.[8]

Secondly, Rescher overstates the case when he claims that the problem of ambiguity is *always* present with belief-contravening hypotheses. His claim is that:

Each and every belief P_1 is a member of a family of related beliefs P_1, P_2, P_3, . . . , P_n of such a kind that, even when P_1 is dropped from explicit membership in the list, the remainder will collectively yield P_1 [either by actually entailing P_1 deductively, or strongly implying it inductively], and are therefore such that one or more of them must also be rejected if $\sim P_1$ is to be assured. (Rescher, 1964: p. 15, or Rescher, 1973a: p. 271. The passage in square brackets is Rescher's footnote.)

But this is false: not all our beliefs form an interconnected network like this. Some beliefs are isolated, so that we can imagine the opposite without creating a contradiction with any other belief.[9] More important, many can be *treated* as isolated.

When the antecedent of the counterfactual only conflicts with an isolated belief, or with one that we can treat as isolated, then the ambiguity of counterfactualization does not arise. This typically occurs when we consider the manifestation conditionals: we can just 'suppose' that the antecedent is satisfied without asking how this could come about. We can imagine a world exactly like ours, except that this piece of zinc is at present in this flask of acid, without making any radical revision to our beliefs: the supposition is, for the purposes of assessing the solubility of zinc in acid, isolated. It is irrelevant how the zinc might come to be in the acid, and we can assume some sort of outside agency at work moving the zinc: if we had to assume that the zinc jumped into the acid, or flew, then we might have problems deciding whether the acquisition of this new and unexpected power was likely to eliminate the zinc's solubility. More pointedly, suppose we want to consider what would happen if it was a hand that found its way into the acid. There may be four different and completely foolproof safety mechanisms to prevent that sort of thing happening, but we do not need to concoct reasons for these failing when we assert that *if* the hand went into the acid, it would be burnt.

So when the counterfactual element is unrelated to the power at issue, we need not inquire how the counterfactual might have come about. Thus at this moment I possess the ability to read car number plates at twenty-five yards (in daylight). But if I am supposing that it was daylight *now* (it being midnight as I write this) I am making a very extreme supposition indeed: the sun's appearance at midnight in these latitudes would indicate that the earth had turned a somersault. Such wild counterfactuals are completely out of proportion to the matter in hand: for we can simply say "If it was as bright as daylight now (no matter how this were to come about), then I could read a car number plate".

This applies also to conditionals about the state of the actor. "If he wasn't drunk, he could read the number plate" does not require a causal story describing how he need not have got drunk tonight. We need not ask ourselves why he got drunk, or what would have changed for him not to have got drunk; we can suppose the actor is now sober without altering any of our beliefs except the belief that he is now drunk. And therefore the problem of ambiguity – of which beliefs to reject and which to retain – does not arise.

10.3—CONDITIONALS IN THE ANALYSIS OF ABILITIES

My general approach to unfulfilled and counterfactual conditionals is that we make sense of them by 'pretending' the antecedent is fulfilled or true (respectively), altering our beliefs as necessary to restore consistency to them, and then seeing whether these beliefs include the conditional's consequent. The major logical difficulty with this process is the problem of ambiguity, but this only occurs in rather untypical circumstances. In this section I shall briefly indicate that the conditionals that arise when we analyse abilities do not give rise to the problem of ambiguity.

As I suggested in the last section, most manifestation, act and choice conditionals can be treated as isolated. Also, some are clearly pointless to contemplate. I think that the only possible problem is with the choice conditional which is part of the analysis of effective epistemic ability.[10] This, to remind you, is the clause that states that if A has the effective epistemic ability to do X then X would result from the actions *that she would choose to do if she chose to do X*. Often we can treat the antecedent ("if she chose to do X") as isolated and simply assume that she does choose X. But it seems that we cannot do this if she strongly *does not* want to do X.

The reason is that usually someone chooses not do some X because her factual beliefs and her desires lead her to consider that not-X would be preferable. In order for us to imagine her choosing to attempt to do X, we must imagine some alteration in her set of beliefs and desires, so that X now appears to be the better choice. There are often many ways for us to do this. But it may make a difference how we suppose that the actor changed her mind, because it would affect the course of action she would choose to pursue – and some courses of action may be successful and others unsuccessful. In such circumstances the question arises: if we suppose she suddenly does want to do X, are we to suppose that she chooses one of the courses of action that *do* result in X, or one of the ones that do not?

Rescher's worry would be that we can counterfactualize our actor's beliefs and desires in a number of different ways so that they are consistent and also lead her to choose to do X.[11] How we choose seems up to us; so how *do* we choose?

But in this situation how we choose is *not* up to us. When we are interested in *effective* epistemic power we are not interested in what someone might do or could do; we are interested in what they *would* do to bring about the required end. And this involves a *prediction* by the analyst, not a *choice*. Recall why we are interested in effective epistemic powers. Our main concern with this particular sort of power is in the practical context when we want to know what other people can do so that we know who to try to persuade to do things we would like done (see pp. 54 and 56). But we are then not interested in those people who are *so* hostile to our desired outcomes that we know that we couldn't persuade, bribe, threaten, cajole or otherwise induce them to try to bring them about. It is pointless to consider whether the Bay of Pigs landings would have succeeded *if* Castro had supported them. Such conditionals are not a problem, because we can simply refuse to consider them – as we refused to consider my cat's habits when a dog.

This gets rid of some ambiguous conditionals, but not all of them. The rest become straightforward when we realize that our interest in power in this context is decidedly as a second-best when we are not able to predict what people *will* do when given persuasion of various sorts (see Appendix I, pp. 211–12). Thus suppose the CIA are interested in someone's power to allow American combat troops to be stationed in her country, and they know that this person would initially be hostile to the idea. The CIA, however, can supply a new belief to the person – namely, if she should help them she could get rich (or, perhaps, if she doesn't help them she could get dead). This new belief, added to the actor's existing stock of beliefs and desires, may well be enough to produce in the actor a consistent set of beliefs and desires, and one that the CIA could predict will lead her to favour the stationing of American troops in her country. They can now go ahead and predict what she'll do and whether it will be effective.

But suppose that we know that what she'll do varies depending on how the CIA work on her: if they offer a bribe, say, she'll certainly make an attempt – she'll try to persuade a few people, make a speech or two, and then she'll give up; if her life is on the line, she'll go flat out, threaten, blackmail, kill – and succeed. Does she then have the (effective epistemic) power or not? The answer is that if we know all this her power no longer matters. We know what she *will* do (in the various circumstances), and that, in *this* context, is better than knowing what she *can* do. We have moved beyond a consideration of her powers.

We do consider people's powers in this context only if we *don't* know (yet) whether we can get the person to do what we want. At that stage we must say that she does have the required power, since it is hardly a limitation on *her* power if the CIA would choose to motivate her the wrong way. But this shows, I think, how different this usage of 'power' is from the others, the moral and evaluative uses. Then, when we say that someone has the power to do something, we mean that she can do it if she wants to. If *she* wants to; not if someone comes along and threatens to blow her head off unless she does it pretty smartish. Someone's power to do things when coerced by someone else (and only when so coerced) is not the sort of power that I imagine you, as a reader of this book, will have at the front of your mind – unless, of course, you happen to have an important post in an organization like the CIA.

I conclude, then, that there are no difficult philosophical problems in dealing with the conditionals that arise in analysing and describing abilities and powers; neither are there paradoxes or unresolvable ambiguities. The problems that conditionals give rise to are of a more practical nature: when we have worked out what we are supposing to be true that is not, and decided which of those beliefs that we think are true we are going to discard, how do we determine whether the conditional can or cannot be reasonably asserted? How do we bring empirical evidence to bear? How do we decide what we should believe?

I have nothing to say about the general epistemological issues involved here, and so I will not discuss these questions further in this, philosophical, part. The questions of how we decide what evidence we should try to obtain and how we go about trying to obtain it are addressed in Part III.

—11—
The family of ability concepts II:
ability and ableness

In Chapter 8 I distinguished generic and time-specific abilities, and have since been considering mainly generic abilities. In this chapter I shall turn my attention to time-specific abilities. The exact difference between the two sorts of ability is given at the end of this chapter: the two sections work towards this statement. (In the process, the label 'time-specific ability' will be dropped, in favour of more accurate terminology.)

11.1—ABLENESS: THE "ALL-IN" CAN

A person's abilities are a property of the person, not of the environment. Like all dispositionals, they carry explicit or implicit references to the conditions in which they apply – and assert nothing about what happens when these conditions do not apply, nor about the likelihood of these conditions occurring. When we learn that zinc has the property of dissolving in sulphuric acid, we neither discover anything about what happens to zinc when it is *not* in sulphuric acid, nor do we gain information about how *often* zinc gets (put) into the acid. Like zinc's property of dissolving in sulphuric acid, a person can have the ability to do something and yet never have the opportunity of exercising this ability, if he never finds himself in the appropriate conditions.

Yet, with people, we are also (indeed, mainly) interested in what they can do given the circumstances that they *do* find themselves in. There is a sense of 'can' in which we are *not* prepared to consider counterfactual descriptive and manifestation conditionals. Whilst we do say "I can read if I have my glasses", we *also* say "I can't read (now); I don't have my glasses". The former 'can' is that of ability; the latter 'can' has been called the "all-in can".[1] This "all-in can" combines the 'can' of ability with the presence of an opportunity.[2]

I shall describe someone who can (in the all-in sense) do something as *able* to do it, and someone who can do something in the generic sense as having the *ability* to do it. This follows a subtle difference in meaning between the two words, captured in the *Oxford English Dictionary*'s definitions of them. The relevant parts are (my emphasis in both cases):

Ability:
2. The quality *in an agent* which makes an action possible; suitable or sufficient power (generally); faculty, capacity (to do or of doing something).

Able:
4. Having the qualifications for, and means of, doing anything; having sufficient power (of whatever kind is needed); *in such a position* that the thing is possible for one; qualified, competent, capable.

(Of course, we don't stick to this difference in ordinary English; I use these terms in a quasi-technical sense.) I shall resurrect the obsolete word 'ableness' as the noun form of 'able', and distinguish between this and 'ability'.

The rich are able to feed off caviar and champagne; the poor have to restrict themselves to beer and pickles, and are unable to eat more expensive food. This is not because of any lack of masticatory ability on their part, but because of the social and economic environment they inhabit. They are unable to eat caviar, whilst having the ability to do so. If we are interested in the distribution of the good things of life – as I argue that we are – this environmental difference is something we should wish to take into account – *particularly* because it may not be due to differences in individual abilities.

Perhaps the nature of the distinction between ability and ableness can be brought out by discussing the following uncharacteristically muddled passage of Kenny's:

The 'can' of ability and the 'can' of [ableness][3] differ from each other in the way they form the future tense. 'I can speak Russian', in the present, according to context, may express either an ability or an [ableness]. Not so in the future.

I can speak Russian tomorrow, we have guests coming from Moscow
is correct; but not,

*I can speak Russian next spring; I'm taking a beginner's course this fall. The future of the 'can' of [ableness] may be either 'I can' or 'I will be able'; the future of the 'can' of ability must be 'I will be able'. Similarly with conditionals. If an ability is attributed conditionally, it must be expressed by 'will be able' or the like; an [ableness] can be attributed conditionally by the plain 'can'. Compare:

If you give me a hammer, I can mend this chair

with

*If you teach me carpentry, I can mend this chair.

It is not difficult to see philosophical reasons for this and connected linguistic differences. (Kenny, 1975: pp. 132–3)

But Kenny has misunderstood the linguistic differences because of an inaccurate philosophical analysis.[4]

First, the 'can' of ability – the generic 'can' – has *no* future tense, since it refers to matters outside time. It is well known that scientific laws are time-less (untensed) statements; so are sentences describing generic abilities. Were the subjunctive mood alive and well in English, we should always use it for generic abilities, since the reference of both is to "present or to unde-fined time, or more truly not to time at all . . . but to utopia, the realm of non-fact . . . or the imaginary" (Fowler, 1968: pp. 596–7). Water can (has the ability to) dissolve sugar because, if sugar *were* put into the water, it *would* dissolve; a carpenter can mend chairs and therefore, if you gave (were to give) one a hammer, he could mend this one.[5]

But *abilities* are not timeless; they do come and go; we gain and lose them. The asterisked sentences refer to the *acquisition* of abilities, not the future exercise of existing ones. If the Russian course is a good one (and if I have the requisite latent ability) then, next spring, I will have the ability to speak Russian. This is not some deviant future tense of the 'can' of ability; "the ability to speak Russian" is simply the object of the verb 'to have', with the future tense supplied by the auxiliary 'will'.

Secondly, the 'can' of ableness. This *is* tensed, because an ableness is an ability with a time attached – or, more long-windedly, it refers not to imagi-nary conditions but to the conditions actually encountered by the agent at the time or times we are interested in. The future tense of 'can' is 'can'. 'Will be able' is, of course, not the future tense of 'can', but has much the same meaning (though 'shall be able' may be better in these sentences). Hence "I can read it tomorrow; I can't today – my glasses are being mended" is correct, though "I shall be able to read it tomorrow; I am unable to today" runs less risk of being misinterpreted.

The 'can' of ableness may specify the relevant times loosely and *appar-ently* generically, referring to those conditions that obtain during a long time span, or generally over someone's life – as when I contrasted the diets of rich people and poor. Hence what distinguishes the 'can' of able-ness from the 'can' of ability is not so much that the former refers to a specific time; rather it is that the former refers to actual conditions whilst the latter refers to imaginary conditions. Put another way, an ability-sentence contains (explicitly or implicitly) counterfactual descriptive and manifestation conditionals; an ableness-sentence cannot contain counterfactual descriptive or manifestation conditionals.[6]

For this reason, social and political power is usually a sort of ableness and not an ability; in social philosophy we are not usually interested in what people could do if they had resources that in fact they do not have. Abilities, it seems, become ablenesses for everybody only in utopia, where opportunities are available to all. The distribution of opportunities in this world is frequently less happy; from which dismal fact stems much of the concern that social philosophy has with power.

11.2—DESCRIPTIVE CONDITIONALS WITH ABILITY AND ABLENESS

Descriptive conditionals were introduced in section 9.1 as telling us the circumstances in which abilities can operate. In special circumstances, people can do things that they otherwise cannot do: when fleeing from the police, non-athletes can leap across rooftops, perhaps. Conversely, my ability to thread a needle disappears when I am drunk. Yet we would not class leaping across rooftops as amongst our non-athlete's abilities (and we do count threading a needle as amongst mine) precisely because these conditions *are* special. Normally when we refer to people's abilities we do so assuming a more or less constant set of background conditions, and certainly if we say "A has the ability to do X" *without* specifying the circumstances in which A can do X, then we are being misleading if the ability can only be used in some bizarre circumstances.

But how do we determine what counts as bizarre and what as standard? Suppose you have a car which won't go because something trivial is wrong with it – it is, shall we say, out of petrol. I have a car which won't go because the engine has just fallen out. It seems reasonable to say that your car can do 70 m.p.h., whilst mine cannot. But why?

One answer has been given by Ayers. He argues that "to replace an old, worn-out engine with an efficient new one is to change the nature of the car" (Ayers, 1968: p. 85). To put petrol in the tank, however, is extrinsic to the car's nature: to say "this car lacks the power to do 70 m.p.h. because there is no petrol in the tank" is an illegitimate quibble, as unjustifiable as saying that the car does not have the power to do 70 because no one is driving it. Ayers argues that, although there are undeniably difficult borderline cases, this "distinction between intrinsic and extrinsic observable properties is evidently empirical" (Ayers, 1968: p. 85).

This is not correct; by introducing a distinction between intrinsic and extrinsic properties, Ayers is either being circular (despite his denials) or falling into the vehicle fallacy – perhaps appropriately in view of his chosen example. We can see that the distinction is not empirical by considering such a difficult borderline case: suppose the timing needs adjusting. Can you convince me that this is intrinsic or extrinsic by citing ever more evidence about the functioning of car engines? I think not. Ayers is quite right that the distinction is not logical or definitional, but it is not empirical either: it is conventional. It depends on the context of the discussion.

We may be interested to know whether the car can go or not because we want to use it at some particular time. If so, its properties *at that time* are what we want to know. If we need the car immediately, lack of petrol may be sufficient for us to say that the car lacks the required powers – as anybody who has ever run out of petrol in the middle of the night in a remote area knows very well. If we need the car for some projected journey next week, then we have time to get the timing adjusted – and maybe even the engine replaced.

The sort of boasting match Ayers is considering is more likely, though, to be concerned with the object's properties in general, rather than those at any specified time. Then we may be interested in those properties that the car *usually* has. Is your car usually out of petrol? Is mine usually without an engine? If you *always* keep your car out of petrol then it never has the opportunity to do 70 m.p.h. – and hence cannot (in the sense of ableness) do it.

But more likely, I suppose, we are discussing generic powers, and apply the same notion of standardness to each car. Then the content of the set of standard conditions is not empirical but conventional – it involves a *decision* on our part. Exactly how we make this decision will depend on the problem in hand: why we are interested in the object's dispositional properties. For we will be interested in what abilities are present in a certain set of conditions, and not interested in what could happen in other conditions. If there is no readily available and widely accepted set of conventional standards to which we can refer, this is probably because such a comparison is not very common. If *we* want to make it, then we have to reach agreement on why we are interested in comparing our cars in such a way; when we have done so, we will find that a suitable set of standards has emerged.

Thus athletics authorities disallow records made when there was a strong following wind: nobody denies that the athlete *did* throw the discus the distance recorded (or whatever), and did so quite deliberately and neither by mistake nor by fluke. Nevertheless it does not count as a record since conditions were so unusually helpful that they did not provide a fair indicator of performance under more standard conditions.

Athletics may be inconsistent here, in allowing records set at the Mexico Olympics to stand even though the thinner atmosphere improved performances in certain events as much as a following wind would have done. The problem was recognized at the time, but it was considered less unfair to allow record performances to stand than to debar all athletes from breaking records at the Games. Nevertheless, in logic, the latter seems the fairer course – or not choosing Mexico City for the Games in the first place.

This judgement has been criticized as merely ground-level chauvinism (why isn't Mexico City taken as standard and Los Angeles considered non-standard?) and it is worth pursuing this somewhat further, as it brings out the sort of standardness involved. For it is important to realize that this dispute cannot be settled by resort to statistics showing how little of the earth's surface is over 7,000 feet above sea level. This is because the standardness at issue is conventional, not empirical: the physicist's 'standard temperature and pressure' is no worse as a standard because it occurs infrequently. The best way of avoiding the dilemma of when an athletic performance should count as a record is by constructing an equation to convert performances at high altitudes to equivalent performances at ground level (or, for that matter, vice versa), thus neither penalizing nor aiding performances under different conditions. But this may not always be possible; and, when it is not, rival views of what is standard may exist.

To summarize.

Generic abilities are things that people can do in certain stated or implied *conditions*; the claim is about what the person could do if those conditions obtained; whether those conditions occur at a certain time (or, indeed, ever) is irrelevant. When no specific conditions are stated or implied, then the ability is taken as referring to a set of *standard* conditions, and it is a matter of *convention* what is to count as standard.

Ablenesses are things that people can do at certain stated or implied *times*; the claim is about what the person could do in the conditions that happen to obtain at those times; whether the person could or could not do the things in question had different conditions obtained is irrelevant. When no specific times are stated or implied, then the ableness is taken as referring to a set of *usual* conditions, and it is an *empirical* matter what is to count as usual.

—12—
Comparing powers

We are usually not interested only in who has the power to bring about what, we also often want to be able to make some comparative judgements: we want to find out who has *most* power, or whether you have more power than I do. The CIA, for instance, want to know who should be approached first with a bribe, or perhaps who should be offered a bigger one. But how we compare powers depends on whether we are comparing abilities or ablenesses, and whether we are interested in one outcome or many.

12.1—COMPARING ABILITIES

Suppose we want to compare our abilities to do some specific thing, such as jumping across a certain chasm. We can do this by comparing those *conditions* in which we each succeed. Your chasm-jumping abilities are greater than mine if, whilst you can jump across it even into the teeth of a gale, I succeed only in ideal conditions. If you succeed in all the conditions in which I succeed, and in more besides, then your ability is clearly greater than mine. Generalizing from this, the more obstacles and the stronger the resistance that you can overcome, the greater your ability.

This is the sort of information we might want to know when picking athletics teams, I suppose. It is also what the CIA would want to know if they had reason to believe that conditions – whatever they might turn out to be – would be similar for everybody, and if they were interested in obtaining just one specified outcome.

The CIA do bribe people for one-off jobs; but they also take people on for long-term contracts in which they are expected to do a *number* of jobs for the organization, not just one. Sometimes this will involve working on several projects simultaneously.

Consider the soldier who, according to Plutarch, brought the news of the victory at Marathon to Athens. He had the ability to run the distance in full armour, even though the effort killed him. If we are interested *solely* in his power to deliver the message, he will do as well as anyone, and is worth bribing.

He could not, however, do this and live. And this means that he would not be any use for future tasks. This might have been a matter of concern for the classical Greek CIA if they had a few more jobs lined up for their willing messenger, and this might have led them to prefer someone else who *could* survive the journey, if anybody had been available. That is, they might not *only* be interested in the messenger's power to run to Athens, but in his power to run-to-Athens-*and*-live. And *this* power, Plutarch says, the actual messenger lacked.

When the CIA consider taking someone on for a long-term contract they don't just want to know what she has the power to do if that is all she does, they want to know what *combinations* of things she can do. The combinations can be thought of as *compossible sets*, in that the actor can do any or all of the actions in each set, together. The original marathon runner could run to Athens or could live, but could not do both together: the two did not form a compossible set for him. Each compossible set can be expressed as a long conjunction, as when we say that the runner lacks the power to run-to-Athens-and-live. Your powers consist of the set of all your compossible sets.

You unequivocally have more abilities than me if your set of compossible sets includes all the sets in my set of compossible sets, and more besides. Of course, everybody has an extremely large, perhaps infinite, number of compossible sets that they have the power to do, but this does not matter here: as long as anything I can do (including all combinations of things I can do) you can do, and you can do more, you have more power than me.[1]

But it is, of course, unlikely that one person's set of compossible outcomes is a subset of anyone else's: we want to be able to make comparisons when each of us has some power that the other lacks. To do this we have to assess the worth of these different outcomes.

In practical contexts there is little difficulty here: the CIA will retain whoever is most powerful in those areas in which they have a particular interest. This means that the KGB may well consider someone to be most powerful (for *their* purposes), whilst the CIA prefer someone completely different. Power, in this sense, is in the eye of the beholder; or, more prosaically, researchers (and potential bribers) will be interested in specific areas of policy, and will want to locate those with particular power in these areas. Unless there is some agreement on the value of the outcomes under discussion, there is no way that we can judge one actor to be definitely more powerful than another. (Unless, of course, she can obtain all the outcomes that the other can, and more.) It is always *possible* that those powerful in one area will turn out to be powerful in another as well, so that the same actors are uncovered by researchers with different interests. But this possibility should not blind us to the logical truth that when two people are looking for different things they may find them in different places.

12.2—COMPARING ABLENESSES

But this conclusion – which sounds very much like that reached by plural-ist analysts of American society – is not adequate when our interest in power is to *evaluate* societies. Here we are interested in comparing people's *ablenesses*, not their *abilities*. A good test of your *ability*, as we have seen, is how large a resistance you can overcome and still bring about the de-sired outcomes. However, your *ableness* is measured by your set of com-possible outcomes, and now the fewer obstacles in your path the better, if that allows you strength (or other resources) to achieve more. The less of your resources you have to expend, the more you have left over for doing other things, and therefore the more powerful you are. What is important here is how many possible goals you can achieve *in total*; it is just not relevant how much resistance might be overcome if you concentrated on one issue.

The practice in political science of considering issues separately has tended to lead to a disastrous neglect of the overall pattern, which can leave an impression that movements attempting change are more power-ful than in fact they are. As a political technique, Tony Benn has advo-cated "the stiletto heel principle: that if you put all your weight on one place you can go through almost anything" (Benn, 1970: p. 19). But those who *have* to concentrate all their weight on one point at a time in order to achieve their ends obviously have less power than those who can spread themselves more widely and still get results. Bachrach and Baratz are undoubtedly correct when they assert that the existence of mobilization of bias and gatekeepers is a limitation on the power of those people who have to fight against such obstacles. Challenging the status quo is likely to be a costly business; and the costs are reflected in a lack of power to achieve more than one goal at a time. Benn is right that much obstruct-ion *can* be overcome; and can, what is more, appear relatively insigni-ficant when we look at issues in isolation from each other. But whilst someone is using up her energies and political resources fighting against the inbuilt conservative tendencies of the political process, she is precluded from attempting a whole range of other things.[2]

Assessing someone's overall power is difficult and requires care, but this is no excuse to claim that we should not even try. If we want to evaluate societies we *have* to try, and make as good a job of it as we can. Those (mainly pluralist) writers who have refused to attempt to do this have simply misunderstood the nature of their dissent from the "elitist" conclusions of Wright Mills and others.

So, having ascertained who has the power to do what, how *do* we reach an assessment of overall power? Well, clearly the power to bring about some disastrous end cannot be a valuable thing; it is only outcomes that are in some way worthwhile that need to be considered. People are the more powerful the more important the results they can obtain are; or, to put this another way, the more these results accord with their interests.

Conceptions of interests, then, play a crucial role in the *aggregation* of separate powers, not in the *identification* of power.[3] If we are content to say that you have power to obtain X and Y, whilst someone else can get V and W, and just leave it at that, then there is no need to bring in any notion of interests. Yet if we want to compare your power with someone else's, or contrast it with what you ought to have, then we have to weigh the importance of the outcomes X and Y to you against the worth of V and W to someone else.

We might, I suppose, decide that this cannot be done. Or we might have, or develop, some conception of human nature that allows us to evaluate the worth of these outcomes. *How* we might do this is not a matter I want to get involved in here. (I touch on it briefly in the final section of this chapter.) A fully fledged theory of interests would be necessary to perform such aggregations and comparisons; I don't possess such a theory but, luckily, I don't need one to elucidate concepts of power.

The result of this intrusion of notions of interest into ascriptions of power is that it is more than likely that two researchers with different views on how to weight the importance of various outcomes will fail to agree on comparisons of power, even though they might agree completely on who has the power to do what. This, again, is just a case of the truism that different things may well be located in different places.

12.3—POWER AND COSTS

Comparisons of power can also be expressed in terms of *costs*. The messenger who dropped dead upon arriving at Athens could do less than a (hypothetical) tougher colleague who would have survived, because the journey *cost* him more. It is important to notice, if we introduce cost in this way, that the cost is measured by the available actions which are foreclosed: that is, by opportunity cost. In the runner's case the opportunity cost was so high that it foreclosed *all* alternatives. But any action that has an opportunity cost will prevent the actor doing something else, since that is what 'opportunity cost' means. (The opportunity cost of an action is a measure of the opportunities foregone by doing that action.)

When we are using the costs of actions to compare *ablenesses*, rather than abilities, it is essential that we compare opportunity costs rather than the raw costs. For consider a store in which each of the goods costs no more than sixpence (as used to be the case in Woolworth's), and outside stand a child with sixpence in his pocket and an adult with a pound note. Then the child is able to buy any of the goods in the store, but the adult's money has more purchasing power because she can always buy a larger combination of goods. The raw cost of buying one item is sixpence to each of them; but the real cost of one purchase by the child is that it rules out buying anything else.

Similarly, it might be that a rich business pressure group and a pressure group composed of poor blacks could each secure the passage of legislation of equal value to them if they lobbied for the same number of hours. But even if this unlikely scenario were true, this would not necessarily mean that the two groups were equally powerful; they would clearly not be equal if the members of the poorer group had to devote themselves full-time to lobbying (thus neglecting their families, perhaps), whilst the members of the business group could simply employ a few lobbyists, with minimal impact on their lives. It is always the case that if the raw costs of an action to two people are the same, the opportunity cost is greater to the poorer of the two.

When we are evaluating societies we are also interested in costs as opportunity cost, but as well we need to consider cost in the sense of the suffering and pain endured in obtaining objectives. If you have to engage in an act of civil disobedience – a demonstration, say – to attain some end, then the cost of that action can be measured by what else you could have done with your time: that is to say, by the opportunities foregone. But if you also run the risk of being beaten up, then this is a cost in a more direct sense – for pain is inherently unpleasant, quite apart from anything else that it might prevent you from doing. Those political prisoners around the world who are currently being tortured are worse off than those who are merely imprisoned in that they are suffering directly, as well as being incarcerated and hence prevented from doing a wide range of things. Such direct suffering is certainly a cost, and should be considered when evaluating the society.[4]

In this context we are interested in people's overall power to satisfy their interests, and in doing this we need to subtract from the value of what they can achieve the cost of achieving it. These direct costs – pain, suffering, fear and the like – are not reflected in the list of compossible outcomes that can be brought about, since they do not themselves prevent one from doing anything. It is, however, clearly not in people's interests to suffer them. So the *overall* interest satisfaction is represented by the value of what can be obtained less an assessment of the direct costs of obtaining it.

12.4—IS POWER CONSTANT-SUM?

We cannot leave this topic of power comparisons without determining whether power is a constant-sum (or, as it is often called, zero-sum) phenomenon. My answer is that power, itself, is never constant-sum. Sometimes, however, the outcome under consideration, the behaviour of the relevant actors, and the nature of the situation are such that it so happens that one person can only gain power when another loses it. This eventuality is peculiar and not typical, and no more makes power inherently constant-sum than the occasional thunderclap makes the weather inherently explosive.

Consider – as always – an example. I enter a beauty competition in which there is a £200 prize, and I win it. This might seem to be obviously zero-sum, since if I win the prize nobody else does. But because *winning* the prize is zero-sum, in this sense, it does not mean that the *power* to win the prize is zero-sum. For it is quite possible that if you had entered the competition – which you did not – then *you* would have won it, for you are far more beautiful than me. You were able to win, since if you had wanted to win you would have done. And it may be the case (as, indeed, it is) that there are many thousands of people – millions – who could beat me in a beauty contest should they bother to enter. But in the example none of these millions did enter, and so I won. I was able to win it (given the quality of the entrants). But, also, you were able to win it (given the quality of the entrants). Your ableness to win the competition would not be lessened because many other people had this ableness too. When we assess powers person-by-person like this, we take the actions of others as given and counterfactualize the preferences and actions only of the actor whose power we are considering (and, of course, the preferences of any others that we predict will be altered if the actor under consideration changes her preferences).

Perhaps another example will be more persuasive. Religious philoso-

phers have considered this issue at some length, for they have wondered
whether the existence of an omnipotent God leaves room for any other
being to have any power. If there is a *constant* sum of power, then God,
being *all* powerful, must have all that there is, leaving none left over for the
likes of you and me. But it does not seem to be required by the idea of an
omnipotent being that nobody else has any power at all. For:

> Although God is able to do all things, we do not think He does do all things. Not
> only do we often ascribe events to human agencies or natural causes rather than
> to divine action, but we allow that some things happen against God's will.
> Although He could intervene to prevent the plans of the wicked from coming
> to fruition, often He does not. (Lucas, 1970: p. 75)

Lucas goes on to say *why* God does not intervene, but this is not relevant
to my point. The point is that human beings can have powers (relatively
limited powers, to be sure) even if we postulate an omnipotent God. Thus
whether I can walk across the room now or not is up to God; He has it in
His power to prevent me or make me. But, also, it *is* in my power to walk
across the room because we know that God will not intervene: when assessing *my* power we have to make some predictions about what God will do,
and it seems to me that the only sane one is to predict that, although He
perhaps *could* prevent me, He *will* not.

So 'power', itself, is not a constant-sum concept. Those writers who think
it is manage to reach that conclusion by restricting their attention to
necessarily conflictful situations (such as winning first prize or an election) and, further, by making the common mistake of using 'power' to
refer to *actions* (such as winning) rather than the capacity to act (being able
to win). By now, I hope that you will not want to make either of these
moves.[5]

12.5—EVALUATION AND THE AGGREGATION OF POWERS

One final point about comparing powers needs to be considered, which
arises when we are engaged in evaluating societies. When we judge
a society it is probably the overall situation within that society that we want
to look at, not that of just one individual or even just one group. (I say
"probably" because a Rawlsian would look only at the worst-off group.)
And this means that we have to treat rather differently those situations discussed in the last section in which you have the power to obtain something, and I have the power to obtain the same something, but you and I
cannot *both* obtain it, simultaneously.

Thus suppose we want to compare two social arrangements. In the first, £400 is to be divided between four individuals and it will be divided equally; none of the four has any power to get more than £100. In the second, £200 is to go to the same four, but through a competition, the winner taking it all. Someone wins, but only because the others were too lazy to enter – any of the others could have beaten the winner if she had bothered to enter. Thus, as I argued in the last section, we can say that each of the four was able to gain the £200 if she wanted.

If we are specifically interested in an individual's power, then this is right. In practical contexts there is nothing wrong with saying that each person has the power to get the money. And if we are engaged in blaming people, because we consider that they had an obligation to try to get the money (to support their aged grandmother, say), then each of the three who did not try is blameworthy. But in this *social* context, we cannot describe the second situation as one in which each can get £200, if we want to contrast it with the first described as one in which each can get £100. As we did when aggregating an individual's power over outcomes, we must consider which outcomes are *compossible* – this time looking at compossibility across actors. In the second set-up the compossible outcomes are all someone gaining £200 and the rest getting nothing; and it is *this* which must be contrasted with the fixed outcome in the first situation. To think otherwise, and to look at the society person by person, is to commit the fallacy of composition.[6]

This does not make 'power' in any way constant-sum, but it does show how careful we must be. And it also suggests that our interest in power is somewhat different in evaluative contexts than it is in the other two. This is indeed the case, as we shall see in the next section and in Chapter 13.

12.6—INTERESTS, FALSE CONSCIOUSNESS AND POWER

In section 12.2 I suggested that when we evaluate societies we must aggregate the outcomes that people can obtain, and see how well people can satisfy their interests. There is, of course, little agreement about what our interests are – or, indeed, about what is meant by the term. And different judgements about the nature of our interests will lead to different judgements about the extent and distribution of our power. (It is a mistake, though, to think that different judgements about the nature of our interests will lead to disagreements about the *concept* of power itself.)

The researcher's ideas on interests – on what goals are valuable – will be part of the moral theory with which he is trying to compare the reality. Such a moral theory might emphasize the satisfaction of wants, accepting whatever these wants might happen to be for any particular individual. On such a theory the value of outcomes will be supplied by the actor herself. Alternative moral theories obviously exist: including valuations based on some notion of need, or prescriptions about what is valuable in life, or sophisticated ways of comparing short-term and long-term wants or establishing 'real' wants.

If interests are identified with wants, then the power to satisfy interests simply becomes the power to satisfy wants; but if we take any other line on interests we open up the possibility that people may not satisfy their interests because they choose not to. In this section I suggest how we should cope with this occurrence. (This is not, strictly speaking, a problem we have with '*power*', but it is intimately connected with the reasons we are interested in power when we evaluate societies.)

Using a different vocabulary, this section discusses people who suffer from false consciousness in not recognizing what their interests are.[7] False consciousness involves failing to utilize the power that one has and failing to acquire powers that one can acquire. It can take several forms. The most contentious – and, I suggest, least common – involves valuing the wrong things, or choosing to pursue the wrong ends. Far more common is endeavouring to reach sensible ends, but choosing inappropriate means to do so. Few people *like* polluted air or would choose it as desirable; many, though, consider (perhaps wrongly) that it is a necessary means to some other end. They would oppose a policy which ran the risk of closing the local (polluting) steelworks down, not because they have a peculiar affection for the polluting factory, but because they see it as a necessary means to enjoying the other good things of life – things which come with a reasonably well-paid job and which arguably are in their interests. False consciousness of *this* kind is similar to false beliefs which prevent somebody realizing all her non-epistemic powers, in that both sorts of lack of knowledge lead her to choose inappropriate means to obtain the given end.

A false system of beliefs is false whatever the reasons for holding it and whatever the forces at work that support it. Whether the consciousness is arrived at through a deep study of all the available sources, or through brainwashing or indoctrination, if it is wrong it is wrong. However, in this context we are evaluating a *society*; and in order to pass a critical judgement on a society we need to establish that those aspects of life in that society of which we disapprove are a consequence of the society's arrangements.

I have suggested that we are interested in power in this context because we want to look at what people *can* obtain rather than what they *do* obtain.

If we discover, within a certain society, some people that are very badly off, then before we criticize that society's arrangements we need to discover whether they are suffering because the society does not give them the opportunities to be any better off, or because they are indeed given the chance and do not take it. But, I am now arguing, even if we establish that the chance is there and not taken, we need to establish why: that is, we need to examine why an actor's (false) consciousness is as it is.

This would be unnecessary if everybody had complete control over their consciousness – over their own beliefs and values. If that were the case, then the failure to exercise power would be the fault of the individual, not the society, and we need look no further than people's power to satisfy their interests. But it is now generally believed that we do not have complete control over the contents of our minds: that it is at least possible that our beliefs and desires are *caused*. If this is the case – and if it is because of their beliefs and values that people fail to exercise their power – then we must try to discover these causes. For if the causes are themselves some aspect of society's arrangements, then these arrangements again stand condemned.

But, unfortunately, it is not this simple: looking at the cause itself is not enough. For if you were genuinely *persuaded* to choose ends that were not in your interests, then you have nobody to blame but yourself; yet your choice has clearly been caused (in a sense) by your persuader. Crucial, then, is the extent to which you *chose* your false consciousness, and the extent to which it was foisted on you.

The range of choice which an actor has over her beliefs and values is an empirical matter, about which little can be said a priori. The success of brainwashing and similar techniques shows that even deep-seated and firmly held values can be altered. We all, what is more, form our values and fundamental beliefs at an early, and impressionable, age: socialization is much more effective than brainwashing because there are no pre-existing beliefs to be altered. It does, then, make sense to say that an actor is unable to hold to certain beliefs and values; and, consequently, unable to make choices that would require these beliefs or values.

The pervasive effects of one's existing beliefs stretch even beyond this: for someone may well be able to change his erroneous beliefs, and yet have no reason to do so. Suppose a person's abilities are such that he could easily get a professional job if he tried. But he is black (and living in a small town in the Southern USA), and has been brought up believing that blacks are intellectually inferior, and unable to do professional jobs adequately (or that in the society in which he lives blacks are never given such jobs when they apply, but are humiliated instead). Let us suppose that both beliefs are totally false; indeed, hidden away in the local library is a study proving conclusively that these beliefs are false. If he ever read this study (and nobody is stopping him), he would be convinced by it, and change his false beliefs to true beliefs. But why should he hunt this study out? He really believes that blacks are inferior or never employed, and he has never come across any opposing evidence in the form of a professional black person, so why should he seek further evidence for what everybody knows already? Somebody (a philosopher) wrote that philosophers examine their life, ideas, and assumptions not only occasionally but full time. But most non-philosophers have better (or, at least, more pressing) things to do with their time than spend it questioning their ideas and assumptions.

In the above situation the false belief does not *force* him to abandon hopes of a professional job – he is perfectly free to try, and may succeed; he, also, is well able to discover that he might succeed. But it would, I think, be *unreasonable* for him to query such a belief that was universally held in his community. If one accepts that it would be unreasonable, then it follows that he can only obtain a professional job if he first does something unreasonable. If we want to consider why he does not obtain a professional job, it seems more reasonable for us to trace this back to the belief of inferiority or discrimination than to his ignorance.

We next need to ask why the belief was so widespread if it was so false. If the whites in the community had done nothing to foster the belief – indeed, had done a lot to dispel it – then we might hold the black community responsible for their false beliefs. But suppose we can show that the white community had (not necessarily intentionally) encouraged this belief to grow. In this case, the white community can be condemned for blacks not obtaining professional jobs, if they would have obtained them under some alternative social set-up.

The above argument has depended heavily on what it would be reasonable for people to do or believe, which is not something that is very easy to establish. We can go part way towards establishing what a reasonable action is by employing parts of rational-choice or game theory: but we still need to attach a probability to the chances of the widespread belief being correct.[8] However, the question of what beliefs a person should reasonably hold given a certain amount of evidence is a very general problem of epistemology, and not one that I can even try to tackle here. Discussing what reasonable people would do is, however, the sort of thing that lawyers seem to manage without too much difficulty, and I have a feeling that fair-minded researchers should not find too large an area of disagreement over what is reasonable in a given situation.[9]

So even if people *can* satisfy their interests, we need to see whether it would be reasonable for them to do so: whether their lack of interest-satisfaction is *their* fault or not. Whether, that is, a different social set-up would lead (or would have led) to their obtaining more interest-satisfaction. We can draw up a sort of chart showing the distribution of overall interest-satisfaction not as it actually *is*, but as it would be if everybody performed as well as they were able (bearing in mind that only compossible outcomes are admissible).[10] This chart can be considered to represent the limits of the society's achievements, the best that could happen within existing social constraints. It is these constraints that we wish to assess. If the best that can happen within them falls short of a realizable ideal, then the society stands condemned.

The family of ability concepts III: active and passive power

13.1—ACTING, FORBEARING TO ACT, AND ABLENESS

Hitherto I have been considering that someone's powers are her possible actions and their consequences. Powers, on this account, involve things which *we do*, not things which happen *to us*: we are able to open and close our eyes, but a nervous tic which does this for us is not an exercise of an ability (or evidence of the possession of one).

But sometimes we are less interested in what a person can *do* than in the outcomes she can produce, including those outcomes which come about without her needing to act at all: we can usefully extend the notion of action to include forbearing, as well as acting.[1] When a person *forbears* to act, she is not merely *not* acting: she is refraining from altering the expected course of events when she *could* have done so. To forbear to do something is, indeed, to do something else; it is, in an extended sense, to perform an action. Leaving the window closed can be considered as much an action as opening the window would be.

Usually the ability to allow events to run their natural course is uninteresting, since everybody must have it.[2] But when the natural course of events is different for different people, and when we are interested in ablenesses (the outcomes a person can produce *given* the conditions she encounters) rather than in abilities, then it would be clearly inappropriate to ignore those outcomes produced by non-intervention.

Such an ableness is exemplified in the sentence "Bernard is able to have a beard (or be bearded)" (said, for example, of an adolescent male). This power clearly does not consist in any *action* that Bernard can do (although the contrary state, that of being clean-shaven, would require an action): the beard just appears. (For the purposes of this example I assume that no artificial ways of inducing the growth of hair, such as implants or hormone treatment, exist.)

Whilst (normally) a man is able to grow a beard although a woman is not, this difference is *not* captured by an analysis in terms of actions and choice. For a woman has exactly the same *actions* open to her as any man – her permanent clean-shavenness is clearly not due to any inability to *do* as much as a man. The difference between men and women on this score is that, whilst both sexes are born beardless, women tend to stay that way whilst men *naturally* become bearded.

It is my contention that this example is not as peculiar as it might appear, and as its complete absence from the philosophical literature on ability might lead one to believe. (Perhaps it is because most of this literature appears under the heading of the philosophy of action that philosophers have tended to ignore abilities which *don't* involve actions.) But rather than discuss ableness-through-forbearance at greater length here, I want to suggest a sense of ableness that moves even further away from a consideration of actions.

13.2—ACTIVE AND PASSIVE ABLENESS

There is a long tradition in the analysis of power, going back to Aristotle, that distinguishes between an *active* power and a *passive* power. Locke expressed this distinction as well as anyone: "Fire has a power to melt gold . . . and gold has a power to be melted. . . . Power thus considered is twofold, viz. as able to make, or able to receive any change. The one may be called *active*, and the other *passive* power." Hobbes, similarly, distinguished in his mechanistic way between an agent and a patient – the agent being a body that does something to another body (the patient). Passive power, the power of the patient to suffer change, is merely the necessary counterpart to the agent's active power to produce change.[3]

Today this probably sounds unacceptably animist; and the distinction between accepting and receiving change would not stand up to scrutiny. Nevertheless, a distinction along these lines makes a lot of sense when applied to *human* powers. I wish to resurrect the term 'passive power' (and coin the unaesthetic 'passive ableness'), though my use will not be exactly that of Locke and Hobbes.[4]

In the last section I suggested that you could have the ableness to produce something if the conditions are such that you could produce it by forbearing to intervene – where 'forbearing' means that you *could* intervene to prevent it occurring, but do not. Forbearing is passive in the sense that it does not involve a bodily act, but it is active in the sense that it involves a choice – a mental act, if you like. That which I call a *passive ableness* or *passive power* is passive in both senses: no choice is involved because you *could not* intervene to prevent the outcome occurring; it would come about *in spite of* anything you might do.

Now this idea clearly needs some defending, because this appears to be a straightforward description of complete powerlessness – and not some unusual sort of power, however much based on tradition it may be. Your inability to prevent the sun rising tomorrow is usually considered (and rightly) to demonstrate your complete powerlessness to make it rise. So I shall now try to state a case for this apparently bizarre idea of calling impotence "passive power".

When I introduced the idea of ability as a two-way dispositional, I pointed out that this had the slightly unfortunate consequence that your 'ability' to understand your native language when it is spoken in your presence is not an ability at all, since you cannot *not* understand it. (See pp. 24–5 and Chapter 4, n. 4.) But, nevertheless, you *do* understand your native language. By contrast, a monoglot Eskimo will not understand your native language. (I assume you are not an Eskimo.) Now suppose you meet a compatriot who has developed the ability to understand speech if she wants to, or not understand if she does not – *genuinely* not understand; not pretend not to understand. Then she *does* have the ability to understand your language, whilst you and the Eskimo lack it. Yet this is hardly a natural way of dividing the three of you into two groups: linguistically, you have far more in common with your compatriot than with the Eskimo. That you *do* understand the language is far more important than whether you can not understand it if you wish. Your power of understanding is passive; but it is no less important to you for that.

So there do seem to be situations in which we would naturally talk of abilities, but would lump together active and passive abilities. And with 'power' (which is less intimately connected with action than 'ability' is) we frequently don't want to differentiate between people who *do* get something and people who *can* get it, but we want to distinguish these people from those who *cannot* get it. A concept of power that includes passive power does this job. (This will be explored further in the next section.)

'Passive power' (even 'passive ability') is not, then, such a stupid notion as it seems at first glance. But is not a passive power no more than an ordinary dispositional power? I originally distinguished abilities from other dispositionals by saying that the former involve choosing whilst the latter do not, and I argued in sections 4.3 and 4.4 that inanimate objects have dispositional properties but no abilities – yet here I am treating people as inanimate objects and arguing that they still have abilities (or at least ablenesses). Does this not mean that I have come full circle; that I am here again interested in 'power' in its widest dispositional sense? The answer is no. Passive powers form only a subset of dispositionals, and this for two reasons.

One difference relies on the distinction between ability and ableness that I drew in Chapter 11. For what we are interested in here are properties that we have in situations that do happen, or are likely to happen. We are not interested in the counterfactual "what would happen if . . ." of generic ability.[5] Indeed, it is normally habitual dispositional properties, and not conditional ones, that are counted amongst our passive powers: that someone receives something passively and regularly is to describe a habitual dispositional property of theirs.

But – secondly, and more importantly – the existence of abilities which do not involve actions on our part does not mean that *everything* that habitually happens to us is normally numbered amongst our powers. To give an extreme example, whilst we all will die, it makes little sense to say that we have a power which the gods lack in that we will not be here for ever. Or, rather, it seems to make sense only if we also want to imply that immortality would be a burden we would rather not bear. Things that happen to us are only classified with our powers if the end result is somehow commendable or approved – otherwise they are *liabilities*. When beards are fashionable, it makes sense to talk about people being able to grow them; when it is considered desirable to be clean-shaven, then possessing facial hair is a liability.

The *Oxford English Dictionary* defines 'liable' as:[6]

> a. Exposed or subject to or likely to suffer from (something *prejudicial*); in older use with wider sense, subject to the operation of (any agency), likely to undergo (a change of any kind). . . .
> b. Subject to the possibility of (doing or undergoing something *undesirable*). (Both emphases mine)

I do not want to elaborate here on exactly what we mean by "something prejudicial" or "undesirable". What I am committed to is that an ascription of an ableness of the involuntary sort entails some sort of commendation, or grudging respect, or (at the least) indifference. Things which happen to us which are harmful or undesirable are liabilities; things beyond our control which happen to us which are beneficial or desirable can stand with our abilities.[7]

As we have seen, the distinction between an ability and a liability is not the same as that between an agent and a patient. But, confusingly, this same difference *can* be synonymous with the agent/patient distinction. Thus the difference between being able, as opposed to liable, to do military service is that in the first case one has a choice, whilst in the second one has none. The implication is that this is an onerous task, which one would rather avoid. It strikes us as odd when a country claims that its young men are able to serve in the army, and it transpires that in fact they have no choice in the matter. But the usage *is* correct within a framework in which military service is considered beneficial[8] – just as it does not sound strange to us to be told that someone is able to take four weeks' holiday a year, even when we learn that he is, in fact, prevented from working for this period (for example if the whole factory closes down). Since we generally feel that holidays (with pay) are good things it seems quite correct to say that someone is *able* (rather than *liable*) to have four weeks' holiday.[9]

It seems, then, that sometimes when we refer to a person's abilities and able-nesses we are interested only in what she can do by acting or intervening; sometimes we want to include outcomes that result if she were to forbear from intervening; and sometimes we want to go further still and include outcomes that will result whatever the actor were do to. These passive abilities and ablenesses are really dispositional properties rather than abilities, but, for some purposes, their similarities with abilities are more important than the differences.

13.3—TWO TRADITIONS IN SOCIAL PHILOSOPHY: ACTIVE AND PASSIVE POWER

In the last section I introduced and defended the notion of "passive power". I suggested there that when we investigate people's power to obtain some given end we sometimes find three sorts of people: those who have the power to obtain it; those who do not have the power to obtain it; and those who do not have the power to obtain it but who get it anyway. I suggested that sometimes we want to lump together people in the first and third groups; when we do, we can say that those in the third group have passive power. In this section I shall suggest that some social philosophers have been interested in passive powers, whilst others have not. My foray into social philosophy is intended merely to be suggestive; I am well aware that it is not remotely exhaustive, and that much more needs to be said on this.

I will contrast those who might be called *romantics* with those who are *utilitarians*, arguing that the latter, but not the former, employ a concept of power that includes passive power. I shall use Marx to illustrate the romantic tradition: doubtless others were truer romantics than he was, but Marx's writings have the virtue of being widely known.[10] The utilitarian tradition is so well known that it does not require any outline here, beyond saying that it is Bentham (and certainly not J. S. Mill) whom I have in mind.

Marx considered that all (or nearly all) human beings possess certain latent powers (to use my terminology rather than his) and that to be truly human was to develop these powers – to transform them from latency to actuality. Under communism, our powers will have developed their true potential; Marx also referred to our 'destination' as being to develop our powers.[11] In other words,

> the end or purpose of man is to use and develop his uniquely human attributes or capacities. His potential use and development of these may be called his human powers. A good life is one which maximizes these powers. A good society is one which maximizes (or permits and facilitates the maximization of) these powers, and thus enables men to make the best of themselves. (Macpherson, 1973: pp. 8–9)

Capitalist society, for Marx and Macpherson, can be criticized in so far as it does not enable people to develop their powers as much as is possible; it can also be praised as an advance on earlier systems which permitted even less development of human powers.

On an individual level we think like this all the time. When we teach a child to speak we are actualizing a latent power, and we unhesitatingly consider this to be a good thing for the child. We would also consider it worthwhile to inquire whether a child who cannot speak is aphasic (and therefore does not possess the latent ability to speak: that is, his capacity for speech is lacking) or merely deaf, so that he has to be taught by different methods. At least in our society, any parent who took no interest in whether their child could speak would be roundly condemned. Similarly, any society which allowed a sizeable proportion of its children to remain unable to talk (or read and write), and took little effort to develop this faculty, could be condemned as not caring enough for the development of its citizens' powers.

Whilst the notion of a developed or merely latent power is a descriptive one, when we turn to consider which latent powers *should* be actualized we face a normative question – for we all have *some* latent powers which are best left latent. (Those who actualize and use *these* latent powers tend to get locked away.) It is therefore a normative decision which of our powers are the important ones: of what, indeed, living the good life should consist.

Marx had very definite opinions on this, which he expressed particularly in his earlier writings. My task in this work, regrettably perhaps, is not to examine Marx's writings, and assess his picture of the fully developed person – it is merely to point out that such a picture existed for Marx. Thinkers in the romantic tradition, who emphasize the importance of the development of 'truly human' powers, must (as a matter of logic) also offer some account of which of our latent powers *are* truly human.

Utilitarians have a different reason for being interested in power, and this demands a different, and wider, conceptualization of power than that which I have considered so far in this section.

Most people have some view about the merits or morality of the way goods (including such intangible, but highly desired, goods as leisure) are distributed within their society; thinkers of a more radically egalitarian stamp, for example, have been appalled by societies in which a few people obtain far more things than others. Some writers, such as Lasswell, have simply defined the powerful as these people: "The influential [or powerful] are those who get the most of what there is to get. . . . Those who get the most are *elite*; the rest are *mass*" (Lasswell, 1936: p. 3). This does not seem a useful approach, for, as I have already argued, one can be powerful and yet not get very much if one does not exercise one's power. If the mass *could* get more of "what there is to get" but do not – because, perhaps, they choose not to exert themselves or just want other things – then we would assess the society differently from how we would if the mass were truly powerless to improve their lot.

But the literature on the concept of power accepts this point and then goes beyond it: to ignore completely the distribution of goods *except* in so far as this distribution is consequent upon an exercise of active power. This is a mistake, and one which we must be careful to avoid. For we must not lose sight of our interest in what people receive passively – what I have called people's passive powers.

Marx, by contrast, was not interested in this passive power: for him the essence of being human was *doing*, not *receiving*. Ollman considers Marx asking:

> What would happen if nature were given in a form which man found adequate? In *Capital* I, Marx mentions the tropics where nature is too lavish, where it is 'adequate', and as a result keeps man in the condition of a child. Instead of

growth there is stagnation. In this instance, nature "does not impose upon him any necessity to develop himself". (Ollman, 1976: p. 99; quoting Marx, 1867: p. 481)

A parsimonious nature is thus a blessing as well as a curse, in that it encourages, as well as forces, us to develop our powers. In short, on this view, achieving things for oneself is better than receiving them from others.

But not all think like this. The utilitarian emphasis on what it is that people can get must include a consideration of what they get anyway, by the simple working out of social forces rather than by exercising power. So the formulation of passive power captures an essential aspect of power – one which all too often merely lurks in the background (if it lurks anywhere at all). Occasionally it reasserts itself, as in a (Marxist) study of contemporary Britain, which was concerned to stress the point that:

> individuals or groups may have the effective benefits of 'power' without needing to exercise it in positive action. . . . What we have in mind is a passive enjoyment of advantage and privilege, obtained merely because of 'the way things work', and because these ways are not exposed to serious challenge. (Westergaard and Resler, 1976: p. 142)

Even Nelson Polsby, no adherent of Marxism, finds himself saying "that many community 'decisions' are unconscious, intended by nobody in the community, and yet have profound consequences for the shaping and sharing [*sic*] of community values" (Polsby, 1963/1980: p. 133). However, Polsby then proceeds to ignore all such decisions. Yet if the social system performs in such a way as systematically to advantage some individuals or groups, it certainly seems odd not to take account of this. It might even be that on this utilitarian perspective – one which emphasizes getting as many valued goods as possible for the least effort – active power begins to pale into insignificance compared with the magnitude of passive power.

The point of this section, then, is to suggest that the romantic emphasizes the power to *do*, the utilitarian the power to *get*: the latter must include passive power; the former must not.

13.4—PASSIVE POWER AND BENEFIT

Perhaps I should just say a brief word about what passive power is *not*, to forestall attacks like the following, which are often made on people who 'confuse' power and benefit.

> Suppose . . . we notice that it rains in Seattle. We speculate that taxi drivers make more money on rainy days. Therefore . . . taxi drivers cause it to rain in Seattle. This conclusion will still be defective even if we are energetic in buttressing some empirical points: we can test the theory that taxi drivers do indeed benefit from rain; we can learn if they know they benefit from rain; we can find out if they actually favour rain. (Payne, 1968: p. 452)

Polsby, who likes quoting this passage, comments:

> Even if we can show that a given status quo benefits some people dispropor-tionately (as I think we can for any real world status quo), such a demonstration falls short of showing that these beneficiaries created the status quo, act in any meaningful way to maintain it, or could, in the future, act effectively to deter changes in it. (Polsby, 1980: p. 208)

Polsby is here quite right; but he is aiming at the wrong target. There is no need to claim that because someone benefits she must *cause* her good fortune, nor that she can control it. All one need do is note that a status quo that systematically benefits certain people (as Polsby agrees it does) is relevant in itself. One can deplore – or praise – such a situation with-out wishing to suggest that the beneficiaries caused it or (*pace* Lukes and Connolly) are somehow to blame for it.

—14—
Beyond personal power

In this chapter I shall extend the account of power developed so far to show how it can cope with power-ascriptions in which the power-holder is not a person; for there is clearly more to consider with 'power' than just the power of (named) individuals. I shall look first at how we can talk about the power of a *position*, and then at how we can talk about the power of a *group*.

14.1—THE POWER OF A POSITION

In both practical and evaluative contexts we frequently want to discover not only the power of individuals but also the power of *positions* within a country. The CIA will consider that it is worth planting an agent in a trade union, in the hope that she becomes president of the organization, if they feel that this position carries with it a considerable amount of power. A skilful incumbent of this position would be more powerful than a mediocre one; a complete incompetent might have no power at all; but nevertheless the power of the position itself is relatively constant. The CIA, of course, will want their nominees to occupy the most powerful positions within the society, and will need to locate such positions.

Perhaps because of this, empirical works on politics tend to fall into two types: the biographical approach (concentrating on the power of named individuals, usually leading politicians) and the institutional. In these latter we are interested in the power of 'the presidency' (or, in British terms, the Prime Minister, Cabinet, civil service, Treasury, and so on) rather than the power of the individuals who happen to have held this office. The power of President Eisenhower may have been small, relative to the presidents who preceded and succeeded him; the power of 'the presidency' in this period was, however, more or less unchanged. For the power of the presidency does not diminish if a President is incapable of using it fully.[1]

When considering the power of a position or role we still need to distinguish between epistemic and non-epistemic conceptions of power. We cannot assume that because we are considering the power of a position rather than a person that it has perfect knowledge: indeed, knowledge itself is a relevant resource which is distributed with great inequality between different positions.[2]

Therefore, in order to cope with the epistemic power of a position we have to make some assumptions about the information available to an incumbent of this position. That is to say, the information available to her *qua* incumbent, rather than as an individual with her own characteristics.

These considerations of the power of a position give rise to problems of their own. For whilst it is easy to talk, at a conceptual level, about an individual *qua* person as opposed to the same individual *qua* holder of a certain position, it is far from easy to make this distinction in practice. Nevertheless, we must attempt to make this distinction.

We can do so by noting that the power of a position stems from the resources which the position carries with it; the possession of these resources is what differentiates two people of roughly equal personal ability, and gives the President more power than the average person in the street. One can get some idea of the power that a position bestows by seeing what resources go with this position. This is what has been understood by a power structure: the political structure allocates resources to people who are the occupiers of certain positions.[3] Thus it has been argued that, in America, "the conception of a 'ruling class' does not apply. Those in the elite group are simply the men who sit in particular chairs at any particular time. The chairs, moreover, have the power rather than their occupants" (Hacker, 1964: p. 142).

It can be a matter of concern whether power *ought* to be distributed between positions in whatever way it is, so we have evaluative reasons for discovering the distribution of power between positions, in addition to the practical reasons mentioned earlier. That great power went with certain positions was one of Mills's themes in *The Power Elite*. The power elite "occupy positions in American society from which they can look down upon" the rest (Mills, 1956: p. 3); they "occupy the strategic places in the structure of American society" (p. 286). Thus one strand in the debate between pluralists and 'elitists' was the question of how much power *did* go with these key positions. Pluralists gave a completely different answer to this question from that which Wright Mills gave, and hence arrived at a different evaluation of the society which they were both studying. We therefore need to be able to reach an assessment of the power that resides in different positions. I think we can do this within my framework by assessing the power-conferring qualities of the resources that go with the position; that is, by comparing what people can do *with* those resources with what they can do without.[4]

14.2—THE POWER OF A GROUP

We often want to know the power of a group or of a collection of individuals, and we can want to know this for several different reasons. Sometimes a group's power can be thought of in exactly the same way as an individual's power. When we consider the power of the Cabinet, or of an organization like Microsoft or an oil company or a trade union, we can treat the collectivity as if it were an individual.[5] These organizations have recognized decision-making mechanisms, and we can sensibly ask whether when they decide on something they can carry it out. This will typically involve asking whether the organization can control its members. But we also need to ask analogous questions when considering an individual's powers, and so there are no new problems of principle here.

Problems do arise, however, when we look at groups that are not formal organizations. In this section I want to show how these problems are resolvable within the individualist methodological framework that I have adopted. We do not need to treat groups as if they were individuals, or impute some mystical group identity or group consciousness to them.

The first step is to realize that groups can be defined in two ways: either *intensionally* or *extensionally*. Intensionally-defined groups are identified by some defining characteristic; extensionally-defined groups by listing their members. I shall argue that these two ways of characterizing groups are used in different circumstances and need to be analysed slightly differently.

In practical contexts the power of groups can be important; after all, if we are interested in bribing people, we might want to know what happens if we bribe two people and ask them to work together. A group in this usage is merely a collection of individuals, and is defined extensionally. Clearly two people working together can often achieve more than the sum of their achievements when they work separately; anybody interested in achieving their ends through the power of others will be aware of this, and on the look-out for useful small groups of bribable people.

The power of groups also obviously arises when we evaluate societies; indeed, groups feature far more often in evaluative discussions involving power than individuals do. The groups we are interested in here are likely to be intensionally-defined groups, such as classes or sectional interests of various kinds, rather than groups defined by naming their members.[6]

I shall start the consideration of group power by considering the simpler case of extensionally-defined groups, which crops up in the practical context. When considering the *non*-epistemic power of a group of people, we simply ask whether there is any combination of sequences of actions that the members of the group could perform which would bring about the desired end. If there is such a combination, then the group has the non-epistemic power to bring about that end.

It by no means follows, of course, if a group of people has the non-epistemic power to bring something about, that any member of the group *individually* has this power. For when considering the power of an individual we consider only what would have resulted from all possible actions that *she* could perform (taking the actions of the other members of the group as fixed); when we consider the non-epistemic power of the *group*, we no longer consider the actions of the other members of the group as fixed – we want to know what they could do if they *all* co-operated.

But, as we have seen, our main interest in this context is in epistemic power, and here we encounter additional factors which we have to consider when dealing with group power. If one (crucial) actor does not know what she is supposed to do, the group does not have epistemic power; each individual has to have the individual epistemic power to do the actions required of her – which implies that she has to know what these actions are. But the main problem with group power – as with any form of collective action – is that *co-ordination* between the individuals is required. Not only does each actor have to know what is required of her as an isolated individual; when working in a group she might need to know what someone else will do, and vice versa. A group has power only if it is able to sort out this problem: if it can manage to co-ordinate satisfactorily, using whatever methods of communication may be available to it.

We can show this by two examples.[7] In the first, you and I, both healthy and reasonably normal people, are standing behind a stalled car. If either of us alone pushes at it, the car will not budge; but if we both push simultaneously, it will move. Suppose that if I asked you to help me push it, you would readily agree; but if *you* wanted it pushed and approached me for help, I would not agree to assist. Then I have individual power to get the car moving (since when I want it moved I can bring this about), but you do not possess this individual power (since whatever you do you cannot move the car).[8] The two of us together as a group, though, *do* have this power if, should both of us want the car moved, we could co-ordinate satisfactorily and succeed in pushing it.

Co-ordination, however, is not always as simple as it is in pushing a stalled car. For consider the second example:

> Suppose that a small group of bandits are holding up a train containing a large number of passengers. How shall we assess the collective power of the passengers with respect to the issue of whether or not they will be robbed? Suppose that the bandits 'have the drop' on the passengers, but that there is a set of sequences of acts, a sequence for each passenger, such that if they performed these sequences of acts, they would disarm the bandits (with no harm to themselves) and foil the robbery. Assume further that each passenger knows which acts would be the most appropriate ones for him to perform as a means to foiling the robbery. This is not enough to ensure that all would perform these acts if all wanted the robbery to be foiled. The rub, of course, is that each passenger has little reason to believe (indeed, has strong reason to disbelieve) that enough other passengers will do their part. Since, for each passenger, it would be very costly if he did his part (e.g., started to disarm the bandit nearest to him) while few others did theirs, each passenger would refrain from doing these acts, and the robbery would succeed. A similar problem arises in assessing the power of a large group of slaves over a small group of masters. If all the slaves acted in unison, they would overwhelm their masters. But it does not follow that they have much (or any) collective power over their masters. Like the train passengers, the problem for the slaves is that each is insufficiently confident that rebellious action on his part would be supported by others. There is an important respect, then, in which 'faith is power'. (Goldman, 1972: p. 238)

The passengers on the train have group power only if they are able to co-ordinate successfully. Thus whilst we counterfactualize the *choices* each member of the group makes, we cannot counterfactualize their beliefs about the actions of the other members of the group: this knowledge, like all other knowledge, has to be kept constant when we consider epistemic power.

Let us consider the stalled car again, and this time let us suppose that you and I have been joined by a third person. It is quite possible that, whilst you and I have group power, the three of us together do not. For it may be that, even if all three of us wanted the car to be moved, each would take the attitude that only two are needed for pushing, so the other two can do it – in which case, of course, the car will never get moved. This is one way a group can lack co-ordination. Indeed, as the group gets larger co-ordination becomes more difficult, even though one might expect that carrying out the task would become easier. The more people there are available to push the car the less effort it is to anybody to push, but the more co-ordination is required to succeed, in that each individual can argue that the car will get pushed anyway, so he need not expend any effort at all. There is a very real prospect, then, that as the group gets larger its power will diminish – a paradox of group size related to the Olson paradox.[9]

If we three can co-ordinate and work out who should push the car, then we can say that the group of the three of us has group power to push the car. This remains true, and significant, even though a subgroup of this group (you and me) also has this power; a group can contain a redundant member without this destroying the group's power. This is for two reasons. As I have just argued, because the two-person group has the power to do something we cannot infer that the group formed by adding another individual to it will still have that power. The three-person group may not be able to co-ordinate properly, so that even if we know that the two of us have power we obtain extra information when we know that the three-person group is also powerful. But also, all that is said when one asserts that a certain group has the power to do something is that they can do it if they choose: it is *not* implied that any member is *necessary* for achieving this end. Bribing the three of us to push the car in such circumstances will certainly be as effective as, if probably slightly more costly than, bribing just you and me.[10]

In the *evaluative* context much talk of power is about the power of groups rather than of specific individuals. We must, at the outset, however, be on our guard against talk that is *apparently* about groups but on closer examination turns out to involve only individual power. When we consider the power of (say) a racial minority within this country we are sometimes, it is true, discussing the power of this group *as a group*, but perhaps more often we are comparing the power of a (typical) individual who is a member of this group with the power of a (typical) individual who is a member of some other group, or an individual in some way typical of the general society. Or again, women often complain about their inability to walk about unmolested at night. But that does not mean that women *as a group* cannot walk unmolested: it means, specifically, that a woman *on her own* cannot do this. But this lack of individual power occurs because the person is a member of a group, and we can say that this group is discriminated against (or, at the least, able to do less than another group – in this case, men). Or, in class terms, a group can be said to lack power because the life-chances open to an average member of that group are less than the life-chances open to an average member of society as a whole. Saying that it is the *group* that lacks power is simply a shorthand (sometimes a confusing one) for saying that individual power is distributed along group lines. This use of 'group power' has been adequately covered under the heading of individual power.

Nevertheless, the power of groups *can* arise in evaluative contexts. Let us suppose we discover that the workers in a certain factory have much less overall power to satisfy their interests than their middle-class neighbours, and that this is because of the preventable injuries they tend to suffer at work. But, also, the workers are allowed to form themselves into a union and, if they did so, may well, collectively, have the power to force the management to introduce safer working conditions. The workers do not do this, as it happens, but, since they could, it would seem to be *their* fault that they fail to satisfy their interests, and not the fault of the social system.

In saying this we are jumping from individual to group power. The workers lack the power to avoid injury not in the sense that the group lacks this power, but because each individual worker lacks it. But there would seem to be little that any individual worker could do about it – one man going on strike brings forth derision, not change. Whilst these workers are badly off *as individuals* they can only do something about it *as a group*. We need, then, to investigate what this group power might be like.[11]

The group here is defined intensionally, not extensionally. When we do want to consider group power in making evaluations, it is invariably intensionally-defined groups that interest us: groups such as classes, or sections of society defined by racial, religious, ethnic, occupational or similar criteria. A consideration of the power of such a group obviously has to take into consideration all the aspects mentioned in the discussion of extensionally-defined groups, in particular the problem of co-ordination. But we have an additional complication when considering the epistemic power of the group, in that it is not very clear what is meant by the group *choosing* anything. Does *everybody* in the group have to choose something for us to say "the group" chose it? If the workers have the power to obtain safer working conditions but only if absolutely everybody in the factory wants them, then this would seem a rather tenuous power. Yet if some small subgroup of the workers have the power to obtain these conditions, against the wishes of the majority, this is surely not the workers (as a group) having the power to do so.

I shall consider this second point first. We have seen that a large group may lack a power that a part of the group has, because of the extra difficulty of co-ordinating the larger group. Suppose this happens with the workers: if they *all* want safer working conditions they fail to get them; if only some want them, then these succeed. Such a story is not necessarily implausible: perhaps too many cooks can spoil broths in factories as well as kitchens. Should we say, in such a case, that the *workers* had the power to obtain the change in working conditions?

I think that we should not. The workers would certainly have the *non*-epistemic power, since there are actions available to them all that would lead to success. But they would seem to lack *epistemic* power if they cannot all co-ordinate: they might succeed if, by luck, a number of people did nothing, but the possibility of succeeding by luck is not what we mean by epistemic power.

So the relevant question is whether they could succeed if they *all* wanted to. But two points must immediately be made about this. The first is that we have to include costs. And we have to include as costs both those costs to individuals that are incurred in the course of performing the required actions and co-ordination costs that arise because an individual has to find out what others are doing in order to know what to do herself. As a general rule of thumb, the larger the group the larger these organization costs; therefore the more costly it is to bring about the required end; and so the less powerful the group. It follows from this, and seems plausible, that the workers' power is greater if a relatively small subgroup can be appointed that, by itself, can obtain their desires than if nearly all of them are required to be active in the struggle.[12]

The second point is that, in evaluative contexts, we would need to look at false consciousness – at whether all workers *can* choose to want safer working conditions and, if they can, whether they have been socialized not to. Some people, for instance, regard such matters as fit only for cissies and not for real macho men. This may be a free, autonomous choice – but we may sometimes think that it is not.

When there is a fair chance that some of the members will not be making autonomous choices, then matters change. It is then very unlikely that *all* workers will choose to want safer working conditions, and so a group that can bring about changes only if they are all in favour of the changes has very little power. If the group of all workers has the power to change working conditions, if they all should want to, and if a smaller subgroup *also* has that power, then the workers as a whole would seem to have greater power to create safer working conditions. The smaller the subgroup required to choose safety, the greater the power of the group as a whole to bring it about.

It must be remembered that we are only interested, in evaluative contexts, in people's power to further their interests – so we have already assumed that the macho-men are misguided. We want to know whether the unsafe working conditions exist because the workers at risk are powerless to do anything about them, or they could eliminate them if they wanted but just do not want. If it only required a very few workers to complain, we would be less inclined to condemn the situation than if it required every single one to speak out.

There is one final matter which needs to be discussed when considering the power of groups, and this involves the notion of group interests. I have argued that the notion of interests enters into our assessments of power when we need to aggregate different outcomes, and that this aggregation will depend on some evaluation of the worth of the different outcomes to the people concerned. When we talk about group interests, however (as distinct from the interests of members of a group), we have a narrower focus. The group interests of (say) farmers are determined by considering what things are of value to farmers *qua* farmers: we are concerned with sectional interests in the double sense that we are considering the interests of a section of society, but we are also considering only a section of the interests of the members of this group. Individual farmers may have interests in clean air or the advancement of the local operatic society; these things may be very important to them as people – but not as farmers. The group interest of farmers is advanced by (amongst other things) high prices of farm products; yet most farmers are *also* consumers of farm produce (bought on the open market) and the group interest of consumers is advanced by low prices. As a whole individual, each farmer has to decide whether high or low prices of food benefit him more: which policy is more conducive to his interests as a person. He may decide that supporting a group campaigning for higher food prices will run against his all-round interest. Nevertheless, such a group could legitimately claim to be acting in the interests of farmers (*qua* farmers) even if its policies were not in the overall interest of any individual farmer.

Thus it does seem that the power of groups can be dealt with within my general framework: group power poses difficulties, but they are not impossible to resolve.

—15—
Power and freedom

15.1—FREEDOMS AND ABILITIES

It has often been remarked that there is a close connection between power and freedom, though there is much disagreement about exactly what this connection is. In this chapter I hope to show that my analysis of 'power' can help us understand why we consider freedom so important and how we should set about analysing it.

I shall start with Isaiah Berlin's highly influential account (Berlin, 1958). He characterized his preferred analysis of freedom as negative, since it involves an *absence* of constraints. To be free is to be left alone to do what one can; it is to be uncoerced. The focus of attention is not on what it is that people are *able to* achieve or obtain; it is on the extent to which they are not forced to act other than they would choose. Thus Berlin approvingly quotes Helvetius:

> The free man is the man who is not in irons, nor imprisoned in a gaol, nor terrorized like a slave by the fear of punishment . . . it is not lack of freedom not to fly like an eagle or swim like a whale. (Berlin, 1958: p. 122 n. 2. There is no reference to the source of the quotation from Helvetius)

Freedom, then, for Berlin, involves the absence of constraints upon our powers. But not all constraints count as rendering us *unfree*: some merely make us *unable* to do something. This distinction between being unable and being unfree is crucial for Berlin, who considers that "You lack political liberty or freedom only if you are prevented from attaining a goal *by human beings*. Mere incapacity to attain a goal is not lack of political freedom" (Berlin, 1958: p. 122; my emphasis).

So it is freedom of interference *from others* that is considered of paramount importance, rather than freedom from *all* interference: to be trapped by an avalanche in a cave is not a diminution of freedom; to be imprisoned in the same cave by an enemy is. To count as an infringement of freedom, the constraint should be brought about by a person, or group of people, or should be something which is traceable back to some person's intervention. Hence one account in the literature is simply that you are only unfree to do something when someone (physically) prevents you from doing it (see Steiner, 1974, or Parent, 1974a).

Many writers have insisted, further, that the actor limiting your freedom must be doing so *deliberately*.[1] Thus:

> to suggest that freedom is at stake is to invite the question of what persons or what social systems are *deliberately* impeding someone's attempts to lead a happy life. To say that someone is not free because not fed is to imply that someone *wants* him to starve. (Ryan, 1965: p. 111; my emphases)

This suggestion, then, further limits the constraints on abilities that can count as making us unfree rather than merely unable.

Still other limitations on constraints have been suggested. One of the oddest suggestions is that only if we make someone *retrievably* unable to do something do we make her unfree rather than merely unable: we can make someone unfree to walk by manacling her legs, but if we chop her legs off "we have no hesitation in saying that [she] is unable, not unfree, to walk" (Day, 1977: p. 264). Yet, I think, we also have no hesitation in saying that chopping off someone's legs is an infringement of her liberty. I suspect that it sounds odd to say that someone without legs is unfree to walk because that is so mild compared with the horrific torture that occurred: it is odd not because she *isn't* unfree to walk, but because she is so much more than *just* unfree to walk. We similarly tend not to say that someone who has just been battered unconscious is thereby made unfree to drink beer; though, even on Day's account, she *would* be unfree to drink beer.

This shows the dangers of relying on what we do and do not normally say: there are lots of logically impeccable things that we do not say, and have good reasons for never saying. Logical oddnesses are only one sort of oddness that can occur in language. So if we want to develop a conception of freedom that regards mutilating people as not infringing their freedom, we need a *reason* for doing so – a reason based on whatever we want the concept of freedom to do. I shall suggest that whilst there *is* a reason for wanting to distinguish lack of freedom from lack of ability, it is a reason that provides no support for Day's bizarre claim.

I think that we can understand why there are divergent accounts of freedom, and disagreements over what constraints are to count as constraints on *freedom*, by considering why there are *any* accounts of freedom. Suppose, instead, that Abel is *only* concerned about his abilities. He will want them enlarged as much as possible, but he won't bother to differentiate between different sorts of constraints on them: if he is unable to get out of a locked room it won't matter to him whether someone locked him in deliberately, did so inadvertently, or if the wind blew the door shut. As far as his concern with his abilities goes, if he is locked in he is locked in, and that's the end of it.

But most of us are interested in more than just our abilities – we are interested in *how we are treated by other people*. Our self-respect – or pride, perhaps – is important to us, and we want to be treated by others in a manner that fits our status. Within a liberal framework this status is usually that of a rational, autonomous human being. If we are not treated in this way we feel demeaned.[2]

I think that it is this sentiment that lies behind our making the fuss that we do about freedom. And I think that this also explains why definitions of freedom differ so much. The reasons are that the sentiments referred to in the previous paragraph are vague ones, and, crucially, people disagree about exactly what treatment is required. Some people – indifferent or thick-skinned or very self-assured – do not worry about how people treat them: like Abel, they do not differentiate between constraints on their abilities. But most of us react to how we are treated, and in so doing react to the symbolic content of the treatment as much as to the actions themselves. Our different readings of this symbolic content, and the different requirements of our notions of self-respect, give rise to the wide variety of analyses of freedom. My claim is, then, that accounts of freedom differ because the various authors are working with different notions of self-respect.[3]

So when Freda is concerned about her freedom, she is not *only* concerned about what she can do, unlike Abel when he assessed his abilities. Yet this does not mean that Berlin-type accounts are necessarily correct. Imagine that you are accidentally locked in a room, or trapped in a cave by an avalanche, and that then, whilst many people could easily free you, nobody lifts a little finger to do so. Some people – Nozick, perhaps – would apparently not feel at all aggrieved if this happened to them. So long as nobody kicks Nozick when he is down, or pushes him down in the first place, he considers that nobody has acted towards him with less than respect – even if everyone ignores his cries for help (Nozick, 1974). Other people feel that their status requires that someone provides aid for them.[4] From this perspective, if someone doesn't let you out of the room when he could easily do so it is as insulting, and insulting in exactly the same way, as if he purposely locked you in the room. It is therefore quite appropriate for those who feel like this to describe both situations as one of unfreedom, for the distinction between being locked in and not being let out is a distinction without a relevant difference for those who do not follow Nozick.

A summary of this section would be that to be unfree is to be unable, where the constraint on the ability is considered to be particularly demeaning to the actor's self-respect: to say that one is unfree as well as unable is to imply that one is insulted as well as injured. But when we come to consider *which* constraints make us unfree and which merely unable, we need a well-worked-out moral theory of self-respect. It is because we lack such a theory, and also lack shared intuitions, that writers disagree about whether certain constraints are 'really' constraints on our freedom. There is common ground within our culture that bad luck or a malign fate does not insult us: offences against our self-respect must be traceable, somehow, to human acts, omissions or constructs. But there the consensus ends. This pluralism cannot be overcome by further investigation of the word 'freedom' or by dogmatic assertions that one's rivals are making linguistic mistakes. Our use of 'freedom' involves, and depends on, the deplorably under-analysed moral notion of self-respect and what self-respect requires. Until agreement is reached on these matters, different writers will (legitimately) use 'freedom' to cover different sorts of things.

15.2—ANALYSING 'FREEDOM'

If I am right that to be free is to lack a certain sort of constraint on one's abilities, then much of the analysis of power can be carried over to apply to freedom, and this can resolve some of the other disputes that occur in the literature on the concept of freedom. I shall discuss just a few such disputes.

The first is whether you are made unfree only if you are actually *prevented* from doing something, or whether threats or obstacles can render you unfree.[5] Most people probably feel that we are less free in a society in which the expression of a range of political ideas is illegal, and punished, than in a society that has no laws against the expression of ideas. But many writers have deemed it unacceptable to say that Freda was unfree to do something when she in fact did it, and so have concluded that laws do not infringe our freedoms – since even in the most totalitarian tyranny people who are brave enough can speak out against the regime, and some indeed do so.[6]

The solution to this dilemma can be seen easily enough if we refer back to the discussion of power and costs on pp. 88–91. If we are interested in somebody's freedom *to do some specified thing*, then making it costly or punishable to do it does not remove the power to do it, and so does not render someone unfree to do it. But, certainly, when one is incarcerated in a dungeon for criticizing the local tyrant, one is then made unable to do a very wide range of things, and hence one's freedom is severely limited. Those who claim that laws do not diminish freedom make the mistake of thinking that we should always split freedoms up into the freedom-to-do-this or the freedom-to-do-that, and never consider freedom in any wider way. Since a law makes it illegal to do something more or less specific, it might seem that it is our freedom to do that specified thing that is being curtailed. But that is not how the law works, at least for most laws.[7] The criminal law deliberately rests on the apparent paradox that we are left free to commit a crime and *then* our freedoms are curtailed, and curtailed in a manner that may well leave us free to continue committing the crime. Thus we can be said to be free to break the law, but punishment is still an infringement of freedom, since it is a constraint imposed on our powers[8] – and the more severe the punishment the greater the overall diminution of freedom. People therefore have more freedom in a society with few rather than many laws (ignoring, for the moment, the freedom-enhancing aspect of laws, in stopping people acting in ways that limit the freedom of others). Hence when evaluating societies – whether we are interested in freedom or in power – we must look at people's aggregate freedom or power, and not at their freedom to do some one thing in isolation.

So far in this chapter I have considered unfreedom as a constraint on an (existing) ability; the second contentious area I want to look at is whether we can be made unfree to do something that we lack the power to do in any case. Does the law that prevents you smoking cannabis limit your freedom if you cannot find any to buy? Or, as has been suggested (by, for instance, Day, 1977: p. 260), is someone neither free nor unfree to do something if they are unable to do it? In other words, if you are unable to do something for two distinct reasons, one of which would count as making you unfree but the other would not, are you unfree or merely unable? Phrasing the question in this way prevents us from confusing it with the quite separate question whether you can be considered unfree *because* you are unable to do something, for instance by being unable to afford it.[9] In that situation, which I have considered already, there is only one constraint, which is of unclear status. Here there are two constraints, each of unambiguous status.

Looking at the situation as two constraints of different sorts helps us to characterize it correctly. If you are interested in your freedoms, to recap, then you are interested not only in whether you can do something but also, and as much, in how others treat you: the constraints they impose on you, and the symbolic meaning of these constraints. By enforcing a law that makes it illegal for you to smoke dope, the government treats you in a certain way which is demeaning (or not) whether or not you can obtain the drug. The *symbolic* meaning is the same whatever the *actual* impact. Hence it seems that if the law would have made you unfree, and not merely unable, had you been able to get hold of dope, then it makes you unfree as well as unable whenever you cannot find any of the stuff. I don't suddenly become unfree to smoke cannabis when a consignment evades the police inspectors at the docks and hits the streets; if I am unfree then, I am unfree all along.

Much the same can be said when you are made unable to do something that you do not want to do anyway. If the laws on drugs limit your freedom, they do so because of the sort of constraint they are, and the implication this has for how others see you: whether you *want* to take the drugs is as irrelevant as whether you *can* take them.[10]

But constraints that stop you doing something you clearly would not want to do may well be seen as supportive and helpful rather than insulting; it depends to a great extent on how they are done and on our attitude to paternalist interference. Hence a tall fence that prevents you throwing yourself over a cliff – that makes you *unable* to do so – would probably be considered by most of us a not inappropriate constraint – it "ill deserves the Name of Confinement which hedges us in only from Bogs and Precipices" (Locke, 1690: sec. 57). This is *not* the difference between feeling free and being free,[11] because whether a constraint counts as an unfreedom or a mere inability is a matter decided by the observer, not the actor. Even if the cliff-walker felt enraged by the fence (perhaps because he enjoys the sensation of danger) *we* would probably not say that he has been treated inappropriately, and hence not say that he was unfree. On my account, we say that someone is unfree if the constraint offends against some notion of self-respect and treatment appropriate to one's status – but it is the speaker's notion of self-respect, *not* the actor's, that is employed.

Finally, if we can limit our freedoms by imposing a *penalty* on everyone who does something, does imposing a tax of the same amount equally limit our freedoms?[12] Usually not, because the symbolic content of a penalty is very different from that of a tax: the criminal law consciously exploits extensive symbolism to make the malefactor feel that she has done wrong, as well as paying a £20 fee for her transgression. (On-the-spot motoring fines, on the other hand, are far more like taxes, and are usually treated as such – with the element of a lottery attached.) But there are certain things that seem to us inappropriate to tax – attending church, perhaps – and a tax on these would be seen as an infringement of freedom. Both taxes and fines limit our ability to do things; either may, but also may not, be a limitation on freedom. It is not simply the *size* of the tax or fine that matters: it is what the levying of a tax or the imposition of a fine says about the way we are being treated.

I have not tried to provide a full analysis of freedom in this section, but I hope that I have shown that freedom can be incorporated successfully and instructively within my general account of power. Our freedoms are very valuable, and I have tried to show both what their value is and how they are valuable in a way different from our powers. Our interest in freedom is almost entirely in the context of social evaluation – this follows from the sort of value that freedom is – and much of the discussion of power in this context applies as well to freedom. The characteristic of freedom is the (implicit) reference to the (under-explored) idea of treatment unfitting to one's status: the genuine differences about whether a constraint of a certain sort makes one unfree usually stem from a different moral perspective on this issue.

To summarize. You are free to do something if there are no demeaning restraints on your power to do it; you lack freedom in so far as restraints which are inappropriate to your status are imposed on you.

—PART III—
How to study power

—16—
Studying power: introduction

So far in this book I have been advancing a thesis about the *concepts* of power – what they are and what they are not. But once we have sorted out what is *meant* by a claim that someone has (or does not have) power, we have to set about establishing whether the claim is *true* or not. So I now want to look briefly at how we can determine just who does have power.

I think this Part is bound to be disappointing, for there is no one method of studying power which guarantees a satisfactory answer. Those who have proposed one, perfect way of going about studying power have been deluded; others, who have searched in vain, have been mesmerized by a social scientists' equivalent of a philosophers' stone. But still there is no reason to conclude that the study of power is just too difficult or that the concept of power is somehow faulty, and all would be delightful simplicity if we could somehow eradicate it from our vocabulary. By now it must be clear that I think that 'power' is indeed not a simple concept – but also not an eliminable one. Not surprisingly, studying power cannot be done mindlessly or mechanically – but it would be completely wrong to abandon such a study because it demands some effort and thought.

We must first remember that we cannot hope to *prove* power ascriptions; nor can powers be directly observed. A claim about a power, like one about any disposition, will go beyond the evidence on which it is based, for "observation is limited to *performance*, to what a thing (or person) in fact does on specific occasions. Its powers and their congeners do not lie open to public view" (Rescher, 1973b: p. 181).

A statement about a person's (active) powers involves a number of counterfactual elements; and counterfactual statements refer (by definition) to non-actual states of the world (or, maybe, states of non-actual worlds). What we can observe – the evidence we can gain – are facts; we cannot observe, nor gain evidence directly about, 'counterfacts'. What we have to do is gain evidence of facts – make observations – and from this *impute* to counterfacts. The ways in which we can move by imputation "beyond overt actual doings to the implicit powers, dispositions, abilities (etc.) of things" (Rescher, 1973b: p. 181) is the subject of this Part. When we see how we can best do this, we shall be in a position to determine what evidence, about "overt actual doings", we shall require. Not all this evidence will be obtainable in practice, but when we understand what we need to do to make a convincing case for a power claim, we shall be in a better position to judge between competing power claims on the basis of admittedly incomplete evidence.

The most convincing way of establishing the truth of a counterfactual is to make the antecedent true, and then see whether the consequent is also true. If we could wave a magic wand to do this (or travel to the appropriate possible world) the issue could be put beyond reasonable doubt. Such a suggestion is not as absurd as it appears, since it is the basis of scientific experimentation: by manipulating the real world we turn a counterfactual into a factual statement, so that we can observe whether or not it is true.

Experimentation involves certain assumptions, however. We have to assume that background conditions are either kept constant or, if they alter, that any changes are irrelevant to the experiment. If we wish to generalize from a series of experiments, we must assume that we are investigating a relatively enduring aspect of reality: that an identical experiment performed under similar conditions but at a different time will produce the same result.

But even waving a magic wand or performing an experiment is not sufficient if there is a possibility that success is due to a fluke. To distinguish between successes through flukes and successes through the exercise of a power we need to perform a series of experiments: one success or failure is unlikely to be conclusive. We would not try to infer my skill at darts from just one throw; we would, if possible, prefer to see how I fared over a larger number – say, a hundred.[1]

The most obvious method of establishing power claims is thus through experiment. In politics, however, there is not much scope for experiments designed to test or falsify hypotheses. But politics is not the only discipline investigating power: power relations within small groups have been much discussed by social psychologists, who *have* been able to develop experimental techniques.

In Chapter 17 I consider experimental approaches that can be used in the study of one such naturally occurring group: the family. We shall see that even here – when we *can* conduct experiments – experiments have a severely limited value. So perhaps political scientists need not feel particularly disadvantaged compared with their colleagues in the more experimental human sciences. Indeed, I shall suggest that the best work on power in families involves no experiments, and was done not by a psychologist but by an anthropologist.

Despite the lack of experimental opportunities, we can gain evidence in other ways. Even harder sciences face this problem: doctors may well feel constrained from scratching a haemophiliac to see whether he bleeds to death – yet there are indirect tests available to establish whether someone suffers from haemophilia. If we lack direct tests we must infer from indirect ones rather than give up or, worse, fallaciously assume that absence of evidence is evidence of absence. Chapters 18 and 19 will examine these indirect methods.

Direct experiments

Perhaps the best way of illustrating the methods of gaining information is to look at a more simple (or, at least, less complex) situation than the ones studied in politics. Such a case would be the distribution of power within the family – and this has the advantage of being a problem to which psychologists have paid a considerable amount of attention. It is interesting to see how practitioners of this discipline have tackled the question of how power is distributed.

A family is a relatively small and self-contained unit. Boundary problems (who counts as in the family and who does not?) can be overcome simply by choosing as subjects those families which meet predetermined criteria. This is not the case normally when we study power. In general, social psychologists are less interested in discovering who is most powerful in some given family – they are concerned with more general questions such as whether men have more power than women in a given culture. Political scientists, however, are concerned with power in a specified community or country. Social psychologists may choose to reject a family from the sample as being (say) too big and extended to be comparable with other families; a political scientist could not simply decide not to study power in the United States because it is so much bigger than most other countries. We are likely to be interested in the United States per se, which we are not about any particular family.

Most families studied have been either a husband and wife, or a husband, wife and child of a certain specified age. For the purposes of illustration here, the family will be considered as a completely autonomous unit; all interactions between the family and those outside it will be ignored. This is obviously unrealistic (although most studies of power in families seem to make this simplification), and any worthwhile study of the family would not ignore the crucial aspect of the family's interaction with the society of which it is a part. But I think that, since this discussion is supposed to be merely illustrative, it is better to keep it simple and clear rather than more realistic but complicated and, perhaps, confusing.

17.1—POWER IN FAMILIES: AN EXPERIMENTAL APPROACH

As one might expect, there are many different methodologies for studying power in families;[1] these derive in part from different notions of what power is, and I shall consider only those that bear some relation to my approach to 'power'.

One of the earliest, and simplest, techniques was developed by Fred Strodtbeck in 1951; Strodtbeck worked with 'husband–wife dyads' in the following way.

> Each couple was asked to pick three reference families with whom they were well acquainted. The husband and wife were then separated and requested to designate which of the three reference families most satisfactorily fulfilled a series of 26 conditions such as: Which family has the happiest children? Which family is the most religious? Which family is the most ambitious? After both husband and wife had individually marked their choices they were requested to reconcile their differences and indicate a final "best" choice from the standpoint of their family. (Strodtbeck, 1951: p. 469)

Winning on a decision (i.e. obtaining one's own original preference as the final family decision) was taken as an indicator of power; the spouse who won most decisions was taken to be the more powerful.

A few years later, Kenkel developed a more sophisticated version of this approach, in which

> Each pair was asked to assume that it had received a gift of $300 [NB This was published in 1957] and was then asked to determine between themselves just how this money should be spent. They were further instructed that the money could not be saved in any form nor could it be spent for items they had previously decided to purchase. (Kenkel, 1957: pp. 18–19)

Here the influential (powerful) spouse is taken to be the one who first suggests the eventual oucome. Decisions on how to spend a sudden windfall might well be considered more important to the family than agreeing which of their friends is most religious or has the happiest children; these latter matters, whilst often not unimportant, are unlikely to prove crucial in the relationship, whilst the expenditure of money could easily be so. Thus, if we wish to generalize from a small set of issues to overall power, Kenkel's choice of issues is preferable.

Kenkel's method is also an improvement in that it to some extent avoids a fairly obvious dilemma with any procedure such as Strodtbeck's. For it is possible that both spouses, when asked to write down their opinions of their friends, are in total agreement. This (a familiar problem in studies of political power) could be because they had always thought alike, *or* could be due to the continual influence of one partner on the other during the course of the marriage. It is extremely far-fetched to assume – when the partners have been living together for years – that the only influence relations working between husband and wife do so during the psychologist's little experiment.

However Kenkel's suggested method does not really avoid this problem. Although he insisted that the money was not to be spent on an item which the couple had already decided to purchase, this might be thought not to exclude an agreed upon shopping-list which ordered the priority of items to be bought whenever there was enough money. People, after all, often daydream about what they would do with the money if they won the pools, so Kenkel would not have been putting a completely new idea into their heads. One problem with this method, then, is that it is not clear how uncontaminated are individuals' expressions of what they want: are they really *their* wants, or have they already been influenced before the experimenter could get to them?

I want to suggest a variant of these methods which retains their essential points – experimental decision-making in hypothetical situations – and yet avoids the problem of the genuineness of each actor's wants. Such a method also is in accord with the conceptualization of power that I have been developing.

I have argued that what someone *actually* wants is hardly relevant to a determination of her power: it is whether she could satisfy *hypothesized* wants that is important. An experiment could be run (in principle) as follows. We would first take on one side just one member of the family, the one whose power we wished to ascertain, and ask her what she would do *if* she wanted to attain some given end. For example, she could be instructed to want to go to see her mother at the next public holiday.[2] She can be told to suggest this to the family, in whatever way she would if she really *did* want to do this. Some decision will be made: she will either succeed in going to see her mother, or fail. Leaving aside the possibility that the result was a fluke, we will be able to discover whether she does, or does not, have the power to go to see her mother at the next public holiday. This will be some evidence relevant to the wider (and more signifi- cant) propositions that she can go to see her mother whenever she chooses and – wider still – that she can see whom she likes when she likes.

It would probably happen – and this is important – that the number of experiments that would have to be run would not be large. For it would scarcely be worth while running an actual experiment if we can discover through questioning that the wife thinks that her husband would dearly love to see his mother-in-law; that the husband, when asked separately, agrees (obviously strongly and sincerely) to this; and that any children are too young to have a realistic say in the matter. Alternatively, if he has beaten up his wife every time she has attempted to see her mother, so that she is now too cowed even to try, an experiment would be a waste of time.

Further, an experiment is not worth running if we have hard evidence that for her to visit her mother is a decision within her competence – that is, one which she could just carry out without even discussing it within the family (or, perhaps, one which she *would* carry out without prior consult- ation – perhaps in secret).

Thus in many ways a better experiment than Kenkel's would be to ask members of the family if they felt that they could purchase a number of items from a list, should they want them, and within the *existing* financial constraints of the family. These items would range over the whole spectrum, perhaps being classified into categories in whatever way is thought most relevant. By asking suitable questions, and where necessary running mock experiments, we could draw up a list of goods which each partner is able to procure.

Another list could be constructed of other family-relevant choices – that is, any choices affecting the family or its members in some way or other. Obvious candidates are questions about where they should live; what employment (if any) each partner should take; how many children should be had, and when; decisions on contraception; and also when, how and how often sexual relations should take place. This list is not, by any means, intended to be exhaustive, but merely illustrative of the sorts of matters that could be investigated.[3] If we are interested in the family in an evaluative context, we also need to acquire information about the costs to each partner of obtaining these things, both in terms of direct pain and suffering and in other opportunities forgone.

17.2—THE DISADVANTAGES OF EXPERIMENTAL APPROACHES

But there are problems in relying on even extensive experimental evidence. One familiar problem with social experiments (particularly psychological experiments) is that the subjects are not the same after the experiment as they were before it (and during it). In this case, the power of the actors can change over time, either through changes in extrinsic factors, or because of changes due intrinsically to the experiment. Experiments carried out on a family ten years ago may well tell us little about power within that family now: the resources of the actors are more than likely to have changed. But, of more immediate interest here, the experiment *itself* can change the situation. Some resources are used up when power is exercised: money is an obvious example. Other resources, however, improve with use and atrophy when neglected: physical strength (up to a point) and any skill which requires practice are cases in point. You may succeed in obtaining something (either in an experiment or in real life) by bribing someone; but if all your money goes in this way, then your power to obtain it disappears until your wealth is restored. Victorious armies at the end of wars are usually unable to defeat forces equivalent to those they have just vanquished; an athlete who has just broken a record is unable immediately to do it again. On the other hand, trial and error works on the principle that one often learns, through failure, enough to enable one to succeed next time.

Experiments, by themselves, thus only tell us what people do *on that specific occasion*: they do not tell us directly even what the same person can do on an identical occasion in the future (or could do in the past). This has to be inferred from the result of the experiment and any knowledge we have of the changes in resources between the time of the experiment and the time in which we are interested.

Secondly, it is difficult to be sure that the expressed preferences of the actors are their actual preferences. We don't know how seriously the family will take games played for the benefit of researchers: it is not unreasonable to suspect that sometimes one spouse may let the other 'win' as a sort of bargaining ploy in a continuing, real-life power game. Further, it may be that subjects do not answer questions honestly (perhaps because honesty would be too painful for them), or, probably as likely, answer erroneously because they simply do not know how they would act if the situation were to arise.

Thirdly, from a single experiment we cannot *observe* whether a success is through a fluke or through an exercise of someone's power.

Finally, we may have difficulties in constructing appropriate background conditions in experimental set-ups. One reason for this is that experimental ethics or common humanity (which seem not always to be the same thing) may prevent us from creating conflicts in marriages that are already unstable.

Experimental evidence, then, is not perfect. There is much that we want to know that cannot be obtained by experimenting; and even the evidence we can get may be unreliable, and not tell us what we want to know. Evidence from experiments must be supplemented by other sorts of evidence.

—18—
Indirect experiments

There are many indirect ways of conducting experiments. In this chapter I shall look at three such ways, which I shall call *thought experiments*, *natural experiments*, and experiments *conducted by others*.

18.1—THOUGHT EXPERIMENTS

Often there is an even better way of establishing a counterfactual than conducting an actual experiment, and that is to carry out a *thought experiment*. Galileo never actually dropped lead weights from the leaning tower of Pisa: to prove his point it was enough to drop them in imagination. I also remember reading somewhere that many theories of the construction of the universe had the big drawback that from the theory one could deduce that the sky at night would be blindingly bright, since the light reaching us from the millions of stars would be far more than that of the sun. We do not require a multi-million pound research grant to discover that this refutes the theory: all we need to do is take notice of the self-evident. In studying power we also should take notice of the self-evident.

That is to say, we must consider – at least briefly – those outcomes which appear of no immediate importance because they are taken for granted: one's power over them (perhaps one's passive power) is assured. In looking at power in families, simply discovering who can do what without even consulting the other partner can take us a long way towards knowing the distribution of power: unspoken assumptions can speak volumes if one listens attentively.

Dahl's study of New Haven can provide us with a political example of how the obvious could be studied. Dahl did not consider unemployment an issue worthy of study, in part because "in New Haven in 1959 only 8% of our sample mentioned unemployment as a problem" (Dahl, 1961: p. 62 n.). Of course unemployment was not a *problem* in 1959, but only because there was not much of it and little prospect that it would increase in the immediate future. Most people took their power to obtain (more or less) suitable jobs for granted; but this power is nonetheless not unimportant for being relatively widespread. Indeed, had Dahl looked at such "non-issues" he could perhaps have *supported* his case – it was, after all, a time when elections could be fought and won under the slogan "You've never had it so good". If all the crucial issues had not been problems in the way unemployment at that time was not a problem, each person's power to satisfy his interests would indeed have been high. This argument, though, cuts both ways: for we must also include outcomes which are of no immediate importance because *failure* is taken for granted.

It is not difficult to draw up lists of those things we take for granted in this way; but just because it is easy to do this does not mean that such lists are unimportant. Indeed, quite the contrary: because we all do take these things for granted, we at least do not have to contend with factual disagreements. It is an instructive exercise to draw up lists for an individual (maybe one representing a group) of those important things he or she can obviously obtain, and those important things he self-evidently cannot. In grossly inegalitarian societies and families, such a procedure will suffice by itself to establish that one person or group has more power than another: it may be that even if the less powerful person has the power to obtain *everything* that is disputable, she still won't have as much power as the more powerful person indisputably has. In such cases, we need research no further.

18.2—NATURAL EXPERIMENTS

Although we might not be able to *create* an experiment that shows what happens if someone wants, or does, a certain thing, we may be lucky in that the person chooses to do it anyway. Suitable experiments sometimes come about *naturally*. Thus another sort of evidence that cannot be ignored is how the family have made *actual* decisions in the past. One must be very careful about the priority of this sort of evidence: on this political scientists have gone badly astray, and need to be taught a lesson by psychologists. What we want is evidence that is reliable and relevant to the central question whether the spouse can succeed in doing certain things should he/she want to. Evidence from actual decisions is only of interest in so far as it is directed towards this goal. That is, our observations of how people actually act lead us to draw inferences about how they *would* act in other situations, or similar situations at other times. One limitation with this sort of evidence is that, except for the most unusual families, the range of decisions made is relatively small: one cannot discover this way whether people can get things they do not in fact want. And (as is well known in political science) we cannot observe, from natural experiments, how little power powerless people have, if the powerless are well aware of their lack of power and so do not bother to try to get something they want but know they cannot get. Nevertheless, much can be learnt by an intelligent use of naturally occurring experiments.

We are unlikely to be fortunate enough to see the people we are interested in trying to obtain the whole range of things we are interested in – and doing so on a sufficiently large number of occasions for us to be happy that the experiment has been conducted often enough to allow safe generalizations. So we will also want to know how *similar* people fare when they attempt to bring about similar things, in similar circumstances in different times or places. The notion of similarity is not a given, of course: it rests on some (usually implicit) theory. But then so does all inference to ascriptions of power: it is only on the basis of a theory of the social process that we can ever generalize or counterfactualize.

18.3—EXPERIMENTS CONDUCTED BY OTHERS

Often our knowledge of experiments (both artificial and natural) will be second-hand, reported to us by the person who observed what happened. Provided we can rely on the probity and acuteness of the reporter, such evidence is as valid as things we observe for ourselves.

As well as reporting to us what they have seen, other people can be more helpful still. For if we cannot perform an experiment or a thought experiment, the next best thing may be talking to people who might know what the result of such an experiment would have been if it had been performed. Expert and informed observers should know such things in many cases, and it is folly (and arrogance) not to avail ourselves of such expertise. Others may know more about an actor or a political situation than we can ever hope to find out in the course of a research project; knowledge gathered over decades of political involvement and observation should not be despised because it is not 'academic', nor rejected merely because it conflicts with the results of a few questionnaires and personal observation of a few months. (Neither, of course, should it be accepted uncritically.)

This is the valid idea behind the misnamed reputational methodology for researching power. If, for instance, we wish to conduct a comparative study of power in a large number of American cities, and we ourselves are not expert on the local politics of every one of these cities, it makes sense to enlist the help of those who *are* knowledgeable.[1] Experts, notoriously, disagree; but nevertheless a picture can be built up by consulting them.

It must be pointed out, to keep clear of confusions that have occurred in the literature, that the object of this approach is *not* to tap reputation for power as a power resource. Reputation for power undoubtedly *is* a power resource (in the next chapter I quote Hobbes to this effect) but this is not what we wish to discover by consulting experts. We don't ask experts who, in the community, has a *reputation* for power; we ask them who *is* powerful – who can get what. The experts are consulted because they might be able to tell us what outcomes would occur if various key actors had certain hypothetical preferences: what would happen if we could run an experiment.

18.4—CONCLUSION

So we can add a lot of useful, and diverse, information to any knowledge we have obtained from running experiments. We have the verbal accounts of the actors themselves; we have knowledge that is so obvious that everybody knows it; we have a great deal of actually observed behaviour, observed both by us and by any others who may be in a better position to see; and we have the results of the thought experiments of informed observers. All this would not be worth saying were it not for the strange belief in the social sciences that there is only one way of gaining information – although disciplines seem to disagree whether that way is through experimentation or observation of past behaviour. It seems that journalists and detectives have developed better noses than social scientists for sniffing out the reliable parts of all the available evidence and deciding what to accept and what to reject.

So have anthropologists; and we are fortunate that at least one intelligent anthropologist has turned his attention to the study of families in a more or less modern part of the world. I refer to Oscar Lewis, and in particular his book *Five Families*,[2] which is an in-depth account of the lives of five families in Mexico. It would be futile for me to discuss his methodology here, or his findings. In any case, the book is not intended to be a study of *power* in the five families, although frequent references are made to those who have (and lack) power in each family. Oscar Lewis does not report any experiments that he conducted, and I would be surprised if he performed any. Instead, his technique of research was first to gain the confidence of the families, and then to observe their behaviour closely over a considerable period, whilst also talking to each member separately when this was possible. The results are detailed descriptions of the families, stemming from intimate knowledge: the account of power and its exercise (and lack of power) in the families is far more detailed and firmly based than could have been obtained through the sorts of experiments that Strodtbeck and Kenkel were advocating. In studying his subjects in detail, and accepting all available sorts of evidence, Oscar Lewis's research provides an example of how research on family power should proceed.

—19—
Resources

The experimental and quasi-experimental approaches discussed in the last two chapters are particularly appropriate for epistemic (and effective epistemic) power. But we cannot infer from your lack of success when trying to bring about something that you lack the *non*-epistemic power to do it, for the failure may be due to lack of skill or knowledge rather than lack of basic (non-epistemic) power. Yet we may be able to infer, from our knowledge of your basic-act repertoire and the resources at your disposal, that you have (or lack) this non-epistemic power. To do this we need some theory connecting resources to power. Such a theory need be neither complex nor complete. We frequently proceed this way as it is. One look at an eight-stone weakling tells us that he will be unable to beat the Olympic shot-putting record – we don't need to collect the results of experiments in which he tries and fails. Examining my bank balance should establish fairly quickly that I am unable to mount a successful take-over bid for ICI; and we would dismiss any suggestion that Britain could invade and conquer America by pointing to the disparate military resources of the two countries. We can, then, infer powers from knowledge of *resources*.

When considering epistemic power we also need to consider the skill with which the actor can handle his resources. Muscles alone do not make champion shot-putters; rich men can conduct take-over bids stupidly; and large and well-equipped armies (it hardly needs saying) can be routed by far inferior forces. So with information on the actor's skill *and* resources available to us, we should be able to deduce his epistemic power.

The second approach to power, then, involves examining resources. This may not be as easy as it sounds, for neither resources nor skill can be directly observed. Skill is, of course, itself a dispositional term. As for resources, whilst we may be able to observe the *thing* that is the resource (the muscles, money or military might) we can only determine *that* it is a resource on the basis of our theory. Current theories of counter-insurgency, for instance, tend to give military firepower a minor role compared with psychological 'weapons'.

Further, the notion of a resource is far from straightforward. It includes, as well as legal powers and instruments of coercion, any customary deference that people receive. (It is well known that the Pope's considerable secular power does not stem from the battalions at his disposal.) Such resources are intangible and difficult to locate. But the difficulties do not stop there.

Most resources are resources only if others recognize them as such: if the things that they can be used to provide are valued by the potential recipients. For:

> [Power's] ultimate seat is – to use an unfashionable word – the soul. It rests on hope and fear, the belief of those who submit to it that its agents can confer on them benefits, from food to spiritual peace, and inflict evils, from hunger to misery of mind. Hence its foundations vary from age to age, with the interests which move men, and the aspects of life to which they attach a preponderant importance. . . . To destroy it, nothing more is required than to be indifferent to its threats, and to prefer other goods to those which it promises. (Tawney, 1931: p. 176)

Whilst it sounds a simple empirical matter to measure the resources that a person has, we can now see that it is not so easy. Behaviouralists, who have objected to identifying power with resources on the ground that resources may not be used fully or properly – and that therefore power may be less than the resources would indicate – have missed a more important point. For the main difficulty with resources is that a resource is not an empirical datum, like a chain of office or a palace: we cannot observe resources directly. We have to infer that things are resources by examining other people's reactions to them; one cannot simply measure resources since the worth of a resource is determined by the effects it produces. (Compare money, which, as the economics textbooks tell us, is only *money* – as opposed to lumps of metal or pieces of paper – when it is widely accepted as such within the economy.) Studying resources is every bit as complicated, and indirect, as studying power itself. In order for the investigator to identify a resource, he needs to have a theory of others' motivations.

This insight has been recognized in exchange theory, which is an attempt to construct a resource-based approach to power. The underlying idea of exchange theory has been clearly expressed by Blau.

Individuals who need a service another has to offer have the following alternatives: *First, they can supply him with a service* that he wants badly enough to
induce him to offer his services in return, though only if they have the resources
required for doing so; this will lead to reciprocal exchanges. *Second, they may
obtain the needed service elsewhere*, assuming that there are alternative suppli-
ers; this will also lead to reciprocal exchanges but in different partnerships. *Third,
they can coerce him to furnish the service*, provided they are capable of doing so,
in which case they would establish domination over him. *Fourth, they may learn
to resign themselves to do without this service*, possibly finding some substitute
for it, which would require that they change the values that determine their
needs. Finally, if they are not able or willing to choose any of these alternatives,
they have no other choice but to comply with his wishes, since he can make continued supply of the needed service contingent on their compliance. In the situation specified, the supply of services inevitably generates power. The absence
of the four alternatives defines the conditions of power in general. (Blau, 1964:
pp. 118–19)

So an individual who can offer a service another requires has, in this
service, a resource. Resources are, however, somewhat wider than Blau
seems to recognize: an individual who can offer another a *dis*service he
would rather be without also has a resource. In plainer language, being
able to beat someone up is a resource as much as being able to provide
help.

Some social psychologists have tried to apply exchange theory to the
family, and I think it is instructive to see how they have done it. It is the
basic tenet of their approach that "The balance of power . . . will be on
the side of the partner who contributes the greatest resources to the marriage" (Blood and Wolfe, 1960: p. 12). But such a bald statement is of little
help when resources are of divergent kinds and incommensurable. If one
of the wife's resources is that she will burst into tears whenever the husband
does something which she does not like, and make the husband feel guilty
and/or compassionate, it may be impossible to assess this resource's worth
in comparison with the greater physical strength or financial security of the
husband. So resource theory is usually used in a relative way: to assert that
if a partner's resources rise, his or her power will rise.

Thus in many families the husband brings money into the family, whilst
the wife does not. This is not to say that the wife does not work, nor even
that she might not work harder. However, her work within the home does
not earn money for the family. Money is a peculiarly pervasive resource
in that it is difficult to do completely without it (Blau's fourth alternative); neither is it likely that the wife is in a position to coerce the husband,
or anybody else, to give up money (the third alternative). If she cannot

obtain money elsewhere – from a private source or by taking employment herself – then she is left in a powerless position unless she has some resource with which she can bargain. It is extremely likely, therefore, that wives who earn money will have more power within the family than those who do not.[1]

The family is not only the basic financial unit within our society, it is also the unit within which sexual relations most often take place. If we presume that sex is desired by both partners, then one can expect the partner who can do best on one of Blau's four alternatives to be more powerful. Ignoring other resources which might give rise to bargaining or coercive possibilities, this is the partner who can either do best at obtaining sex elsewhere, or who can best resign themselves to doing without it or finding a substitute. If we assume that, for whatever reason, the couple is isolated on a sexual equivalent of a desert island, each is necessary to provide the sexual gratification of the other. A partner who can increase his or her ability to gratify the spouse (or who can raise the spouse's sexual desire) should increase in (non-epistemic) power.

One writer has extended resource theory by assuming that:

> The desire for sex is normally far stronger for the male than for the female. Since it is a strong motive for the male, it holds strong potential bargaining power for the female. Some wives exploit this bargaining power, and get substantial concessions from husbands in return for sex, such as clothes or vacations. (Kuhn, 1966: pp. 534–5)

In the absence of other factors, we might then want to conclude that wives have more power in marriages than husbands.[2]

The problem with this inference (the questionable nature of the assumptions aside), as is hinted at in the final sentence of the quotation, is that some wives would be unable to take advantage of their superiority in resources – or would feel such a deep-seated (and perhaps indoctrinated) revulsion to such sexual bargaining that they would choose not to engage in it, and thus leave this resource untapped. Whilst non-epistemic power may, therefore, be there, epistemic power would be lacking.

Kuhn himself notes, in a passage on the power of children, that we need to consider skill at manipulating resources, as well as the resources themselves.

> Being unable to disaffiliate, young children occupy an inherently weak bargaining position. Some nevertheless discover some things highly desired by parents which they can withhold or destroy, and some unwary parents may find themselves making huge concessions to presumably helpless children.

One such device is to trade heavily on the parents' desire that the child be happy. This has limitless possibilities if the parents do not catch on, since the child can withdraw the desired state from the parents as often or as completely as he chooses, and can also restore it at strategic moments. A second device is to work on the parent's desire to be a "good" or "unselfish" parent in the eyes of the rest of the family, friends, or neighbours. A third gambit uses the parent's desire to be loved by the child, which can be parlayed by some children into truly spectacular returns. (Kuhn, 1966: p. 534)

Thus from resources alone one cannot infer epistemic (or effective epistemic) power – we need a knowledge of resources *and* skill. All the resources in the world will not help someone who does not know how to use them; others can perform miracles on very limited resources. Thus if we know that the husband has more resources than the wife we cannot infer that he can (epistemically) gain more than she unless we also know that he is no less skilled at handling these resources than she is. This may be a difficult comparison, since the skill needed to handle his resources may be a totally different sort of animal from that required to get the best out of hers.

Sometimes, however, the amount of skill required is so minimal that it is not being presumptuous to assume that the actor possesses it. If (to take a commonly used example, though not one usually found in families) you have a gun and are prepared to use it, we do not have to ask ourselves searching questions about whether you know how to stick it in someone's back and ask him to hand over his money.

So, to employ a resource-based approach, we require a theory of social interaction that enables us to identify (and evaluate) resources, and, if we are interested in epistemic power, we require some knowledge of the actor's skill at utilizing his or her resources. If we know this, we can make an assessment of the things that someone could get if she wanted them. Once we have developed our theory, this approach does not involve a study of actual occurrences, or questioning the actors as to what they think the outcome will be, or an experimental mock-up of a real-world situation. From the theory, observation of resources, and assessments of skill at using them (if required), we can read off the actor's powers.[3]

Little more needs to be said when applying a resource-based approach to social and political situations. One drawback, more pronounced here perhaps than in studies of intra-familial power, is that it is all but impossible to test the theory on which the approach rests – the theory that allows us to determine what things *are* resources, and how effective different sorts of resources are likely to be. Since it is rarely possible to test such theories adequately, they tend to be turned into dogmas. This is unfortunate, and has given a bad name to attempts to study resources. I hope what I have said here has cleared the name of resource-based approaches to at least some extent.

Unfortunately I cannot here even begin to elaborate a theory of the political process that will tell us what things are resources. One could do worse than start with the list Hobbes provided:

> to have servants, is power; to have friends, is power: for they are strengths united.
>
> Also riches joined with liberality, is power; because it procureth friends, and servants . . ..
>
> Reputation of power, is power; because it draweth with it the adherence of those that need protection.
>
> So is reputation of love of a man's country, called popularity, for the same reason.
>
> Also what quality soever maketh a man beloved, or feared of many; or the reputation of such quality, is power; because it is a means to have the assistance, and service of many.
>
> Good success is power; because it maketh reputation of wisdom, or good fortune; which makes men either fear him, or rely on him. (Hobbes, 1651: ch. X)

And so on.

There are also other sorts of resources, which Hobbes overlooked. Some groups with apparently very few resources can maybe have more power than we would initially expect, by procuring the help of others who are richer in resources: the possibility of doing this is itself a resource. Protest activity involves an apparently resourceless group making life difficult or unpleasant for another group in order to mobilize support; the support can then be used to obtain desired outcomes.[4] Being able to be a nuisance is a resource, and one which needs to be taken into account in any analysis of resources. Playing on the conscience of others is another tack open to those lacking in tangible resources: sometimes lying down in the path of tanks can turn them back. Such resources – the resources typically possessed by the weak – should not be overlooked. But neither should they be exaggerated: typically they are the sort of resource that cannot be used often.

When we need to assess incommensurable resources disagreements start that are, to some extent, at the core of the recent academic debate on power, particularly that between pluralists and elitists. For one of the differences between these schools of thought hangs on the question how important a political resource the vote is. Pluralists and elitists agree that, by and large, votes are evenly distributed throughout Western societies, whilst almost all other conceivable resources are very unevenly distributed. If there is a modicum of equality within these societies, it must be because votes are more important than other resources, such as money, control of the means of production, or occupation of the key positions within society.

As yet, we are not very far advanced towards developing a theory of the political process that allows us to evaluate these divergent sorts of resources. If we are to choose between these two competing accounts of the distribution of power within Western societies, we need to employ one of the other approaches, rather than a resource-based one.

A resource-based approach is, though, likely to prove sufficient in other contexts, particularly that of individual responsibility. Frequently also in considering practical politics it may be clear which positions or actors hold the most resources and hence power. It might be very clear who the most powerful *individuals* are, even if far less clear if a small elite group possessing one sort of resource has more power than a large mass possessing another sort of resource.

Evidence based on resources is, then, neither necessarily the whole story nor an irrelevance.

—20—
Studying power

There are three important conclusions to be drawn from this discussion. The first is that we do not *observe* power: our evidence is used in *indirect* ways to establish the truth of, or reasonableness of asserting, counterfactuals that cannot be tested directly. And there is no easy, mechanical way of establishing how much power someone has; the connection between a justifiable assertion that someone has power and the evidence for this assertion is often complex and subtle.

Secondly, the assessment of raw observations depends at crucial points on a theory of the social process. Therefore, power cannot be studied in isolation. Most of the empirical disagreements about power are about the validity of different *theories*, not simply *factual* disputes: theories on which the counterfactualizations depend. Since all ascriptions of power depend on theories, the main requirement in studies apparently about power is to provide evidence for (or against) such theories. In this, the study of power becomes no different from the study of society; that is, a separate research project to 'study power' is a non-starter.

The third is a plea for methodological tolerance. It is just silly – if one prefers, it is unscientific – to reject evidence on the a priori ground that it does not fit some criterion of 'hardness'. We need to be willing to consider various, very different, types of evidence. But all the time we need to combine this eclectic attitude with a firm understanding of how different sorts of evidence help us, and how we should treat them.

I have suggested that there are five different approaches to gaining evidence about power, which should be used in conjunction with each other. These are:

(a) experiments;
(b) thought experiments: considering the obvious;
(c) natural experiments: examining the relationship between actual

preferences and outcomes;

(d) consulting experts: getting others to conduct direct and indirect experiments;

(e) resource-based approaches.

The three standard methods of studying power – which have now become known as the decisional, reputational and positional methods – are fairly close approximations to the last three of my methods, although none of them in their 'classical' formulation quite gets at the information we require. The reputational approach tends to confuse experts' assessments of power with reputation as a resource. The decisional approach ignores preferences not expressed in overt political action; is issue-oriented instead of interest-oriented; and tends to commit the stiletto-heel fallacy by ignoring the costs of successful action.[1] The positional approach tends to take the worth of the resources accompanying major positions for granted.

When starting to embark on empirical work on power, the first thing to consider is *why* you are interested in power; I have suggested that the answers to this question can be divided into three categories – my three contexts.

The next question is: power to do *what*?

In the moral context there is no difficulty: someone is blamed for not doing something, and his defence is that he could not have done it. Here both the accuser and the defendant agree on the outcome under consideration, and the question is to decide whether the defence is correct.

Power in practical contexts refers to whatever outcomes you as researcher happen to be interested in – we may well ask ourselves why you choose to concentrate on an apparently insignificant issue, but such doubts are not relevant to your analysis of power on that issue. If your main interest in life is to get the street in which you live named after you, then you might be willing to go to great lengths to see who could bring about such a change. Everybody else might consider this obsession of yours verging on the insane, but that need not alter the accuracy of your assessments of who has the power to do this. Obviously, you are only interested in practical power because there is an outcome (or range of outcomes) about which you are concerned. These will be the ones you choose to research into.

As we would expect, it is in the evaluative context that matters become complicated. I have argued that here we need to investigate the extent to which different people can satisfy their interests. So you would need to have some account of interests, to know what you want to look for. This may not be particularly difficult or contentious. Thus Crenson based his well-known study (Crenson, 1971) on the surely acceptable assumption that polluted air is not in the interests of those who breathe that air. It is not difficult to draw up a list containing items that all would agree it was in one's interest to have or enjoy: one could start with health (and psychic health) and the conditions likely to promote it. The working conditions described so graphically (and poignantly) in the chapter in *Capital* on the working day (Marx, 1867: ch. X) are so clearly injurious to health that not even the factory owners could claim that they were in the workers' interests. Neither can it be disputed that working conditions in many industries now are unsafe and dangerous: it is not in somebody's interest to contract pneumoconiosis or asbestosis, or to run the risk of receiving fatal doses of radiation.

The crucial aspects of most people's lives involve safe working conditions, adequate food and housing, a reasonable amount of leisure, and sufficient financial resources to ensure both a certain amount of comfort and freedom from worry about their ability to continue to enjoy these things. Others may add or subtract items from this list: I intend it to be suggestive rather than exhaustive. My main point is that reaching agreement on people's interests, at least in broad terms, may not be as difficult as many have supposed.

Having established *what* it is that you are interested in, you need to establish *whose* power you wish to examine. This will depend again on your purpose: the reasons that you want to compare societies, or the evaluative criteria against which you want to test your chosen society.

Having got that straight, the first thing to do – I suggest – is examine the obvious: things that there can be no doubt at all about. You could start by looking at things affecting an individual's life-chances which are obviously beyond his immediate control, at least at reasonable cost. A great deal of such information can be gathered from official statistics, broken down into appropriate groupings. These statistics tell us what *does* happen, rather than what *could* happen; but in a large number of cases they tell us of things that happen to people which are to a great extent beyond their control. Differential life-expectancy based on class, for instance, is unlikely to be explained by suggesting that the working class choose to live shorter lives, or even that they choose to live riskier ones. More miners than office-workers die through unforeseeable and unpreventable accidents at work,[2] and more contract disabling diseases because of their working conditions. The only way a miner can avoid such risks is by ceasing to be a miner – a choice that, in most cases, involves costs justifiably thought to be excessive. And if we are interested in the power of a representative miner, rather than a given individual who happens to be a miner, we must assume that he remains a miner. (If he moves and takes a job in a steelworks he obviously ceases to be a representative miner.) In so far as we are interested in the comparative ability to satisfy their interests of representative miners and office-workers, these facts cannot simply be ignored.

Neither, of course, can the incidence of work-related diseases in office workers be overlooked. One must distinguish, however, between statistical correlations and correlations beyond the control of the actor to alter. Thus the higher incidence of heart disease amongst managers, brought about by the tendency of this group to be overweight and unfit, may well be something which it is within their capabilities to do something about at little cost – by, for instance, eating less. Similar physical effects caused by stresses which are an integral part of doing the job (well) cannot be so dismissed. It is self-evident that a miner cannot be held responsible for contracting pneumoconiosis, in that it is beyond anybody's powers to avoid this disease when working in dust-laden conditions. It is less self-evident – although it may well be true – that managers can do nothing to avoid ulcers. Thus a commonsense approach to such statistics will not provide all the answers, but it most certainly provides a start. There has been a tendency in the literature to overlook such obvious facts of life (and death) – as if somehow by being obvious they cease to be important.

An example of what happens when we ignore these is an own goal that Polsby scores when he attempts to criticize Crenson's study of Gary, Indiana. Polsby suggests that the apparent lack of concern in Gary about polluted air was because the inhabitants prefered to have a polluting steel complex that gave employment, rather than no polluting steelworks and no jobs (Polsby, 1980; pp. 216–17). But posing the choice in this way precisely highlights the lack of power of those who lived in Gary: in the 1960s (when Crenson's study of Gary was done) most of us took the power to obtain employment without having to breathe foul air for granted. Polsby therefore supposes that Gary's populace had even less power than Crenson suggested: for Crenson was at least prepared to consider the possibility of employment being provided without pollution, whilst Polsby, by implying that we should reject this possibility out of hand, obviously thinks that it is clear that Gary's citizens were indeed extremely powerless.

Having got as far as possible by looking at the obvious and conducting thought experiments – and consulting experts who can conduct thought experiments for you – the next step would be to conduct any direct experiments that could be carried out or, failing this, look at natural experiments. That is to say, you can look at what is happening in the areas that interest you.

This will involve a procedure not unlike the decisional method employed by the pluralists. But the *interest*-oriented approach that I am advocating is very different from their *issue*-oriented approach, for concentrating on issues is to attack the problem from the wrong direction. Dahl's study again provides a good illustration. When setting out to study New Haven, he wondered which were the most important issues currently being considered. Having settled on a suitable range, he then studied who won and who lost on decisions taken within these issues. But even granting that he did choose the most important issues, many people must have been unaffected by these issues, and more concerned about other things. Indeed, the apparent practice in New Haven of leaders tackling just one problem at a time, and associating their administration's prestige (and large sums of money) with this project, meant that anybody who was not particularly bothered about this matter would be left out in the cold. Different people occupy different positions in society, and so what might be a very important matter to one may be irrelevant to another. Education policy, for instance, is obviously very important to many: but not directly to old-age pensioners, the childless, or those who do not expect their life-chances to alter very much whatever education they receive.[3]

If we wish to discover the power of various groups it is wrong, therefore, to consider the apparently most important issues, and to investigate the distribution of power on these issues. Dahl has been heavily criticized for his choice of issues; but it is looking at issues *at all* that is the mistake. Rather we should discover which are the most important *outcomes for each group*, and to what extent a group, or a member of that group, has power over the outcomes of most importance *to it*.

The other weaknesses of attempts to locate power through studying the making of actual decisions stem from the mistaken notion that power can be directly observed: that a research project studies power itself, rather than coming up with evidence from which power can be inferred. The implications of the counterfactual nature of power have not been fully absorbed. Because of this, the sorts of decisions chosen for study have fallen into too narrow a range. The decisions investigated have involved major and overt political issues: the sorts of things that take up the bulk of the legislature's time. I suggest that a view from the 'bottom', based on people's interests, will produce a much wider list of outcomes than the elite-oriented view has typically come up with, and one that may support the common attitude that politicians spend most of their time talking about matters of no concern to the average man or woman.

Thus we need to look also at other issues. These would include issues which never come to a head because those seeking change anticipate the reactions of the powerful, or do not possess enough resources to gain attention for their grievances; issues which rarely hit the headlines but are nevertheless important because they are always there (such as unsafe working conditions); issues which are not considered because existing routines define them as not political; and issues which look beyond the making of legislation to how it is enforced. All such issues are about matters having a considerable impact on people's lives, and the power they have over their lives; a study of power is highly selective, and biased, if it ignores such issues.[4] If we first consider interests, and the outcomes associated with them, we are more likely to come up with a list of matters for study that includes issues of each of these sorts.

But you may find that naturally occurring experiments are not that helpful because the people and groups that you are interested in do not try very hard to bring about many things that you have identified as in their interests. You want to know whether they *could* bring these outcomes about, and so you will want to look at other (analogous) times and other places, to see what happened there. You will also need to look at your subjects' *resources* – particularly their political resources that might enable them to further their interests through the political process. How important this information is will depend on what sort of resources your subjects possess, and how well equipped you are with theories that allow you to infer from these resources to power.

When we come to look at political power, you must not forget to look at the mobilization of bias, and the rules and routines that allow some people a lot of power and others, with apparently comparable resources, none at all.[5] An example of the importance of rules is provided by Northern Ireland before the imposition of direct rule in 1972: the existence, and location, of the border with the South, combined with the rules of majoritarian representative democracy, ensured that the Protestant population had the power to do a wide variety of things that the Catholics could not do.

You may also want to look at passive power – people obtaining outcomes without having to exert themselves or even try to obtain them. (Passive power is relatively easy to research into, as it does not involve trying to assess counterfactuals.)

Finally, you may decide that significant numbers of people have a considerable amount of power that they seem not to exercise. If so, then you will need to ask *why* they choose not to act in their interests: is it because they just do not want to, or is it because significant barriers are placed in the way of their wanting to? (On this, see section 12.6.)

In my opinion the study that comes nearest to the approach I am suggesting here is John Gaventa's study of power and powerlessness in Appalachia (Gaventa, 1980). First, Gaventa adopted a commendably eclectic methodology. He studied documents and records of contemporary events and also immersed himself in the history of the area; he interviewed as many people as possible and himself observed the decision-making process; he even, as a community activist, helped to set up social experiments. He also acted as an investigative journalist in trying to uncover the secrets of exactly who owned most of the land in the area. And throughout he showed a deep understanding of the culture of the inhabitants of the area, and how the world looked to them.

Secondly, Gaventa adopted an interest-oriented approach. His study starts out by establishing that "Central Appalachia is a region of poverty amid riches; a place of glaring inequalities" (p. 35). The distribution of *actual* interest-satisfaction contrasted markedly with the American democratic ideal. There were two main reasons for this: the people in the valley that Gaventa studied had hardly any power, and they did not use what they had. The lack of power took two main forms. First, the Appalachians got absolutely nowhere when they tried to insist on their legal rights. Thus when they tried to get the rating laws enforced against the coal owners they were refused a hearing; and they could not bring pressure to bear on the (British) landowners because the landowners' complex of holding companies proved impossible to penetrate. And, secondly, they got warned off by threatened (and actual) violence. But even when outside agencies, such as the radical wing of the United Mine Workers of America and governmental anti-poverty programmes, *did* provide resources, these were largely spurned. To explain this, Gaventa shows how these helpful outsiders appeared rather differently to the inhabitants of the valley, whose culture (itself a rational response to their deprivation) branded them as threats. Even the little (non-epistemic) power they did have they were unable to use. At the end of Gaventa's very persuasive – and quite moving – story, the social order stands condemned even more than the statistics of distribution of wealth had suggested.[6]

Power, then, *can* be studied along the lines I have suggested. But there is no short cut that takes us straight to the power. We can only reach conclusions about power in a society by first having a deep understanding of that society.

—PART IV—
Measuring power

—21—
The power of votes: introduction

For many writers the ultimate goal when assessing power is to be able to *measure* it: to discover that you have thirty units, or whatever. It should be clear by now that I consider such an endeavour to be often unnecessary and usually prohibitively difficult, since we do not have the required information. Yet for several decades now mathematicians have been exploring numerical indices of power, which do allow us to measure power (or so it is claimed).

Unfortunately the study of power indices is in a mess: several rival indices are in existence, each with its adherents who want to apply 'their' index to every conceivable situation. Much of this literature shows great mathematical sophistication, which unfortunately means that it cannot be read by non-mathematicians; but most of this sophistication is unnecessary, and this Part can be read by anybody who does not faint at the sight of a number. For what those who have constructed mathematical power indices lack is not mathematical sophistication, but common sense. Perfectly good indices are applied in hopelessly wrong ways, leading to clearly bizarre results. (Some support for this sweeping claim will be provided in due course.) What I try to do in this Part is show how power indices can be used intelligently. Hitherto mathematicians (and others who have developed these indices) have all too often been in the position of a child with a new toy: they have wanted to play with it all the time, whether appropriate or not. (This, I think, is a general danger affecting all who try to develop tools for research, and one to which I myself find it all too easy to succumb.) An outsider, a non-mathematician, can, perhaps, find it easier to see the worth of these different tools (or toys); I hope that that is what I do in this Part.

The best place to start considering numerical measures of power is the simplest; and this is measuring the worth of *votes*. Votes are a resource, and usually a highly visible one: we have perfect knowledge about the actors' resources if we know both how the votes are distributed and the method of aggregating votes to determine the winning outcome. For the purposes of this Part I shall assume that the vote is the only relevant resource: I ignore the possibility of one actor producing a gun and coercing others to vote his way, or of some actor's wealth allowing her scope for bribing other actors. This is, of course, unrealistic. For this reason the indices developed here have more relevance in certain evaluative contexts (in which we want to consider only constitutionally permissible resources) than in painting an overall picture of who can get what in the real world.

Votes, in short, are nice and easy because they come with numbers already attached to them; in constructing a mathematical index we just need to manipulate these numbers in the correct way. In the wider world we have to evaluate the significance of incommensurable resources – which is to say that if we want to construct a numerical index we have to supply the basic numbers. The power of votes would seem, then, an appropriate place to start in an attempt to construct a mathematical index of power.

I will also be making some further simplifying assumptions which delimit the issues which I consider here. I shall assume that epistemic and non-epistemic power are identical, since all that the voter is required to know is how to vote. This means that I will not consider any occasions when sophisticated voting is more efficacious than straightforward voting, and I shall restrict my attention to situations in which the voter does best by voting for her first preference.[1] Secondly, I shall not consider the possibility that one voter might influence another, whether by persuasion, bargaining, log-rolling or force. I shall be thinking of the voters voting without communicating with each other and without knowing (or caring) how the others have voted. This is, of course, a very static portrayal of even the most elementary elections. But we shall see by the end of this Part that even with these simplifications there are complexities enough to be both interesting and useful.

This Part, then, is very much a first step in the construction of numerical indices. I think that it is amazing (and humbling) that such basic work still needs to be done in an area in which many accomplished theorists have been working for over thirty years; I also think that it shows the crying need for establishing a clear conceptualization of power before embarking on complications – mathematical or any other. I hope that this part of the book provides some justification for the approach to power that I adopt, by showing how it can help us talk sense where many others (with or without elaborate symbology) have talked nonsense.

In this Part I shall look in turn at how votes give us power in the sense of ability and power in the sense of ableness, and finally look at the evaluative question of how we should *create* power – by giving people votes – if we hold to some common democratic ideals.

Distinguishing between ability and ableness is very important here. An absolute dictator, whose vote is the only one to count, will have absolute power; but so will the chair of a committee (with the casting vote) when the committee is so evenly balanced that a tie will inevitably result. But these cases are different and, as we shall see, require different approaches. For the dictator is powerful (ex hypothesi) *whatever* anyone else does; the committee chair only when the other members vote as predicted. The dictator has much greater ability than the chair, since his power is present in a wide range of background conditions (in this case, assumptions about the actions of others). The chair's ability may be very restricted indeed if she can cast a vote only when the vote is otherwise tied. So when measuring *ability* we make no assumptions about how others will vote, and investigate the range within which the actors' votes are decisive; when measuring *ableness* we *do* include our knowledge of likely voting behaviour.[2]

But as well as *measuring* people's power, you have a strong interest in *increasing* your own. One way of doing this, of course, is by obtaining more votes; but you might also be able to increase your power by changing the rules that aggregate the votes and determine the winner. Indeed, we might *all* be able to increase power if we adopt the best set of rules. How we should do this is the topic of Chapter 24.

Doubtless numerical indices of power have many other uses beside the three chosen for consideration here; and they can be developed in much more sophisticated ways. Nevertheless, I think that, however these extensions are done, they should be based on the groundwork provided here. That is my main claim in this Part.

—22—
Measuring ability

22.1—THE PENROSE INDEX

The CIA agent, in considering power within a society, must ask himself which actor in the society is the most powerful, and how this actor's power compares with the power of other powerful actors. When these actors all have votes (and only votes) and the CIA's concern is with bringing about some desired outcome through the voting process, the agent is interested in the power of actors relative to each other. In qualitative terms he is interested in discovering who the most powerful actor is; quantitatively, he may want to know how much each actor is worth, to him, before deciding the size of the bribe to offer. The 'worth', in this sense, will depend on the actor's power. Indices of power can be thought of as attempting to assess the value of each person's votes to a potential briber.

In section 12.1 I suggested that you have more ability (to obtain some outcome) than I have if you can obtain it in conditions in which I cannot obtain it, and not vice versa. In elections, the relevant conditions are how other people vote. If you have any voting power at all, there will be some configurations of the votes of others in which your vote is decisive; and, unless you are a dictator, there will be some configurations in which it is not. Those configurations in which your vote is decisive are the conditions in which you have power: in those conditions, you can ensure that the motion passes, should you wish, and you can defeat it.

Thus imagine you have one vote on a three-person committee, whilst the other members have two votes each (and a simple majority is decisive). (This I shall call Committee I.) Then you have the power to decide the outcome only when the other two members vote against each other; if they agree, you are powerless. But if you think this is bad, notice that the same goes for the other members as well – even though each has twice as many votes as you, neither can outvote the other one and you combined. It seems that although the number of *votes* is unequal, the power is equal (or, at least, symmetrical).

Now suppose the committee is expanded (to become Committee II) by admitting a fourth person, who is also given two votes. At a stroke, your power is wiped out altogether. For *however* the other members vote, at least two of them must vote together, thus obtaining the required majority of four votes. (If one voter abstains, then we are back – in effect – with a three-person committee, and you again have some power. However, it is widely thought that voting power that depends on the abstention of others is not significant, so we can assume here that the relevant, standard conditions are those in which everyone votes.)

We can see, then, that a voter's power cannot be assessed by simply observing how many votes she has: having one vote is as good as having two if there are two other voters with two votes; it is useless if there are three such voters.

Looking again at the four-person committee, we can say unequivocally that someone with two votes has more power than you have with one, since she has power when the other two voters disagree (whatever you do) and you do not. This is perhaps easiest to show in a little diagram, showing all the voting combinations: in these figures + indicates that the actor votes for the measure, and – that she votes against. (Later, when abstention is admitted, this will be represented by 0.) The first eight columns of Figure 1 show that when A and B agree they always win, so that then neither C nor D have (active) power; the second eight columns show that when A and B disagree C has power but, even here, D does not.

However, we cannot make comparisons of the powers of the members

Figure 1—Voting in committee II

A (2 votes):	+	+	+	+	–	–	–	–		+	+	–	–	+	+	–	–
B (2 votes):	+	+	+	+	–	–	–	–		–	–	+	+	–	–	+	+
C (2 votes):	+	+	–	–	+	+	–	–		+	+	+	+	–	–	–	–
D (1 vote):	+	–	+	–	+	–	+	–		+	–	+	–	+	–	+	–
Outcome:	+	+	+	+	–	–	–	–		+	+	+	+	–	–	–	–

with two votes this simply. It is true that B has power when A votes against C, and C has power when A votes against B, but these events are not the *same*: clearly, C voting against A is not the same event as B voting against A. So to compare the voting power of B and C we need to compare those voting configurations in which each has power. When we come to consider ableness we will compare them by assessing their actual probability of occurring, and investigate the ideological positions of the voters. However, abilities are not compared in this way, but by assessing the importance (to us) of the various background conditions. And since it is difficult to see why any one voting configuration is privileged over another, there seems no reason to do anything other than weight them all equally.

This last step is a most important one, because it at once allows us to create a *numerical* measure of power. If all the possible voting configurations are given equal weight, then you have more power than me if you have power in more voting configurations or, in other words, if the probability of a voting configuration occurring in which you have power is greater than the probability of one occurring in which I have power. We can then say that A, B and C all have equal power in Figure 1, because each has a 50:50 chance of having power.

Figure 2—Committee III: Penrose index

B (25 votes):	+	+	+	+	+	+	−	−	−	−
C (25 votes):	+	+	−	−	−	−	+	+	+	+
D (24 votes):	−	−	+	+	−	−	+	+	−	−
A (26 votes):	+	−	+	−	+	−	+	−	+	−
Outcome:	+	−	+	−	+	−	+	−	+	−

A (26):	+	+	+	+	−	−
C (25):	−	−	−	−	+	+
D (24):	+	+	−	−	+	+
B (25):	+	−	+	−	+	−
Outcome:	+	−	+	−	+	−

A (26):	+	+	+	+	−	−
B (25):	−	−	−	−	+	+
D (24):	+	+	−	−	+	+
C (25):	+	−	+	−	+	−
Outcome:	+	−	+	−	+	−

A (26):	−	−
B (25):	+	+
C (25):	+	+
D (24):	+	−
Outcome:	+	−

A third example will give an idea of how this index works. Suppose that in Committee III the votes in a four-member committee are nearly, but not quite, equal: A is given 26 votes, B and C 25 each, and D only 24, with again a simple majority (51) being required to pass a motion. Then each actor has power only when the others happen to vote as in Figure 2 (where the actor whose power is under test is put last). We can see from Figure 2 that A has power in five configurations, B and C in three each, and D in only one. So there is a considerable disparity in power, despite the small range of votes. Further, the number of possible voting configurations for three voters is 8 (that is, $2 \times 2 \times 2$), so we can say that A's index of power is $\frac{5}{8}$, B's and C's are $\frac{3}{8}$, and D's is $\frac{1}{8}$.

We have now arrived at a numerical index of power with (I hope) a clear understanding of what this index measures. This index is not new – it was developed as long ago as 1946 by Lionel Penrose[1] – but it has not received the attention due to it. This is a pity, since, as we shall see, it is very useful. Instead, the recent literature has been more interested in two other indices, one developed by Shapley and Shubik and the other by Banzhaf.[2] Since there is widespread misunderstanding in the literature about the properties of these two indices, I shall briefly describe them here, in a non-mathematical way.

Shapley and Shubik's and Banzhaf's indices both require the two assumptions which I made when producing Penrose's index: they are measures of ability, not ableness, and they restrict their attentions to voting configurations in which no one abstains and all possible remaining configurations are weighted equally.[3] But in addition both make a further assumpton, and one which usually is *not* warranted. They both assume that there is a fixed amount of power to go around, and their index measures the proportion of it that each actor has. The sum of the power of all the actors therefore is always a constant: usually it is fixed at 1, so that the indices run from zero (no power) to one (all the power).

I have already argued (in section 12.4) that it is usually not justifiable to assume that there is a constant amount of power, and in Chapter 24 I shall illustrate how applying either of these two indices leads to absurdities, precisely because of this constant-sum assumption. Here, though, I shall simply present the indices and I shall show what they do tell us.

22.2—THE SHAPLEY–SHUBIK INDEX

When Shapley and Shubik presented their index in 1954, they derived it from three premises which they claimed were intuitively necessary: (1) symmetry: relabelling the actors makes no difference to their power; (2)

the actors' powers sum together to a constant; and (3) additivity: the power distribution in a committee system composed of two strictly independent parts is the same as the power distribution obtained by evaluating the parts separately.[4] Shapley proved (in Shapley, 1953) that these constraints give a unique index, which can be calculated as follows:

> The power index . . . is equal to the chance that a state [or any other sort of actor] has of being "pivotal" on a ballot – i.e., of casting the deciding vote for or against a proposal – if we assume that the order of voting is determined by lot and that each state has an identical probability of voting "aye". The exact value of this probability turns out to be irrelevant to the definition. In numerical work it is convenient to assume that all states always vote "aye", and to define the pivotal state as the one that clinches the majority. (Mann and Shapley, 1964: p. 153 and n. 3)

Thus to calculate the Shapley–Shubik index for Committee III we write down all the (24) voting orders, and count how many times each actor is pivotal in their sense. This is done in Figure 3, with the pivotal actors in brackets and, as an aid, the cumulative vote after the first two have voted shown. Remember that A has 26 votes, B and C 25 each, and D 24,

Figure 3—Committee III: Shapley–Shubik index

A(B)CD	A(B)DC	A(C)BD	A(C)DB	AD(B)C	AD(C)B
51	51	51	51	50	50
B(A)CD	B(A)DC	BC(A)D	BC(D)A	BD(A)C	BD(C)A
51	51	50	50	49	49
C(A)BD	C(A)DB	CB(A)D	CB(D)A	CD(A)B	CD(B)A
51	51	50	50	49	49
DA(B)C	DA(C)B	DB(A)C	DB(C)A	DC(A)B	DC(B)A
50	50	49	49	49	49

	Total number of pivots	Shapley–Shubik Index
A	10	$\frac{10}{24} = \frac{5}{12}$
B	6	$\frac{6}{24} = \frac{3}{12}$
C	6	$\frac{6}{24} = \frac{3}{12}$
D	2	$\frac{2}{24} = \frac{1}{12}$
Total	24	1

and the pivotal voter is the one that takes the total to 51 or above. We can see from Figure 3 that the actors' Shapley–Shubik power indices are A $\frac{5}{12}$, B $\frac{3}{12}$, C $\frac{3}{12}$ and D $\frac{1}{12}$.

But what do these numbers indicate? Many writers have criticized the Shapley–Shubik index on the grounds that their sense of a pivotal actor – the actor who brings up the majority when all vote the same way – is just irrelevant, for who cares how many times someone is pivotal if everybody agrees anyway?[5] But it is important to realize that counting up the pivotal actors is a way of *calculating* the index; it is not an account of what the index is designed to *measure*. Shapley and Shubik themselves are sometimes careless on this point. However, for them the strength of their index is that it, alone, conforms to the three premises I cited earlier (pp. 160–1). But, unfortunately, the significance of these premises – particularly the third one – is not intuitively obvious. Yet it turns out that *Shapley and Shubik's index is a measure of the amount it is worth bribing an actor*, given certain assumptions. Shapley and Shubik do realize this, since they state – almost in passing – that if votes were for sale we might expect their relative prices to be in the same ratio as their Shapley–Shubik values (Shapley and Shubik, 1954: p. 212). But nowhere in the extensive literature on this index is this idea explored.

To see how the index works as a bribe index, consider again the simple three-person committee, Committee I. This committee is going to vote on a series of issues which are of immense interest to your local CIA agent – so much so that he would give £2 million of the CIA's money to ensure his desired outcome on them. The CIA agent does not know the form these motions will take, so he does not know how many he will want to pass and how many to fail; therefore he assumes he is as likely to want a motion to pass as to fail. Further, he knows nothing of the preferences of the members of the committee, except that each of the members is as likely to favour his preferred outcome as to oppose it. If the votes of the three members can be bought at a price – the price being the maximum each can extort – the Shapley–Shubik index tells how much each can expect to get.[6]

But each committee member is likely to vote the way the CIA agent wants half the time anyway (by the last assumption), so the final decision will be the one he wants half the time even if he does not bribe anyone. Therefore he would be foolish to pay out in bribes more than *half* the amount by which he values the outcomes: that is, there is only £1 million going for bribes.

Suppose you (a committee member) approached the agent and offered to vote as directed by him for a fee. If he could rely on your support, the chances of his preferred outcome occurring would rise from $\frac{1}{2}$ to $\frac{3}{4}$, irrespective of whether he wanted a motion passed or defeated.[7] So his gain in value would be a quarter of the £2 million, or £$\frac{1}{2}$ million. That is the maximum amount you could ask.

But, having bribed one voter, the agent will not rest content, since he still might lose: he will be on the look-out to bribe another voter as well. If he does so, he will ensure success, since two people on this committee can always outvote the third. The rise in the probability of success from bribing the second voter is again $\frac{1}{4}$ (it is $1 - \frac{3}{4}$), and so this person too is worth £$\frac{1}{2}$ million to the agent. It is easy to see that if you had been bribed second, and someone else first, you also would have been worth £$\frac{1}{2}$ million to the agent. You can, then, expect to get £$\frac{1}{2}$ million if bribed first, or £$\frac{1}{2}$ million if bribed second – but, of course, nothing if you are too slow and offer your services only after the other two have been signed up. We can assume (and this is the last assumption) that, in the long run, the order of bribing is random, so that you have an equal chance of being bribed first or second – or third (that is, not at all). You can then expect to receive the average of $\frac{1}{2} + \frac{1}{2} + 0$ million pounds – that is, $\frac{1}{3}$ of the million. And this ($\frac{1}{3}$) is your Shapley–Shubik index of power on that particular committee.

Now this might, of course, just be a coincidence: one illustration (particularly a very simple one) is not a proof. Since I have promised to avoid heavy mathematics I will not give a formal proof here,[8] though in Appendix 4.2 I explore the nature of the Shapley–Shubik bribe index in somewhat more detail.

One point, though, must be made, as it has been often overlooked and allows us to see why the Shapley–Shubik index has been unfairly criticized. This is that the index is considerably more general than I have been indicating, since we can weaken one of the assumptions.

In the previous calculation I assumed that you and your colleagues on the committee were as likely to vote for a motion as against, and that the CIA agent was as likely to want a motion passed as defeated. These two assumptions are not both necessary; if we drop either one, we still arrive at the same index. That is to say that if the agent is indifferent, in the long run, between passing and blocking motions, it does not matter what the probability of each of the committee members voting for a motion is, as long as it is the *same* probability for each member. (See the quotation from Mann and Shapley given on p. 161.)

This finding allows us to make sense of Shapley and Shubik's rather odd account of their index, an account which has justifiably given rise to much confusion. They say:

Let us consider the following scheme: There is a group of individuals all willing to vote for some bill. They vote in order. As soon as a majority has voted for it, it is declared passed, and the member who voted last is given credit for having passed it. Let us choose the voting order of the members randomly. Then we may compute the frequency with which an individual belongs to the group whose votes are used and, of more importance, we may compute how often he is *pivotal*. This latter number serves to give us our index. It measures the number of times that the action of the individual actually changes the state of affairs. (Shapley and Shubik, 1954: p. 210)

Now, on the face of it, this is just a non sequitur, since:

the pivot, so understood, does *not* in the relevant sense change the state of affairs. Since we have a group of individuals "all willing to vote for some bill", it makes no difference who happens to provide the vote that gives the measure the winning margin, since, *ex hypothesi*, if any of the remaining members of the body had replaced that person in the sequence, he would have voted for the measure instead. (Barry, 1980b: p. 276)

But we can now see why Shapley and Shubik's conclusion is correct. We get their result by assuming that there is a group of individuals all willing to vote *against* some bill, and that we are willing to bribe enough of them to ensure that it passes (and to bribe no more), when the order of bribing is random. Then the pivotal actor *is* the one that ensures that the bill passes whilst otherwise it would not. And the index is the probability of each actor being pivotal.

It may still seem odd to give the *whole* value to the pivotal actor, and nothing at all to any actor bribed prior to the pivot. (Indeed, how can you 'bribe' someone by paying them nothing?) But this does not matter; it just makes the calculation much easier. If we assume instead that all actors vote for a bill with some probability p, then each actor before the 'pivot' gets some pay-off for switching her vote – and the index turns out to be the same anyway. When p is set at zero we have a degenerate case – which is very handy for *calculating* the index, but very misleading for *describing* it.

In conclusion, let us return to Shapley and Shubik's assumption that their index always sums to a constant.

A bribe index, of the sort described here, *must* sum to a constant, since we have assumed that the briber has a fixed sum of money which he is prepared to shell out in bribes. Shapley and Shubik's second assumption is therefore perfectly justified *in this case*. That is why their index works as a bribe index. It works here not because there is a constant amount of *power* to go round, but because we are interested in expressing what power there is as a proportion of a constant amount of *money*. That is why, at the beginning of this chapter, I said that the CIA agent is interested in the actors' powers *relative to each other*. As we shall see, this is not always how we compare powers, and for other purposes Shapley and Shubik's index is no use, precisely because of their constant-sum assumption.

The Shapley–Shubik index is, then, an index of voters' expected long-term gains from being bribed, under the assumptions that it is equally valuable to pass or to block a motion, that all voters have the same probability of supporting a motion (although it does not matter what this probability is), and that we rule out (or ignore) the possibility of abstentions.

22.3—THE BANZHAF INDEX

Banzhaf's index is usually presented as a variant, and simplification, of Shapley and Shubik's.

If you look back at Figure 3, you will see that the first two entries in the top row differ only in the ordering of the actors after the pivot, and yet each counts when calculating the index. It is not easy to see why the ordering of the actors after the pivot is relevant to anything; indeed, it is not clear why the ordering *before* the pivot should matter either. Banzhaf's procedure is simply to proceed as in Figure 3, but only to count configurations in which the decisive actors (the pivot and those to its left) are different.

This index has been suggested, apparently independently, by J. S. Coleman and by Rae as well as by Banzhaf; it was also hinted at a bit earlier by Riker. Shapley himself has adopted it.[9]

The rationale behind Banzhaf's index is that Shapley and Shubik's index

appears inappropriate, for it is implicitly based on the assumption that the probability that a coalition will form is proportional to the number of different orders that can exist in that coalition. It seems more reasonable to assume that each distinct coalition has the *same* probability of forming.[10]

(We are not here interested in coalitions, but the same point can be made about subsets.) Thus he suggests an index where each subset or coalition is counted once only, instead of once for each ordering of it. With this index

> the ratio of the power of legislator A to the power of legislator B is the same as the ratio of the number of possible voting combinations of the entire legislature in which A can alter the outcome by changing his vote to the number of combinations in which B can alter the outcome by changing his vote. (Banzhaf, 1965: p. 331)

But there is nothing new about this property, since Penrose's index had it. Indeed, Banzhaf's index is simply Penrose's index multiplied by whatever constant is required so that the sum of the actors' indices is 1. For instance, Figure 2 gave Penrose indices for A, B, C and D of $\frac{5}{8}, \frac{3}{8}, \frac{3}{8}$ and $\frac{1}{8}$, respectively; the respective Banzhaf indices are $\frac{5}{12}, \frac{3}{12}, \frac{3}{12}$ and $\frac{1}{12}$.

So what does this index tell us? The answer is simple: nothing at all. (This is now being slowly recognized by the mathematical fraternity.) When we know that A's Penrose index is $\frac{5}{8}$ we know that $\frac{5}{8}$ is the probability of her being in a position to sway the vote (given the equal weighting assumptions of section 22.1).[11] It is also the amount that A could ask to be bribed when no other actors have been bribed and the briber expects to gain two units if the result of the vote is his favoured one. When we know that the Penrose indices are in the ratio $5:3:3:1$ we know somewhat less, since we know the *ratios* of these amounts, but not their absolute size. The Banzhaf index simply expresses this ratio as a fraction – but not a fraction *of* anything. The denominator, which is the sum of the numerators, is a numerical artefact which conveys no information. The Banzhaf index is simply a less informative version of Penrose's index, and should be banished. Despite this, as we shall see in Chapter 24, Banzhaf's index has been much used by American courts as an index of power, and used quite inappropriately.

22.4—THE LMDS INDEX

One reason that Banzhaf's index has appeared preferable to Shapley and Shubik's is that it is much easier to calculate[12] and often ends up with identical (or nearly identical) results. (In all the examples I have used so far, the two indices agree.) It was also felt by its protagonists that, when the indices differed, the Banzhaf measures were intuitively preferable. For instance, in their original article Shapley and Shubik calculated the powers of the various members of the UN Security Council (as it was constituted in 1954), and concluded that the five permanent members had 98.7 per cent of the power (nearly 20 per cent each) whilst the six non-permanent members shared the remaining 1.3 per cent, at just over 0.2 per cent each. But, in a detailed breakdown of the calculations of this index, Coleman argued that this put the permanent members' power too high. His index (identical to Banzhaf's) allocated only 90.5 per cent of the power to the five permanent members, making the ratio of a permanent member's index to a non-permanent member's roughly 10:1 as against Shapley and Shubik's 100:1 (Coleman, 1971: pp. 274–6). Coleman found his result preferable.

But it is by no means clear why he should have done so, since it is not clear what these ratios are supposed to *mean* (at least, if we are not interested in bribing UN delegates). Often what these exercises are doing is simply attaching numbers where numbers ought not to be attached. The argument about power in the Security Council is similar to two children arguing whether Liverpool is ten or a hundred times as good a football team as Luton. As the children grow up they realize that it usually does not make sense to say that one team is so many times as good as another, since this usage of 'good' is not quantifiable on a ratio scale. Hopefully, as political science grows up, it will realize that it makes no sense to construct a ratio (let alone a cardinal) scale of power, except in specific and carefully described ways.

What all these indices do achieve is an *ordering* of the members according to their power, rather than placing them on a cardinal scale. But there is a still simpler index which gives the same ordering under the restrictions we have so far accepted. This index I call a lexicographic MDS (or LMDS) and is derived from a suggestion by Alvin Goldman (in Goldman, 1974b). Let us define a minimal decisive set (MDS) as a decisive set of voters which is of the minimum size possible in that no member can be excluded without the set ceasing to be decisive. It is similar to the idea of a minimal winning coalition in coalition theory, but I call it an MDS to avoid the inference that the winning set should be a co-ordinated coalition – it can be completely fortuitous that a certain set occurs on an issue.

Goldman derives two conclusions about power from the idea of a minimal decisive set:

(I) Ceteris paribus, the larger the number of minimal decisive sets for [some outcome X] to which A belongs, the greater is A's power over X.
(II) Ceteris paribus, the smaller the size of the minimal decisive sets for X to which A belongs the greater is A's power over X. (Goldman, 1974b: p. 239)

If we allow condition (II) to dominate condition (I), we always get the same ordering as any of the indices discussed in this chapter, although I will not give a proof of this here.[13] That is, if we rank MDSs in order of size, with the smallest ranked highest, then the actor who occurs in most MDSs of the smallest size is the most powerful, the one who occurs in the second largest number of MDSs of the smallest size is next powerful, and so on. Members who are tied on the MDSs of the smallest size can be differentiated by those of the next smallest size, and so on down the hierarchy. The ordering is lexicographic in that no matter how many times someone occurs in a larger MDS this cannot outweigh just one appearance in a smaller MDS. Thus for Committee III, MDSs are {AB}, {AC} and {BCD};[14] taking the two-member MDSs, A occurs in two, B and C in one each, whilst D is not in any; B and C cannot be distinguished when the three-member MDS is considered. The power ordering is thus A > B = C > D.

22.5—CONCLUSION

The LMDS is an adequate and parsimonious way of providing a power *ordering* if we just want to discover who the most powerful member in some voting system is, or whether someone has more power than someone else. If we are selling shares or buying politicians, however, we need a numerical index and the correct one will be Shapley and Shubik's (or Penrose's if only one actor can be bribed). If we do need a numerical index of ability, which measures the probability of the conditions being such that an actor has power, then we should use Penrose's index.

—23—
Measuring ableness

When we require a measure of ableness rather than ability we want to concentrate on those conditions which the actors find themselves in, rather than on some standard set of conditions. Here, this means investigating power given the actual (or predicted) voting pattern of all the other voters. The assumption that all configurations count equally has to be replaced by an assessment of which configurations will occur, and how often.

The discussion of the various indices in the last chapter should put us in a position to see how an index of ableness can be created: we proceed as we did before when creating the Penrose index, but attach appropriate weights to the various different configurations. So in the three-person committee in which you have one vote and the others two each, if we know that the others are deadly enemies and will always oppose each other then you are always powerful, since your vote ensures that you will always win. Conversely, if the others will always vote together, then they will always win and you are powerless.

Such knowledge is obviously useful to the CIA in determining who to bribe.[1] An index of power as ableness could also be very useful in helping to solve a possible constitutional problem that was much discussed in Britain in the 1970s and 1980s: that of who should form a government if a general election produces a hung Parliament. This problem did actually occur, since after the British general election of February 1974 there was a brief constitutional crisis when it was not clear which of the two major parties could command more support in the Commons. The Queen, traditionally above party politics, was faced with the unpleasant prospect of either sacking the defeated Prime Minister against his will, or doing nothing and thus allowing the Conservative Party (seemingly the less powerful of the two) the undeserved advantage of having the first attempt at forming a new government simply because they formed the outgoing government.

(The election result was Labour 301 seats, Conservatives 297, Liberals 14, 11 assorted Ulster Unionists, and 12 others.) In fact, the Conservative leadership admitted defeat, but not before making an attempt, of dubious constitutional ethics, to stay in power. What was needed, clearly, was an index which would tell us which party had most power in the Commons; undeniably the Labour Party, as the largest single party, had the most power-as-ability, but which one had the most ableness?

In this chapter I show how a modified Penrose index is what we require in such situations.

23.1—FORMING A GOVERNMENT: THE CONSTITUTIONAL REQUIREMENTS

There has been considerable discussion of what should happen immediately after an election which fails to produce a party with an overall majority. This discussion has mainly drawn on the experiences of other countries (mainly European and Commonwealth) or has probed precedent to try to work out what the British constitutional position now is.[2] There has been little sustained consideration of what elections are supposed to be, and how the results should be analysed in the light of this. For instance, it has been plausibly argued that there is no constitutional obligation on a Prime Minister to resign before meeting the new Parliament irrespective of the election result (see, e.g., Bogdanor, 1983: pp. 110–12), and despite the realization "that whoever is *first* asked by the Sovereign to form a government will enjoy a considerable advantage" (Bogdanor, 1983: p. 119). Yet if the election result, and that alone, is supposed to determine who should form a government, this position is indefensible: the outgoing Prime Minister should not have first crack, simply because he or she was Prime Minister before the election. Instead "the principle of parliamentarism, that a government must command the confidence of Parliament" (Bogdanor, 1983: p. 118) seems the appropriate one, with the person most likely to command the confidence of Parliament being the first to be asked to try to form a government. What we need is a more sophisticated way of determining this than is obtained by just adding up the seats each party has won.

Even then it is unclear what is meant by "commanding the confidence of Parliament". Does it mean enjoying the support of a parliamentary majority, or merely being able to survive? How the phrase is interpreted is clearly of great importance, since the former interpretation would seem to require a coalition government, whilst on the latter reading a minority government would suffice.[3] I shall adopt the interpretation that the 'winner' of an election is the person (or party) least likely to be defeated in a vote of no confidence, but the procedure outlined here can easily be adapted to the more positive requirement of discovering the person best able to secure the passage of their legislation.

The required index will involve at least four factors: first, the distribution of votes (from which the abilities can be calculated); second, the effects of allowing abstention; third, the effects of the likely pattern of voting, which typically will not be random; and fourth, the effects of a member's defection from his party's line (which can include involuntary abstention through sickness and death, if one wants to take this into account). The importance of these four factors should be obvious. The abilities are clearly crucial, other things being equal – which they rarely are. The likelihood of abstentions can be very important: a member who never takes his seat or votes can be ignored. Differential abstention – and non-random voting generally – can make an immense difference to the distribution of power. Thus if there were three parties (Conservative, Labour and Irish Nationalist) with 6, 5 and 2 votes respectively, and it was known that the Irish would always abstain on non-Irish matters, whilst the Conservative and Labour parties were wholeheartedly agreed about Ireland and would always vote together on such issues, then the Conservatives are as safe as if they had an overall majority.[4] The importance of defection likewise needs no stressing: if there are groups within a party who agree with the other party's line on an important issue (for example the European Union or a statutory incomes policy) then the party is weaker than if no such groups existed – at least if these groups will press their views to the lengths of voting against their party or abstaining on a vote of confidence.

My aim, then, is to construct an index such that the four factors above are taken into account; this index could be used to decide who to ask to be Prime Minister, without appearing to be engaged in party squabbles. Of course, the actual likelihood of the occurrence of the last three factors is a contentious matter, and may well be difficult to assess – but I am not a magician attempting to pull a non-existent rabbit out of an empty hat. All I am doing is providing a way of aggregating four diverse sets of data once these data have been agreed upon – and also (and equally important) pointing out what information it is that we require.

23.2—THE EPW INDEX

Penrose's index is not quite what we want in these circumstances. Your Penrose index, to recap, tells us the probability that you will be in a position such that if you vote for a motion it will win *and* if you vote against the motion it will lose. It is an index of active power.

But the constitutional criterion described in the last section does not refer to this; it requires us to calculate simply the probability of your avoiding defeat, and it simply doesn't matter whether you could have swung the vote the other way should you have so chosen. In other words, our index of power here must include passive power – winning so convincingly that even if you had chosen to vote against yourself the remainder of the voters would *still* have expressed confidence in you. Such an index is given by calculating your *expected probability* of *winning*, and I shall call it the EPW index.

As a measure of *ability*, when we are making the equiprobability assumptions of the last chapter, there is a simple mathematical relation between the EPW and Penrose indices. It is not difficult to see that even if someone has no votes at all (or a Penrose index of zero) she will still get the outcome she prefers half the time on average, since whatever the outcome that the others vote for there's a $50:50$ chance it is the one that she wants. Nobody, then, has an EPW index of ability less than one-half. Conversely, nobody has an EPW index greater than one – for since it measures the *probability* of something happening it can never exceed one.

The EPW index measures the sum of an actor's active and passive powers. Her active power is shown by her Penrose index, and she has passive power (given the equiprobability assumptions) on half those occasions on which she lacks active power. The EPW index is therefore equal to $P + \frac{1}{2}(1 - P)$ (where P is the Penrose index); simplifying,

$$EPW = \tfrac{1}{2}(P + 1).$$

The EPW index therefore runs from $\frac{1}{2}$ (no active power: $P = 0$) to 1 (complete active power: $P = 1$), as we saw in the last paragraph that it must.[5]

But when we drop the equiprobability assumptions, there is no necessary connection between the EPW and Penrose indices, since an actor's passive power varies depending on how the others vote. So when we are constructing an index of ableness that is to include passive power, we must use the EPW index and cannot use the Penrose index.

An index that measures the expected probability of an actor winning is very simple to understand, if usually very tedious to calculate. In the next section I shall discuss how we can develop it to provide the index that the last section required.

23.3—THE INDEX DEVELOPED

In the last section I briefly described how the EPW index worked under the equiprobability assumptions; in this section I show how to extend it when we drop these assumptions. But first I shall see what happens when we allow abstentions, retaining the equiprobability assumption for the time being.

We saw in section 22.4 that when abstentions are not allowed, the actor with most (active) power is the one that does best in the lexicographical ordering of the minimal decisive subsets. Often this gives an appropriate ordering when abstention is allowed as well.[6] When member A abstains, the power of the other actors is distributed according to the lexicographical orderings of their MDSs: we can simply ignore A's presence.

Now when actors have commensurable votes, it is clear that if any member A has more power than another (B) without abstentions, she cannot have less power when abstentions are allowed. For A to have more power than B it is a necessary condition (although, of course, far from a sufficient one) that A has more votes than B. But clearly, however abstentions occur, if A has more votes than B, B can never outvote A. Thus the only difference in the ordering is that if A and B are equal in power without abstentions but not equal in votes, then they need not still be equal in power when abstentions are allowed; and, conversely, A and B can be equal in power in certain circumstances after abstentions when they are not equal when everybody votes.[7]

We can, then (when votes are commensurable), define: A has more power than B if and only if A is ordered above B in some lexicographical ordering of the minimal decisive sets, calculated with and without the abstentions of the other members.

With a simple majority required, this simply says that A has more power than B if and only if A has more votes than B.[8] This is, of course, not particularly enlightening; but, perhaps because of its obviousness, it does seem undeniably correct.

But this procedure will not work when we drop the equiprobability assumptions; then we need the EPW index. We can calculate your EPW index, allowing for abstentions, by averaging the probability of the eventual decision being in favour of the motion when you vote for it, and the probability that the committee's decision is against the motion when you oppose it. When you abstain, you are showing no interest in the outcome, and so what the eventual outcome is is of no concern to us. We measure the power given by resources (here, votes) by seeing what you can obtain when you use these resources; what happens when you let them lie idle is not of any relevance.[9]

Thus in Committee I when abstentions are possible we have 27 configurations (including that in which all actors abstain) as shown in Figure 4.

Figure 4—Voting in committee I with abstention

A (2 votes):	+ + + + + + + + + 0 0 0 0 0 0 0 0 0 − − − − − − − − −
B (2 votes):	+ + + 0 0 0 − − − + + + 0 0 0 − − − + + + 0 0 0 − − −
C (1 vote):	+ 0 − + 0 − + 0 − + 0 − + 0 − + 0 − + 0 − + 0 − + 0 −
Result:	+ + + + + + + − − + + + + − − − − − + − − − − − − − −

A's probability of being on the winning side when she expresses a preference is $\frac{15}{18}$, whilst C's is only $\frac{12}{18}$. We can see from this both that A is now more powerful than C (without abstentions they had the same power) and that the EPW of A has gone up whilst that of C has gone down, for without abstentions both their EPWs were $\frac{3}{4}$. Abstentions, then, make a difference to each actor's power, and may even result in the most powerful actor losing this position.

I have assumed so far that each actor abstains one-third of the time, but this obviously need not be the case. Thus in Figure 4, A has more power than C because she outvotes C when B abstains. But if B is very unlikely to abstain, then A has very little more power than C. So it is obviously of some importance to both A and C to know how often B will abstain, for A's power relative to C depends on this information. (Assuming for the moment that when B does vote he votes randomly with respect to A and C.) That such information is important in practice is shown by the amount of speculation immediately after the February 1974 general election about the frequency with which the Ulster Unionists would vote on matters not affecting Ireland.

Let us now drop the random-voting assumption, and instead predict how people are likely to vote. We have already seen that, in our three-person committee without abstention being allowed, when any two actors are so antagonistic that they will always vote against each other, the third will always win: for when there are only two ways for A and B to vote, and if one votes one way the other votes the other, whichever way C votes will win by 3 votes to 2. When two voters quarrel in this way, the third always has more power than either of them, even if she has fewer votes.[10]

Allowing abstentions does not alter this: so long as A abstains only if B does (and vice versa), C will still win. If, however, A's and B's antagonism extends only to never voting the same way, then, with abstentions allowed, the situation is more complicated. We can see what happens by showing all the possibilities with A and B never voting the same way (see Figure 5). With all these possibilities equally probable, A can expect to win 9 times out of every 12 that she expresses a preference, whilst C's probability of winning is 10 out of 14. Since A's probability of success, at 0.75, is slightly higher than C's (0.71), A has more power than C (as does B, of course, since the EPW of A and B are identical).

Figure 5—Voting in committee I with quarrelling voters

A (2 votes):	+	+	+	+	+	+	0	0	0	0	0	0	0	0	0	−	−	−	−	−	−
B (2 votes):	0	0	0	−	−	−	+	+	+	0	0	0	−	−	−	+	+	+	0	0	0
C (1 vote):	+	0	−	+	0	−	+	0	−	+	0	−	+	0	−	+	0	−	+	0	−
Result:	+	+	+	+	−	−	−	+	+	+	+	−	−	−	−	−	−	+	−	−	−	−	−

If we are interested in whether party A or party C should be invited to form a government by the criterion of section 23.1, we are only interested in whether a motion (of no confidence) can be passed against her opposition. For A the probability of this is $\frac{1}{6}$, since of the six columns in Figure 5 in which she votes −, only one results in a + outcome. For C, though, the probability of failing to defeat a motion is $\frac{2}{7}$. Thus A will be far more secure than C as a government.

For a second illustration of the effects of non-random voting, and how we can accommodate it, we can consider Committee III (A: 26, B: 25, C: 25, D: 24, simple majority), and let us suppose that B and D are ideologically fairly similar, to the extent that we hypothesize that for each time they vote against each other (that is, one supports a motion that the other opposes) they will vote together six times (including when both abstain), and one will abstain whilst the other does not four times. Assuming voting is random within these constraints, their frequency of voting is as set out in Figure 6.

Figure 6—Frequency of non-random voting

B:	+	−	0	0	+	−	+	−	0
D:	−	+	+	−	0	0	+	−	0
Frequency:	1	1	2	2	2	2	4	4	4

Should A or B be invited to form a government? Again we construct EPW tables, shown in Figure 7. (Since we are only interested in a party's ability to defeat votes of censure, we need only consider those occasions on which the prospective governing party opposes a motion. In the tables the party on the top line is the (putative) government; the weight is the likelihood of this voting pattern occurring, given the above information about B's and D's voting; and the result is weighted accordingly, to determine A's and B's probability of defeat if they are the government. I put D immediately after B to make the tables easier to follow.) Thus B is likely to be defeated on 11 out of 63 motions, A on 12 out of 66. Since $\frac{11}{63}$ is less than $\frac{12}{66}$, B is likely to be defeated less often than A, and so B should be invited to form the government.

Notice that A's *active* power is still very much greater than B's: the chances of its vote being crucial are $\frac{41}{66}$, compared to B's $\frac{29}{63}$. But active power is not here what we are interested in: a government survives a vote of censure equally successfully whether through the strength of its own vote or the improbability that other parties support the censure motion. So long as our estimates of the probabilities of voting patterns are accurate, passive power is as important as active power. This shows why we must here compare EPWs, which include the actor's passive power, rather than Penrose indices, which do not.

A procedure along these lines is going to be essential if there is a hung Parliament in Britain in the near future, particularly if the Alliance obtain most seats. For 'the Alliance' are, formally, two separate parties, and there is likely to be considerable – and heated – argument about whether they should be treated as two parties or one. If – suppose – the Alliance won 250 seats (made up of 150 Liberals and 100 SDP), Labour won 200 and the Conservatives 175, which is the largest single party? If the Alliance counts as a party, then it is; but if not, Labour is. If the Conservative leader resigned on being so soundly defeated, who should be invited to try to form a government? On current thinking, it should be the leader of the largest party, but this gets us back to the question of what *is* a party?[11] Even in February 1974 this problem could well have arisen, for "if the 11 Ulster Unionists had been willing to accept the Conservative Whip, would Mr. Heath who 'lost' by 297 to 301 to Harold Wilson, have 'won' by 308 to 301?" (Butler, 1983: p. 149 n. 11).

Clearly, party labels are less important than likely voting behaviour. If the Liberals and SDP will always vote together, we can treat them as one bloc; if not, we cannot. This will involve difficult – and doubtless contentious – predictions about whether the Alliance will remain together when they have to take tough decisions. But such predictions are what we

Figure 7—Committee III: EPW index with non-random voting

Weight:	4	4	4	4	4	4	2	2	2	2	2	2	1	1	1	1	1	1	1	1	Total
B (25):	−	−	−	−	−	−	−	−	−	−	−	−	−	+	+	+	+	+	+	+	
D (24):	−	−	−	−	−	−	0	0	0	0	0	0	+	−	+	+	+	+	−	0	
A (26):	−	−	0	0	+	+	0	0	0	+	+	−	−	0	0	+	−	0	+	+	
C (25):	−	0	+	−	0	+	−	0	+	−	0	+	−	0	+	0	+	−	0	+	
Weighted − :	4	4	4	4	4	4	2	2	2	2	2	2	1	1	1	1	1	1	1	1	52
result + :																					11

Weight:	4	4	4	2	2	2	2	4	4	4	4	2	2	2	1	1	1	2	2	4	4	4	4	2	2	2	4	4	4	4	Total
A (26):	−	−	−	−	−	−	−	−	−	−	−	−	−	−	−	−	−	+	+	+	+	+	+	+	+	+	+	+	+	+	
B (25):	−	−	−	−	−	−	0	0	0	0	0	0	0	0	0	+	+	−	−	+	+	+	+	+	+	+	−	0	+	+	
D (24):	−	−	0	0	0	+	0	0	0	+	+	−	−	0	−	−	0	−	−	0	+	+	+	−	0	+	−	0	+	+	
C (25):	−	0	+	−	0	+	−	0	+	−	0	+	−	0	+	−	0	+	−	0	+	−	0	+	−	0	+	−	0	+	
Weighted − :	4	4	4	2	2	2	2	4	4	4	4	2	2	2	1	1	1	2	2												54
result + :																															12

require, not attempted analyses of when a political party is not a political party.

This process needs to be taken a step further. In my simple illustrative examples I have not differentiated between *parties* in a legislature and *people* with weighted votes in a committee. This was justifiable because parties were being considered as completely homogeneous and united: as if the party leader disposed of the party's vote just as a holder of stock votes at a shareholders' meeting. This, of course, is an inaccurate picture of most legislatures – even the British, which has a stronger party discipline than most. We need no reminding that a few maverick (or principled) MPs can make a party whip's job very difficult. So there seems little doubt that party A has more power than party B if A's members have stronger party discipline than B's. It is, of course, usually very difficult to predict in advance exactly how stable a party will be; but it has to be done if we are to construct the appropriate index.

This sort of factionalism can be considered as a special case of non-random voting. In Committee III there are 100 legislators: if they all voted or abstained randomly there would be 3^{100} possible different combinations. But they are grouped into four parties which, until now, I have taken to reduce the possibilities to 3^4 by the assumption that members of the same party never vote against each other. When we drop this assumption, we simply consider any defector as a new party – or, better, we consider a 'party' as a label that describes how people tend to vote, a shorthand for likeminded voters. Thus suppose (still with Committee III), that in party A there are four members who always vote with party B – not such an unlikely occurrence in America, for example. Then, whatever party label these four wear, we can consider them as part of party B for voting purposes. B will then be the largest single party and, ceteris paribus, the most powerful.

Perhaps more realistically, we can suppose that this faction in A thinks like B to the extent that there is a one in three probability of it choosing to vote with B whenever A and B do not vote the same way, except that when A and B vote against each other, this faction (call it A$'$) will only abstain.[12] We have seen that party A can expect to be defeated on only $\frac{4}{27}$ of the votes; when A$'$ deserts it, however, it is defeated on $\frac{9}{27}$ of the votes. As A$'$ votes with A on twice as many motions as it rebels on, A can expect to be defeated on $\frac{17}{81}$ of the motions. When B is the government it can expect to lose $\frac{6}{27}$ of the votes of confidence; aided by A$'$, however, it loses only $\frac{4}{27}$. Thus it can expect, overall, to lose on $\frac{16}{81}$ of the motions, which gives it the better index.

All that remains to do now is to put this together. Thus if in Committee III we expect both the modifications suggested in the preceding pages to occur (both non-random voting and defections from A), we can simply construct a figure to see what happens. This is done in Figure 8 for the alternatives of A and B forming the government. As we might expect, A is shown to be unequivocally less powerful than B. Although B is not the largest single party, when we take into consideration the known ideological similarities between B and D, and the faction A′ which is frequently sympathetic to B's line (and prepared to extend this sympathy to voting with B), B is then in the strongest position. It would, I assert, be perverse to invite A to form a government in such circumstances.

23.4—CONCLUSION

All the spadework has now been done to apply this index, measuring power to remain undefeated as a government, to the situation as it stood after the last result had been declared on 2 March 1974. However, it would require an expert on British party politics, which I am certainly not, to hazard a guess at the effects of abstention, non-randomness and defection. But from playing with some figures, it would seem that these effects would have to work very strongly indeed in favour of the Conservative Party for this party to have had a stronger claim than the Labour Party to form a government. In short, unless Mr Heath could have substantiated a claim that his party would have been invariably supported by the Liberals or Ulster Unionists, or that there was likely to have been a considerable and frequent defection from the Labour Party, and none from the Conservatives, then he had clearly lost the election and should have resigned immediately – or been forced to resign.

It is possible, using the method I have developed, to calculate the size of the deviations from randomness necessary for a smaller party to have the stronger claim. In general this will give a set of simultaneous equations with an infinite number of solutions. Even if we cannot guess at accurate figures for the various variables, it may be obvious from the magnitudes required for a smaller party to have the best claim to govern whether this claim is justified. I suggest that, in the 1974 Parliament, the Conservatives' claim was probably not justified.

To conclude. This chapter provides a first attempt at developing an index of ableness. The mathematical complications have been kept to a minimum in order to show clearly to non-mathematicians how the index works.[13] It is really very simple – the difficulties lie in obtaining the re-quired estimates of voting intentions. But we should not try to avoid

Figure 8—Committee III: EPW index with non-random voting and defections

```
Weight : 12 12 12 12 12 12  8  4  6  6  6  6  6  4  2  6  4  2  6  3  3  3  3  3  3  2  1  3  3   Total

B (25) :  -  -  -  -  -  -  -  -  -  -  -  -  -  -  -  -  -  -  -  -  -  -  -  -  -  -  -  -  -
D (24) :  -  -  -  -  -  -  0  0  0  0  0  0  0  +  +  +  -  -  -  0  0  0  +  +  +  +  +  +  +
A (22) :  -  -  0  0  0  +  +  +  +  0  -  -  0  0  0  +  +  -  -  -  0  0  0  +  +  -  -  -  0  +
A'(4)  :  -  -  0  0  0  +  +  +  0  -  -  0  0  0  +  +  -  -  0  0  0  +  -  -  0  +  -  -  0  +
C (25) :  -  0  +  -  0  +  -  0  +  +  -  0  +  -  0  +  +  -  0  +  -  0  +  +  -  0  +  -  0  +

   -  : 12 12 12 12 12 12  4  6  6  6  6  6  4  2  6  4  2  6  2  3  3  3  3  2  1         162
   +  :                    8  8  4  6  6  6  4  2  6  3  3  3  3  3  3  3         27
```

```
Weight : 12 12 12  6  6  3  3  6  6  6 12 12  8  4  6  4  2  6  3  3  3  2  1  6  4  2  6  8  4 12 12   Total

A (22) :  -  -  -  -  -  -  -  -  -  -  -  -  -  -  -  -  -  -  -  -  -  -  -  -  -  -  -  -  -  -  -
A'(4)  :  -  -  -  -  -  -  -  -  -  -  -  -  -  -  0  -  -  0  -  -  -  0  -  -  0  -  -  0  -  -  -
B (25) :  -  -  -  -  -  -  0  0  0  0  0  0  0  0  0  +  +  +  -  -  -  0  0  0  +  +  +  +  +  +  +
D (24) :  -  -  0  0  0  +  +  -  -  0  0  0  0  +  +  +  -  -  -  0  0  0  +  +  -  -  0  0  +  +  +
C (25) :  -  0  +  -  0  +  -  0  +  +  -  0  +  -  0  +  +  -  0  +  -  0  +  +  -  -  0  +  -  0  +

   -  : 12 12 12  6  6  3  3  6  6  6 12 12  8  4  6  4  2  6  3  3  3  2  1         149
   +  :                    4  4  2  6  6  1  2  6  3  3  2  8  4 12 12         49
```

(In these tables, A′ is only shown defecting when this would make a difference to the result; this does not impute any motives or foresight to A′, it merely makes the diagrams somewhat smaller.)

B is defeated on 27 out of 189 votes of no confidence, whilst A is defeated on 49 out of 198, which is significantly more.

these difficulties by adopting apparently more objective procedures, such as allowing the outgoing Prime Minister to continue until defeated by Parliament (which gives the incumbent an inbuilt advantage), or concentrating solely on the number of seats a party has (which favours single-party minority government over coalitions, and puts too much weight on the definition of a party). There is, I suggest, a strong need for the formation – now, before the problems arise – of a Constitutional Court (consisting perhaps of respected ex-politicians, constitutional lawyers, and experts on contemporary politics) which has widely recognized impartiality and which can perform the required calculations. *Any* decision reached after an indecisive election will be contentious, and it is quite wrong to try to minimize the contention by adopting some rule that is clear-cut but arbitrary.[14] The EPW index provides the rule that should be followed.

—24—
Creating power

Votes do not grow on trees, nor do we acquire them naturally in the way we acquire many other resources. Votes are human artefacts, created by us (collectively) and for us (individually), and created, one hopes, for a purpose. In this chapter I shall show how we can create votes in the manner best designed to secure the purpose for which they are created.

As I did in the last chapter, I shall concentrate on one specific problem which requires the use of appropriate power indices. As we shall see, the main attempts to deal with this problem have used a completely misguided approach – which is worrying because some American courts have based their judgements, on an important constitutional issue, on this erroneous argument. The problem concerns weighted voting in legislatures and other assemblies of representatives.

24.1—THE PROBLEM OF WEIGHTED VOTING

In the late 1960s and the 1970s, the American courts had to decide a large number of cases brought to determine whether weighted voting was constitutional at state and county level, and if so how the weights should be determined.[1] The issue had arisen in large part as a consequence of the famous Supreme Court decision in *Baker* v. *Carr* which declared that it was unconstitutional for constituencies to differ significantly in size. One way of conforming to the decision would be to redraw constituency boundaries so as to produce equal-sized constituencies, and this is probably what the Supreme Court expected to occur. But often the constituency boundaries follow natural geographical or social lines (between townships, for instance) and there are good reasons for retaining them. Several states have tried to bring their legislatures into line with the Court's decision, without redrawing boundaries, by allocating a different number of votes to each representative. That way, it was felt, the principle of "one person, one vote, one value" could be maintained.

Most of these suggestions were thrown out in the courts on grounds not connected with voting strength; for "can a legislator with nineteen votes be expected to make nineteen times as many . . . telephone calls as his fellow representatives [with one vote]; will he be permitted to have nineteen secretaries and control a proportionately large number of patronage positions?" (Banzhaf, 1965: p. 322 n. 21). Or have representation on nineteen times as many committees? These drawbacks to weighted voting could presumably be circumvented somehow, but the more important point is that the effect of weighted voting is frequently not that intended by its proponents. Suppose we have a legislative area with 90,000 voters, divided into five constituencies: one of 50,000 voters, and four with 10,000 in each. If we allocate votes proportional to population, with five votes for the representative of the largest constituency and one for each representative of the others, then the largest constituency has an overall majority (5 votes out of 9) and the remaining 40,000 voters are effectively disenfranchised. Conversely, if the five constituencies are divided so that four contain 20,000 voters each and one only 10,000, then when weights are allocated proportionate to voters each representative is equally powerful, so that weighted voting makes no difference at all. In these cases weighting the votes of legislators clearly does not give electors votes of equal value, and so does not meet the Supreme Court's requirements.

But in some cases weighted voting is essential: for example at gatherings such as the British Trades Union Congress. Such a congress avoids objections on grounds other than voting power (or does so to a much greater extent than in the case of legislatures) since the sole function of the annual congress is to meet to consider motions. Further, as the largest union (the Transport and General Workers' Union) has 1,632,957 members, whilst the smallest one (the Cloth Pressers' Society) has only 16, we cannot (equitably) allocate one vote to each union, nor (practically) allow each union to elect one delegate for some chosen numeraire.[2] Redistricting into single-member constituencies of larger size also appears uninviting, as this would mean lumping small unions in with large ones to elect a delegate, which would almost certainly be effectively to disenfranchise them.

Weighted voting, then, is the answer. But how weighted? In practice, of course, each delegation's vote is weighted by the number of members of that union; but as I have just shown this frequently gives results differing widely from those intended.

That, then, is the problem of weighted voting: if we feel that we cannot redistrict into equal constituencies, how should we allocate the weights to the representatives?[3] In discussing this problem, I shall interpret it as concerned with ability rather than ableness: that is, we should adopt the equiprobability assumptions of Chapter 22, rather than try to assess how people will vote. The comparable problem with ableness is how to detect and eliminate gerrymandering; I will not consider that here.

24.2—TWO FAILED SOLUTIONS–I: BANZHAF'S APPROACH

This "problem of weighted voting" was raised in 1946 by Lionel Penrose, but it has been John Banzhaf III who has done most to bring it to our attention. Banzhaf is described as both a lawyer and a mathematician, and he developed his power index in order to act as a consultant for people contesting the validity of weighted voting schemes before the American courts. In this he has had some success, the most significant being the case of *Iannucci* v. *Board of Supervisors of the County of Washington*, in which the New York State Court of Appeals "explicitly cited the Banzhaf index to turn down a weighted voting scheme" (Grofman, 1982: p. 118).[4] As a consequence, a "New York mathematician and consultant" called Lee Papayanopoulos has managed "to supplement his income ... by providing New York counties with [computerized] weighted voting schemes acceptable under the Iannucci guidelines" (Grofman and Scarrow, 1979: p. 175).

This is rather worrying, because the Banzhaf index is completely inappropriate for doing this job. When I previously discussed this index (in section 22.3) I did not have much to say in its favour; but, even apart from that, here both it and the Shapley–Shubik index are out of place. That is because of the constant-sum assumption that they both contain.

I can show this best perhaps by means of an illustration: consider again Committee III (in which A has 26 votes, B and C 25 each, D 24, and a simple majority decision rule operates). I have shown already that the Penrose indices of the four actors are $\frac{5}{8}, \frac{3}{8}, \frac{3}{8}$ and $\frac{1}{8}$ respectively, and their Shapley–Shubik and Banzhaf indices are $\frac{5}{12}, \frac{3}{12}, \frac{3}{12}$ and $\frac{1}{12}$ (see pp. 159–60, 161–2, 166). Suppose that there is now a proposal to introduce a change from a simple-majority decision rule to a rule that 76 votes or more are required to win. Under such a rule the actors' Penrose indices would become $\frac{1}{4}, \frac{1}{4}, \frac{1}{4}, 0$. Thus *every* actor's Penrose index (and therefore also her expected probability of winning) would be decreased by such a change: everybody would be made unequivocally worse off. Yet the Banzhaf and Shapley–Shubik indices under such a voting rule are $\frac{1}{3}, \frac{1}{3}, \frac{1}{3}, 0$, so that both B and C would seem, according to the Banzhaf index, to prefer this change, since their indices rise from $\frac{3}{12}$ to $\frac{4}{12}$. This is patently absurd, and is purely a result of the constant-sum nature of indices such as

Banzhaf's – for as the Penrose indices show, *everybody* has lost power due to this change. Expressing the resulting powers as a proportion of a constant hides this fact.

Further, if the change had been made so that the majority required was 76, and then it was suggested that the majority be reduced to 74, the Penrose indices of everybody would increase until they were all the same at $\frac{3}{8}$ (since with a majority of 74 required, no two actors have enough votes together to pass a motion, but any three do). That is, everybody would be made better off by this change. Yet everybody's Banzhaf (and Shapley–Shubik) index would now be $\frac{1}{4}$, so that the Banzhaf index of everybody except D would have fallen.

We can now see how erroneous it is to assume that power always sums to a constant, for this is simply false. When we alter the voting rules we create or destroy power, because we change the probabilities of voting configurations occurring in which people's votes are crucial. The Shapley–Shubik and Banzhaf indices miss this.

We saw in Chapter 22 that the Shapley–Shubik index was not an unreasonable way of comparing the powers of different actors on a given occasion. We can see now that it *is* a totally unreasonable way of comparing the power of a *given* actor on *different* occasions. When we compare the powers of actors, with the rules fixed, we can treat the power *as if* it summed to a constant; indeed, in a sense it does (a rather trivial sense), since with both the votes and the rules fixed the total sum of power cannot vary. But when we want to compare the powers generated by different rules, or by different distributions of votes, we cannot divide the index through by the total amount of power *on that occasion* and then compare *across* occasions, since we will be dividing through by different numbers.

If this isn't clear already, a simple example might help. Suppose you have three apples and I have six; we might then say that you had $\frac{1}{3}$ of the total number of apples. If you were then to throw one apple at my pile, and send four of my apples (plus yours) flying into a passing cement-mixer, you would now only have two apples, but your proportion of the total would have risen to $\frac{1}{2}$. Assuming that apples are constant-sum (which is no more senseless – or meaningless – than assuming that powers are constant-sum)[5] you have gained by this destructive act. But only dogs in mangers and their acolytes would advocate measuring one's stock of possessions simply as a proportion of the total. Similarly with power. You do not gain by increasing your proportion whilst decreasing the absolute amount that you can effect. If you had to choose between two or more sets of voting rules, or allocations of votes, you would be sensible to choose the one that maximized your Penrose index (or EPW), and not the one that maximized your Shapley–Shubik or Banzhaf index.

We have here a point of considerable importance, which gives rise to the general question: what *principles* should we adopt by which to allocate votes? Banzhaf seems to have adopted an *equality principle*: that votes are to be allocated to legislators in a way that ensures that the legislators' power is proportional to the population they represent; in other words, that each voter should have equal power irrespective of the group he is in. Since the equality principle is comparative, Banzhaf's index would seem appropriate, since it is the ratios of the actors' Penrose indices: it measures their *relative* power.

But it is easy to show that the equality principle, by itself, cannot be an acceptable basis for allocating votes. If we take the equality principle seriously, we must accept that the best allocation of votes is the one that best equalizes voters' powers. In practice, those allocations that pass the Banzhaf test (as accepted, for instance, in the Iannucci case) come pretty close to equality. But in all cases there is a distribution of votes that *exactly* equalizes power, and is therefore to be preferred on the equality principle. This is the distribution that gives nobody any votes at all and (therefore) decides each issue by tossing a coin. Everybody then has a 50 per cent chance of being on the winning side, irrespective of their constituency; that is, everybody's power would be exactly equal – although equal to zero. If it really *is* equality that we are concerned about, this would be our ideal. But, as I have suggested, most people would find this dog-in-the-mangerishness indefensible. (Would you willingly destroy all your three apples provided you also got rid of all my six? If not with apples, why with power?)

Banzhaf's procedure *only* compares power *ratios*; it therefore considers that the equality principle, alone, should govern the allocation of power. I have suggested that this is indefensible; that we need (also) to take into account the absolute amounts of power that people have, and try to maximize these. My interpretation of what democracy is about is that it involves some attempt to *maximize* popular power, not (merely) *equalize* it. If you agree with this interpretation, you will reject Banzhaf's procedure. If you do not agree with this interpretation you will still reject Banzhaf's procedure, since you will want complete equality, which is only obtained by deciding issues on the toss of a coin. Either way, Banzhaf's procedure fails.

24.3—TWO FAILED SOLUTIONS–II: THE SQUARE-ROOT RULE

Banzhaf's solution fails because it concentrates exclusively on equalizing power and not at all on maximizing it. The second proposed solution fails because it concentrates exclusively on maximizing power and not at all on equalizing it. But the proposal is very simple, and elegant, and we can learn a lot by seeing why it fails. The proposal is simply that each legislator should be allocated votes proportional in number to the *square-root* of the number of people she represents. This was originally proposed in Penrose's 1946 article, and reasserted in Fielding and Liebeck (1975); Banzhaf has also apparently advocated it.[6]

But why the square-root? The reasoning behind this rule is usually presented in a mathematically complicated way, full of weird symbols, but it is really quite simple. It can be presented in two rather different ways, starting from apparently different principles but both arriving at the square-root rule. Leaving out the mathematics, these run as follows.

The first starts by thinking of the problem as one of trying to ensure that the legislators vote for the 'correct' outcome, which is the outcome that would have resulted if the issue had been decided by a referendum. This is not an accurate portrayal of the theory of representative democracy, but does work well as a model of certain two-stage voting procedures, for instance those sometimes employed by trade unions on strike ballots and the like (and, indeed, by the American Electoral College). In these procedures, the branches vote on the issue and each sends a delegate to a delegate conference, with the delegate mandated to vote for the branch's preferred outcome. The delegate casts the *whole* of the branch's vote for the outcome preferred by the branch's majority, however small that majority; and the delegate conference decides the matter on a majority vote of delegates.

We can think of this process as not really a two-stage *voting* procedure, but a two-stage *aggregation* procedure: aggregating the members' votes first into blocs of branches, and then into the overall outcome. Now often this two-stage process will produce a different result from the more direct one-stage method of simply counting up the members' votes across all the branches. For instance, if one branch has over half the membership, and votes by a small majority against a strike, then (if delegates have votes proportional to their membership) the union as a whole will decide not to strike, even if all the other branches are overwhelmingly in favour of striking. And vice versa.

Such an occurrence may well be thought to be unsatisfactory – if the union goes to all the trouble of balloting its members, it is unfortunate if the majority still lose. The obvious way round this is simply to count up all the votes, but if this is impossible for some reason the problem becomes one of arranging the rules of the delegate conference to minimize this discrepancy. This could be done by forcing the delegates to cast only the number of votes by which the majority won in their branch, since this would produce the same result as straightforwardly counting all the votes. But

suppose that we cannot trust the delegates to limit their votes in this way[7]
– suppose they will always cast *all* their votes for their branch's preference.
Then what we require is some estimate of what the likely size of the majority in each branch is. It turns out that, if we make the equiprobability
assumption that everybody has the same probability of voting for a strike
irrespective of which branch they are in, the likely size of the majority in a
branch is proportional to the square-root of its membership.[8] So if the
number of votes each delegate is given is proportional to the square-root
of the number of members she represents, the probability of the two-stage
aggregation producing a different result from the one-stage aggregation will
be minimized.

   This is the first argument for the square-root rule. It holds when (and
only when) our sole concern is to do the best we can to ensure that the
delegate conference produces the same result as a referendum. If this is
an accurate description of the requirements for the American Electoral
College (for instance), then it seems that the square-root rule should apply
and the size of each state's delegation be proportional to the square-root
of its population.

The second argument proceeds from the premise that the object of democracy is to maximize the amount of power in the system. It turns out that
this is achieved by adopting the square-root rule.[9]

   The drawback with this approach is that it completely ignores the distribution of power. To see this, cast your mind back to the three- and four-
member committees, Committees I and II. Suppose that your one vote on
these committees comes from representing 100 members, whilst the other
delegates represent 400 each; and the square-root rule is applied to give
you one vote to their two. Yet – as we saw on pp. 157–9 – in the three-
member committee your power is equal to that of the others (with a
Penrose index of $\frac{1}{2}$), whilst in the four-member committee you have no
power at all. Adopting the square-root rule can easily lead to the disenfranchisement of one (or more) of the groups.

   The startling aspect of this is that *despite* this disenfranchisement, this
procedure *does* maximize the total amount of power that the actors have.
To show this requires some elementary mathematics and so I relegate my
demonstration of it to Appendix 4.4. In that appendix I show that this result
is completely general: if we have any even number of groups, all of which
are the same size except for one which is smaller, the total power is maximized when the smallest group's delegate has no power, irrespective of
how tiny the difference in size is between that group and the others. If there
are only four groups, this will involve effectively disenfranchising nearly a
quarter of the entire voting population.

A word, perhaps, about what this means. We sometimes say that you are "effectively disenfranchised" if your vote has no chance of making a difference – so that if you live in a constituency in which 90 per cent of the voters are certain to vote Labour, then there is no point in voting. Considering power as *ableness*, you do indeed have little or no power. But that is not what is meant here. Here everyone in the constituency has no power because the *delegate* (or MP) is denied any power – in effect, is denied a vote. And this, again, does not mean that on each motion some delegate or other is denied a vote, with delegates suffering this misfortune in turn so that in the long run it evens out. The delegate that is denied a vote is always the same one. It is in this strong sense that up to a quarter of the population can be disenfranchised.

It is unlikely, I think, that any democrat could defend such an outcome. I suppose really hard-line maximizers might be happy with this, just as some utilitarians have professed to be totally indifferent to the distribution of happiness. But the basic principle that everyone should have at least *some* power does seem to be central to democracy. The simple principle that power should be maximized must therefore be rejected. We are thereby forced to conclude that the square-root rule does not solve the problem of weighted voting.

The main reason that I have rejected both Banzhaf's approach and the square-root rule is that neither embodies an acceptable democratic principle: I think that we should reject both the principle of equality of power and the principle of maximization of power. So what principle *should* we adopt?

It seems to me to be clear that we should adopt some combination of these two principles: either a principle of equality subject to maximization constraints or a principle of maximization subject to equality constraints. Perhaps maximizing the total of the worst-off group (Rawls's principle) is an intuitively sound compromise; or perhaps you favour some more complicated trade-off between equality and maximization.[10] In section 24.5 I shall suggest how any such principle can be applied. But first, in the next section, I shall argue that we have the strongest reason to try to avoid the problem by avoiding two-stage aggregation if we possibly can.

24.4—WHY DIRECT DEMOCRACY IS PREFERABLE TO INDIRECT DEMOCRACY

My argument in this section follows from yet another principle that we could adopt when dealing with this sort of a problem. It is a principle which I have already implicitly invoked when rejecting the equality principle, and is *the principle of Pareto Optimality*. This principle, applied to power, states that a set of voting rules (S) is to be preferred to another (T) if in S every individual has at least as much power as that *same* individual has in T, and at least one individual has more power in S than in T.

Notice that this principle does not attempt to trade off one person's gain in power with another's loss, nor does it try to compare two systems which contain different individuals. The Pareto Optimality principle in this form is, indeed, usually taken to be uncontentious but far too weak to come up with any definite solutions to interesting problems, because usually a very large number of different outcomes satisfy it. It is, however, all we need to show that for any indirect democracy (that is, two-stage aggregation process) there exists a direct democracy that is preferable. This argument does not depend on the representative in an indirect system 'usurping' power from the people (although, of course, she might). There is simply less power to go round in any indirect democracy than in a direct one. We can see this by ignoring the representative altogether, and considering an indirect democracy as a two-stage aggregation process (as was done on pp. 187–8), with delegates acting solely as mouthpieces.

Let us assume first that equality has been achieved: that the voters are allocated to groups of exactly equal size, within which they have one vote each, and that each group casts one vote in the final delegate stage. Everybody's power is, then, equal.

Now it is not difficult to see that an individual's power in the two-stage process (measured by his Penrose index) is the product of his power in his group and the power of his delegate.[11] And it is also a well-established result (which is proved in Appendix 4.3) that a voter's Penrose index, in a group with N members who have one vote each, is approximately $\sqrt{\dfrac{2}{\pi N}}$ (provided that N is not very small).

Let there be N voters in all, split into m groups containing n voters apiece, so that mn = N. Then in a direct democracy, each individual's power is $\sqrt{\dfrac{2}{\pi N}}$, since each has one vote in the constituency of the whole. In a two-stage aggregation each voter's power in his *group* is $\sqrt{\dfrac{2}{\pi n}}$, and each delegate's power is $\sqrt{\dfrac{2}{\pi m}}$, since there are m delegates. Each individual's overall power in the two-stage process is then $\sqrt{\dfrac{2}{\pi n}}$ times $\sqrt{\dfrac{2}{\pi m}}$.

If each individual has less power in the two-stage process (as I claim), the loss in power will be given by his power index in the one-stage process minus his power index in the two-stage process; that is, by

$$\sqrt{\frac{2}{\pi N}} - \sqrt{\frac{2}{\pi n}}\sqrt{\frac{2}{\pi m}}$$

But since mn = N this reduces to:

$$\frac{1}{\sqrt{N}}\left(\sqrt{\frac{2}{\pi}} - \frac{2}{\pi}\right) = \frac{0.1613}{\sqrt{N}}$$

There is thus a loss of power associated with indirect democracy. We can get an impression of the magnitude of this loss by expressing it as a proportion of an individual's power in the direct democracy. Dividing the expression for the loss of power by $\sqrt{\frac{2}{\pi N}}$, and simplifying, we see that the proportionate loss in power is $1 - \sqrt{\frac{2}{\pi}}$, which is slightly over 20 per cent.

Thus each individual can expect to lose more than a fifth of his power if the aggregation of votes changes from a direct to an indirect method. By the Pareto Optimality principle a direct democracy is, then, to be preferred to an indirect democracy.

This result is perhaps surprising enough for it to be worth showing how this loss occurs, and demonstrating that it does not represent an uninteresting peculiarity of the Penrose index, but indeed captures something real. This can be shown by considering a simple example. Let there be just nine individuals, and let them be divided into three groups of three for the two-stage voting procedure. In this case we cannot make the square-root approximation to the Penrose index, but from the exact formula (see Appendix 4.3, p. 228) we can calculate that each voter's loss in power is $\frac{35}{128} - \frac{32}{128} = \frac{3}{128}$.[12] We can see how this loss occurs by examining those voting configurations in which the two methods of aggregating votes give different results.

When the voters vote in one large group, a voter has active power if (and only if) the other voters divide 4–4 – his vote is then decisive. When the voters are grouped, he has active power if (and only if) the other groups split 1–1 *and* the other members of his group split 1–1. This can occur when only three others vote for a motion (his group splits 1–1; the others 2–1 and 0–3); it can fail to occur when the others do split 4–4 (his group votes 2–0; the others both 1–2). We can calculate the difference in power of actor i of group I by comparing these different configurations, as in Table 1.[13]

In (a) and (b) i is crucial when votes are aggregated in groups, whilst powerless otherwise, and so gains power when voting is in groups; in (c) and (d) he has no power in his group, and so loses power when votes are grouped. The expected probabilities of these configurations occurring are $\frac{6}{128}$, $\frac{6}{128}$, $\frac{9}{128}$, $\frac{6}{128}$, respectively, giving an expected loss of $\frac{3}{128}$.

We thus see that the power of each individual is less because the probability that anyone will be in a position to bring about his desired outcome is less in an indirect system than in a direct one. Indirect methods of aggregating votes are simply less efficient at satisfying wants than direct methods, and this loss of efficiency is reflected in a loss of power. In so far as one of the objects of democracies is to increase every individual's power over decisions affecting his own life, we must choose direct aggregations of votes in preference to indirect ones.

Table 1—How power is lost

Group	Actor	(a)	(b)	(c)	(d)
	i				
I	j	+	−	+	−
	k	−	+	+	−
		+	+	+	+
II		+	+	−	+
		−	−	−	+
		−	−	+	+
III		−	−	−	−
		−	−	−	−

24.5—HOW TO SOLVE THE PROBLEM OF WEIGHTED VOTING

The first (and best) way of solving the problem of weighted voting, then, is by avoiding it altogether and aggregating the votes directly, as in a plebiscite or referendum. This is always preferable except when there are very strong arguments against simple aggregation. The advocates of *representative* (rather than direct) democracy do have such arguments (or so they claim); but I can see no adequate reason for continuing with institutions like the United States Electoral College, for which these arguments do not apply.

If we decide that we do want a two-tier system of aggregation or voting, in spite of the loss of power involved, then we should endeavour to create (nearly) equal-sized constituencies and give the representatives one vote each. This ensures that all voters have (nearly) equal power, and as much of it as is possible given that each should have some power.

If *this* is impossible or deemed undesirable – because we have natural boundaries of pre-eminent importance which divide the population into unequal-sized groups – then we should adopt a procedure along the following lines. It is long-winded and messy, but at least it ensures that we obtain the outcome we desire.

It is important to realize that we can very rarely obtain the distribution that ideally we would want, even if we care very little about maximization. This is because for any fixed number of groups there is a finite number of possible distributions of the delegates' power between which to choose, whilst there is an infinite number of possible distributions of people between the groups. Therefore there is a vanishingly small probability of being able to allocate power to the delegates so that each voter has the same (non-zero) power, irrespective of the group that he is in.

An example will, as usual, help. Suppose that our voters are divided naturally into just three groups – denoted A, B, C. When the delegates or representatives meet to vote on the final outcome, they can be allocated votes essentially in five (and only five) different ways. Let us suppose (to simplify the discussion) that group A is the largest, and C the smallest, with B in the middle; we then always want to give B's delegate at least as many votes as C's, and A's delegate at least as many as B's. If we express the *votes* allocated to A's delegate (not the power) as $v(A)$, then we require $v(A) \geqslant v(B) \geqslant v(C)$. We can further simplify by requiring that at least a simple majority of the votes cast is required to pass a motion.[14]

Then, however we allocate votes, we will produce one of the five distributions of power shown in Table 2 (where k is the number of votes required for a motion to pass). *Whatever* allocation of votes we choose, one of these five rows will occur; there are no other possibilities. But, further, rows (iv) and (v) are both Pareto-dominated by row (iii); so if we accept the Pareto Optimality principle we would never choose either of these alternatives as desirable. This gives us only three different distributions of power to choose between. If it so happens that the distribution which we want to produce is one of these three, then we're in luck; but if the distribution is any other one at all, then we will be disappointed: we *have* to choose one of these three, and the question is simply which one of them is best.

Table 2—Possible distributions of power with three groups

	Minimal decisive subsets	Other winning subsets	Example A B C k	Penrose index of delegate (×4) A B C
(i)	A	AB, AC, ABC	5 3 1 5	4 0 0
(ii)	AB, AC	ABC	5 3 1 6	3 1 1
(iii)	AB, AC, BC	ABC	1 1 1 2	2 2 2
(iv)	AB	ABC	5 3 1 8	2 2 0
(v)	ABC	–	5 3 1 9	1 1 1

So how do we choose? The first thing we would need to do is to decide on the principle on the basis of which we would choose: fancy mathematics is no good to us if it gives us something we didn't want anyway. I have already suggested that if we want to maximize power, irrespective of distribution, we should adopt the square-root rule; but not if we *do* care about distribution. If we want some trade-off between equality and maximization we need to formulate our principle very carefully, and then proceed slowly, step by step. I do not want to suggest exactly what trade-off we should adopt: I shall first show how to proceed if we adopt Rawls's maximin principle, and then suggest a possible alternative.

Rawls's principle states that "we are to adopt the alternative the worst outcome of which is superior to the worst outcome of the others" (Rawls, 1971: p. 153). Applied to our problem this requires us to select the row in which whoever has least power in that row has more power than whoever has least power in the other rows. We can see at a glance that row (i) can never be acceptable, since in it the delegates from both B and C have no power at all (and hence the individuals in B and C have no power). This leaves only rows (ii) and (iii) left for consideration, for in these every delegate has at least some power.

Rawls's principle (I shall assume) is to be applied to the *members* of the groups, rather than to the delegates; that is, we want to maximize the minimum that any individual achieves. Now we saw in the last section (p. 190) that we can discover an individual's power in a two-stage aggregation by calculating the product of his power in his group and the delegate's power in the second-stage vote. Let us denote the power of any individual in group A by P_A (assuming that everyone has one vote in his group, so that everyone has the same amount of power in that group). The delegates' powers are shown in Table 2. Multiplying these, we can rewrite the last section of Table 2 to show each *individual's* power in rows (ii) and (iii): see Table 3.

Table 3—Penrose index of individual (×4)

	A	B	C
(ii)	$3P_A$	P_B	P_C
(iii)	$2P_A$	$2P_B$	$2P_C$

But it is always the case that the larger the group, the smaller each individual's power in that group is (see pp. 228–9). Therefore it is clear that the people with least power in row (iii) are the members of group A. Members of group A *might* also be the least powerful group in row (ii), if $3P_A < P_B$. In this case row (ii) is clearly to be preferred, since A-members always do worst of the three, and do better in row (ii). When $3P_A > P_B$, then in row (ii) members of group B do worst (members of C never come off worst, since $P_B \leqslant P_C$). Then, we choose between the rows by comparing A's power in row (iii) with B's power in row (ii): A's is less if $2P_A < P_B$ in which case (maximizing the minima) row (ii) is to be chosen.

We therefore should choose row (ii) if either $3P_A < P_B$ or $2P_A < P_B$. But the former inequality is redundant, since it is always more restrictive than the latter one. The criterion of choice is that we choose row (ii) if $2P_A < P_B$, row (iii) if $2P_A > P_B$, and we are indifferent between the rows if $2P_A = P_B$.

Finally, it is shown in Appendix 4.3, and was mentioned in the last section, that, for largish numbers, an individual's power in a group in which everyone has one vote (and a simple majority rule operates) is inversely proportional to the square root of the number of people in the group. Denoting the number of people in group A by a (etc.), we see that row (ii) is to be preferred when $\dfrac{2}{\sqrt{a}} < \dfrac{1}{\sqrt{b}}$, that is, when a > 4b.

So, for three groups, Rawls's principle reduces to a very simple decision rule: give every group's delegate one vote unless the largest group is more than four times the size of the second largest group, in which case allocate votes so that the largest group's delegate and either of the other delegates can pass a motion together, but the two smallest groups' delegates together cannot.

With more than three groups the relevant decision rules start getting far more complicated because the number of real alternatives to decide between increases fairly rapidly – for instance, with four groups there are five alternatives (after the elimination of Pareto-dominated distributions and those giving someone no power at all). With large numbers of groups we would require a lengthy computer programme to calculate the appropriate decision rule. Nevertheless it is possible to do this, and if we are serious about preferring Rawls's principle we should be prepared to take the time to ensure that we are applying it.

But there are reasons for not adopting Rawls's principle since it is not clear that we want to look *solely* at the power of the least well-off group, irrespective of its size. When the largest union at the TUC has 1,600,000 members and the smallest has 16, it seems perverse to allocate votes to delegations by seeking to maximize the power of the sixteen people, thereby largely ignoring the power of $1\frac{1}{2}$ million. In short (in the three-group example) it would seem reasonable to choose row (i) if group A is *very* big compared with groups B and C, even though this deprives some people of power altogether.[15] In the extreme, if B and C have four members each and A has four million members, neither the principle of equality nor the principle of maximization would advocate choosing row (ii) over row (i).

But how big does the biggest group have to be for it justifiably to get complete power? I want to suggest (somewhat tentatively) the *principle of minimizing losses*. The argument for this is as follows.

The democratic ideal is simultaneously to give people equal power and maximize the total amount. This can be achieved by giving everyone one vote and deciding issues by a simple majority. When a two-stage process is adopted there is a considerable loss of power (as I showed in the last section), but *given* that we have a two-stage process the democratic ideal is achieved by having equal-sized groups, giving each person one vote within groups and each group one vote at the second stage. That is the ideal two-stage process, but we have assumed that we *cannot* have equal-sized groups. Then the next best, I suggest, is to adopt the procedure that minimizes the losses that result from the deviation from this ideal.

This principle suggests that we *only* count losses, and that we ignore any gains in power that the deviation from equality might provide. Such gains are added bonuses, as it were, for those fortunate enough to get them; but not of the same order of significance as others' losses. (Minimizing the losses and allowing gains to offset losses is, of course, the same as maximizing the total power.)

So we first calculate the benchmark of the amount of power a voter would have in a two-stage process with equal groups. If there are N voters overall, split into m groups, then each equal-sized group would contain $\frac{N}{m} = n$ voters. Then each individual's power would be the product of his power in a group of that size and his delegate's power with equal voting: that is, P_nP_m. From this we subtract the individual's power under the various different weightings of his delegate's votes. Taking these from Table 3, and adding row (i) back from Table 2, we have Table 4.

Table 4—Loss of power of individual (×4)

Row	A	B	C
(i)	$4P_nP_3 - 4P_A$	$4P_nP_3$	$4P_nP_3$
(ii)	$4P_nP_3 - 3P_A$	$4P_nP_3 - P_B$	$4P_nP_3 - P_C$
(iii)	$4P_nP_3 - 2P_A$	$4P_nP_3 - 2P_B$	$4P_nP_3 - 2P_C$

We want to calculate the total loss of power for each row (ignoring negative losses), and to choose the row with the least loss. To find the *total* loss for each row we have to add up all the individual losses, which gives us (since $P_3 = \frac{1}{2}$)

Total loss in (i): $a(2P_n - 4P_A) + 2bP_n + 2cP_n$
Total loss in (ii): $a(2P_n - 3P_A) + b(2P_n - P_B) + c(2P_n - P_C)$
Total loss in (iii): $a(2P_n - 2P_A) + b(2P_n - 2P_B) + c(2P_n - 2P_C)$

where any number in brackets which is negative is set at zero.

It transpires that row (i) should be chosen, and A's delegate given enough votes to win on her own, when group A is roughly eleven times the size of group B and C together.

The point of this section is not really to persuade you of the merits of my principle of minimizing losses, but to show how, *whatever* principle we choose, we can find the distribution of power that provides the best approximation to that principle. The problem of weighted voting can be solved. It can be solved by being very clear what we are trying to achieve (which principle we are adopting), and then comparing the possible outcomes with our ideal. This is usually a messy procedure, and lengthy; but it does give us whatever we want in the end.[16]

Conclusion to Part IV

In this Part I have tried to show how we can arrive at numerical measures of power, given knowledge of the actors' resources. I hope that I have demonstrated the necessity of carefully working out first what it is that we want to measure, and then using the method appropriate for measuring just that: if we want to know the actors' expected income in bribes (under the equiprobability assumptions) then we need the Shapley–Shubik index; if we want to know who has most power in a legislature we require the EPW index; and if we want to create power in accordance with our normative ideals we should use Penrose's index. If we want to measure power for some other reason, then we may have to create another index.

The approaches described in the last three chapters are rather elementary, and can usefully be extended in a number of directions. Thus we might want to include, under the heading of how to create power equitably, the problem of measuring – and avoiding – gerrymandering. Gerrymandering occurs when voters have equal power-as-ability but systematically unequal power-as-ableness. An approach similar to that of Chapter 24 is required, but replacing the equiprobability assumptions by assessments of likely voting patterns.

A further development in measuring power as ableness would be to look more closely at the different patterns of voting that are likely to occur on various different issues; work out exactly which votes each person is likely to win; and assess the importance of these victories to the actors. This will enable us to produce a measure of interest-satisfaction.

We can, then, measure power, at least when that power is produced by resources that are readily comparable, such as votes. But, as usual, we must be careful how we do so – and we must have an adequate understanding of what the power is that we are trying to measure.

—25—
Epilogue:
understanding concepts

My account of 'power' is now completed. It will have to stand or fall on its own merits; but if it stands up it will provide some support for the more general claim that my approach to the analysis of concepts is the correct one. In this chapter I shall attempt to elucidate the view of concepts that I have arrived at in analysing 'power'.

Probably the best way of describing my position is by contrasting it with two that have been put forward recently: William Connolly's essential contestability thesis and Felix Oppenheim's reconstructionist position. It is my view that both these approaches are wrong, but that each contains one very valuable insight. I shall discuss these two insights in the first two sections of this chapter, then discuss the essential contestability thesis, and finally conclude with a summary of my own approach.

25.1—CONCEPTS AND CONTEXTS

Why do we use the concepts that we do? Concepts are not somehow *given* to us; they are *chosen*; and chosen for a purpose. How they are used depends on this purpose. This is Connolly's insight:

> To describe is to characterize from one or more possible points of view, and the concepts with which we so characterize have the contours they do in part because of the point of view from which they are formed. (Connolly, 1974/1983: p. 23)

All our concepts are in our conceptual vocabulary for some reason, and if we fail to understand what this reason is we will miss their point.

And this is what Oppenheim does in his *Political Concepts*. He wants to "construct a language of political inquiry that could be used by all political scientists regardless of their ethical or ideological views" and regardless of whether they are trying to attack, defend, describe or explain existing power structures (Oppenheim, 1981: p. 152). Oppenheim thinks that those who have different moral points of view need a definition of 'power' that is acceptable to all, whatever their point of view, so that they can communicate with each other (p. 157). He therefore fails to ask what reasons we have for talking about power – what the point of the term is – and as a result his whole discussion takes place in a vacuum: it is literally point-less. I think that this is why his book is both so arid and so full of unsupported dogmatic assertions. It is not a fruitful method of "construct[ing] a language" to deliberately avoid considering the reasons we want the language, and what the sort of things are that we want to say in it.

Indeed, it is not a fruitful method of constructing *anything* to proceed in ignorance of what the thing is supposed to be for. If we want to choose (or construct) a knife we want to know whether it is to slice bread or spread butter with. People use knives for different reasons, and what knife-makers do *not* do is come up with some neutral, all-purpose knife that is allegedly acceptable to all would-be knife users. The same applies to constructing a language. Oppenheim's approach, far from providing a language in which people with different interests can communicate, destroys communication. For, like knife-makers, we need to discover what people use language for, and then create a vocabulary of specialized terms, each one of which is the one best suited for each task. That is what I have tried to do in this book.

25.2—THE DESCRIPTIVE AND THE NORMATIVE

In the last section I endorsed Connolly's view that we choose to describe things by certain criteria because of our belief in the importance of these criteria, and that these beliefs are often moral ones. But this view does not commit us to the quite different view that descriptive and normative elements are inextricably intertwined within the terms we use. Here I side firmly with Oppenheim: philosophical analysis should always aim to separate the normative from the descriptive.

It is of course true that in ordinary speech descriptive words often carry normative implications, for it would be incredibly tedious to be restricted to separate descriptive and normative vocabularies, so that each time we used a descriptive term we had to attach to it an appropriate normative qualifier. We are normally lazy, and develop linguistic habits that reflect this – habits which usually do no harm, and, indeed, produce the richness that is in our language. But when confusion *is* created, one of the first steps should be to disentangle the different ideas lumped together under one term, and see to what extent the dispute is engendered by the disputants simply talking at cross-purposes.

The use of descriptive concepts in normative contexts should not be allowed to cause problems: there is nothing evaluative in the concept of oxygen, even though I most certainly prefer the air I breathe to contain it. Similarly, even if we have very strong views on what the distribution of power in a society ought to be, this does not make the concept normative. We first have to establish the existence and distribution of power within a society – that is, provide a description of it – before praising or condemning it for conforming to our hopes or fears. Thus the (normative) job of sorting out what the world ought to be like is different from the (descriptive) job of seeing what the world *is* like.

This conclusion does not contradict the point made in the last section, and I find it odd that anyone should think it did. Perhaps an example will help. Suppose you disagree with somebody about whether to condemn some country or regime for its persecution of racial minorities. Then there are two completely different things you could be disagreeing about. You could be disagreeing about what is to *count* as persecuting a racial minority; or you could agree about that, and be disagreeing about whether this persecution does, as a matter of fact, go on. Now 'persecution' is clearly an evaluative term: there is something linguistically odd about asserting that a lot of persecuting is going on and all the better for it. But it also has a descriptive content. One can rephrase the claim that persecution is occurring into the two statements that treatment of a certain sort is happening and that that treatment is to be condemned. If the speaker *cannot* rephrase the claim like this, then that shows that it is false or empty: the speaker has to have *some* descriptive content in mind when using the term 'persecution', otherwise he is just saying that he condemns the society for no reason at all. Sometimes our language does run away with us like this, and we use terms like 'persecuting' carelessly, because they are more impressive than purely evaluative terms in that they combine condemnatory feeling with a descriptive basis for this feeling. But, as philosophers, we should be careful not to use language carelessly.

In short, there just is a logical difference between saying that in South Africa black people were frequently arbitrarily arrested and deported to a 'homeland' they had never seen, and saying that such treatment is wrong – even though we wouldn't bother to say the former unless we thought it *was* wrong (or perhaps had some other compelling reason for making the point), and even though we can, if we wish, combine both statements by saying that black people were persecuted. Philosophical analysis consists precisely in unpacking the logically separate claims that are boxed together into a sentence. To do this unpacking properly we need to sort the claims out into descriptive ones and normative ones, since each sort is rebutted and supported in completely different ways.

Connolly rejects the familiar distinction between normative and descriptive in favour of his essential contestability thesis: which is that concepts like 'power' give rise to interminable conceptual debates that we have reasonable grounds to believe will persist. I think that this thesis is quite misguided – indeed, incoherent. It is philosophically wrong, and hence is politically dangerous. (This is relevant since one of its alleged advantages is that it is politically radical. It is not. If anything it is conservative, since conservatism is always helped by muddled thinking; real radicalism requires clarity.)

Even at first glance the essential contestability argument appears suspect. I consider that the object of philosophical analysis is to solve conceptual conundrums; to resolve disputes; not merely to explain how they arise. To say that disputes about a term like 'power' are inevitable is not to advance our understanding very far; it amounts to either a dereliction of philosophical duty or an admission of failure. For the conclusion that there are philosophical disputes which cannot be rationally resolved is one which should be reached with the greatest reluctance: every conceivable attempt at reaching a solution needs to be tried before the hunt can be finally abandoned. The onus of proof, in short, lies firmly on the shoulders of those who advance the essential contestability thesis.

I do not think that the case for the essential contestability thesis can be made out. Indeed, I think it is false, and can be shown to be so; any apparent plausibility it has is gained by blurring a crucial distinction: between a *concept* and a *word*.

25.3—CONCEPTS AND WORDS

Connolly uses the three words 'concept', 'word' and 'term' interchangeably; but this is an elementary mistake. If I mispronounce a word I don't thereby mispronounce a concept; someone can think in concepts of which they are unaware (for instance, liberal individualism or romantic love), whilst one cannot think in *words* of which one is unaware. Concepts and words occupy different logical categories: words are the symbols that we use to refer to concepts.

Often one word does service for many concepts. Then the argument could arise of which concept the word is representing in a given instance. But this is not a conceptual dispute, *about* concepts; it is a verbal one. If the person who used the word were around we could ask him which concept he meant, and, if he remembers and was thinking straight at the time, he could now tell us. If he cannot tell us, then there is a fair chance that he was muddled at the time, and did not quite know what he was trying to say – an all too frequent occurrence for each of us, alas.

Connolly's discussion of essential contestability cries out for a distinction between concepts and words. For instance, there is supposedly something called a "cluster concept" (Connolly, 1974/1983: p. 14). 'Politics' is a cluster concept because "to call something 'political' or part of 'politics' might include reference" to eight (or more) different "dimensions", "criteria" – or "concepts" (pp. 12–14).

> Radicals . . . are prone to call certain corporate decisions political because these practices are thought to conform to items 2, 3, 4, and 6, whilst their opponents resist these efforts on the grounds that . . . the more important criteria [are] 1, 5, 7, and 8. (Connolly, 1974/1983: p. 14)

It should be crystal clear from this sentence that Connolly is considering the usage of the *word* 'political', which he thinks is used by radicals and their opponents to refer to different concepts. These eight concepts (or criteria) are vaguely expressed but are quite distinct, and are taken as being sufficiently unambiguous that we can recognize that they *are* quite distinct. How much clearer to say that 'politics' is a word that is used to refer to a range of different concepts!

We can then realize how empty the disagreement is that Connolly erects between radicals and others. Unlike Christmas presents, concepts do not come with detachable labels that can somehow get muddled up, giving rise to endless disputes about which label should be attached to which conceptual package. The label is supposed to help us to locate the appropriate concepts: if it does not do this, then it should be scrapped and replaced by one that does the job efficiently. Which label is used is arbitrary – a matter of convenience. It is not something worth arguing over; and certainly not the basis of an important philosophical thesis.

However, this sort of argument is sometimes not quite empty, but rather more sinister. Words sometimes take on a life of their own: they gather a penumbra of emotive overtones around them. Words like 'violence', 'freedom' and 'democracy' are now like this. If you can somehow redefine them so that they do your bidding, you have gained a big advantage over your opponent. That is, if you can attach to yourself the words with a positive aura and to your opponent the words with a negative aura, you are half-way to winning the argument before you even start it. This is what Stevenson (1944: p. 210) called a "persuasive definition", and it

seems to be what Connolly has in mind when he advocates "new concepts" built "upon old and familiar ideas", and considers that pushing
for one's own position on a contested concept is to engage in politics
(Connolly, 1974/1983: pp. 203, 205; and 1983: p. 227). To use Connolly's own
example, if you can extend the notion of racism to include 'institutional racism' you have thereby "shifted the burden of evidence away
from the blacks and towards the elites, and thus the balance of political
pressures has shifted perceptibly too" because "all those who do not remain
(or do not want to be considered) old-fashioned racists" have to prove that
they are not party to institutional racism either (Connolly, 1974/1983:
p. 202).

This is a neat political trick, and one which radicals should be aware of
– if only because those who have the power *really* to manipulate language
like this tend to be far from radical. But such tricks have absolutely nothing
to do with philosophy and absolutely nothing to do with sorting out
concepts. There is no doubt that institutional and old-fashioned racism
are different concepts; that Connolly's "militant black activists" do not
like either; and that they can save themselves the trouble of showing
exactly what is wrong with 'institutional racism' if they can label it so
that it seems like another sort of old-fashioned racism. This is a move
that only a dishonest philosopher should applaud. If there *is* something
wrong with 'institutional racism' (and I agree with Connolly that there is)
then this can be shown by reasoned argument, rather than by linguistic
sleight-of-hand.[1]

25.4—CONCEPTUAL ANALYSIS

Concepts and words are, then, different things and need to be discussed in
quite different ways. And it is (at best) quite senseless to argue about
what *the* concept is that a word refers to. In this book I have tried to show
that we use the word 'power' to refer to a large number of different concepts, and that we do not get anywhere by asking which of these is *the*
"concept of power". Looking at words – at their usages, definitions and
derivations – can help us to get a start, because they show us the sorts of
concepts that we are interested in. But once we have started, and have got
down to discussing the concepts themselves, then facts at the verbal level
are no longer a help. Hence the method I have adopted in this book. Part
I looked at words and ordinary language, in order to see what sorts of things
people are bothered about when they talk of power, and what sort of
concepts are involved; Part II consisted of a detailed examination of these

concepts; and Parts III and IV considered ways of studying and measuring that which is denoted by these concepts.

My approach stems from the belief that concepts are like tools, that we use them to do certain jobs, and that we need to choose the concepts that are as suitable as possible for the job that we intend them to do. This approach helps us to dissolve many disagreements between users of 'power', and to bring other disagreements into clearer focus. Briefly, disagreements may be of three kinds.

The first, and most trivial, sort of disagreement is that people can be simply interested in different things. In this book I have distinguished between three different contexts, and within each context there are differing emphases. The CIA don't want to know the sorts of things about a society that a fervent democrat, worried about the society's practices, does. One wants to intervene; the other wants to evaluate. It will not be surprising if the CIA analyst and the democratic ideologue will employ slightly different concepts to achieve their differing ends.

Thus it should be clear that I certainly do not want "to save philosophy from political engagement by endowing it with a neutral method to adjudicate between competing perspectives", as Connolly thinks contemporary analytical philosophy seeks to do (Connolly, 1983: p. 221). I have not tried to adjudicate between competing perspectives, but rather the opposite: I have tried to show that some arguments ostensibly about power (or about 'power') are really arguments between competing perspectives. The CIA analyst and the democrat do not disagree about the distribution of power: they have such different perspectives that they never reach the point of disagreement. More subtly, the utilitarian celebrating the amount of power to satisfy wants is not disagreeing with the romantic bemoaning the lack of power for self-development. What sort of power we should concentrate on is not for me to say here: that depends on which of the many competing perspectives we should adopt. And deciding *that* involves an exercise of quite a different sort from the one that I have been engaging in in this book. That exercise is however helped no end by realizing that the different perspectives are not fighting over a single concept of 'power'; they are employing different concepts. When we have worked out which concepts are appropriate to each perspective, then we are in a position to start choosing between the perspectives. We can scarcely do this when we don't know what a key term in the perspective's vocabulary is supposed to mean.

The second kind of disagreement is about concepts themselves. Much of this book is concerned with an analysis of concepts: trying to explore their logic. Often this consists in drawing distinctions; sometimes in suggesting that a possible one is a distinction without a difference. Thus in section 8.3 I drew a distinction between actual powers and latent powers, but argued that this distinction only holds when the powers are generic, not when they are time-specific. Conceptual points like this are crucial for straight thinking.

The third sort of problem which might seem to arise involves the relationship between the previous two kinds. Given that we agree what we want to investigate; given that we agree on the concepts available; which ones do we use? But this is just not a problem. In formulating exactly what it is that we want to investigate we will have used concepts – and these are then the concepts to apply. If the formulation of the problem is vague, then we need to go back and reformulate it more exactly. This is why it is so important that we understand *clearly* what we are trying to say.

Conceptual disputes are thus only of the second kind. I do not believe that there are unresolvable conceptual disputes; I believe that with a lot of hard thinking we can get the logic of our concepts sorted out. I hope that I have shown how this can be done – or, at least, commenced – with concepts of power. So I cannot shrug off criticism of my analysis by saying that it all depends on one's point of view, and this happens to be mine. My analysis is open to criticism; and if it can be shown that I have made mistakes then I will have to alter or withdraw the analysis. That, I believe, is how philosophical analysis should proceed. And this admission of vulnerability perhaps provides a suitable note on which to end.

—*Appendix 1*—
The redundancy argument rejected

Abilities, in my vocabulary, are those (peculiarly human) powers that differ from ordinary dispositionals in that (in suitable conditions) they are exercisable by the powerholder at will (see section 4.3). But recently several different and influential schools of thought have attempted to deny any use at all for such a concept, since it assumes that people do have wills and exercise real choices – are, in a word, autonomous. B. F. Skinner, for one, has argued strongly against such a notion, claiming that "Autonomous man serves to explain only the things we are not yet able to explain in other ways. His existence depends upon our ignorance, and he naturally loses status as we come to know more about behaviour" (Skinner, 1972: p. 20). Likewise Poulantzas and his followers have poured scorn on those of us who cling to the "humanist problematic of the subject" instead of seeing people as "bearers" of an "objective system of regular connections" (e.g. Poulantzas, 1969: p. 295). Both behaviourist and structuralist would agree that it is the goal of scientific practice to reduce contingency through further specification of particular theories, or their replacement with more determinate theoretical systems, and that something is contingent when it is unpredictable in the terms of a specific theoretical system.[1] They require, then, a theoretical explanation of human choices, not ideological assertions about free will and moral responsibility. And when we perceive the world in that "scientific problematic" in which people do not make choices, there is clearly no room for any concept that relies on their choices. My concept of power-as-ability, then, becomes unacceptable.

Perhaps the same point can be put another way. It would seem to make as little sense to say "Although I know that she would never do X, nevertheless she *could* have done so, and therefore she has the power to do so" as it does to say "Although I know that this lead weight would never float up to the ceiling, nevertheless it *could* have done so, and therefore it has the power to do so". Lead weights do not have the power to defy gravity, but why should we treat psychological (and other) generalizations, that are backed by evidence and tell us what people will do, any differently from physical generalizations that are backed by evidence and tell us what objects will do? It would seem that, as we obtain greater knowledge about the social and psychological worlds we inhabit, concepts of ability occupy an ever contracting space until they drop out altogether.

I shall call this argument (in its various forms) the Redundancy Argument. I think that it is fallacious; and I think that in showing this I can show how power-as-ability is useful in the contexts that I described in Chapter 6. I also think that this helps show why these are probably the *only* contexts that employ this concept.

The Redundancy Argument depends on the possibility that we can, in principle, obtain knowledge of what people will do. Now there are, very schematically, two sorts of ways in which we may know what events happen (will happen, etc.). We may know what happens because, simply, we were there: we have the evidence of our senses. Or – an alternative form of this first sort – we may have reliable second-hand evidence: we may know what happened because we read about it in a book, or saw a film of it, which we have very good grounds for believing. Such knowledge might cover the future as well as the past: we may time-travel, or we may bump across a book of our life that tells us, in minute detail, everything that has happened and will happen to us, and is so accurate on those points which we can check that we have great faith in those parts which we cannot check.[2] Our knowledge of *our* lives is of this sort, except that we only have knowledge of the past (and present).

Secondly, we may know (inductively) what social, psychological (etc.) laws hold in our world, and thus work out from them what happens (in the standard Hempellian way). This would give us more complete knowledge since we would not only know what has happened and what will happen, but we would know the truth of counterfactuals: what would have happened if some change had been made (if Hitler had invaded England in 1940 . . .).

But we must look somewhat closer at what believing in a psychological law involves. A scientific law is a human construct: we do not discover laws (as we discover objects), but we infer to them from evidence. If we claim that we know a scientific law we assert that we believe that this law will hold in the future; asserting a law involves believing that certain counterfactuals are true. Psychological laws can be divided into two kinds – which I shall call weak and strong – depending on what sort of counterfactual they are intended to sustain. A weak psychological law tells us what sorts of *choices* a person will make; such a law does not deny that she can (in an important sense of 'can') choose something else. Strong psychological laws relate to phobias and the like, and these *do* deny that the subject can choose otherwise.

When we assert a weak psychological law we do not intend to rule out the possibility of it being broken. It predicts an agent's choices and the very fact that it is a *choice* that is predicted necessarily implies that the agent could choose otherwise. (For that is what making a choice *means*: one cannot make a choice which of only one alternative to have.) That is, you might believe, on the basis of very good evidence, that something will occur – that I will choose to drink a cup of coffee within the next five hours – without intending to imply that I can do nothing to prevent this, that it will happen no matter what.

Strong psychological laws, on the other hand, *are* intended to carry this implication. When we describe someone as an agoraphobic we mean that she *cannot* go into open spaces: not that it just happens that she doesn't like them and so doesn't go in them, but that she *cannot* go in them. In this, strong psychological laws are like physical laws: the agoraphobic cannot choose to go into open spaces, just as the lead cannot soar into the air.

Now I believe there are limitations on the amount of such knowledge we can have. Whether we have the knowledge in the form of strong laws or observations of the future does not matter, so I shall choose a graphic science-fiction example to illustrate my case.

Suppose I time-travel to this time next week. I see myself board a train to go and give a lecture in another university. Twenty minutes later I see the train crash and I see myself killed. (Or I read this description in the book of my life; a book which, remember, has proved so accurate that I cannot but believe it.) I return from this journey in time rather upset; a week later I face the prospect of going to give the lecture, and wonder what I should do.[3] I am faced with two incompatible beliefs: beliefs both of which I hold very strongly indeed. I believe that I know what will happen in the future: I will catch the 10.30 train and be killed. But I do not want to be killed, and if I can manage not to catch that train I will not be killed when it crashes. And I also believe that it is up to me whether I catch that train or not: it is a matter solely of *my* choice.

If I argue rationally, I think that I will catch the train.[4] If I reject the belief that I time-travelled – I put it down to a hallucination – then I will catch the most convenient train, which is the 10.30. If I *do* believe that I saw the future (not *a* future, but *the* future) then I must believe that I will catch the 10.30. It is senseless to argue that, since I saw the 10.30 with me on it crash, I will not catch the 10.30 – for if I do not catch the train what I saw was not my future. If I stay at home because I expect the 10.30 to crash, then whether it crashes or not what I saw was not the future as it actually happened. Thus if one believes one saw the future, one must believe that one is *fated* to catch the train and die; if one does not believe one saw the future there is no reason to miss the train and inconvenience oneself. Either way, I will catch the train.

I cannot believe both that I have a choice whether to catch the train, and that the train will crash with me on it. (Keeping the background assumption that at no time do I want to be killed in a train crash.) For if I believe that the train will crash with me on it, then I believe that I will catch the train; but I would not *choose* to catch a train that I knew was going to crash (not, at any rate, for so trivial a reason as giving a lecture; and when other trains were available earlier in the day). So if I caught the train believing it was going to crash I must have caught it not through my choice. Since I presumably was not physically dragged there by anybody, I must conclude that I do not have a free choice on the matter: that somehow I am a puppet on invisible strings or a lifelike robot. It is not just that my choice was *predictable*; it is that I have no choice at all.

I cannot conceive what it would be like to consider a future (even a short one) in which I felt unable to make choices. I therefore think that I would choose to disbelieve that I had knowledge of the future: I would consider that my time-travelling was really a hallucination, or that the book of my life was some elaborate and extraordinarily good hoax.[5] Of course, I might really be a well-disguised automaton and not an agent; but I cannot see how I could *believe* I was such a robot.

So I maintain, at the end of all this, that a belief that I will know my own future is untenable.

If I do not believe that my actions are foreordained, then I am interested in my own abilities. For when I want to know what to do I want to know what I can bring about: if I cannot bring about something then I will not try. If I have perfect knowledge of my powers then I will know exactly what things I can bring about. This is obviously very important knowledge, the sort of thing we are constantly asking ourselves: it is the knowledge on which we base our choices. And (to repeat) each of us must think that he makes choices, even if maybe no one else does.

So the first area where the Redundancy Argument fails is in the practical context when we ask "what can *I* do?"

The difficulties that I have been describing do not arise if I see *your* future. There is no tension between believing that I know what you will do and believing that you are an autonomous agent, since just because I see what you do (whether in the future or in the past) does not mean that you could not have chosen to do some-thing else. So Skinner, if he is to remove the notion of autonomous agents from our conceptual vocabulary, must believe that we can obtain what I have called *strong* laws governing human behaviour – *all* human behaviour.

Such a claim seems extremely implausible. The claim is not that we do what we choose to do and this choice is predictable; it is that we never, ever, make any choices at all. It would mean that all of us, all the time, were suffering from phobias such that we could not but do whatever we do do. But we normally think of phobias, and the like, as exceptional states, so that people who suffer from them are different from the rest of us. And even Skinner – when he was being a psychotherapist rather than a philosopher – tried to *cure* people of their phobias, so that they could, for instance, go into public places *when they wanted to*.

As I have already declared, I think that I make choices. I also think that I am not particularly special in this: I think that you do, too. So I think that we will never obtain a comprehensive set of strong psychological laws; we are each of us doomed to making many choices in our lives.

The result of this is that we can still use counterfactual moral reasoning. Because something occurs it does not follow that it could not have been prevented. Because I can *predict* that you will kill your next-door neighbour (or because I saw you do it) does not mean that you are (or were) *forced* to do so. The principle 'ought implies can' restricts blame to actors whose acts (and omissions) could have been different. Skinner, of course, would deny any point in blaming and punishing people for things they have done; but his argument here is a practical and moral one, not a logical one. There is still room for those who wish to censure people to do so, and to ask, before they do so, whether the accused could have acted differently. For this they will need concepts of power-as-ability. This is the second context in which we need such concepts – the moral context, in which we ask whether someone could have prevented some disaster.

The evaluative context, in a sense, presupposes that we do have a practical interest in our own powers, as I have argued here that we do. If we do, then we will want as wide a range of powers as possible, and we will criticize social set-ups in which our powers are limited. Since we can change the extent and distribution of powers by changing the social system, we are interested in evaluating the social system to see if it *should* be changed. This is the evaluative context.[6]

Thus all the three contexts I distinguished in Chapter 6 arise even when we have theoretical or observational knowledge that allows us to predict everybody's choices. But currently, of course, we lack such knowledge, and there are no signs that we will obtain it in our lifetimes. This ignorance gives us another reason why we are interested in people's powers: if we do not know what they *will* do, it may be useful to know what they *can* do. In fact, it is useful in three distinct ways, two within the practical context and one in the moral context.

In our practical life we often want to know what people will do, so that we can plan our lives around them as comfortably as possible. We also want to know how they will react to various possible actions of ours. If we can't predict their choices, it may be some consolation to know that if they can't do something then they won't do it.[7]

Confusion has often crept in here, since there are some things that people could do but we know they will not. Since our main interest here is in what people will do, we tend to dismiss powers that people will not exercise as of no interest to us. But this does not mean that people *lack* the power to do things they will not do. Stanley Benn has put this well:

> If Jones tells us that Smith has the power to carry ten pounds weight of stones in his pockets to and from work each day, our reaction is an incredulous "But why should he want to?" But that is not to say, with Hobbes, that power is conditional upon will [that is, that if Smith does not will to do it he thereby lacks the power to do it]; rather that the only interesting powers are the ones that someone might conceivably exercise, and that we are puzzled to know the point of attributing any others. (Benn, 1972: p. 207)

Knowing people's powers may, then, be a useful stand-in for being able to predict their actions. For instance, one of the advantages of not living in a police state or under an absolute tyrant is that you can be fairly sure that you will not be arbitrarily arrested and incarcerated for years – and because no one *can* do this to you, not because you accurately predict that at the moment no one *wants* to do this. Such safeguards are indeed very important for our peace of mind.

That is one concern with power. But we also want to know what people can be persuaded (or bribed) to do for us. We again want to know what they *will* do (if persuaded), not what they could do but might choose not to. But, as a first step in our calculations, it is certainly helpful to sort people out into those who can bring about whatever interests us and those who cannot; that way we will not waste time trying to persuade the wrong people.[8]

Thirdly, there is the concern with alibis. This is similar to the previous cases, but about the past. I know someone robbed the bank, but I do not know if it was you who did; if I know that you could not have done, then I can eliminate you from my inquiries.

So we can see how all the reasons for using concepts of power which I described in Chapter 6 arise.

Yet the Redundancy Argument does show that power-as-ability will not appear in any ideal predictive theory, since we will want to predict (if possible) what people *will* do rather than what they have the *power* to do. So we can see why those who – like Skinner and Poulantzas – view the job of the social sciences as prophesying the future have no time for concepts of power. Compared with Poulantzas's grand project of understanding how capitalism reproduces itself, my concerns in this book may seem rather trivial. But each must plough his own furrow. Just because 'power' is of no use in Poulantzas's project, does not mean it might not have other uses. (And conversely, just because it is of importance in other areas does not mean that Poulantzas must have to find a use for it.) If you are prepared to accept our everyday "humanist problematic of the subject", you will be able to find plenty of important work for my notion of power-as-ability.

—Appendix 2—
David Lewis and
his amazing possible worlds

In this appendix I sketch the reason why I prefer a suppositionist approach to counterfactuals to a possible worlds approach.[1]

The advantage of a suppositionist account is that it allows us to have *isolated
beliefs*,[2] which can be counterfactualized without requiring any change at all in our
other beliefs, and which are therefore not ambiguous. More important, some beliefs
can be treated *as if* they were isolated. When we consider a counterfactual claim
made with a certain purpose, we can simply ignore knowledge that we have that is
not relevant to that purpose. If we are interested in a counterfactual claim about
the way that the European economy would have developed without the coloniza-
tion of Africa, we can simply suppose that the continent of Africa never existed,
even though we know full well that the earth cannot just have a hole in it (and that
the consequential geological changes would have completely altered the shape of
Europe anyway).[3]

Yet possible worlds cannot be treated piecemeal like this. Possible worlds, like
real worlds, cannot contain contradictions. To some this seems an advantage; but to
me it seems unnecessary. I also think it can be misleading. If we are to consider the
set of nearest possible worlds to ours in which the European economy did not have
access to the resources of Africa, we clearly cannot include a world like ours but
with a whole continent removed. That world, whilst possible, is not like ours at all.
Yet, for the purposes of this counterfactual supposition, it might be the most appropriate "world" to consider. Even more appropriate is the completely *im*possible
world of our earth with a hole in it.

The possible-worlds people would reject this, and their main reason for doing so
is that for them a suppositionist approach has a grave drawback: it does not allow us
to call counterfactual statements true or false. On the suppositionist view, counterfactuals can be more or less justified, they can be sensible or stupid, but they cannot
be *true or false*. The possible-worlds people consider that this is not good enough: all
other statements are true or false; counterfactuals should be, too. Whilst an account
like Rescher's is very much along the right lines, they say, we need to go beyond it:

> Now that we have found an answer to the question 'How do we decide whether
> or not we believe a conditional statement?' the problem is to make the transi-

tion from belief conditions to truth conditions; that is, to find a set of truth conditions for statements having conditional form which explains why we use the method we do to evaluate them. The concept of a *possible world* is just what we need to make this transition, since a possible world is the ontological analogue of a stock of hypothetical beliefs. (Stalnaker, 1968: p. 169)

David Lewis's ontological commitments are even stronger:

> I believe there are possible worlds other than the one we happen to inhabit. If an argument is wanted, it is this. It is uncontroversially true that things might be otherwise than they are. I believe, and so do you, that things could have been different in countless ways. But what does this mean? Ordinary language permits the paraphrase: there are many ways things could have been besides the way they actually are. On the face of it, this sentence is an existential quantification. It says that there exist many entities of a certain description, to wit 'ways things could have been'. I believe that things could have been different in countless ways; I believe permissible paraphrases of what I believe; taking the paraphrase at its face value, I therefore believe in the existence of entities that might be called 'ways things could have been'. I prefer to call them 'possible worlds'. . . .
>
> I emphatically do not identify possible worlds in any way with respectable linguistic entities; I take them to be respectable entities in their own right. When I profess realism about possible worlds, I mean to be taken literally. (Lewis, 1973: pp. 84–5)

I see no necessity to take the paraphrase at its face value; indeed, most of the progress of recent philosophy has consisted in *not* taking the ontological commitments of ordinary language literally. Lewis Carroll, over a hundred years ago, satirized brilliantly the absurdities involved in drawing ontological commitments from common usage:

> "Who did you pass on the road?" the King went on . . .
> "Nobody," said the Messenger.
> "Quite right," said the King: "this young lady saw him too. So of course Nobody walks slower than you."
> "I do my best," the Messenger said in a sullen tone. "I'm sure nobody walks much faster than I do!"
> "He can't do that," said the King, "or else he'd have been here first." (Carroll, 1871: pp. 281–2)

Lewis seems to take his notion of a possible world so literally that he almost seems to be saying sometimes that we determine the truth-value of a counterfactual by establishing the possible world to which it refers, and then going to this world and seeing if it holds. But, however much science-fiction we read, it is *logically* impossible for any of us to go to any other world; as Lewis is quite aware, we are forever doomed to exist in the world we do exist in, and only that world. We can daydream of other worlds; but that is not the same as travelling to them.

> If worlds were creatures of my imagination, I could imagine them to be any way I liked, and I could tell you all you wish to hear simply by carrying on my imaginative creation. But as I believe that there really are other worlds, I am entitled to confess that there is much about them that I do not know, *and that I do not know how to find out*. (Lewis, 1973: p. 88; my emphasis)

But if I do not know how to find out whether something is true in another world, how does this other world help us? *All* the evidence we can possibly possess is obtained from this world, sorted and classified in this world, and then transported into a fictional other-world, which we then construct as best we can. This is how I read the account if it is to make any sense at all. And this is little different from Rescher's approach, except introducing the (possibly heuristically useful) dramatic metaphor of a possible world.

I do not see how we can accept the real existence of possible worlds. Yet if we do not, we cannot use possible worlds to make counterfactuals true or false: they remain merely assertable or not assertable. I do not myself see this as a problem: in the social sciences the best we can ever do is determine whether a statement can justifiably be asserted. Truth, as opposed to justifiable belief, remains always beyond our grasp.

For these reasons, whilst I admire the brilliance with which Lewis executes his project, I cannot accept that his account is an improvement on the suppositionist approach developed in the text. So, when *I* use the words "possible world", I do so merely as a metaphor, without any ontological commitments. I think that when we assert a counterfactual we do not invite the listener to embark on a trip to another world; we play Alice's favourite game – "let's pretend".

—*Appendix 3*—
Jon Elster on counterfactuals

The discussion of counterfactuals by Jon Elster is by a long way the best and most acute in the social sciences.[1] It is full of penetrating insights, and the general approach seems to me to be very much along the right lines. Yet it also contains several small but important mistakes, which I shall try to point out in this appendix. This is a worthwhile task in itself, precisely because Elster's account is the best there is. I also hope that in this appendix I show the worth of my own discussion of these issues in this book.

Elster constructs what he calls a "basic paradox" of counterfactuals. In section 1 of this appendix I argue that this "basic paradox" is neither basic nor paradoxical. In section 2 I discuss an example of Elster's that he thinks illustrates the basic paradox; I argue that it in fact illustrates something else, and I suggest why Elster's analysis is wrong – from which follows an important conclusion about power. Finally, I look at another of Elster's examples; again I suggest that his account of it is wrong; and I use this to make a further point about the nature of the counterfactuals sometimes involved in discussing power.

This appendix is, then, consistently critical – although also, I hope, constructive. I would, nevertheless, like to reiterate my genuine admiration for Elster's work, which is simply streets ahead of that of everybody else.

A3.1—THE BASIC PARADOX OF COUNTERFACTUALS

Elster's "basic paradox of counterfactuals" runs as follows.[2] To evaluate a counterfactual we need a theory that tells us whether the consequent would indeed occur given the antecedent; to be any use this theory must be as strong as possible; but if it is any good as a theory it will also tell us that the antecedent is impossible, and hence tell us to dismiss the counterfactual as absurd. The problem is that the *same* theory has two roles:

> [it] permits us to conclude from the hypothetical antecedent to the hypothetical consequent, [and] it also serves as a filter for the acceptance or the rejection of

the antecedent itself. . . . The stronger (i.e. the more deterministic) the theory, the better grounded is the conclusion from antecedent to consequent, but the more vulnerable is also the legitimacy of the antecedent. (Elster, 1978: p. 184)

The point may be brought out more clearly by an analysis of the famous counterfactual put forward by Fogel that if the railroads had not been invented, this would not [have] had any large impact upon the development of the GNP of the United States in the nineteenth century. In order to determine the truth of the consequent (given the antecedent) we should have to know (among other things) if the internal combustion engine would have been invented earlier; in order to answer this question we should need a theory linking socioeconomic conditions to technological change, but this theory might very well have the unhappy side effect of being incompatible with the antecedent, so that the question can be put legitimately only if it cannot be answered. This delicate balance needed for a successful counterfactual – we must assume sufficient theoretical knowledge to permit us to determine the truth value of the consequent, but not so much as to endanger the legitimacy of the antecedent – constitutes a major unresolved problem in the logic of the social sciences. (Elster, 1976: p. 254)[3]

But this paradox cannot be *basic* to counterfactuals, since it arises, even on Elster's account, only in special circumstances – when the *same* theory plays the two roles he mentions. Such situations are rarer than Elster seems to realize, and Fogel's counterfactual is not one of them.

Fogel's concern was to evaluate "the proposition that railroads were indispensable to American economic growth during the nineteenth century" (Fogel, 1964: p. vii), which involves asking, counterfactually, what would have happened if the railroads had not (been) developed. But Elster's version of this counterfactual's antecedent – "if the railroads had not been *invented*" – is itself an invention by Elster: Fogel never even mentions the possibility that it was because they remained uninvented that the railroads were not developed. Instead he throws out a few reasons why railroads might have remained insignificant – for instance "that the sparks thrown off by belching engines would set fire to buildings and fields" (Fogel, 1964: p. 2) – all of which were reasons suggested by the railroad's early critics, *after* its invention.

It is only by distorting Fogel's counterfactual so that its antecedent is about inventions that Elster can use it to illustrate his paradox. But Fogel's real counterfactual contradicts only an isolated belief (that the railroads developed in the nineteenth century), and so we can happily suppose its antecedent true. If asked to explain how this could have come about, all we need to do is exercise our imagination. We may suppose, for instance, that when the first railroad was opened some local preacher described trains as the transport of the devil; that the first train crashed with great loss of life; and that consequently there was a total rejection of this diabolical form of transport.[4] (This example is not even particularly far-fetched. I have heard it authoritatively argued that powered lighter-than-air balloons were a viable form of transport a century later, but that the great publicity given to the crashes of the Hindenburg and the R101 effectively ended their development.) Once we suppose that the railroads did not catch on – for whatever irrelevant reason – we can ask what then *would* have happened. This will probably require a theory about inventions and technological change; but this is the sole role that such a theory plays in considering Fogel's counterfactual.

It is, indeed, not surprising that it is unusual for one theory to play the double role Elster mentions. For there is something absurd or pointless – not paradoxical – in asserting a counterfactual that requires a theory that itself invalidates the hypothetical antecedent. When we catch ourselves doing this, we withdraw the counterfactual.

Consider a simple example. On pp. 76–7 I used the conditional "If he wasn't drunk, he could read the number plate" to illustrate my thesis that not all counterfactuals are ambiguous – that is, that we can treat the antecedent as an isolated belief. Whilst it is unlikely that being unable to read number plates would drive one to drink, examples in which the same theory plays both Elster's roles do occur. For instance, we could imagine a potentially brilliant student who was embarrassed by his intelligence, and, trying to be accepted as "one of the lads", drank to excess. We could not say, simply, "If he wasn't drunk, he would be able to pass the exam brilliantly" – by this story, it is precisely because of his brilliance (and character) that he drinks.

In such circumstances we cannot treat the drunkenness as an isolated belief, to be simply assumed away, as we could in the number plate example. We must either alter our theory, or refuse to countenance the counterfactual. In the former case we would have to reinterpret the bald "If he wasn't drunk he would be able to pass brilliantly" as "If his character was different and therefore he didn't drink, then . . ." or "If he didn't come from a community in which you are thought a cissy if you don't go down the pit, he would . . ."; but we would hardly be tempted to try "If he didn't drink, because he wasn't brilliant, then he would fail the exam anyway". The counterfactual is used to make a point, and, in this context, it is clear what the point is and there is no ambiguity. But we can make much the same point by asserting and then withdrawing the counterfactual: "If he wasn't drunk he would pass brilliantly; but, alas, it's because he is brilliant that he drinks". These situations are better called tragic than paradoxical.

Asserting and then withdrawing a counterfactual in this way can be a powerful rhetorical device; it can also be a useful way of gaining knowledge. *Reductio ad absurdum* proofs work like that: we suppose something to be true, see what follows from this supposition, find it unacceptable, and so reject the original supposition. We could always, of course, instead reject some theory used in the deduction – or even the rules of logic; but in most practical cases to do so would be extremely bizarre.

I thus claim to have resolved Elster's "basic paradox of counterfactuals": first by showing that it is not basic; and secondly by showing that, when it occurs, it is not paradoxical. Most counterfactuals do not employ the same theory in the two competing roles, and so we can treat the antecedent as an isolated belief. Those counterfactuals that do employ the *same* theory in both roles are simply not assertable – not, at any rate, once we have realized that the theory does rule out the antecedent. To realize the contradiction and then want to assert the counterfactual anyway is to want to have one's cake and eat it, a feat sometimes possible to undertake but always impossible to achieve (cf. Elster, 1978: p. 71, and ch. 4, passim).

A3.2—TWO CHOICE CONDITIONALS

In section 4.3, introducing ability, I referred to its 'two-wayness' – that if I have the ability to do something it must be up to me whether I do it or not, which means I must also have the ability *not* to do it. Abilities, it seems, go in pairs, like two sides of a coin; you have the ability to do some X *only* if you also have the ability not to do X: take away one, and the other vanishes with it.

But, Elster has pointed out, this surely give rise to a dilemma.[5] If we want to assert:

(A) De Gaulle had the power to safeguard France's independence,

it seems that we must *also* be prepared to argue that:

(B) France would have *lost* her independence if de Gaulle had so wanted.

But "it seems . . . clearly absurd to assume that de Gaulle *could* have wished for France to lose her independence" (Elster, 1978: p. 185). I shall accept here that counterfactual (B) *is* "absurd" to the point of being meaningless. But I shall demonstrate that it is also irrelevant, so that there is no absurdity in asserting de Gaulle's power in (A).

First, it is true that if de Gaulle *literally* could not have chosen France's dependence then he lacked the effective epistemic ability to protect her *inde*pendence. For a choice – to *be* a choice – means that the chooser could have chosen differently; if he could not have chosen differently, he had no choice. Add this to my analysis of effective epistemic ability and we have the following argument:

(1) If A has the effective epistemic ability to do X, then A has the ability to choose to do X (from section 9.4);
(2) If A has the ability to choose to do X, then A has the ability to choose not to do X (from above);
Therefore,
(3) If A has the effective epistemic ability to do X, then A has the ability to choose not to do X;
That is,
(4) If A lacks the ability to choose not to do X (i.e. *must* choose X), then A lacks the effective epistemic ability to do X.

But, as I suggested in section 9.5 (pp. 69–70), by "cannot choose" we mean more than that it would go against everything he held dear and valuable; we mean that he is clinically unable to choose it. Now maybe de Gaulle had a phobia about France's independence, in the strict, clinical sense. Then he would, indeed, have lacked the ability to choose other than as he did; he would, there-fore, have lacked the effective epistemic ability to bring about France's depend-ence. But, even then – if the suggested counterfactual (B) about de Gaulle were demonstrably false – this would not matter for the truth of Elster's claim (A).[6]

To have the effective epistemic ability to do X, you must indeed have the ability not to do X – but *not* the *effective epistemic* ability not to do X. The ability-not-to-do-X that is required here is only the *non-epistemic* ability not to do X. All that is required, that is, is that there must be *some* action open to you that does not lead to X.[7]

For consider an example. Suppose you go into a maze. Not wanting to get trapped overnight, you mark the path you have taken, so that you can follow it back. You then have the effective epistemic ability to leave the maze. But suppose that, if you didn't want to leave, you would strike out boldly in the other direction – and, to your astonishment, find yourself stumbling out anyway. That is, you lack the effective epistemic ability to stay in the maze. This would not mean that you lacked the ability to leave the maze after all. It would only be if you couldn't stay in the maze *whatever* you did (including sitting down) that your ability to leave would come into question. (For then you wouldn't be *able* to leave but would be *forced* to leave.)

So it is the *non-epistemic* ability not to do X that is necessary for the effec-tive epistemic ability to do X. And this ability does not contain a choice condi-tional at all. So we do not need to ask ourselves whether de Gaulle would have made France dependent if he had so wanted; we merely need to ask whether France would have remained independent *no matter what* de Gaulle did. If not, de Gaulle's power to safeguard France's independence would seem to have been established. Thus it is, as we would expect, an empirical matter whether de Gaulle had the power to keep France independent, and not a question that implies any absurdity.

Therefore, the 'two-wayness' of ability does not require, as a second choice con-ditional, "If A were to choose not-X, not-X would result"; it requires, instead, merely that there must be a string of basic actions (W′) that A could do, and were A to do W′, not-X would result. The "other side of the coin" of an ability (whether epistemic or not) is a *non-epistemic* ability.

We can now see why this example about de Gaulle does not illustrate Elster's basic paradox of counterfactuals. The difference is that in the "basic paradox" the counterfactual *that we wish to assert and test* has an antecedent that we cannot assert without abandoning a theory that we need in order to test the truth of the coun-terfactual itself; in the de Gaulle case it is another counterfactual (one that, I argue, we do not need to assert) that has the troublesome antecedent.

A3.3—EFFECTING AND AFFECTING AGAIN

Elster contrasts his example about de Gaulle with one about Nixon: "[C] Nixon had the power to end the Vietnam War: therefore [D] the Vietnam War would have gone on had Nixon so wanted" (Elster, 1978: p. 185, or 1976: p. 253). Since there is nothing absurd about pretending that Nixon had wanted the war to continue, the absurdity that Elster found in his de Gaulle example does not arise here.

But the power claim in (C) is about the power to *end* the war; not the very different power to *continue* the war. I have stressed in this book that we should be very careful to specify the power that interests us, and not slide into considering a very different power. And I have argued that you can have the power to effect something even if it would have happened anyway (see my discussion of the rain-making machine on pp. 30-2). There is no oddity in saying that the Vietnam War would have ended anyway *and* Nixon had the power to end it. What we mean by this is that Nixon could have ended it *even if* it would not have ended anyway. (Why should we be interested in this? Perhaps we want to decide whether an American President could end some other war that shows no sign of ending anyway, and we think this situation is otherwise analogous to the Vietnam War in 1970.)

Elster's assessment about Nixon's power was as follows:

> If we say that Nixon had the power to end the Vietnam War, this statement has little interest if the war would have been ended no matter what he did; the statement has substance only if Nixon could have made the war *continue* had he so wanted. (Elster, 1976: p. 253)

We can now see, I think, that Elster followed the wrong track at the semi-colon: he introduced a counterfactual *about Nixon's wants*, when he should have introduced a *historical* counterfactual supposing that the war would *not* have ended anyway. In my terminology, the claim does not imply a counterfactual *choice* conditional but a counterfactual *descriptive* conditional.

I hope that this reinterpretation of Elster's examples has served to show the point of my analysis. With it I think we can make sense of counterfactuals that have hitherto been considered problematic or paradoxical.

—*Appendix 4*—
The properties of the power indices

In this appendix I provide some backing for the statements in Part IV about the mathematical properties of the power indices. On the whole I provide illustrative examples rather than mathematical proofs, so that this appendix is still accessible to the non-mathematical reader.

In the first section I give an example in which the Penrose/Banzhaf and Shapley–Shubik indices produce different orderings of power between the actors, and in section 2 I use this example to demonstrate how the Penrose and Shapley–Shubik indices can both be considered indices of the value of bribing the actors. Section 3 looks at the mathematics of Penrose's index. Finally, section 4 illustrates how the square-root rule can maximize aggregate power whilst denying power to large groups of actors.

A4.1—THE VICTORIA CHARTER

The British North America Act of 1867 granted self-government to Canada, but specified that amendments to the Canadian Constitution could only be granted by the British Parliament. This was changed by Canada's Constitution Act of 1982. The delay in 'patriating' the Constitution was the result of the Canadian provinces' inability to agree to a formula by which Canadians themselves could amend their constitution. Many alternative formulas were suggested; the one which the federal government proposed when it presented its patriation bill in 1980 is known as the Victoria Charter. Although the Victoria Charter was eventually rejected, in favour of a formula which gave less power to Ontario and Quebec, it was not rejected because of the strangeness of its mathematical properties. The Victoria Charter is, then, a good example of the sort of constitutions that constitution-makers propose. We can see how our various indices of power work by applying them to this real example. (I have chosen this proposal, rather than the one adopted, because it is simpler and also because it shows the differences between the indices more clearly.)

Under the Victoria Charter, a constitutional amendment would be passed only if it was approved by *all* of the following groups of provinces:

(a) Ontario;
(b) Quebec;
(c) two of the four Atlantic provinces (New Brunswick, Nova Scotia, Prince Edward Island and Newfoundland);
(d) British Columbia and one central province (Alberta, Saskatchewan, Manitoba) *or* all three central provinces.

This complicated procedure is impossible to translate into a simpler one in which each province has a number of votes with a given total ensuring that an amendment passes.

The power indices of the provinces are shown in Table A4.1. From this we can see readily that the Penrose/Banzhaf indices do not always produce the same ordering as the Shapley–Shubik index: on the Penrose/Banzhaf indices an Atlantic province is judged to have *more* power than a central province, whilst Atlantic provinces do *less* well than central ones on the Shapley–Shubik index. (This was first pointed out in Straffin, 1977.) This striking difference only holds when, as here, the votes are not expressible directly as numbers; but, even so, one would have expected that such results would have made those who have used these indices ask insistently exactly what the indices are supposed to be measuring.

Table A4.1—The Victoria Charter: indices of power

	Penrose index (×512)	Banzhaf index (×202)	Shapley–Shubik index (×168)
Ontario	44	44	53
Quebec	44	44	53
Each Atlantic province	12	12	5
British Columbia	33	33	21
Each central province	11	11	7
Total (of all provinces)	202	202	168

In the next section I use the Victoria Charter as an example to support the contention of section 22.2 that the Shapley–Shubik index is a measure of an actor's worth to a potential briber.

A4.2—'BRIBE INDICES'

To construct a measure of each actor's worth to a briber, the first thing that we need to do is to calculate the probability that a motion will pass anyway, without any bribes being made. To do this we need to make assumptions of the likely support for motions. Since we are here measuring ability, not ableness, we can assume that each actor is as likely to support a constitutional amendment as it is to oppose it, so that the probability is $\frac{1}{2}$ that it will support the amendment. (As was suggested on pp. 163–4, the magnitude of this probability turns out to be irrelevant so long as it is the same for everyone.)

To calculate the probability of an amendment passing, we need to calculate the probability of it being passed by each of the four groups of provinces that the Victoria Charter specifies. By inspection, we can see that the probabilities that groups (a), (b), and (d) each individually pass an amendment is $\frac{1}{2}$, whilst the probability that group (c) passes one is higher, at $\frac{11}{16}$, since an overall majority is not required. The probability that *all four* groups of provinces pass an amendment is the product of the probabilities that each group alone passes the amendment (assuming – as we do – that votes are cast independently by the provinces) – which is $\frac{11}{128}$. Similarly, the probability that an amendment will fail is $\frac{117}{128}$. Therefore a potential briber will pay up to $\frac{117}{128}$ of the value to him of an amendment to ensure that it *passes*, but only $\frac{11}{128}$ of the value of the amendment to *block* it.

The next calculation is to see what difference bribing just one province makes to the probability of an amendment passing or failing. It is not difficult to see that the probabilities change as shown in Table A4.2.

Table A4.2—Increase in probability of success for bribing just one actor (×128)

	Province bribed							
	Ontario or Quebec		An Atlantic province		British Columbia		A central province	
	Pass	Block	Pass	Block	Pass	Block	Pass	Block
Probability after bribe	22	128	14	120	$19\frac{1}{4}$	$125\frac{1}{4}$	$13\frac{3}{4}$	$119\frac{3}{4}$
Probability before bribe	11	117	11	117	11	117	11	117
Difference	11	11	3	3	$8\frac{1}{4}$	$8\frac{1}{4}$	$2\frac{3}{4}$	$2\frac{3}{4}$

These numbers are the Penrose power indices of the provinces: the probability that a province can swing the vote either way.[1] Expressing these numbers as the proportion of the total power gives the Banzhaf index.

But to calculate the full bribe index we need to look at the worth of an actor if bribed second. Unlike the simple example discussed in the main text (pp. 162–3), it now makes a difference who has been bribed first: Ontario could ask for a bigger bribe if Quebec had been bribed already than if British Columbia had been. Table A4.3 shows how much each province could ask when bribed second. (To simplify, I have done the calculations for representative provinces only.) The *average* each province can expect to receive when bribed second is one-ninth of the total in the relevant column.[2]

Table A4.3—Increase in probability of success for bribing a second actor (×512)

Province already bribed	Province to be bribed second							
	Ontario		New Brunswick		British Columbia		Alberta	
	Pass	Block	Pass	Block	Pass	Block	Pass	Block
Ontario	–	–	24	0	66	0	22	0
Quebec	88	0	24	0	66	0	22	0
New Brunswick	56	32	–	–	42	24	14	8
Nova Scotia	56	32	8	16	42	24	14	8
Prince Edward I	56	32	8	16	42	24	14	8
Newfoundland	56	32	8	16	42	24	14	8
British Columbia	77	11	21	3	–	–	11	11
Alberta	55	33	15	9	33	33	–	–
Saskatchewan	55	33	15	9	33	33	11	11
Manitoba	55	33	15	9	33	33	11	11
Total	554	238	138	78	399	195	133	65

We then need to continue, and calculate the average each actor receives when bribed third, fourth, fifth . . . and so on down to last. I will spare you the individual tables, which are very large as there has to be a separate line for each different combination of bribed actors. A summary of these tables is shown in Table A4.4.

Table A4.4—Increase in probability of success for bribing an actor (×64,512)

Position bribed	Province							
	Ontario		New Brunswick		British Columbia		Alberta	
	Pass	Block	Pass	Block	Pass	Block	Pass	Block
1st	5544	5544	1512	1512	4158	4158	1386	1386
2nd	7756	3332	1932	1092	5586	2730	1862	910
3rd	10535	1687	2331	651	7203	1491	2401	497
4th	13842	648	2610	288	8838	612	2946	204
5th	17528	144	2640	72	10200	144	3400	48
6th	21328	0	2304	0	10896	0	3632	0
7th	24912	0	1584	0	10512	0	3504	0
8th	28000	0	672	0	8736	0	2912	0
9th	30464	0	0	0	5376	0	1792	0
10th	32256	0	0	0	0	0	0	0
Average	19216.5	1135.5	1558.5	361.5	7150.5	913.5	2383.5	304.5
Combined	10176		960		4032		1344	

The "Combined" row in Table A4.4 is the average of the passing and blocking indices. Dividing through by 192, we obtain the combined indexes:

Ontario, Quebec:	53
Each Atlantic province:	5
British Columbia:	21
Each central province:	7
Total (of all provinces):	168

This, as we have already seen (see p. 223), is the Shapley–Shubik index.

I do not expect many of you will want to bother to check the details of this calculation,[3] but I hope that by giving the exact numbers I have given an idea of what the Shapley–Shubik index, as a bribe-index, represents – and, more importantly perhaps, what it does not represent. This example does not constitute a *proof* that this bribe procedure always produces the Shapley–Shubik index, but it may be more persuasive to a non-mathematician than an incomprehensible proof. I am sure such a proof could be obtained, but I have not spent much time looking for it, since I am not primarily addressing mathematicians. I will leave it – as they say – as an exercise for the interested reader.

Nobody has considered the Shapley–Shubik index as a bribe index before, and so nobody (including, it seems, its inventors) has quite understood its significance. We are now in a position to do so. The Penrose index, as we have seen, is the worth of each actor to a potential briber if that actor is the *only* actor to be bribed (or, alternatively, if she is always the first to be bribed). The Shapley–Shubik value is the worth of each actor to a potential briber if the briber expects to bribe sufficient actors to ensure victory. The Shapley–Shubik index has been much criticized in the literature for 'weighting' each winning combination by the number of orderings of that combination (and, in addition, the number of orderings of voters not in that combination – of actors *after* the pivotal voter). We can now see the significance of these weights. The weights are a (much) simpler method of calculating the bribe to an actor, since in order to calculate the bribe we need to know the probability that she will occupy each of the possible places in the bribing order.

It is not difficult to see from the first row of Table A4.4 that the Penrose value which an actor has for *passing* legislation is always the same as her value for *blocking* legislation, and that the same holds for the Banzhaf index. This is because an actor only has active power when she can ensure that the motion is passed *or* defeated, whichever she should prefer. In calculating the Banzhaf or Penrose index, then, we need not distinguish between the power to pass a motion and the power to block it.

With the more complete approach, which eventually gives Shapley and Shubik's index, we *do* arrive at a separate value for passing and blocking legislation. This is also not difficult to understand: in situations in which a subset of actors can block a motion but cannot pass it, their worth to a potential briber will be different depending on whether he wants the motion passed or blocked. The Shapley–Shubik value turns out to be the average of the passing and blocking values when we go through the complete bribe procedure, considering each position. It is therefore somewhat misleading of Shapley and Shubik to say that an index of blocking power would be exactly equal to an index of passing power (Shapley and Shubik, 1954: p. 211). This result does in fact occur, but only because what Shapley and Shubik call their measure of power to pass a motion is *already* an average of passing power and blocking power. So we can calculate separate Shapley–Shubik indices for passing and blocking legislation, as I do here. Note that not only are these indices different, they produce a different ordering: New Brunswick would be a better bet to bribe than Alberta if you want to *block* a motion, but a much worse one if you want to *pass* one.

We can also see from Table A4.4 why New Brunswick does better than Alberta on the Banzhaf index, and worse on Shapley and Shubik's. If no other actors have been bribed, New Brunswick does better than Alberta – and this is what the Banzhaf index measures. But as more and more other actors get bribed, Alberta quickly overtakes New Brunswick, becoming the better bet after three others have been bribed, and then pulling away strongly.[4] It is Alberta's stronger position when a third or more of the provinces are certain to vote for a constitutional amendment that ensures it a better Shapley–Shubik index.

So we must be careful when bribing politicians to use the correct index. If we sit in an office, and voters come to us offering to be bribed, and we do not know who, if anybody, has already been bribed, we should use the Shapley–Shubik procedure to determine how much to offer. If, on the other hand, we have to go and hunt out people we want to bribe, we should use the Penrose index to determine who to go for first. As I have shown, just because someone can expect to get most *on average* does not mean that she is the best person to approach first. If we want to know who to attempt to bribe first, we should use Penrose's procedure; and if we then want to know who to go for next, we should recalculate the index, to show specifically who is worth most when bribed second, after our first choice (and her, specifically) has already been bribed. The Shapley–Shubik index does not tell potential bribers *who* to bribe; instead it gives average expected receipts of bribes *if* the order of bribing is random.

But the debates on the Canada Constitution Act show clearly that the protagonists were less interested in their *ability* than in their *ableness*: they wanted to know their power, given the likely voting behaviour of others. (This recognition of common interests was, of course, the reason that the Victoria Charter grouped certain provinces together, ensuring that either the Atlantic provinces or the central provinces could – if unanimous – veto any proposed change. This feature was not incorporated into the eventual Canada Constitution Act.)

It is not difficult to see how we can amend Shapley and Shubik's procedure if we do have information on the likelihood of various actors voting together, or on the probability that any specific actor will seek to change the status quo. All that is required is to include this information when calculating the various probabilities, instead of making the equiprobability assumption.

Hitherto it has not been shown how Shapley and Shubik's index can be extended to produce an index measuring ableness: we have now seen that, using the interpretation of it as a bribe index, we have little difficulty in doing this. How much practical use such a bribe index of ableness is seems to me less clear: for most purposes we would seem to be more interested in an absolute rather than relative power index (see Chapter 24). But, by producing a bribe index of ableness, I hope I have been of some service to the CIA and other philanthropic bodies acting on our behalf, who may now find it easier to invest their (our) money wisely. And who knows – if the mechanics of bribing is better understood, they may pursue this course more often, instead of resorting to the cruder mechanism of assassination.

A4.3—PENROSE'S INDEX

I now turn to explore further the properties of the Penrose index when the actors have commensurable votes. We saw in section 22.1 that a voter has some active power only when the votes of the others are cast so that the majority on an issue is less than the number of votes she has – so that she can sway the vote. In general, if actor A has a votes, there are N voters in all, and the required majority for a motion to pass is k, then A's Penrose index is the probability that the number of positive votes cast by the other $(N - 1)$ voters is at least $(k - a)$ and less than k.

When each person has one vote only, the probability of this occurring (of A's vote being able to swing the decision) is (by the formula for the binomial expansion):

$$\frac{(N-1)!}{(k-1)!(N-k)!}\left(\frac{1}{2}\right)^{N-1}$$

For a simple majority voting system, k is $\frac{N}{2}+1$ for N even, and $\frac{(N+1)}{2}$ for N odd. Thus, under a simple-majority voting system, the Penrose index (P) reduces to:

$$P=\prod_{t=1}^{s}\frac{2t-1}{2t}$$

where $s=\frac{N}{2}$ for N even, and $s=\frac{N-1}{2}$ for N odd. For example, when N = 10,

$$P=\frac{1\times3\times5\times7\times9}{2\times4\times6\times8\times10}=0.25$$

It should be obvious that as N increases, P decreases – for one's chances of determining the outcome in a small committee are much greater than one's chances in a large one.[5]

When the number in the committee is large, we can use an approximation to the binomial expansion which gives:

$$P \sim \sqrt{\frac{2}{\pi N}}$$

For $N > 100$ this is accurate to four places of decimals. This approximation cannot be used in assessing power with weighted voting, as the binomial distribution only applies when the number of votes each actor has is the same. But when the actors do have equal votes, it is highly accurate.

A4.4—THE SQUARE-ROOT RULE

It might seem that the square-root approximation to the Penrose index provides some support for the square-root rule discussed in section 24.3. The argument would run as follows. It was shown in Chapter 24 that an individual's power in a two-stage aggregation process, as measured by his Penrose index, is the product of his power in his group and the power of his delegate (see p. 257 n. 11). But his power in his group, we now see, is inversely proportional to the square-root of the number of voters in his group (assuming each voter has one vote). Therefore if each delegate is given a number of votes proportional to the square-root of the number of voters she represents, every individual's power will be equal in the two-stage process.

But the last step in this argument is fallacious. It *is* true that every individual's power is equal if the *power* of each delegate is proportional to the square-root of the number of voters she represents. In that case each individual's power, in the two-stage process, is proportional to $\sqrt{N} \sqrt{\frac{2}{\pi N}}$, which is a constant irrespective of the number (N) in the individual's group. But it should by now be a well-established result that we do not achieve our desired distribution of *power* by distributing *votes* in the desired pattern. In fact, as I stated in section 24.3, the square-root rule seems to *maximize* power, at the expense of giving highly undesirable distributions. In this section I will show that if we have any *even* number of groups, all of which are the same size except for one which is smaller, then total power is maximized by the square-root rule, but at the cost of giving the smallest group's delegate no power at all, irrespective of how tiny the difference in size is between that group and the others.

Let there be m groups of size n, and one group of size $(n - \alpha)$ where α is very small in comparison to n. Further, let $(m + 1)$ be even. Then if we allocate votes to the delegates by the square-root rule, we have m delegates with $\sqrt{n}$ votes each, and one with $\sqrt{(n - \alpha)}$. Since m is an odd number, the votes of the m delegates together must produce a majority for one side or another of at least $\sqrt{n}$ votes. Therefore the delegate of the smallest group, who has $\sqrt{(n - \alpha)}$ votes, is effectively disenfranchised – since however she votes the outcome will have already been determined, since $\sqrt{(n - \alpha)}$ is less than $\sqrt{n}$.

I now need to show that, nevertheless, the square-root rule maximizes power. We can think of the delegate voting stage, under the square-root rule, as consisting of m voters with equal votes, each of which has a Penrose power index of P_m, and one voter with no votes having a Penrose power index of zero. The only plausible alternative is to give all $(m + 1)$ delegates equal votes (since α is very small in comparison to n), when each will have a Penrose power index of P_{m+1}.

As we have seen the power of an *individual* voter is the product of his power in the group and his delegate's power. The power of voters in the larger groups is P_n; in the smallest group it is $P_{n-\alpha}$. An individual's power under the square-root rule is therefore $P_n P_m$ if he is in a large group; and zero if he is in the smallest group. The total sum of the individuals' power under the square-root rule is therefore $nmP_n P_m$. Under the alternative distribution of equal votes to all delegates, the total sum of power is $nmP_n P_{m+1} + (n - \alpha)P_{n-\alpha}P_{m+1}$.

The square-root rule maximizes power, then, if:

$$nmP_n P_m > nmP_n P_{m+1} + (n - \alpha)P_{n-\alpha}P_{m+1}$$

or, regrouping, if:

$$m\left[\frac{P_m - P_{m+1}}{P_{m+1}}\right] > \frac{(n - \alpha)P_{n-\alpha}}{nP_n}$$

But, for $(m + 1)$ even,

$$P_{m+1} = \frac{m}{m+1} \cdot \frac{m-2}{m-1} \cdot \frac{m-4}{m-3} \cdots \frac{1}{2}$$

and:

$$P_m = \frac{m-2}{m-1} \cdot \frac{m-4}{m-3} \cdots \frac{1}{2}$$

(from the formula for Penrose's index, given on p. 228). Thus,

$$\frac{P_m}{P_{m+1}} = \frac{m+1}{m}$$

Substituting this in the last inequality, the LHS becomes:

$$m\left[\frac{m+1-m}{m}\right] = 1$$

Hence the square-root rule maximizes power if $\dfrac{n}{n-\alpha} > \dfrac{P_{n-\alpha}}{P_n}$

We can see from the way the expansion of the Penrose index behaves that if this inequality holds for $\alpha = 1$, it holds for all larger values of α. (This is because $\dfrac{n}{n-\alpha}$ increases faster as α increases than $\dfrac{P_{n-\alpha}}{P_n}$ does.)

With $\alpha = 1$, when n is odd, $P_{n-1} = P_n$, so the inequality holds, since $\dfrac{n}{n-1} > 1$.

When n is even and $\alpha = 1$, $\dfrac{P_{n-1}}{P_n} = \dfrac{n}{n-1}$, so that the total of power is the same under the two arrangements. (With n even and $\alpha > 1$, it is easy to see that the inequality holds and the square-root rule maximizes the power.)

Therefore even though the square-root rule disenfranchises the smallest group, it still maximizes the power.

Notes

Introduction

1 Some of the examples are now very out of date: for instance "the Alliance" (p. 176) no longer exists in British politics (it was an electoral pact between the Liberal and Social Democratic Parties, which have now combined into one party, the Liberal Democratic Party). I have left most of these anachronisms unaltered, since any more modern examples will also date quickly.

2 See Haugaard (1997) for a good discussion of recent work on power in sociological theory.

3 Though they have usually mistakenly awarded the credit for revealing these fallacies to me, and not to the person to whom it belongs, who is Anthony Kenny.

4 See, for instance, Isaac (1987a and 1987b); Barnes (1988); Dowding (1991 and 1996); and Ball (1993). Dahl, unfortunately, still uses 'power' and 'influence' as synonyms (Dahl, 1991: chs 2–4).

5 See, for instance, Isaac (1987a and 1987b); Barnes (1988); and Ball (1993: p. 551). Wartenberg (1990) remains committed to 'power-over'. Dowding (1991 and 1996) and Ledyaev (1997: pp. 92–101) take probably the most sensible approach, and make room for both 'power-to' and 'power-over'; Dowding gives a somewhat cautious priority to 'power-to', whilst Ledyaev prefers 'power-over'.

6 For instance: "Foucault's notions of power and knowledge are so divorced from common speech that I need to recall how he arrived at them" (Hacking, 1981: p. 28). See also Taylor (1984: pp. 90–1).

7 Aron (1964: p. 256). The internal quotations are from Littré.

8 Aron then says that usage has blurred this distinction between potential and act: "In French it has become common to term '*Pouvoir*' the man . . . that decides in the name of the collectivity or takes decisions of a kind that affect the collectivity" (Aron, 1964: p. 256). Hence, presumably, Foucault's obsession with denying the perspective that sees *pouvoir* as necessarily wielded by a sovereign. This dual use of '*pouvoir*' – as an action and as a person – is present in English, but the contrast appears less significant as neither is the main use of 'power'.

9 The original French is "le pouvoir n'existe qu'en acte" (Foucault, 1982a: p. 236). It may be of interest to contrast the two halves of Foucault (1982b): the first half was written by Foucault in English (and seems to me largely unexceptionable, if also not very interesting); the second half is translated from Foucault's French, and reads very oddly in English. That Foucault's translators are unaware of the difficulties in rendering '*pouvoir*' in English is shown in the editor's 'Notes on Terms and Translations' in the most recent English collection of Foucault on power. He writes: "For all the complexities of Foucault's thought and usage, his 'political vocabulary' largely allows of straightforward translation. One can readily gloss [sic] *pouvoir* as 'power' . . ." (Foucault, 2001: p. xlii). Would that it were all so

simple! For a more aware, although brief, discussion of the nuances of *pouvoir* and *puissance* in Foucault, see Spivak (1992). She points out, correctly, that "Foucault insisted upon the difference between . . . *pouvoir* and *puissance*" and that "it is a pity that there is no word in English corresponding to *pouvoir*" (Spivak, 1992: pp. 152, 150).

10 The two contemporaneous works are Lukes (1986b: passim) and Said (1986: p. 151); others who have asked this question more recently include Rae (1988: p. 34), Dowding (1991: p. 164), Ball (1993: p. 549), and Allen (1999: p. 1).

11 See Buckle (1988). Buckle (1990) reprints most of this article, though omitting the (important) footnotes.

12 An adult human in a coma is a more difficult case. Arguably, someone in a reversible coma is in a somewhat similar position to a foetus (as discussed below); however, on this approach, someone in an irreversible coma would lack moral standing, if he or she has permanently lost the crucially relevant powers.

13 Or, of course, not done to it.

14 Exactly what sort of powers *are* able to give rise to moral standing is a huge question that I cannot touch on here.

15 'Common morality' may be wrong here. But the advocates of the potentiality argument seek to rely on this common morality in ascribing moral standing to an embryo, in order to claim that killing it is wrong in the same way that killing a baby (or an adult) is wrong.

16 I draw a distinction between generic and time-specific powers (pp. 48–9); and Buckle draws a distinction between deontological and consequentialist forms of the potentiality argument. The two pairs go together. Buckle's deontological form refers to the generic (although latent) powers of a specific (and continuing) entity. His consequentialist version, like my time-specific one, collapses the distinction between latent and actual powers, and simply predicts what powers will be present at a specified future time. It is the deontological form of the argument I am discussing in the text.

17 Compare my p. 84 with Buckle (1988: p. 249 n. 3).

18 We can see that use of the idea of what would happen "in the natural course of events" is misleading when used in a potentiality argument. Although aborting an embryo *in utero* involves an intervention in the natural course of events, whilst failing to implant an embryo *in vitro* does not, this is not relevant to the moral standing of the embryo concerned.

The phrase "the normal course of events" is even more unhelpful, managing to be misleading in two different ways, since it can be taken as making reference either to what is statistically usual (in a case such as this) or what is required by prevalent norms. Neither idea is appropriate here.

19 Buckle (1988: p. 247; or 1990: p. 106; my emphasis). See also Buckle (1988: p. 249 n. 3), in which he states that the appropriate standard conditions "must . . . be understood in terms of biological normality, that is, in terms of the proper functioning of the relevant biological process. . . . [The point is] that potential can be frustrated or inhibited, and so depends on 'sympathetic', or at least non-inhibitory, environments in order to be expressed. The appeal to the normal (i.e. in this case, biologically functional) course of events must be understood to be an appeal to an environment which is assumed to be appropriately sympathetic."

20 Tooley's full argument is much more complicated than this simple *reductio ad absurdum*, but this is enough to show that the potentiality argument is liable to spread moral standing very widely indeed.

21 I am not sure that this distinction between "properties of its own" and properties provided externally holds water; but it is clearly crucial for an adequate potentiality argument. (See, further, n. 39 below, and pp. 83–4.)

22 Unfortunately, Sen's writings are scattered through a large number of diverse publications, and he has not (yet) produced a definitive or complete account. Like other commentators on his work, I have had to reconstruct his views as best I can.

23 For instance, GNP ignores life expectancy (Sen, 1987: pp. 34–5). If life expectancy dramatically decreased from 70 years to 60, GNP per capita could well *in*crease, as the last ten years of our lives are rarely the most productive, even when we are completely healthy.

24 Exactly what is to count as a 'functioning' can be, of course, highly contentious; but this difficulty is not relevant to my discussion here. In any case, Sen does not attempt to give an exhaustive account of functionings; he appears to think (as do I, on p. 147) that there are enough obvious and uncontentious examples of functionings for us to readily understand what we mean.

25 See, for example, Sen (1993: pp. 40 and 45) or Sen (1987: p. 37).

26 This dichotomy may suffice for Sen's purposes, but that it is in general over-simple is shown by people (often young girls) who over-diet, sometimes literally starving in the midst of plenty. Anorexia and bulimia are now recognized as diseases that prevent a person choosing to eat (cf. pp. 68–9), whilst many other over-dieters seem to be so influenced by the constant bombardment of images of an 'ideal', over-thin, figure that they choose to starve in the hope of becoming their ideal (cf. pp. 93–7). A concern for starvation in the developed world would have to include a consideration of such occurrences.

27 For instance, "The capability approach to a person's advantage is concerned with evaluating it in terms of his or her actual ability to achieve various valuable functionings . . ." (Sen, 1993: p. 30); or "a functioning is an achievement, whereas a capability is the ability to achieve" (Sen, 1987: p. 36).

28 One such instance is in Sen (1990: p. 121), though I do not think the usage there is significant. Crocker (1995: p. 168) argues that Sen would do better if he thought of his capabilities more as powers.

29 Sen himself alludes to this story about Capability Brown (in Sen, 1993: p. 30 and p. 44 n. 36).

30 To be pedantic, someone in an advanced stage of starvation might indeed be too weak to eat, and so might lack the ability to eat, as well as lacking the ableness. For some purposes, we might wish to distinguish these two cases: providing food to someone who did lack the ability to eat would be no help to them.

To be further pedantic, Keith Dowding has quoted the passage I have just referred to on p. 81 to criticize my notion of ableness: "The poor do have the ableness if they break the law – steal caviar or stage a revolution after which it is equally rationed. They may not be able to steal caviar if it is too closely guarded, or if the potential costs of revolution are greater than its potential benefits they thus remain unable to eat caviar. But in these cases their lack of ableness is based upon their abilities, though not their masticatory ones. Thus the distinction between the two [ability and ableness] is a normative one . . ." (Dowding, 1991: p. 52; a similar idea is expressed in Dowding, 1996: p. 49). I (mainly) disagree. Firstly, let us suppose that there is absolutely nothing you can do to get hold of caviar; you therefore lack the ableness to eat it. But you do have the *ability* to eat it: if it were placed in front of you, you could gobble it up. This difference between ableness and ability (you lack the former; you have the latter) is factual, not normative. Your lack of other abilities (to fly to the Caspian Sea, or whatever) is simply irrelevant. Secondly, suppose Dowding's first sentence holds: there are things you could do to get caviar, but they are illegal. I consider this – briefly – on p. 249 n. 10 to ch. 12, and stand by what I say there. In addition, Sen has argued better than anyone that famines are often caused by the existing legal system (the lack of entitlements some have to purchase food): see, for instance, Drèze and Sen (1989: passim). As a response to famine, it is hardly useful (even when it is, in Dowding's sense, true) to say "Oh, the starving could always *steal* some food, so it is not true to say that they are unable to eat". Instead we need to change the system of entitlements. This is indeed a normative conclusion; but we need a (non-normative) distinction between ableness and ability to reach it. Finally, I disagree with the second half of the second sentence quoted; I think that high costs do not necessarily render people unable (see pp. 56, 69–70, 89–91).

31 See, for instance, Barry (1988a: pp. 314–17), discussed below: pp. xxxix–xli.

32 Cohen (1993: p. 24). Sen rejects this characterization (at Sen, 1993: pp. 43–4). I think that Sen has a good case: he writes almost as often of functionings as "beings" as "doings". But my main interest in this is that both Sen and Cohen seem to accept the importance of passive powers (although not, of course, this name for them). I anticipate Cohen's discussion – and his association of the activist position with Marx – on pp. 102–5.

33 I am rather ashamed that, when writing this book, I seem to have forgotten Marx's Eleventh Thesis on Feuerbach: "The philosophers have only *interpreted* the world, in various ways; the point, however, is to *change* it" (Marx, 1845: p. 30). My defence is that I think that understanding the world is a difficult enough task to accomplish; and trying to change the world before we have properly understood it is likely to lead to disaster. In this book I am only trying to understand some of the *concepts* with which we seek to understand the world, so that I am at two removes from the activist's concerns. Nevertheless, changing the world for the better should remain the ultimate goal.

34 The best attempts to analyse 'empowerment' that I have seen are Wartenberg (1988) and Allen (1998 and 1999). The most depressing (for the purposes of this book) is Friedman (1992), a widely used text, which seeks to develop a radical advocacy of anti-poverty strategies, yet defines 'political power' as "the access of individual household members to the process by which decisions . . . are made" (Friedman, 1992: p. 33). Friedman seems quite unaware of Bachrach and Baratz's and Lukes's efforts to combat this emphasis on decision-making: more than thirty years' work on providing a radical analysis of power has just passed him by.

35 Allen (1998: p. 27; or 1999: pp. 20–1; emphasis in original only in the latter version). This would seem to be empowerment of the sort Cohen calls "athletic" (see p. xxv), but, in this case, this is deliberate: the aim here really is getting people to be able to *do* things, rather than be the passive recipients of assistance.

36 Harré expressed the same ideas again, in almost the same words, in Harré and Madden (1975: pp. 86–7 and 92). But cf. Harré (1986: p. 284): "one must note that some beings have the tendencies [i.e. dispositions] they do because of their internal or intrinsic natures, whilst others acquire tendencies dependently through the influence of environmental influences on them".

37 Martin (1996: p. 176; see also pp. 178–9). Martin first presented this argument in print in his (1994).

38 See, for instance, Prior (1985: p. 9) and Lewis (1997).

39 It is actually much more complicated than this, for Buckle's position requires us to distinguish, within external interveners, between magical injections and ordinary feeding. This depends on an Aristotelian notion of an entity's 'natural' development and powers, which I cannot pursue here.

   A similar idea doubtless underpins the description of athletes who take certain performance-enhancing drugs as 'cheats'. These drugs can perhaps be thought of as giving an athlete *new* powers, that are in some sense not truly theirs; on the other hand, something like extensive training at altitude can be thought of as developing the athlete's *own* powers. This would seem to be the intuitive idea; whether it can be sustained seems to me doubtful.

40 Barnes (1988: pp. 61 and 62). Barnes's passage in full on his pp. 61–2 makes this point very forcefully.

41 Isaac (1987a: pp. 74–5); his (1987b: p. 21) is only slightly different.

42 When I first borrowed this example, on p. 32, I was not teaching *Leviathan*. I now am, and have discovered that I lack the power to get all but a handful of my students to read it. Whether this indicates a failing on my part, or says something about the structure of Irish universities – or, indeed, about the nature (intrinsic or otherwise) of contemporary students – I leave as an open question.

43 Of course, when we have established that a power exists we might want to explain *why* it exists. But that does not point to a property of 'power': anything and everything cries out for explanation. Crucially, we learn nothing about what the concept of power is by knowing that we might want to explain why a particular power exists.

44 Barry (1988a) is a long review. Dowding, in (1990) and (1991), looks at aspects of this book in some detail; see also Dowding (1996).

45 See Chapter 11, and index entries under "ableness".

46 Barry (1988a: p. 308). This idea that power necessarily involves the ability to overcome resistance is repeated throughout Barry (1988a). By contrast, the definition of political power Barry provided in an earlier article was "the ability of an individual or group to change the outcomes of some decisionmaking process from what they would otherwise have been in the direction desired by the person or group" (Barry, 1980b: p. 272): there is no mention here of resistance, although there is later in the article (Barry, 1980b: pp. 296–300).

47 See Barry (1988a: pp. 310–14).

48 If you don't like thinking about God, the same would apply to an absolute dictator: we could render him powerless by not resisting his power.

49 Barry's discussion of his other illustrative example, that of voting in a legislature, undermines his case further, for in this context Barry accepts that ableness is a type of power (Barry, 1988a: p. 312; quoted on p. xxxv). In his example, your bloc has 30 votes, and there are two other blocs, with 40 and 30 votes each; Barry agrees with me that your bloc would be powerful if the other blocs are always opposed to each other, and would have no power if they always voted together (Barry, 1988a: p. 311). But what if on some issue they could not care less, and so they both abstain? Barry would have to say that you then have no power at all (because you win the vote without overcoming any resistance or opposition). I cannot believe that anyone would accept that. So the "no resistance, no power" claim must be abandoned.

50 See Barry (1976); now reprinted in Barry (1991).

51 I did have a chapter on bargaining power in an earlier draft, but I dropped it because I did not think it said anything particularly interesting, and it took me away from the main line of argument that I was trying to develop in the book. I do readily concede that any *complete* account of power (whatever that would look like) would have to include a fully developed account of bargaining power. But (I assert) it would have to be compatible with the framework sketched in this book.

52 "A has power over B to the extent that he can get him to do something that B would not otherwise do" (Dahl, 1957a: p. 80).

53 Barry (1988a: p. 312). The phrase "all the power" in the penultimate sentence is careless, since it may be taken to imply that everybody else must have *no* power. Better would be something like "all the power he could have".

54 Dowding (1991: p. 60). In Dowding (1996: p. 48) a similar passage appears; the last sentence is identical except that MJ has changed sex.

55 That is, active power; for passive power see below, pp. xxxix–xli.

56 As I originally put it, all too briefly, we are "investigating power given the actual (or predicted) voting pattern of all the *other* voters" (p. 169; emphasis added). See also the similar passage on p. 91.

57 The first "sometimes", that is; on the second "sometimes" the vote is determined whatever BJ should do. It is easy to see that the *average* power of each of the other eight Justices is half that of MJ.

I should perhaps point out that there is an apparent problem in this analysis of Barry's example. Barry, in setting up the example, has assumed that BJ is a member of a bloc that will all vote together. In my discussion above I have taken BJ as an individual actor, and said (in effect) that he is powerful if (and only if), were he to vote against his bloc, he could defeat it. One could argue that that is inconsistent with the original assumption, which is that here we have cohesive blocs. But I think that Dowding has provided the answer to this worry. As he says, both MJ and BJ have their reasons for voting as they do; but when we are investigating the power of any one Justice we are asking what he or she could do (or could have done) if their reasons had been different. This is an essential part of the counterfactual analysis that I propose in this book.

58 See, for instance, Dowding (1991: pp. 82, 137–8). Note, further, that Barry-luck is not to be confused with "the law of anticipated reactions", although the exact relationship between the two is complicated. The paradigm of Barry-luck is: others give you the outcome you want even though you do nothing to these others, you could do nothing to them, and everybody else knows you could do nothing to them. The paradigm of being powerful via "anticipated reactions" is: others give you the outcome you want even though you do nothing to these others, but you *could* do something to punish those who did not bring it about for you, and everybody else knows that you could punish them (and suspects that you *would* do so). I will not explore here exactly how we should treat intermediate cases (such as others providing you with what you want because they suspect – wrongly – that you could punish them) because I am only trying to explore the relationship between luck and power.

59 Ironically, perhaps, Barry has used this sense elsewhere when he wasn't writing about power. In Barry (1988b: p. 26) he characterized an outcome as due to luck if "almost exactly the same causal sequence might have produced a very different outcome". (See also the almost identical passage in Barry, 1989: p. 219.) This would seem to describe MJ's position fairly accurately.

60 See also Dowding (1991: pp. 152–3) and Dowding (1996: ch. 4). Systematic luck would seem to apply only to Barry-luck, since Dowding-luck (as defined here) can *not* be predicted methodically.

61 This paragraph and the following one are borrowed from Morriss (1995: pp. 183–4).

62 I should also mention that I introduce the idea of passive power gradually in Chapter 13, to solve certain problems revealed in the discussion of 'ability' (e.g. being able to understand your mother tongue, when spoken in your presence). Nobody, to my knowledge, has objected to these uses. In my view the contentious uses of 'passive power', discussed here, get considerable support from the *un*contentious uses developed in Chapter 13. I do not consider the term 'passive power' linguistically odd, nor the idea contradictory. It is in keeping with my general account of power as a dispositional, though here not a 'two-way' dispositional (see pp. 24–5, 100). It is true that usually we are more interested in the human powers that require the power-holder to act to activate them. But sometimes our 'mere' dispositions do matter. The power to hear is a 'mere' disposition, the power to speak a 'two-way' one; but those who are deaf lack an important human power as surely as do those who are dumb. I think that the further move from a conditional dispositional to a habitual one (pp. 22–4, 101) can be similarly defended (as with the example of being able to grow a beard, on pp. 98–9, 101).

63 See Barry (1988a: pp. 317; also pp. 318 and 320–1).

64 Barry (1988a: pp. 315–16). He continues this point, to reject my criticism (on p. 106) of a passage from Polsby. I think Barry is making the same mistake Polsby made.

65 The phrase is Adam Ferguson's, in his (1767: p. 119).

66 Structures that are unalterable – if there are any – are not sociologically interesting, in this context at any rate. But most structures are alterable with sufficient imagination – although the cost of altering them might make doing so undesirable.

67 Dowding makes a similar point at the very end of his book: Dowding (1991: p. 175).

68 Actually, in the example that would be pretty pointless, since she will be on the winning side anyway.

69 On p. 255 n. 4, I specifically put to one side considerations of bargaining and log-rolling.

70 In section III.iii I rejected the claim that this difference would make you lucky, rather than powerful: see pp. xxxvii–xxxviii.

71 Note that this conclusion does *not* depend on you being better at using your resources than I am at using mine. Compare Dowding (1991: pp. 76–7) where he claims that he avoids the

vehicle fallacy because his actors may use their "external" resources with differing degrees of efficacy (depending on their skill, and other "internal" resources), so that these external resources do not determine their power. It is certainly the case that a skilled operator can get a lot from meagre resources, but this difference between epistemic and non-epistemic power (see pp. 52–6) is not what I am relying on here. What I am saying applies as much to non-epistemic as epistemic power.

72 We are here ignoring the possibility of abstentions; suppose, if you wish, that an Abstention always counts as a No vote, or two votes are always required to pass a motion.

73 Felsenthal and Machover put this point more formally: "the voting power of a voter . . . is not a localized property of that voter in isolation, but a global property that involves the whole structure of the [voting situation]" (Felsenthal and Machover, 1998: p. 236).

74 For a careful analysis of Rawls's discussion of equal opportunity, see Barry (1988b).

75 Kingman Brewster was a leading American educationalist and public servant for over 25 years before his death in 1988: between being President of Yale (for fourteen years) and Master of an Oxford college, he was a Democratic appointee as US Ambassador to Great Britain. He could be thought of as being on the left of the American Establishment.

76 Those, like Connolly, who take a radical attitude to American society might suppose that it is no coincidence that this label is both so popular and so misleadingly used. It is another example of the importance – at the level of ideological struggle, as well as disinterested love of clarity – of a correct understanding, and use, of our key terms: in this case, of "opportunity" (cf. pp. 202–4).

A similar conclusion is reached by Rae (Rae, 1981: ch. 4), but by an instructively mistaken route. Rae thinks " 'equal opportunity' is not a very useful concept, because it blurs at least two conceptions" (Rae, 1981: p. 65), which he calls *prospect-regarding equal opportunity* (in which actors have the same *probability* of attaining some X), and *means-regarding equal opportunity* (in which actors have the same *instruments* for attaining X). His conclusion, similar to mine, is that "the ideological (or moral) appeal of equal opportunities is vitally connected to its prospect-regarding form, but its practical implementation is almost always means-regarding" (Rae, 1981: p. 73; see also his pp. 66–7).

I agree with the conclusion, but the analysis of both prospect-regarding and means-regarding equal opportunity is flawed. The discussion of prospect-regarding equal opportunity is mistaken, because to interpret it in terms of a *probability* is to lose sight of the nature of an opportunity, which refers in some way to the background circumstances within which an actor acts. You and I might genuinely have equal opportunities to obtain some end (become rich, say), but I (unlike you) might not be interested in becoming rich, and so not use these opportunities. My *probability* of becoming rich will be close to zero, yours very high; but our *opportunities* may still be equal. (For the importance of the distinction between a capacity and a probability see Barry [1980b: pp. 296 and 300].)

The idea of *means-regarding equal opportunity* is even more fundamentally wrong, for although "equal opportunity" *is* often used in this sense, there simply is no such thing. If I give Harold a CD of Beethoven's Ninth Symphony, he has the opportunity to listen to it, for he has a CD player and excellent hearing; if I give the same CD to Daphne this is not an opportunity for her, for she is deaf. To say that they have equal opportunities because they are given the same means (or instruments or resources) is nonsense (and insulting nonsense as well). If their opportunities really are equal, then they must be equally able to succeed with the opportunities they have, and if they have different abilities this will require appropriately different means. This will, in short, be prospect-regarding equal opportunity, as revised above (with "capacity" replacing "probability"). Means-regarding equal opportunity is, then, not equality of opportunity at all, which is why it "has great ideological power if means-regarding equal opportunity becomes confused with equality of prospects" (Rae, 1981: p. 67): for then something that is not equality of opportunity is passed off as if it is.

77 For this claim, see Johnston (1995a); another version of it is found in Brams and Fishburn (1995). Perhaps I should stress here that these authors are talking about a priori power as

ability (in my terminology); that is to say, they are assuming that we know nothing about how voters are likely to vote, and we are ignoring any influence the voters may have on the voting strategies of others. We are measuring, simply and solely, the worth of a specified number of votes to a voter. For (critical) comments on Johnston's article, and his replies, see Garrett, McLean and Machover (1995), Johnston (1995b), Morriss (1996), Johnston (1996), and Garrett and McLean (1996). For a more formal discussion of this fallacy (and others), see Felsenthal and Machover (1998: pp. 211–20 and ch. 7).

78 It may be worth reminding the reader of this distinction, because not all writers on mathematical power seem to be aware of it: see, for instance, Garrett and Tsebelis (1999) for an article that quite ignores it. For further discussion of this article see the remaining articles in the July 1999 and January 2001 issues of *Journal of Theoretical Politics*, particularly Felsenthal and Machover (2001).

79 Felsenthal and Machover (1998: p. 35). This distinction is important, but I am not happy with seeing it in terms of the voter's *motivations*: apart from anything else, it would get very messy indeed if some voters are motivated by policy considerations and others by office-seeking ones. I prefer to see this distinction as representing two different reasons why some outside analyst might be interested in ascribing power to the voters; this is in general conformity with the approach in this book. Adopting this approach allows us to realize that when the power-ascribing analyst is *also* a voter, she does not need to make any assumptions about the motivations of her fellow voters.

80 Felsenthal and Machover (1998: p. 36). To forestall any misunderstandings that might be caused by the use of the word 'influence' in the definition of I-power, it may be necessary to point out that Felsenthal and Machover are *not* looking at a voter's influence in the sense of her ability to persuade other voters to vote the way she would like them to; 'influence' here is used simply to refer to an actor's ability to use her vote to bring about a preferred outcome. It is a property solely of the mathematical structure of the votes, and has nothing to do with the personal characteristics of the voters.

81 Felsenthal and Machover call this the *Banzhaf measure* in their (1998), although in their (2000) they opt for the term *Penrose measure*, more in agreement with my usage here. I have two reasons for preferring my nomenclature. The first is that Penrose deserves the credit for discovering this index: he did so nearly twenty years before Banzhaf (see Penrose, 1946). The second is that Felsenthal and Machover make a careful distinction between the Banzhaf measure and the (normalized) Banzhaf index, and stress that it is the Banzhaf *measure* that is appropriate here (see their 1998). The more careless readers of Felsenthal and Machover's book may not fully take this crucial distinction on board. This possibility is enhanced because we can use the Banzhaf index quite legitimately when we want to compare the powers of *different* actors (when the allocation of votes, and the quota required to pass a motion, remain fixed). Here it does not matter whether we use the Penrose or Banzhaf indices, since the *relative* size of two actors' power is the same on both measures. In short, you will never go wrong if you use the Penrose index in measures of I-power, whilst if you use the Banzhaf index where the Banzhaf measure (i.e. Penrose index) is appropriate you will go badly astray. See also Felsenthal and Machover (2000: p. 7).

82 Again, to forestall misunderstandings, I should perhaps point out that phrases such as the spoils of victory, or prize of power, are ambiguous – and usually metaphorical – verbal representations of what is supposed to be a clear mathematical concept. Some victories bring more spoils than others, and then there is more to divide up. But what we are trying to measure here is unaffected by the size of the purse; the question is what *proportion* of it each can get. This *is* a zero-sum (or constant-sum) notion.

83 Felsenthal and Machover (1998: pp. 191–2). At (1998: p. 45) they also prove my conjecture (pp. 166, 224, 226–7) that the Penrose index gives a measure of the worth of an actor to an outside briber if only *one* actor is to be bribed.

84 Felsenthal and Machover (1998: pp. 60–1 and 72–5); their (2000: pp. 24–6) is somewhat less technical. Instead of examining my first conjecture (which is not of interest to them),

Felsenthal and Machover prove that adopting my square-root rule maximizes the number of voters who get their desired outcome, and minimizes the expected *number of voters* who lose out through adopting a two-stage rule, in that they are in the majority of the whole electorate yet nevertheless lose the vote in the two-stage process.

Felsenthal and Machover also rightly point out (1998: p. 75) that these two results require setting the number of votes needed to pass a motion at just over half the total vote; I assume this condition, but do not say so.

85 See Felsenthal and Machover (1998: pp. 63–72) for the proof and further discussion; for a slightly less technical account see their (2000: pp. 22–3).

86 For another discussion of the need within democratic theory to be concerned with maximization as well as equalization, see Nagel (1988: particularly pp. 74–6). Nagel distinguishes between 'isocracy' (the requirement of equal power) and 'politicracy' (the requirement of maximizing power).

87 Felsenthal and Machover (1998: pp. 134–41). One factor Felsenthal and Machover consider which I do not is that it may often be sensible to abandon (or question) the equiprobability assumptions which underlie my discussion on pp. 192–7, where I am only considering voting power as ability. In this they are quite right; but the move from an ability measure to an ableness measure is a big one, and really lies outside the scope of their book.

At this point I would like to add an admission of failure. On p. 184, in explaining that in Chapter 24 I am considering only power as ability, I say "the comparable problem with ableness is how to detect and eliminate gerrymandering". Barry, in his review of this book, has called this "a pregnant sentence which is unfortunately not followed up" (Barry, 1988a: p. 318); and, after a brief elucidation of what the problem is, he concludes: "The jurisprudence that has grown up around this in the USA is quite mind-boggling and could, I think, be used to illustrate the great difficulties that lie in the path of those who seek to deploy the concept of power as ableness" (Barry, 1988a: p. 319). I can only concur here with Barry. I did look at some of this American jurisprudence, and my mind very quickly got about as boggled as it has ever been. To deal with this adequately would require a lengthy article – probably a lengthy book – on this topic alone; I rapidly decided I could not touch on the issue here. But the problem seems to me to lie less in deploying a concept of power as ableness – which, as I argue in section III above, seems to me to be not that difficult – and more in trying to work out both how democratic theory requires us to approach (benign) gerrymandering and also what principles (if, indeed, any) underpin the American courts' attitudes to the question. It is a big – and important – issue; but one best dealt with separately from a consideration of the concept of power.

88 Felsenthal and Machover (2000: p. 20; see also pp. 42, 45–6 [Tables 6, 9, 10] for illustrations of this effect). Although they describe this result as a "theorem", they have, at the time of writing, not yet provided a proof; the result was first given by Penrose (1952: Appendix), also without proof, but has subsequently been completely ignored. Note also that it seems to hold only when certain requirements are placed on the distribution of weights; but these requirements are not stringent, so that the result is likely to occur in practice in almost all bodies except the smallest. There are also some possible, though unlikely, distributions of votes that would leave a voter as a dummy, with no power at all: see my p. 229. I believe that, these exceptional cases aside, the powers and weights in large bodies are indeed very close to being proportional, although, when the quota is set at just over half, the voters with the larger weights have slightly more power than their weights would indicate: often up to about 5 per cent more.

1—Prologue

1 Perhaps I should say here that the writers I criticize are invariably those for whom I have the greatest respect, and from whom I have learnt most; frequently I was initially convinced that they were right, and my disagreements with them reflect changes in my own views. I

would like it to be understood that even if everything I say about somebody seems hostile, I am still grateful to him for helping me form my ideas. A critical mention is really also a compliment, even if a back-handed one, since I have not bothered to criticize or distance myself from writers who I feel had nothing of importance to say.

2—Power and influence contrasted

1 See, for instance, Simon (1953: p. 368 n. 3) or Dahl (1957a: p. 80).
2 The dictionary goes on to give many other technical senses.
3 Bagehot states that the British monarch has "the right to be consulted, the right to encourage, the right to warn" (1867: p. 111). These rights give the monarch considerable influence. But no constitution, even an unwritten one, could give such influence explicitly.
4 In later editions of his *Modern Political Analysis*, Dahl referred to Pitkin's "interesting attempt to clarify the meaning of various influence terms" (Dahl, 1984: p. 20 n. 2) but in his text he completely ignored her complaint quoted here.

3—Dispositional concepts

1 The quotation from Dahl is from his (1968: p. 410), in which he follows Simon (1957: p. 5). For Hobbes see his (1655: ch. 10). Hume, in *A Treatise of Human Nature*, states baldly that "the distinction, which we often make betwixt *power* and the *exercise* of it, is . . . without foundation" (Hume, 1739: p. 171); but later he comments that "tho' this be strictly true in a just and philosophical way of thinking, 'tis certain it is not the philosophy of our passions" (p. 311), and he then modifies his account, considering "it may justly be concluded, that power has always a reference to its exercise, *either actual or probable*, and that we consider a person as endow'd with any ability when we find from past experience, that 'tis probable, *or at least possible* he may exert it" (p. 313: my emphases). Such equivocation is not uncommon amongst those who equate power and its exercise whilst knowing intuitively that they are wrong to do so.

4—Power as a dispositional concept

1 See, for example, the careful analysis by Reeve (1982).
2 And omissions. Connolly considers that someone can *exercise* power by *refraining* from helping others when he could do so, provided that he could reasonably be expected to understand the harm he was causing by not acting (pp. 102, 106). Connolly also includes as an *exercise* of power that sense of 'having power' in which the powerholder does not need to act because his actions are anticipated, and he is given what he wants without needing to bestir himself (pp. 101–2).
3 In sections 6.2 and 6.3 I shall discuss how power and responsibility *do* connect.
4 This has the odd-sounding consequence that understanding Greek or English does not count as a human ability – although it is a human dispositional power (and certainly is not a *non*-human ability). This apparent difficulty is resolved in section 13.2.
5 Wrong (1979: p. 4) defines power as intended influence, as do many others.
6 See Oppenheim (1981: p. 46), Georgiou (1977), and, to an extent, White (1971).
7 See Connolly (1974/1983: pp. 104–6) and Lukes (1974: pp. 51–2).
8 Gibson offers two arguments; the second has already been considered and dismissed on pp. 20–1.
9 *De facto* power; not the *de jure* power of Power₅, which the Prime Minister possibly lacks.
10 This idea is explored further and in greater detail in Chapter 8.
11 The quotations are from Hume's *Treatise of Human Nature*, section vii, part I, and St Augustine, *The City of God* XIV, ch. 24. For Danto's discussion see Danto (1973: pp. 116–19; also the rest of ch. 5 and pp. 151–3).

5—Power and influence: the differences concluded

1 But compare Lukes's later version, in an excellent survey article: "The absolutely basic common core to all conceptions of power is the notion of the bringing about of consequences, with no restriction on what the consequences might be or what brings them about" (Lukes, 1979: pp. 634–5).

2 I owe this example to Fowler (1968: p. 13). The ease with which people confuse 'affect' and 'effect' is partly explained by an unfortunate oddity in the English language: the noun corresponding to the verb 'to affect' is 'an *effect*'; and there is no noun 'an affect'. So "the brandy has an effect on his recovery" does not mean that it *effects* it, but that it *affects* it. Hence *an effect* is something caused; it is not restricted to something accomplished. Perhaps this muddle has added to the confusion over the two very different verbs.

3 See Goldman (1972: section I and p. 241, and, particularly, n. 4).

4 For a further discussion of effecting and affecting see Appendix 3.3 (p. 221).

5 Goldman, in his (1974b: p. 233), does talk of power being over *outcomes* (and *control* over issues), but he does not investigate the difference this makes, apparently considering it merely a different terminological decision.

6 The *OED* gives seventeen different senses of 'power', of which at least four can be considered senses of social power (senses 1, 4, 5 and 6); only one of these senses can be followed by 'over' (sense 4). The *OED* gives thirty different quotations to illustrate the usage of this one sense of power, and in only *one* of these is the phrase 'power over' employed. If 'power' *was* normally followed by 'over' in our discussions of politics, the compilers of the *OED* would assuredly have noticed.

7 Perhaps this form of horse-trading (doing favours for people to put them in your power) is what American politicians have in mind when they contrast being powerful with being influential. See, for instance, Manley's discussion in his (1970: pp. 121–35).

8 This way of drawing the contrast is Ted Benton's: see Benton (1981: p. 174).

> Stanley Benn has found an equivocation of this sort in Hobbes, who
>> seems to oscillate between two conceptions of confrontations of powers. In the first place, there is the simple competition for a common objective, the success of one contender implying simply failure for the rest. . . . By contrast, there is a contention that arises from the effort of one man to control another, to win power over *his* power. . . . In the first case, the powers that are matched are the powers to gain primary objectives, like desired objects, jobs, or sweethearts, [and thereby the powerful indirectly affect those who fail to gain such objectives]; in the second, they are powers *against* each other, the power to inflict harm or confer benefits, used to induce compliance. (Benn, 1972: pp. 210–11)

9 *Why* this very limited conception of power has proved so congenial I leave to the future sociologist – or psychologist – of social science. Maybe a suggestion is that seeing power as harming others is characteristic of men at the third stage of the Freudians' four-stage personality typology (the phallic stage), whilst women, and men at other stages, conceptualize power very differently (see McClelland, 1975). It may be that when people rely on their intuitions about power they tell us less about power than they realize; but more about themselves.

10 See Carmichael and Hamilton (1968), and cf. Aberback and Walker (1970). Of course, achieving black power would have involved *affecting* people in ways they might not have liked, since it would have meant reducing the power of many whites. But the goal desired was that of giving black people more power over their own lives, *not* more power over other (white) people.

11 Connolly is someone who takes this last tack (Connolly, 1974/1983; pp. 86–8), overlooking that it is unclear why what he *is* interested in should be labelled 'power'.

12 Richard Peters has claimed that Hobbes's theory of power rests on a similar suppressed empirical claim that is hidden because he uses two definitions of power (a narrow one and a wide one) and fails to distinguish between them. The wide sense is an ability to obtain something; the narrow sense assumes the inevitability of conflict (Peters, 1956: p. 139).

13 I agree with Fowler that "the compound preposition 'with respect to' . . . should be used not as often, but as seldom, as possible" (Fowler, 1968: p. 521). It needs treating with great care and suspicion if muddled thinking is to be avoided. See also Fowler's strictures on those who misuse the word 'relationship' (pp. 514–15).

6—Why we need concepts of power

1 I have exchanged the order of the first two sentences to fit this passage into my text. The first omitted passage lists a few more concepts like 'power'; all the other omissions are of the word 'political' – omitted because Wolin's remarks apply equally well to non-political senses of the word 'power'.

2 To be more accurate, what we want to know here is the harm someone *would* do us, rather than the harm they *could* do us. We can safely antagonize powerful people if they are very tolerant. For an extended discussion of this difference see Appendix 1.

3 From a speech in 1881, quoted, without source, in Eccles (1981: p. 389).

4 The terms are Goldman's, from his (1970: p. 197).

5 Connolly considers that "when we see the conceptual connection between the idea of power and the idea of responsibility we can see more clearly why those who exercise power are not eager to acknowledge that fact. . . . Those who exercise power over others typically seek to deny it or to hide it." (Connolly, 1974/1983: p. 97). But this is simply factually false. Rulers have typically *revelled* in their power, and have gone to great lengths to impress their rivals and their subjects with the extent of their power. (For many examples of this, drawn from Renaissance Italy, see Martines (1980: chapter 12), though studies of most other times and places will reveal a similar ostentation). It is only people who are interested in evading responsibility who wish to deny their power. Most really powerful people have not been interested in this in the slightest – they have been interested in power for practical, not moral, reasons.

I think Connolly's mistake here is a good example of the errors one so easily falls into by forgetting that others have been interested in power for reasons rather different to one's own.

6 In Chapter 15 I argue that the other emphasis I have mentioned – the concern with freedom – can be best understood as a concern with certain sorts of obstacles to our power – with 'power' here still understood as the capacity to effect.

7 I write "empirical" responses because there is also, of course, the normative response that things are indeed as the critic has described them, and a good thing too.

8 The moral context, being concerned with the power to bring about certain specified outcomes, and at a given time, does not really lend itself to theoretical speculation.

9 Amongst people who have suggested this are Dahl (e.g. 1965: pp. 88–9); Goodin (1980: p. 2); McLachlan (1981: p. 406); March (1966); and Russell (1938: pp. 10–11). It is perhaps noteworthy that the people who have concluded that 'power' is a term without much utility tend to see it as part of an explanatory theory. See, for instance, March (1966).

10 I suspect that this provides a further reason why so many analyses of power are so odd: the writer was looking for a term that could explain, and dumped the label 'power' on one of the ones that came along. Actions (which can be described as exercises of power) *can* feature in explanations. This may explain why so many writers, particularly the ones that think of themselves as 'scientific', blur the distinction between having and exercising power.

11 This conclusion is from Dahl (1965: p. 89; my emphasis); for the two premises see, inter alia, his (1963: p. 6, or 1957a: p. 80) and his (1968).

7—The family of ability concepts: introduction

1 Von Wright, for one, looks mainly at generic abilities in his (1963) – see, for instance, von Wright (1963: pp. 50–1). Goldman's analysis is in Goldman (1972: particularly pp. 225–6 and n. 4; and 1974a: p. 264).

2 Time-specific abilities, when they are fully spelt out, include both references to time;

hence Goldman is right to insist that a (time-specific) ability statement has two temporal components: one has the ability at time t_1 to do X at (or by) time t_n. See Goldman (1972: pp. 225–6 and 230–1; 1974a: pp. 263–4).

3 The first quotation is from von Wright (1971: p. 68); the second from Danto (1973: p. 28). See also ch. 2, ch. 3 sec. III and ch. 4 sec. IV of Danto's book, and the slightly different definition given by Goldman in (1970: ch. III sec. 4).

4 The term is Goldman's, from his (1970: p. 21). See, further, ch. 2 of his book.

8—The family of ability concepts I: epistemic, non-epistemic and latent abilities

1 The terms are again Goldman's, from his (1970: p. 203 et seq.); see also his (1972: p. 265 n. 7). This distinction has been referred to in passing in the literature, though only Goldman and Carr (1979) discuss it, and neither goes into much detail. The distinction is sometimes referred to as that between 'knowing how' (my 'epistemic ability') and 'ability' (my 'non-epistemic ability') (e.g. by Carr, 1979, and Chisholm, 1976: p. 54). This seems to me unfortunate for two reasons. First, know-how is only *part* of what is required for an epistemic ability: the relevant basic actions are also needed. I may be an excellent armchair theorist on shot-putting; I may even be an excellent coach; but unless I do something about my muscles I will never be any good at putting the shot. Know-how, or skill, is what turns a non-epistemic ability into an epistemic one; it is not a separate sort of ability. Secondly, the relation between knowledge and epistemic ability is not necessarily straightforward: it is always possible that as someone finds out more he simply becomes more confused, until he no longer knows what to do. We have all at times failed to accomplish something which we would have done easily had we known less.

2 But we may have to be careful how we describe the ability in which we are interested – see Chapter 9 (p. 67 and nn. 13 and 14). Note also that ability-claims can be phrased either as the ability to *do* something (an action) or as the ability to *bring about* something (a state of affairs). Which way they will be phrased depends on the interests of whoever is making the claim; neither is in any way philosophically privileged or to be favoured for general philosophical reasons. In this part of the book I shall usually talk generally of someone's ability to do something, but this is to be taken as including the ability to bring about some state of affairs – "do" is to be interpreted as widely as possible, to include every verb that can stand between "ability to" and "something".

3 Some philosophers have argued that the non-epistemic sense of ability and power is the *only* correct one, and that any reference to the actor's intentions is a blunder, no matter what the context. One such argument, made by Ayers (in his 1968) amongst others, is based on the sound dictum of medieval logic *ab esse ad posse*, which is then incorrectly applied to the analysis of abilities. The dictum means that what is is possible: if something occurs then it is possible that it occurs. Applied to actions this becomes: if somebody does something, then it is possible that she does that thing. But it is mistaken to infer from this that if somebody does something then she was *able* to do it – in every sense of 'able' we might want to use. It does not follow from someone doing something that she has the epistemic ability to do it; but that it does not follow does not mean that an epistemic concept of ability contradicts *ab esse ad posse*. We have room amongst our concepts for both epistemic and non-epistemic ability; we need both; and we can have both without running foul of any dicta of medieval logic.

4 That latent abilities are distinct from present abilities when the ability is generic, but not when it is time-specific, is the reason for one of the disagreements between David Braybrooke and Alvin Goldman (see Braybrooke, 1973: pp. 370–1; Goldman, 1974a: pp. 264–5). Goldman (in Goldman, 1972, to which Braybrooke's article is a response) opts to analyse time-specific power, and thereby, as Braybrooke rightly points out, "obliterate[s] the difference between having power and being able to acquire power" (Braybrooke, 1973: p. 371). But *given* this decision (which Braybrooke does not question), Goldman is right to obliterate this distinction, and right to claim that "Nixon, in 1940, had the power to nominate Burger Chief Justice in 1970". (Braybrooke, on p. 370, asserts that this claim is "absurd", which Goldman denies at his 1974a: pp. 264–5. It may well be that the claim *is* absurd – it is a very odd claim to want to make – but it is neither false nor meaningless. There are many true statements that it would be absurd to assert, and Braybrooke has here come up with one of them.)

9—The ifs and cans of abilities

1 The example in this sentence is Alan White's, from White (1975: p. 34).
2 The two manifestation conditionals are of the same sort in that both are *necessary* for the power's manifestation. The manifestation conditional for a natural power (or mere disposition) also states a *sufficient* condition for the power's manifestation; but this is not, of course, true for an ability, because of ability's 'two-wayness'. This crucial point is the subject of the next two sections.
3 I return to descriptive conditionals in section 11.2.
4 As White asserts in White (1975: p. 35).
5 Though choosing, wanting and trying are all different, I shall treat them together; the differences do not matter for this discussion. Note, also, that I reserve the term 'choice conditional' for conditionals of the form "if A chose/wanted/tried, then . . ." that are manifestation conditionals. Not all conditionals of this form are manifestation conditionals, as we shall see, and those that are not will not be called choice conditionals.
6 The example is Kenny's, from his (1975: p. 141). See also Danto's discussion of voluntary erection, pp. 27–8, above.
7 The example discussed in this paragraph is White's (White, 1975: p. 31). This emphatic usage probably occurs more often when time-specific abilities are being discussed than it does for generic abilities, and serves to emphasize that, at the time(s) in question, the circumstances were such that I was able to do it at will. See, further, section 11.2.
8 David Carr's example (Carr, 1979: p. 397). Carr tries to use this example to illustrate the difference between an epistemic and a non-epistemic ability, considering that the fugitive's ability has "much the same sense" as someone being (non-epistemically) able to hit the bull's-eye at darts if they have done it just once. But however one reads the example of the leaping fugitive it does not illustrate *that* distinction.
9 For a discussion of "if I wanted to *enough*" where the conditional *is* the choice conditional, see pp. 68–9. I have assumed in the text that the fugitive can choose to leap at other times and, were he to try to leap, would fail to reach the other rooftop: he normally lacks this athletic ability. To describe him as having the ability if he *wants* to enough, though, may be stretching the notion of wanting further than it should go. For a discussion of phobias, in which the conditional "I could, if I (only) wanted to" is meant quite literally, see p. 68.
10 A suggested counter-argument to my conditional analysis (in, for example, Taylor, 1966: ch. 5) is that it is incoherent to talk about trying to raise an arm or wiggle a finger – for just what does this trying consist of? We do not try; we just *do*. But I think this is false, even for the basic actions here mentioned: you can try and fail to do a basic action. Presumably this would happen if, unknown to you, you had lost some members of your repertoire of basic actions and then discovered the loss (Chisholm, 1976: p. 85). I agree that, for basic actions, one cannot fail by doing the wrong thing: all non-epistemic abilities must also be epistemic abilities. However, it is invalid to argue that because this is the case for basic actions it is also true for more complex actions: here possibilities for error abound. There is certainly a logical gap between going to Boston and trying to go to Boston – otherwise nobody could ever lose their way!
11 This is explored further in Chapter 11.
12 I argue for this proposition in Appendix 1.

13 This example is an adaptation of Quine's (Quine, 1953: pp. 141–2). See Quine (1953: ch. VIII, or 1960: pp. 141–56) for discussion of referential opacity.

14 Carr, after making this point with an amusing example (Carr, 1979: pp. 407–8), introduces a doubt backed by another example:

> Oddly enough, some substitutions in knowing how contexts seem to be safe enough. For example the same magician's performance might be described as: (14) A display of conjuring tricks or alternatively as: (15) A performance of prestidigitation. Now it seems clear enough that if the magician knows how to bring about (14), then he also knows how to bring about (15) . . . ([even though] he might be unaware that 'prestidigitation' means much the same thing as 'conjuring'). (Carr, 1979: p. 408)

But if what we are interested in is the ability to prestidigitate *as distinct from* the ability to conjure, then our unlearned magician does lack the ability, since he does not know how to prestidigitate. Usually, of course, we don't want to test people's abilities and vocabularies simultaneously; but someone might justifiably claim to have been unable to obey the notice 'Expectoration Prohibited' if she didn't know what it meant (unable in the epistemic sense, of course).

15 Phobias work in two different ways: one can be somehow unable to *choose* a certain end, or unable to *act* in the appropriate ways. Kleptomaniacs might be unable to stop themselves wanting to steal, and thus steal perfectly conscious of what they are doing; on the other hand, they might find themselves stealing without even realizing it, and thus be unable to prevent themselves. Similarly, agoraphobics might be unable to choose to venture into open spaces; or they may pass out whenever they *do* so venture. In the former cases, they do have actions available to them which will enable them to break the phobia, but do not have the epistemic ability to do them; in the latter cases they lack even the non-epistemic abilities. It is the former type of cases that are being discussed here.

16 The body can be strengthened, and perhaps the will can too – but these would be latent abilities rather than currently existing ones.

17 This only scrapes the surface of the problems with weakness of will. For fascinating insights into what lies underneath see Jon Elster's work, particularly Elster (1979: ch. 2). I should just like to comment that if you can bind yourself against your future self, as Ulysses literally did, then presumably you are (now) *not* unable to choose (and try) to obtain the end in question – you are able to bypass your weak will, as it were, and ensure that it does not get the chance to fail you.

18 For the argument that all ability-claims contain *two* choice conditionals – "if A chose not-X" as well as "if A chose X" – see Appendix 3.2 (pp. 219–20) where the argument is rejected.

10—How to interpret conditional sentences

1 Compare, for instance, the entries under the headings 'Contrary-to-fact conditionals' and 'If' in the *Encyclopaedia of Philosophy*: Walters (1967) and Aune (1967).

2 I briefly discuss the approaches to counterfactual conditionals of David Lewis and Jon Elster in Appendices 2 and 3, respectively.

3 For the suppositionist approach see Mackie (1973: pp. 92–108).

4 In unfulfilled conditionals the antecedent refers to an event that has not taken place; in counterfactual conditionals the antecedent is, as a matter of fact, false. A belief-contravening hypothesis is a conditional in which the antecedent is *believed* to be false. The conditionals that arise in discussions of power are assessed by referring to the current state of belief in the social sciences – and can only be assessed in that way. What social scientists call "facts" are merely statements generally believed in the discipline to be true: conditionals that contradict such beliefs will be those that concern us here. Conversely, complications of the kind that arise when someone believes something to be false, and supposes it true, when it was true all along, do not arise in the analysis of power. So we can analyse counterfactual, unfulfilled and belief-contravening conditionals together.

For Rescher's analysis, see particularly his (1964); also his (1973a: ch. 11) and (1961). For some philosophical underpinning of his views on conditionals see his (1973a) and, particularly, his (1973b) – although I think that, for our purposes, his analysis as stated here can stand on its own.

The example I discuss here can be found at Rescher (1964: pp. 11 et seq.) or Rescher (1973a: pp. 268 et seq.).

5 Rescher (1964: p. 15, or 1973a: p. 271).
6 For a brief defence of my use of the suppositionist approach, and not the dominant 'possible worlds' approach, see Appendix 2. In that appendix I conclude that we can talk of possible worlds as a useful metaphor, but that we should not accept the 'possible worlds' approach in full. Philosophers should be warned that when I use the phrase "possible world" in the main text of this work, I am using it in the loose, everyday sense, meaning something like "an imaginative reconstruction of how some aspect(s) of our world might possible have been different". In Appendix 2 – and only there – "possible worlds" is to be understood in David Lewis's sense. (What this difference is will be explained there.)
7 It may be that the properties "being a cat" and "being a dog" are exclusive by definition, so that it is a logical truth that a cat cannot (simultaneously) be a dog. If so, the words "cat" and "dog" in (C2) and (C3) can be replaced by "pet" and some doggie-like description, respectively. But it must be understood that (C2) is not to be read as "If I had a dog, not a cat, it would bark" but as "If the animal which at present is my pet were to become suitably doggie-like, it would bark". There is, of course, no *logical* absurdity – at least within the analytic tradition – in supposing that my cat, currently purring contentedly in front of the fire, turns in the next hour into an alsatian. (If such great changes are to be ruled out as logically impossible, how could caterpillars ever become butterflies?)
8 Rescher himself makes this point, in a slightly different way, in his (1975: ch. 9).
9 One of my arguments in Appendix 2 against David Lewis's "possible worlds" approach is that it does not allow isolated antecedents.
10 Manifestation conditionals would seem obviously to be isolated – but see the discussion of them in the next chapter (section 11.2). An act conditional is not really a conditional at all, but the existence claim that there exists a string of A's basic actions which would result in X. Since it is part of the *definition* of a basic action that A can do it when she wants to, and that she *can* want to do it, no problems of ambiguity arise with basic actions.
11 More accurately, we restore consistency to *our* beliefs about *her* beliefs. *We* can consistently believe that *someone else* has an inconsistent set of beliefs and desires (people often do, after all).

11—The family of ability concepts II: ability and ableness

1 The term is Austin's (Austin, 1956a: p. 229).
2 Contrary to what some writers have suggested – for instance Austin (1956a: p. 230), Ayers (1968: pp. 103–4) and Kenny (1975: pp. 131–5) – there is no "can of opportunity": examples that have been offered are all 'all-in cans' for which the generic ability is so obvious that it is taken for granted. Thus Ayers considers that "The general ability to read may be possessed by someone in circumstances that make reading impossible, while an illiterate in a library may have the opportunity but not the capacity" (1968: pp. 103–4). But we would not say that the illiterate in the library can read, just because he is surrounded by books; or, if we did say it, we would withdraw it on discovering his illiteracy. For an opportunity is not *distinct* from the ability: what is an opportunity for someone depends on the nature of his abilities. That is why if you give somone who is illiterate a book you

don't give him the opportunity to read, any more than you give someone who is blind the opportunity to read by handing them your reading glasses – although without them *you* lack the opportunity to read. Situations become opportunities only when they dovetail with abilities.

3 "[Ableness]" replaces Kenny's "opportunity" in this passage, since there is no "'can' of opportunity" and Kenny's examples use the 'can' of ableness.

4 Kenny distinguishes ten senses of 'can', and twenty-two subsenses (Kenny, 1975: p. 131), but he fails to distinguish epistemic and non-epistemic abilities, or – crucial here – present and latent abilities.

5 Possibilities for confusion when considering the past are even greater than for the future, since most English verbs have the same form in the subjunctive and in the past indicative. Compare "if you gave a carpenter a chair, he could [subjunctive] mend it" with "you gave the carpenter the chair yesterday, so that he could [past indicative] mend it". The former contains no reference to time.

6 The next section expands on, and explains, this paragraph.

12—Comparing powers

1 One infinitely large set can be smaller than another infinitely large set. For instance, the set of all even integers is infinitely large but it is smaller than the set of all integers, since it is a proper subset of it.

2 For Bachrach and Baratz, see their (1962). For some evidence that the American polity was resistant to the stiletto heel of protest groups see Lipsky (1968 and 1970) and Gamson (1975).

3 Note that in the *practical* context a completely different idea of interest cropped up: I suggested that the researcher will value the outcomes according to whatever she is interested in (pp. 87–8). In the evaluative context the interests are those of the people in the society that is being researched.

4 Cohen's distinction between difficulty and cost in Cohen (1978: pp. 237–40) seems analogous to mine between opportunity cost and direct cost, although he expresses it in a different way.

5 Some of the implications of making the mistake of treating power as constant-sum are shown in Chapter 24, particularly section 2.

6 See Elster (1978: pp. 99–105); and see also Jerry Cohen's excellent analysis of a similar problem, in his (1983).

7 It should perhaps be immediately stated that such beliefs are *false* only if we accept the values and beliefs of the researcher: "different consciousness" would be a more appropriate term. Of course, if the correct values can be definitively established then any other belief system would be false in the full sense. I do not think that there are such truths about values, but whether there are or not is irrelevant for my discussion here.

8 Rational-choice theorists usually distinguish between situations of risk – with known probabilities for the various outcomes – and uncertainty. In situations of uncertainty – which is how they would characterize those I am considering here – they employ criteria of choice such as minimax or minimax regret. (In laymen's terms these involve hedging one's bets so one ensures that one does not lose – or lose out on – too much.) But such choice criteria treat the beliefs on which the actor bases his choice as ones about which he has no information, which is precisely not the case here: he has *very good grounds* for believing his beliefs to be true. To assimilate this case to that in which he has no grounds at all for believing them is to miss the point of the example. So an assessment of the strength of these grounds must be included in our consideration of what a reasonable choice would be.

9 For an outstanding study that employs exactly this approach see Gaventa (1980), discussed on p. 151.

10 We would probably also want to rule out certain sorts of actions as impermissible or irrelevant – for instance, illegal ones. Any ability we have to redistribute wealth by theft cannot be used to defend capitalism, however desirable such redistribution might be; neither can advocates of state socialism draw support from any efficiency gains that might be created by an illegal private sector and black markets.

13—The family of ability concepts III: active and passive power

1 As von Wright, for instance, does (von Wright, 1963: p. 48).
2 Everybody who has actions open to them has the *non-epistemic* ableness to 'bring about' whatever occurs when they forbear from intervening – but not necessarily the *epistemic* ableness. If you did not know that that outcome would eventuate were you to forbear to intervene (and you did not know any actions of yours that would bring it about), then you would lack the epistemic ableness to procure it.
3 The passage from Locke is from Book 2, ch. 21, sections 1–2 of Locke (1689). For Hobbes see Hobbes (1655) chs IX and X, particularly pp. 127–8 (which is in ch. X, section 1).
4 Locke, it seems, changed his mind about active power, and in his later writings used the term in my sense rather than that in the passage quoted. On this see Mattern (1980).
5 The ability to understand a language would seem to be an exception.
6 There is also the sense, which is not relevant here, of 'bound or obliged by law'.
7 The English language can be very confusing at times – and it is so here. For despite their similar appearance 'ability' and 'liability' come from completely different roots: the latter is not 'li-ability' and so is not to be contrasted with 'ability'. As the definitions make clear, 'ability' refers to the possibility of an *action*, whilst a liability is something (harmful) that is likely to happen *to* one. What I understand by a passive ability or passive power is a sort of positive liability: the regular receipt of something *beneficial*. Having passive power is thus akin to holding a sinecure: the benefits arrive regularly and without requiring any effort or even action on the part of the recipient.

For a discussion that in many ways parallels mine here, see Alan Ryan's exploration of the evaluative uses of the suffixes '-free' and '-less' in Ryan (1965: pp. 101–3).
8 This argument was made by the National Organization for Women. Elshtain (1985: p. 43) reports that in 1981 NOW filed a legal brief challenging all-male military registration on the grounds that "compulsory, universal military service is central to the concept of citizenship in a democracy", and that women, who were not registered for the draft, were thereby being treated as less than full citizens.
9 Perhaps we can assimilate the agent/patient and ability/liability distinctions by noting that your passive powers and ablenesses refer to things you *must* do or receive, but only that subset for which we can safely assume that if you *had* had a choice, you would have (should have?) chosen them anyway. Hence, when we refer to something as a passive power we imply that, although you are a patient, you are no worse off for being a patient rather than an agent: being a patient is not a liability to you.
10 I am not intending to engage in arguments about the correct interpretation of Marx; it just seems to me that this interpretation puts the case I want to put peculiarly well (and is, incidentally, correct). If you favour a rival interpretation of Marx's writings, then please try to imagine that the person I here call "Marx" is some fictional invention of my own: it is the argument that I put forward that I consider important, not whether or not the actual Marx would have agreed with it.
11 According to Ollman (1976: p. 280 n. 25), who refers to *The German Ideology*. It is sometimes unclear whether Marx wanted us to develop our powers, or develop *and use* our powers. (See the apparent equivocation in the quotation from Macpherson in the text.) But on Marx's conception of human nature the two claims probably amount to much the same thing.

14—Beyond personal power

1 It is, however, possible that a long series of weak Presidents could so weaken the position that it was no longer possible for any President to exercise much power – but that
is a different point. Neither am I trying to deny that it is very difficult to study 'the
presidency' without merely chronicling the acts of individual Presidents – in the main
because each incumbent changes the nature of the office and leaves it in a different state
from that in which he found it. Perhaps there should be a sign over the entrance to the
White House reading "Please leave the presidency in the condition that you would like to
find it".

2 For intelligent discussions of the importance of different distributions of information see
Kuhn (1966: pp. 642–53) and Bartlett (1974).

3 We must be careful not to confuse Mills's notion of structure with that used by recent structuralists. The structures of structuralists leave no room for power because they tell us what
will happen rather than what people are enabled to do: see Appendix 1.

4 For a further consideration of resources as a source of power see Chapter 19.

5 Even here there are problems. When considering Yale's power in New Haven, should we
restrict our attention "to circumstances where acts taken by Yale as an institution by
persons authorized to act and acting for it are involved", as Polsby suggests (Polsby, 1980:
pp. 181–2)? Or when people are worried about "the power of Yale" do they include things
that Yale administrators and employees can do in their private capacities?

6 The power of groups does not arise in moral contexts: we do not hold a group responsible
for anything that we cannot blame its members, as individuals, for.

7 Both taken from Goldman (1972) – pp. 236 and 238, respectively.

8 We must not confuse power with strength here. I do not have the strength to push the car,
but I have the power to get it pushed. Since you will help me if asked, I can treat your
strength as a resource of mine – I control it as I control my own strength.

9 See Olson (1965). I suspect that a lot of the apparent callousness associated with big-city
living stems from this paradox. For the more people there are around to help somebody
in distress, the less pressing it is for any given individual to come to their aid; the greater,
therefore, the likelihood that *nobody* will assist. This is a possible explanation of people
watching someone get murdered without even bothering to call the police – cases of which
are from time to time given great publicity. One such murder, of Kitty Genovese in 1964,
created the academic sub-discipline of "bystander studies"; for a fascinating survey of
research see Sheleff (1978), who confirms that empirical research shows that "the more
bystanders there are, the less likely it is that any one of them will respond" (p. 13) –
although he does not mention the explanation for this that I have suggested here.

10 It is on this point that Goldman goes uncharacteristically astray in his discussion of group
power. He considers that the group cannot contain redundant members, because he has in
mind a different reason for studying group power from any that I have mentioned. He
wants to allocate power to *individuals* via groups by adopting "some sort of distributive
principle: if a group of persons has collective power with respect to an issue, then every
member of the group has [some] power with respect to the issue" (Goldman, 1972: p. 240).
It is this distributive principle that I want to reject. For what it allows is that someone who
is completely powerless *on his own* to bring about something, can have some power if,
should others also want to bring it about, then it occurs. But this notion of 'some power'
can never be of any use to us. We cannot use it in the context of individual responsibility:
we cannot blame A for the non-occurrence of X when A, on his own, could do nothing
about this however hard he tried. Neither are we interested in this sort of power in practical contexts: we will not bribe A to bring about X in such circumstances. Nor is this a
useful idea in the context of social evaluation. In all cases we want to know who is able to
do what, and not who would be able to do something *if* others agreed with him (which,
unfortunately, they do not).

If, then, we are interested in group power it is because we want to know how much power that *group* has; it is not a way of getting at some other sort of *individual* power.

11 It might seem that I am agreeing here with Alvin Goldman's account criticized in the last note, in that I am distributing to individuals power that is collective. This is, however, not so. *Individual* workers gain safer working conditions through *collective* action. But this means that the things obtained through exercises of collective power go to individuals; it does *not* mean that each individual has some individual *power*. The power to obtain things and the things obtained must be kept distinct.

12 When we wish to consider what it is reasonable for groups to do – as we did for individuals in section 12.6 (pp. 95–7) – we need to notice that costs can fall in two sorts of ways. The costs may be borne by the group, as a whole, or by certain specific individuals within the group – and the latter is no less important when considering group power than when considering individual power. For, although the total costs to the group may be low, if the costs falling on some crucial individual are high (more than she could reasonably be expected to bear) then this can destroy the effective power of the whole group. The costs imposed on this individual would make it unreasonable of her not to drop out of the group; and if she does withdraw support the group will fail (because, ex hypothesi, this individual is crucial to the group's success). So in such a case the group effectively lacks power unless it can somehow redistribute the costs within it so that it demands less from a few crucial individuals.

15—Power and freedom

1 Berlin himself seems contradictory on this point. Thus he says both that "the extent of my freedom seems to depend on . . . how far [possibilities] are closed and opened by *deliberate* human acts" (Berlin, 1958: p. 130 n., my emphasis; see also p. 122) and that my freedom is limited when "other human beings, directly or indirectly, *with or without the intention of doing so*" block my possible actions (1958: p. 123, my emphasis; see also his 1969: p. xi).

2 For a fascinating discussion of the importance of treating people as befits their status, see Cupit (1996).

3 A somewhat similar account is offered by David Miller, but he suggests that "the appropriate condition for regarding an obstacle as a constraint on freedom is that some other person or persons *can be held morally responsible* for its existence" (Miller, 1983: p. 72; my emphasis). Miller then goes on to show how other criteria (for instance that the obstacle must be deliberately imposed) are "unsatisfactory" (p. 73). My proposal, on the contrary, shows how these alternative criteria can *all* be satisfactory: the underlying logic of the concept of freedom leaves room for different conceptions, giving rise to different criteria. I think that the claim that only deliberately imposed constraints limit freedom is not conceptually wrong or unsatisfactory; it is a legitimate notion of freedom that follows from a particular view of self-respect, although one that, as it happens, I do not share.

4 The aid could be provided by the state, a compatriot or a passing stranger; the relevant status could be thought of as being a human being, a member of a community, or a future or past benefactor of others: see, for instance, Titmuss (1970), Walzer (1983), Godwin (1793) and Hart (1955) respectively.

5 For examples of the former position see Steiner (1974) or Parent (1974a); for examples of the latter view see Benn and Weinstein (1971) or Oppenheim (1981: ch. 4).

6 Those who have claimed that if someone did something she could not have been unfree to do it, and have drawn the conclusion that laws do not infringe freedom, include Parent (1974b: pp. 155–6, 157 and 160) and Cassinelli (1966: pp. 32–6).

7 Some laws do attempt to *prevent* our doing things, rather than threaten to punish us if we do them. All laws involving censorship, licensing, and impounding forbidden goods aim to prevent our doing things, and thus make us unfree to do them (subject to the proviso in the next note).

8 Some have denied that being imprisoned for breaking a *just* law is an infringement of freedom. My account gives some credence to this view, since it can be argued that being imprisoned is not, in itself, inappropriate treatment – not if you deliberately broke a just law, received a fair trial and an appropriate sentence, etc. Maybe what I say in the text only applies uncontroversially if the law is unjust.

9 Oppenheim, for instance, runs these two together (Oppenheim, 1981: pp. 84–8).

10 Some have argued that present wants are irrelevant, for the different reason that you might change your mind. But if my account of the difference between power and freedom is correct, you can dislike restrictions on your *powers* for this reason, but not on your *freedoms*.

11 Contrary to Oppenheim (1981: p. 91).

12 See Benn and Weinstein (1971: pp. 204–5).

16—Studying power: introduction

1 Often it is easier to establish the absence of an ability than its presence. If, when aiming at the bull, I hit it with my first dart, this might be a fluke and so is not conclusive evidence of my skill; if, however, I miss the board altogether, then it is fairly clear that I am a novice at the game. We tend to employ a commonsense notion of the laws of probability in such cases. Thus Kenny appears to me to be on the right lines when he writes:

> Of course it is on the basis of people's performances that we attribute skills and abilities to them; but a single performance, however successful, is not normally enough to establish the existence of ability. (I say 'not normally' because a single performance may suffice if the task is sufficiently difficult or complicated to rule out lucky success. Pushing one's wife in a wheelbarrow along a tightrope stretched across Niagara Falls would be a case in point.) (Kenny, 1975: p. 136)

However it is not the difficulty of the task that is the key factor; rather it is the improbability of lucky, or flukey, success. The Ministry of Transport sensibly consider that successfully reading just one number plate at a distance of 25 yards is adequate evidence for the ability to read all such plates at a similar distance.

17—Direct experiments

1 See, for example, Cromwell and Olson (1975) and the two review essays Safilios-Rothschild (1970) and McDonald (1980) for a large range of references.

2 This example is taken from Oscar Lewis's descriptions of family life in Mexico, discussed below.

3 Less obvious candidates for those who only see enlightened marriages include who the partners can see or talk to, and whether they can go out of the house. There are also passive powers – but no less important for that – such as living without fear of assault.

18—Indirect experiments

1 For a study employing this reasoning see Crenson (1971).

2 Lewis (1959). See also his further work on these families, such as his (1962) and (1970).

19—Resources

1 For a heated but not particularly helpful exchange on the empirical support for this hypothesis, see Safilios-Rothschild (1970: pp. 547–9), Bahr (1972) and Safilios-Rothschild (1972), and the works cited therein. Most of the in-depth studies of families – which I consider more valuable – that I have seen support the resource theory. All Oscar Lewis's five families either act on it or believe it – for instance Guillermo Gutierrez dates the loss of the upper hand in his marriage to the day he allowed his wife to start earning money (Lewis, 1959: pp. 163–4). See also the comments of American couples expecting their first child, reported in LaRossa (1977). Here, though, the situation is complicated since some wives thought they would gain in power, despite stopping paid employment: they thought that their new role as a mother would provide compensating resources. One wife even said that she would be able to threaten to leave her husband, taking the baby with her, whilst before the baby's arrival any such threat would have been empty, since if she left her husband she would not have deprived him of anything he valued much.

2 Though these other factors are presumably more important, since the wife can only force "concessions" from her husband – which shows where the real power lies. Even so, Kuhn uses his conclusion to justify sexual double standards to prevent women from becoming too powerful. (For a brief justification of the assumption about differential sexual desire see Kuhn (1974: pp. 419–20).)

3 In Part IV I discuss how we can calculate the actors' powers when we have knowledge of the distribution of one important resource – votes.

4 For an intelligent study of protest activity as the attempt to mobilize the support of others, see Lipsky (1968) and (1970). Lipsky's account of the dynamics of protest activity leads persuasively to the conclusion that protest is a weak resource, and also one that demands a great deal of skill to use effectively – and precisely the sorts of skill that those without other resources are unlikely to have.

20—Studying power

1 On the contrast between issue-oriented and interest-oriented approaches see below, particularly p. 149; on the stiletto heel fallacy see p. 88.

2 By this I mean unforeseeable and unpreventable *by the victim*, not (necessarily) by the employer; and the overall accident rate may be highly predictable.

3 It is no coincidence that formal education is probably the middle-class issue par excellence. Those who expect that their children will have a chance in the scramble for the few professional jobs – jobs that crucially demand a good education – will be (justifiably) obsessed with the issue. But those who realize that their children's chances of gaining one of these jobs are slim, whatever the educational system, because they are so severely disadvantaged by other factors, will have little interest in educational reform. If the realistic choice is between the mine and the steelworks (if there is choice at all), then educational policy does not make much difference to one's life when compared with the conditions of work in these jobs.

4 For a critique of a study that does systematically overlook all such issues, and in which I expand on some of these points, see Morriss (1975).

5 For a discussion of power stemming from rules and routines see Parry and Morriss (1974).

6 This summary does scant justice to Gaventa's book, which I recommend you to read in full. For the incidents mentioned in this paragraph, see sections 6.1 and 9.2 for the two failed attempts to exercise power, *passim* for the violence, and Part III (and *passim*) for the discussion of the region's culture. It seems to me, incidentally, that Gaventa is much more successful in establishing his claims about power than he is in showing that he is following Steven Lukes's "three-dimensional" account of 'power'.

21—The power of votes: introduction

1 Sophisticated voting is only advantageous when issues are partitioned into more than two outcomes: a complication I shall not consider. It should not be difficult, however, to extend the analysis developed in this chapter to include cases of sophisticated voting. In such cases, unlike those considered here, an individual's epistemic voting power may well differ from her non-epistemic power – depending how sophisticated she is.

2 The assumptions made when measuring ability have been put more formally by Doug Rae (1969: p. 44).

22—Measuring ability

1 Penrose (1946). See also his (1952). A similar approach is offered in Coleman (1973).

2 See Shapley and Shubik (1954) and Banzhaf (1965), respectively.

3 As we shall see, Shapley and Shubik's index applies under slightly more relaxed assumptions. But these will do to get us going.

4 Shapley and Shubik (1954: p. 378 n. 7). The exact meaning of this third premise need not concern us here; for a brief discussion see Luce and Raiffa (1957: pp. 245–55).

5 See, for instance, Barry (1980b: pp. 276–8).

6 Instead of thinking of this process as bribing legislators, it is perhaps less distasteful to consider it as buying shares in a company, provided that we are only interested in buying the shares to influence the company's policy, and not for investment purposes. The index will tell us how much we should be prepared to pay for shares of each type as they come on to the market, provided that we know how much we could expect to gain (or to lose) from the company's policies.

7 If you would vote for his preference, he would only lose if both the others voted against. The chances of this occurring are $\frac{1}{2} \times \frac{1}{2} = \frac{1}{4}$. So his preferred outcome would win $\frac{3}{4}$ of the time.

8 The mathematically inclined can consult Shapley (1953); non-mathematicians will probably be willing to accept my word that the coincidence of results in this example is found quite generally.

9 See, respectively, Coleman (1971), Rae (1971), Banzhaf (1965), Riker (1964) (the hint occurs in the Addendum), and Riker and Shapley (1968).

10 Coleman (1971: p. 276). See also Banzhaf (1965: pp. 330–1 n. 32) for a similar complaint.

11 Strictly speaking, we need not assume that the probability of every voter voting for a motion is $\frac{1}{2}$. We can assume that, on any one vote, each voter's probability of supporting a motion is unknown and is independent of all other voters' probabilities of supporting the motion, provided that the pattern of each voter's probability of supporting a motion is a symmetrical distribution about $\frac{1}{2}$. This relaxation of the assumptions, producing the Penrose/Banzhaf index, is very different from the relaxation (described on pp. 163–4) that produces the Shapley–Shubik index.

12 The mathematical expression of the Shapley–Shubik index for an actor i is given by:

$$\sum_{S \subset N} \frac{(s-1)!(n-s)!}{n!} [v(S) - v(S - \{i\})]$$

where N is the set of all voters and S is any subset of N; $v(S)$ is the value of a set (which is 1 if it is winning and 0 if it is losing); and lower-case letters are the number of members in the set denoted by the corresponding capital letter. The Banzhaf ratio is given by the same formula without the factorials, which is clearly simpler. But for a more convenient (if less comprehensible) way of calculating the indices see Owen (1982: pp. 198–211).

13 For a long while it was thought that the Penrose, Banzhaf and Shapley–Shubik indices always produced the same ordering (see, e.g., Allingham, 1975), but it is now known that this is not always the case. In fact, one of the proposals for amending the Canadian constitution produced different orderings. This proposal (the "Victoria Charter", put forward in 1971) involved two-stage voting (see the discussion in Appendix 4.1), and then the different premises of the Penrose/Banzhaf and Shapley–Shubik indices can make a difference. (Banzhaf's premises do not include Shapley and Shubik's additivity condition, mentioned on p. 161, which is replaced by some even obscurer conditions.)

However, when we have more straightforward rules, which allow every actor to be allocated votes which are directly commensurable, then it is a simple matter to show that the Penrose, Banzhaf and Shapley–Shubik indices all produce the same ordering. This is the case, for instance, in unicameral (but not in bicameral) legislatures. It is only when this commensurability condition holds that my LMDS index *always* gives the same orderings as the other indices.

14 It must be stressed that the meaning of a minimal decisive set is not the same as the similar idea employed in Banzhaf's procedure for calculating his index. Banzhaf's procedure looks at those sets which are winning but would lose if some vital member were dropped; my minimal decisive sets are winning and *all* members are vital in this sense. Thus in this example, Banzhaf's procedure includes {ABC}, since this is not winning if A drops out; mine excludes it since it is winning when C drops out.

23—Measuring ableness

1 For bribe indices of ableness – the equivalent of the Shapley–Shubik index for abilities – sce Appendix 4, pp. 227–8.

2 See, for instance, Butler (1983) and Bogdanor (1983).

3 See the discussion in Bogdanor (1983: chs 7 and 8 and, particularly, pp. 118–21 and 133–7).

4 Of course, the Nationalists and Labour would probably try to engage in log-rolling, but that is another matter that I will not consider here. If these parties do form a coalition this will be reflected by their always voting together, which is considered under non-random voting.

5 Notice that I am not saying here quite the same as Brian Barry does in his apparently similar discussion in his (1980b: pp. 284–302). Barry defines 'success' as "the probability of getting the outcomes you want", and characterizes success as the sum of luck and decisiveness. "Luck is the probability of getting what you want without trying and decisiveness is the increase in the probability of getting what you want that occurs if you try" (p. 300). Luck, then, is the probability of getting what you 'want' should you nevertheless abstain, and decisiveness is defined residually as success minus luck. Decisiveness, so defined, is always no greater, and usually less, than my notion of active power. On Barry's account an absolute dictator is decisive only half the time, and lucky the other half (when the decision would have gone the same way had he not tried to affect it). I think that my active/passive distinction draws the line in a more useful place.

6 This holds whenever votes are commensurable: that is, all voting resources can be ranked and compared with each other.

7 This is the case in Committee III when one member abstains.

8 This is not always the case for other decision rules. For example, when A has 95 votes, B has 3 and C 2, and a two-thirds majority is required, B and C have the same power, as even when A abstains B cannot secure a two-thirds majority over C's opposition.

9 Some have gone sadly wrong by allowing abstaining voters to be pivotal. For instance Fishburn appears ready to assert (Fishburn, 1973: pp. 53–5) that, in a three-member committee, you have more power with 51 votes out of a hundred (with the remainder split unevenly) than with 98 votes (with the others split evenly) – 9 per cent more power, in fact. You also have the same amount of power, on his index, if you have 1 vote (with the others split 98, 1) as you do if you have 32 (with the others divided 35, 33), whilst it is not difficult to see that you are considerably better off with 32.

10 For a completely mistaken discussion of a similar situation, coming to the conclusion that the power of such 'quarrelling' members can increase, see Brams (1975: pp. 181–2, or 1976: pp. 189–90). Brian Barry is quite right to comment that "Brams is like someone who owns a broken thermometer and says that the fact that it does not register a higher temperature when it is put in a flame shows us something new and interesting (albeit counter-intuitive) about the nature of heat" (Barry, 1980b: p. 284). Brams's mistakes lie in unintelligently

extending Shapley and Shubik's and Banzhaf's indices when allowing non-random voting, and – more important – using these indices at all for comparing power in this way: we have to use the Penrose or EPW indices. For more on this last point see Chapter 24.

11 The same problem could occur in determining the Leader of the Opposition. "The Minister of the Crown Act of 1937 requires [the Speaker] to designate as Leader of the Opposition the leader of the party, 'having the greatest numerical strength in the House' [excluding the Government party, presumably]" (Butler, 1983: p. 141). Even if the Alliance had a leader, does it count as a party?

12 In fact, it would make no difference if they carried their rebellion to the point of voting against their party in such cases; since it makes no difference, they might as well not do it if this would run the risk of being disciplined.

13 It is obviously tedious to calculate an index by tabulating all the possible voting configurations and counting the number of times that each actor wins (or avoids defeat), and there are simple techniques that reduce the labour considerably. But I have been trying to ensure that the logic of the procedure is not obscured by sophisticated technical accretions.

14 Both David Butler and Vernon Bogdanor take the inconsistent line that the decision should be made by the monarch alone, but at all costs without being contentious. They fear that "if the Sovereign comes to be accused of partisanship, she could be embroiled in the kind of political controversy which could prove perilous to the institution of constitutional monarchy" (Bogdanor, 1983: p. 89); it could be perilous because "it does not enhance the authority of the office of head of state if the holder feels forced, however unavoidably, into actions which many voters regard, however misguidedly, as partisan" (Butler 1983: pp. 124–5). But if the monarchy is to retain discretionary powers, it must be deemed strong enough to use them; if it is as insecure as Butler and Bogdanor imply, it should abandon its remaining political powers. Choosing procedures simply to protect the monarchy (rather than reflect the outcome of the election) may have been acceptable to political conservatives in the eighteenth century, but surely not in the twentieth.

24—Creating power

1 For a survey of some of the courts' judgements on this issue, see Grofman and Scarrow (1979).

2 Figures are for 1982, taken from TUC (1983: pp. 642, 636).

3 It amazes me how little this problem is recognized. For instance, two eminent writers in the field, in a book promisingly entitled *Fair Representation: Meeting the Ideal of One Man, One Vote*, aim "to establish a solid logical foundation for choosing among the available methods of apportioning power in representative systems" (Balinski and Young, 1982: p. ix). Yet these experts simply *assume* that "a distribution of seats exactly proportional to the populations of the states is, of course, the ideal solution" (Balinski and Young, 1982: p. 67). As we have seen this assumption is quite wrong (in spite of the "of course"). Balinski and Young's entire book is concerned with the 'problem' raised by the impossibility of allocating seats *exactly* proportional to population if we can allocate only whole numbers of seats to the states, and not fractions. This 'problem' becomes irrelevant when we realize that we don't want to allocate seats proportional to population anyway.

4 The full reference to the *Iannucci* case is *Iannucci* v. *Board of Supervisors of Washington County, New York* (1967) 282 N.Y.S. 2d502.

5 The constant-sum (or zero-sum) assumption is probably helped by the frequent description of power as a relationship: power over others. If you have power over me, then it seems as if what you gain I lose, so that, overall, powers cancel out – much as the total debt in a closed economy is always zero, since your debts are someone else's credits (and vice versa). This analogy does not hold even when power over people is under consideration; and certainly not for power over outcomes, which is what both Banzhaf and Shapley and Shubik are considering.

6 Grofman and Scarrow (1979: pp. 170–1, 176–7) describe Banzhaf's use of the square-root rule.

7 It is in a branch member's interest to agree in advance that the delegate will cast as many votes as possible, in spite of the possibility that the delegate may be voting against the member's preference. The probability of a member being in a majority in his branch is always greater than the probability of being in a minority, since the majority must be greater than the minority; therefore, each member's power is increased if the delegate casts the maximum possible vote.

8 Proving this is where the mathematics comes in; but it is a well-established result in probability theory, and I do not think anything would be gained by proving it here.

9 This can be proved independently, but also follows quickly from the previous result. The square-root rule maximizes the probability that a majority of voters wins overall; it therefore maximizes the sum of the individuals' expected probability of winning; it therefore maximizes the sum of the Penrose indexes of power.

10 It is amazing that this problem has received so little attention in the literature on democracy: one would have thought that there would be at least *some* discussion of the basic principle of democracy, and yet I am not aware of any. I suspect that this omission stems from the unthinking acceptance of an equality principle, probably aided by an assumption that there is a constant amount of power.

11 This can be shown by looking at an individual's expected probability of winning. There are two ways in which an individual can eventually win: if he is in the majority when voting for his delegate and his delegate is then in the majority; or if he is in the minority when voting for his delegate but his delegate is then outvoted. His expected probability of winning in a two-stage system is thus

$$EPW_i = EPW_G EPW_D + (1 - EPW_G)(1 - EPW_D)$$

where EPW_i is i's overall expected probability of winning, EPW_G is his expected probability of winning within his group, and EPW_D is his delegate's expected probability of winning in the second stage convention. Simplifying this, and substituting $EPW = \frac{1}{2}(P + 1)$ (from p. 172) we have

$$P_i = P_G P_D$$

where P_i is i's overall Penrose power index, P_G is the index of his active power within the group, and P_D is his delegate's active power in the second stage.

12 This is a much smaller loss, proportionately, than occurs in general. With small numbers the proportionate loss fluctuates considerably. In this example it is only 8.6 per cent, whilst with four people split into two groups of two each it goes as high as 33 per cent. I chose this example simply because it is easier to see what is happening with odd numbers, which do not require tie-breaks. But the proportionate loss is always less when m and n are odd.

13 I could also draw in further columns in which pluses and minuses are interchanged throughout. But – hoping this makes things easier to follow – I have treated them as permutations of the four basic configurations.

14 This simplification does not exclude anything; a minority which is able to *pass* a motion is adequately represented by the row(s) in Table 2 in which that minority is able to *block* a motion, since we are assuming that the phrasing of motions is random.

15 This is a common complaint against Rawls's principle. Rawls takes an extremely timid attitude towards risk, and it is not clear how this can be justified – certainly Rawls fails to do so.

16 In many cases we can make reasonable approximations which simplify the calculations. I have not discussed these here, since my concern has been with the logic of the process, not

with the mathematical tricks that make it easier to carry out. As we saw when discussing Shapley and Shubik's index, concentrating on the techniques of the calculation can easily obscure the logic of the process.

25—Understanding concepts

1 A term which has suffered an analogous extension is 'discrimination'; I try to make sense of it in Morriss (1986) – an article which provides a further illustration of the approach to concepts and words advanced in this chapter.

Appendix 1—The redundancy argument rejected

1 This formulation is Bob Jessop's, from his (1976).
2 For this notion of a book of life see Goldman (1968).
3 Not all time-travelling will involve seeing such unfortunate results. But people do die in train crashes and if they had perfect knowledge of the future would have to know this. Whilst we can construct stories – even sad ones – in which the conflict I point to does not arise (Goldman does, in his 1968: section XI) this is only a part of the future, and I think we currently have excellent grounds for believing that unwelcome events like train crashes *will* happen in the future.
4 Compare Newcomb's Problem (introduced by Nozick in Nozick, 1969) and the now considerable literature on it.
5 Jon Elster reaches the same conclusion: "When I act, it is logically impossible for me to regard myself as a fully determined mechanism whose behaviour can be predicted by myself and be incorporated as a basis of my future plans" (Elster, 1980b: p. 214). For a fascinating, if brief, further development of this see Elster (1979: pp. 171–2). The opposite view is taken by David Lewis (in his 1976), but the example he chooses to discuss (can time-travelling Tim kill his grandfather?) allows him to evade the exact problem that I discuss here.
6 Some people go further. You may have the power to get something if you choose, they say, but you may also be fed distorted information so that you do *not* choose it. Your choice then is not really autonomous – there is a sense in which it is not *your* choice. For a consideration of this suggestion see section 12.6.
7 'Can' here being taken in its non-epistemic sense – see sections 8.1 and 8.2.
8 As before, if we know that we could not possibly prevail on the person to help us, then we have no interest in their power: once the CIA accepted that Castro was unbribable, they probably did not bother to speculate what he could have done for them if he *had* been bribed. But that, of course, does not make Castro any less powerful.

Appendix 2—David Lewis and his amazing possible worlds

1 I shall assume that the reader has knowledge of the general logic of possible world accounts of counterfactuals. The main works are Stalnaker (1968), Pollock (1975), and, particularly, Lewis (1973).
2 On isolated beliefs see Chapter 10 (pp. 76–7). Elster makes a similar point to mine; he calls an isolated belief "an accidental or exogenous fact" (Elster, 1978: pp. 186–7).
3 Barry's example: see his (1980a: p. 140).

Appendix 3—Jon Elster on counterfactuals

1 See Elster (1978: ch. 6, and 1976). For discussion of Elster's work see Barry (1980a) and Elster's reply (Elster, 1980a), and a symposium in *Inquiry* 23 (1980).

2 The "basic paradox of counterfactuals" can be found at Elster (1978: pp. 184–5, and 1976: pp. 253–4).

3 The reference in this passage is to Fogel (1964). Elster has a more extended discussion of Fogel's counterfactual in Elster (1978: pp. 204–8). See also Elster (1980a: pp. 146–7).

4 When I wrote this sentence, I was unaware that the first train *did* cause loss of life, and, what is more, of a very eminent person. At the opening of the Manchester–Liverpool Railway in 1830, the (British) Foreign Secretary was run over and killed. It is perhaps surprising that, after such an ill-fated start, rail transport was not abandoned.

5 For Elster's discussion of this example see Elster (1978: pp. 185–6, or 1976: pp. 253–4).

6 In n. 15 of Chapter 9 (p. 246) I distinguished two types of phobia: those that work on choice and those that work on actions. If de Gaulle had a phobia of this latter type, so that – *whatever* he chose – he acted to safeguard France's independence, then he would indeed lack the ability to do so (though safeguarding France's independence would still be one of his powers, in the purely dispositional sense). Of course, Elster does not think de Gaulle had a phobia of either sort. What he means, I think, is that it seems clearly absurd to assume that de Gaulle *would* (not *could*) have wished for France to lose her independence.

7 In section 13.2 I argue that even this demand is not strictly necessary, but here we can accept it, and consider only active power.

Appendix 4—The properties of the power indices

1 The numbers in the first row of Table A4.2 are the probabilities of a motion passing (failing), given that the province at the head of a column votes for (against) it, and that all other provinces vote for (against) half the time. The probability of a motion passing is the product of the probabilities that each group of provinces votes for it. Hence if Quebec is certain to vote for a motion, its probability of passing is $1 \times \frac{1}{2} \times \frac{11}{16} \times \frac{1}{2} = \frac{22}{128}$; if only British Columbia is certain to vote for a motion, the probability of its passing is $\frac{1}{2} \times \frac{1}{2} \times \frac{11}{16} \times \frac{7}{8} = \frac{19\frac{1}{4}}{128}$. The probability of a motion failing can also be easily worked out, by calculating the probability of it not passing.

The increase in the probabilities, calculated in this way, is not *definitionally* the same as the Penrose index, since the latter is the probability that the actor is in a position to determine the vote. However, when we make the assumption that unbribed actors are equally likely to vote for and against motions, the increase in probabilities is always the same as the Penrose index.

2 Thus the probability of a motion passing if Quebec is bribed first and Ontario second is $1 \times 1 \times \frac{11}{16} \times \frac{1}{2} = \frac{11}{32}$. The gain from bribing Ontario is thus $\frac{44}{128} - \frac{22}{128} = \frac{22}{128}$ or $\frac{88}{512}$. If Ontario is bribed after British Columbia, the probability of a motion passing is $1 \times \frac{1}{2} \times \frac{11}{16} \times \frac{7}{8} = \frac{77}{256}$; Ontario has thus added $\frac{154}{512} - \frac{77}{512} = \frac{77}{512}$. The other entries in Table A4.3 are calculated similarly. When we know that Ontario is bribed second but we do not know who has been bribed first, it seems reasonable to assume that each of the nine contenders is equally likely to have been first. The expected gain for bribing each province second is thus the bottom row of the table divided by 9.

3 I can provide further details to anybody interested.

4 The main reason for this is that in New Brunswick's group only two out of four provinces are required to vote for a motion for that group to assent to it, so that, if two of the other three are certain to vote for it, New Brunswick's vote is of no extra worth. As the number of voters bribed increases, the probability of this increases, and so New Brunswick's value declines. Alberta's vote, on the other hand, is still significant even if the other two central provinces are already pledged to vote in favour of the change.

5 But an increase of one extra member which raises the number on the committee from an even number to an odd one does not decrease an individual's power. This is because a group of, say, six members has to include a tie-breaking procedure which comes into effect

when the vote is split 3–3. When the tie-break has a fifty–fifty chance of approving or defeating the proposal, it is exactly the same, mathematically, as adding another member who has a fifty–fifty chance of supporting or opposing a proposal. Thus whether one is in a group of six people which tosses a coin when it ties, or in a group of seven people, one has the same power and EPW – assuming, as we do, that votes are cast independently and at random, and voters cannot abstain.

Bibliography

In this book references are abbreviated to the author's surname and the original date of the work's publication. In the bibliography I give the publication details of the editions which I used, with the year of publication given when appropriate. When an article is noted as reprinted somewhere, page numbers refer to this reprint.

Two books which are important for this study have been reissued in second editions, which reprint the first editions (with identical page numbers) and then add new chapter(s). When I refer to material in the first edition (and, therefore, also in the second edition) I describe the work as Polsby (1963/1980) or Connolly (1974/1983); for the new material present only in the second edition I give the date of publication of the second edition only. On the other hand, later editions of Dahl's *Modern Political Analysis* are so different from the first edition that they are best treated as completely different books.

Aberback, J. D. and Walker, J. L. (1970): 'The meanings of black power: a comparison of white and black interpretations of a political slogan', *American Political Science Review* 64: pp. 367–88.

Agee, P. (1975): *Inside the Company: CIA Diary* (Harmondsworth: Penguin).

Allen, A. (1998): 'Rethinking power', *Hypatia* 13: pp. 21–40.

Allen, A. (1999): *The Power of Feminist Theory: Domination, Resistance, Solidarity* (Boulder, Colorado: Westview Press).

Allingham, M. G. (1975): 'Power and value,' *Zeitschrift für Nationalökonomie* 35: pp. 293–9.

Aristotle (c. 330 BC): *Metaphysica*, translated by W. D. Ross: *The Works of Aristotle* vol. VIII (Oxford: Oxford University Press, 1908).

Aron, R. (1964): '*Macht*, power, *puissance*: prose démocratique ou poésie démoniaque?', *European Journal of Sociology* 5: pp. 27–51. Reprinted in Lukes (1986a).

Aune, B. (1967): 'If', in *The Encyclopaedia of Philosophy*, ed. P. Edwards (New York: Macmillan) vol. 4, pp. 127–9.

Austin, J. L. (1956a): 'Ifs and cans', *Proceedings of the British Academy* 42: pp. 109–32. Reprinted in Austin (1970) pp. 205–32.

Austin, J. L. (1956b): 'A plea for excuses', *Proceedings of the Aristotelian Society* 57: pp. 1–30. Reprinted in Austin (1970) pp. 175–204.

Austin, J. L. (1970): *Philosophical Papers* (second edition; Oxford: Oxford University Press).

Ayers, M. R. (1968): *The Refutation of Determinism* (London: Methuen).

Bachrach, P. and Baratz, M. S. (1962): 'Two faces of power', *American Political Science Review* 56: pp. 947–52. Reprinted in Bell (1969).

Bagehot, W. (1867): *The English Constitution* (Glasgow: Collins, 1963).

Bahr, S. J. (1972): 'Comment on "The Study of Family Power Structure: A Review, 1960–1969"', *Journal of Marriage and the Family* 34: pp. 239–43.

Balinski, M. L. and Young, H. P. (1982): *Fair Representation: Meeting the Ideal of One Man, One Vote* (New Haven: Yale University Press).

Ball, T. (1976): 'Review of S. Lukes, *Power*, and J. Nagel, *The Descriptive Analysis of Power*', *Political Theory* 4: pp. 246–9.

Ball, T. (1993): 'Power', in R. E. Goodin and P. Pettit, eds, *A Companion to Contemporary Political Philosophy* (Oxford: Blackwell).

Banzhaf, J. F. (1965): 'Weighted voting doesn't work: a mathematical analysis', *Rutgers Law Review* 19: pp. 317–43.

Barnes, B. (1988): *The Nature of Power* (Cambridge: Polity Press).

Barry, B. (1974): 'The economic approach to the analysis of power and conflict', *Government and Opposition* 9: pp. 189–223.

Barry, B. (1976): 'Power: an economic analysis', in B. Barry, ed., *Power and Political Theory* (London: Wiley) pp. 67–101. Reprinted in Barry (1991).

Barry, B. (1980a): 'Superfox', *Political Studies* 28: pp. 136–43.

Barry, B. (1980b): 'Is it better to be powerful or lucky?' *Political Studies* 28: pp. 183–94, 338–52. Reprinted in Barry (1991).

Barry, B. (1988a): 'The uses of "power" [review of P. Morriss, *Power*]', *Government and Opposition* 23: pp. 340–53. Reprinted in Barry (1991).

Barry, B. (1988b): 'Equal opportunity and moral arbitrariness', in N. E. Bowie, ed., *Equal Opportunity* (Boulder, Colorado: Westview Press).

Barry, B. (1989): *A Treatise on Social Justice,* Vol. I: *Theories of Justice* (London: Harvester-Wheatsheaf).

Barry, B. (1991): *Democracy and Power: Essays in Political Theory* I (Oxford: Oxford University Press, 1991).

Bartlett, R. (1974): *Economic Foundations of Political Power* (New York: Free Press).

Bell, R., Edwards, D. V. and Wagner, R. H., eds (1969): *Political Power: A Reader in Theory and Research* (New York: Free Press).

Benn, A. W. (1970): *The New Politics: A Socialist Reconnaissance* (London: Fabian Society Tract No. 402).

Benn, S. (1967): 'Power', in *The Encyclopaedia of Philosophy*, ed. P. Edwards (New York: Macmillan) vol. 6, pp. 424–7.

Benn, S. (1972): 'Hobbes on power', in M. Cranston and R. S. Peters, eds, *Hobbes and Rousseau* (New York: Anchor Books) pp. 184–212.

Benn, S. and Weinstein, W. (1971): 'Being free to act and being a free man', *Mind* 80: pp. 194–211.

Benton, T. (1981): 'Objective interests and the sociology of power', *Sociology* 15: pp. 161–84.

Benton, T. (1988): 'Review of P. Morriss, *Power*', *Sociology* 22: pp. 491–3.

Berlin, I. (1958): *Two Concepts of Liberty* (Oxford: Oxford University Press). Reprinted in Berlin (1969) pp. 118–72.

Berlin, I. (1969): *Four Essays on Liberty* (Oxford: Oxford University Press).

Blau, P. M. (1964): *Exchange and Power in Social Life* (London: Wiley).

Blood, R. O. and Wolfe, D. M. (1960): *Husbands and Wives* (New York: Free Press).

Bogdanor, V. (1983): *Multi-party Politics and the Constitution* (Cambridge: Cambridge University Press).

Brams, S. J. (1975): *Game Theory and Politics* (New York: Free Press).

Brams, S. J. (1976): *Paradoxes in Politics* (New York: Free Press).

Brams, S. J. and Fishburn, P. C. (1995): 'When is size a liability? Bargaining power in minimal winning coalitions', *Journal of Theoretical Politics* 7: pp. 301–16.

Braybrooke, D. (1973): 'Two blown fuses in Goldman's analysis of power', *Philosophical Studies* 24: pp. 369–77.

Brewster, K. (1983): 'The voluntary society', in S. McMurrin, ed., *The Tanner Lectures in Human Values* IV (Salt Lake City: University of Utah Press).

Buckle, S. (1988): 'Arguing from potential', *Bioethics* 2: pp. 227–53.

Buckle, S. (1990): 'Arguing from potential', in P. Singer, ed., *Embryo Experimentation: Ethical, Legal and Social Issues* (Cambridge: Cambridge University Press).

Butler, D. (1983): *Governing Without a Majority: Dilemmas for Hung Parliaments in Britain* (London: Collins).

Carmichael, S. and Hamilton, C. V. (1968): *Black Power: The Politics of Liberation in America* (Harmondsworth: Penguin).

Carr, D. (1979): 'The logic of knowing how and ability', *Mind* 88: pp. 394–409.

Carroll, L. (1871): *Through the Looking-Glass and What Alice Found There*, in *The Annotated Alice*, ed. M. Gardner (Harmondsworth: Penguin, 1970).

Cassinelli, C. W. (1966): *Free Activities and Interpersonal Relations* (The Hague: Martinus Nijhoff).

Chisholm, R. (1976): *Person and Object: A Metaphysical Study* (Le Salle, Illinois: Open Court).

Cohen, G. A. (1978): *Karl Marx's Theory of History* (Oxford: Oxford University Press).

Cohen, G. A. (1983): 'The structure of proletarian unfreedom', *Philosophy and Public Affairs* 12: pp. 3–33.

Cohen, G. A. (1993): 'Equality of what? On welfare, goods, and capabilities', in M. Nussbaum and A. K. Sen, eds, *The Quality of Life* (Oxford: Oxford University Press).

Coleman, J. S. (1971): 'Control of collectivities and the power of a collectivity to act', in B. Lieberman, ed., *Social Choice* (New York: Gordon & Breach) pp. 269–300.

Coleman, J. S. (1973): 'Loss of power', *American Sociological Review* 38: pp. 1–17.

Connolly, W. E. (1974/1983): *The Terms of Political Discourse* (first edition: Lexington, Mass.: D. C. Heath; second edition: Oxford: Martin Robertson).

Crenson, M. A. (1971): *The Un-Politics of Air Pollution: A Study of Non-Decisionmaking in the Cities* (Baltimore: Johns Hopkins Press).

Crocker, D. A. (1995): 'Functioning and capability: the foundations of Sen's and Nussbaum's development ethic, Part 2', in M. Nussbaum and J. Glover, eds, *Women, Culture and Development* (Oxford: Oxford University Press).

Cromwell, R. E. and Olson, D. H., eds (1975): *Power in Families* (New York: Wiley).

Cupit, G. (1996): *Justice as Fittingness* (Oxford: Oxford University Press).

Dahl, R. A. (1957a): 'The concept of power', *Behavioral Science* 2: pp. 201–15. Reprinted in Bell (1969).

Dahl, R. A. (1957b): 'A rejoinder', *American Political Science Review* 51: pp. 1053–61.

Dahl, R. A. (1961): *Who Governs? Democracy and Power in an American City* (New Haven: Yale University Press).

Dahl, R. A. (1963): *Modern Political Analysis* (first edition; Englewood Cliffs, New Jersey: Prentice Hall).

Dahl, R. A. (1965): 'Cause and effect in the study of politics', in D. Lerner, ed., *Cause and Effect: The Hayden Colloquium on Scientific Method and Concept* (New York: Free Press) pp. 75–98.

Dahl, R. A. (1968): 'Power', in *International Encyclopaedia of the Social Sciences*, ed. D. L. Sills (New York: Free Press) vol. 12, pp. 405–15.

Dahl, R. A. (1984): *Modern Political Analysis* (fourth edition; Englewood Cliffs, New Jersey: Prentice Hall).

Dahl, R. A. (1991): *Modern Political Analysis* (fifth edition; Englewood Cliffs, New Jersey: Prentice Hall).

Danto, A. C. (1973): *Analytical Philosophy of Action* (Cambridge: Cambridge University Press).

Day, J. P. (1977): 'Threats, offers, law, opinion and liberty', *American Philosophical Quarterly* 14: pp. 257–72.

Dowding, K. (1990): 'Ability and ableness: Morriss on power and counteractuals', *Government Department Working Papers*, 10 (Uxbridge: Brunel University).

Dowding, K. (1991): *Rational Choice and Political Power* (Aldershot: Edward Elgar).

Dowding, K. (1996): *Power* (Buckingham: Open University Press).

Drèze, J. and Sen, A. K. (1989): *Hunger and Public Action* (Oxford: Oxford University Press).

Dunn, J. (1979): *Western Political Theory in the Face of the Future* (Cambridge: Cambridge University Press).

Eccles, T. (1981): *Under New Management: The Story of Britain's Largest Worker Cooperative* (London: Pan).

Elshtain, J. B. (1985): 'Reflections on war and political discourse: realism, just war, and feminism in a nuclear age', *Political Theory* 13: pp. 39–57.

Elster, J. (1976): 'Some conceptual problems in political theory', in B. Barry, ed., *Power and Political Theory* (London: Wiley).

Elster, J. (1978): *Logic and Society* (London: Wiley).

Elster, J. (1979): *Ulysses and the Sirens* (Cambridge: Cambridge University Press).

Elster, J. (1980a): 'The treatment of counterfactuals: reply to Brian Barry', *Political Studies* 28: pp. 144–7.

Elster, J. (1980b): 'Reply to comments', *Inquiry* 23: pp. 213–32.

Felsenthal, D. S. and Machover, M. (1998): *The Measurement of Voting Power: Theory and Practice, Problems and Paradoxes* (Cheltenham: Edward Elgar).

Felsenthal, D. S. and Machover, M. (1999): 'Minimizing the mean majority deficit: the second square-root rule', *Mathematics of Social Sciences* 37: pp. 25–37.

Felsenthal, D. S. and Machover, M. (2000): *Enlargement of the EU and Weighted Voting in its Council of Ministers* (London: Centre for the Philosophy of Natural and Social Sciences, London School of Economics); available at www.lse.ac.uk/votingpower.

Felsenthal, D. S. and Machover, M. (2001): 'Myths and meanings of voting power: comments on a symposium', *Journal of Theoretical Politics* 13: pp. 81–97.

Ferguson, A. (1767): *An Essay on the History of Civil Society* (Cambridge: Cambridge University Press, 1995).

Fielding, G. and Liebeck, H. (1975): 'Voting structures and the square root law', *British Journal of Political Science* 5: pp. 249–56.

Fishburn, P. C. (1973): *The Theory of Social Choice* (Princeton: Princeton University Press).

Fogel, R. W. (1964): *Railroads and American Economic Growth* (Baltimore: Johns Hopkins Press).

Foucault, M. (1982a): 'Le sujet et le pouvoir', in M. Foucault, *Dits et écrits 1954–1988* (Paris: Gallimard, 1994) Vol. IV: pp. 222–43.

Foucault, M. (1982b): 'The subject and power', Afterword in H. Dreyfus and P. Rabinow, *Michel Foucault: Beyond Structuralism and Hermeneutics* (Chicago: University of Chicago Press).

Foucault, M. (2001): *Power (The Essential Works of Foucault 1954–1984* Vol. 3; ed. J. D. Faubion) (London: Allen Lane).

Fowler, H. W. (1968): *A Dictionary of Modern English Usage* (second edition, revised by Sir E. Gowers; Oxford: Oxford University Press).

Friedman, J. (1992): *Empowerment: The Politics of Alternative Development* (Oxford: Blackwell).

Gamson, W. A. (1975): *The Strategy of Social Protest* (Homewood, Illinois: Dorsey Press).

Garrett, G. and McLean, I. (1996): 'On power indices and reading papers', *British Journal of Political Science* 26: p. 600.

Garrett, G. and Tsebelis, G. (1999): 'Why resist the temptation to apply power indices to the European Union?', *Journal of Theoretical Politics* 11: pp. 291–308.

Garrett, G., McLean, I. and Machover, M. (1995): 'Power, power indices and blocking power: a comment on Johnston', *British Journal of Political Science* 25: pp. 563–8.

Gaventa, J. (1980): *Power and Powerlessness: Quiescence and Rebellion in an Appalachian Valley* (Oxford: Oxford University Press).

Geach, P. T. (1960): *Mental Acts* (London: Routledge & Kegan Paul).

Georgiou, P. (1977): 'The concept of power: a critique and an alternative', *Australian Journal of Politics and History* 23: pp. 252–67.

Gibson, Q. (1971): 'Power', *Philosophy of the Social Sciences* 1: pp. 101–12.

Godwin, W. (1793): *An Enquiry Concerning Political Justice*, ed. I. Kramnick (Harmondsworth: Penguin, 1976).

Goldman, A. I. (1968): 'Actions, predictions, and books of life', *American Philosophical Quarterly* 5: pp. 135–51.

Goldman, A. I. (1970): *A Theory of Human Action* (Englewood Cliffs, New Jersey: Prentice Hall).

Goldman, A. I. (1972): 'Toward a theory of social power', *Philosophical Studies* 23: pp. 221–68.

Goldman, A. I. (1974a): 'Power, time, and cost', *Philosophical Studies* 26: pp. 263–70.

Goldman, A. I. (1974b): 'On the measurement of power', *Journal of Philosophy* 71: pp. 231–52.

Goodin, R. E. (1980): *Manipulatory Politics* (New Haven: Yale University Press).

Grofman, B. (1982): 'Alternatives to single-member plurality districts: legal and empirical issues', in B. Grofman, A. Lijphart, R. B. McKay and H. A. Scarrow, eds, *Representation and Redistricting Issues* (Lexington, Mass.: D. C. Heath).

Grofman, B. and Scarrow, H. (1979): 'Iannucci and its aftermath: the application of the Banzhaf Index to weighted voting in the state of New York', in S. J. Brams, A. Schotter and G. Schwodiauer, eds, *Applied Game Theory* (Würzburg: Physica Verlag) pp. 168–83.

Hacker, A. (1964): 'Power to do what?', in I. L. Horowitz, ed., *The New Sociology: Essays in Social Science and Social Theory in Honor of C. Wright Mills* (New York: Oxford University Press).

Hacking, I. (1981): 'The archaeology of Foucault', *New York Review of Books*. Reprinted in Hoy (1986).

Harré, R. (1970): 'Powers', *British Journal for the Philosophy of Science* 21: pp. 81–101.

Harré, R. (1986): *Varieties of Realism: A Rationale for the Natural Sciences* (Oxford: Blackwell).

Harré, R. and Madden, E. H. (1975): *Causal Powers: A Theory of Natural Necessity* (Oxford: Blackwell).

Hart, H. L. A. (1955): 'Are there any natural rights?', *Philosophical Review* 64: pp. 175–91.

Haugaard, M. (1997): *The Constitution of Power: A Theoretical Analysis of Power, Knowledge and Structure* (Manchester: Manchester University Press).

Hobbes, T. (1651): *Leviathan*, ed. J. Plamenatz (London: Fontana, 1962).

Hobbes, T. (1655): *De Corpore*, in *English Works* vol. 1 (London: John Bohn, 1839).

Hoy, D. C., ed. (1986): *Foucault: A Critical Reader* (Oxford: Blackwell).

Hume, D. (1739): *A Treatise of Human Nature*, ed. L. A. Selby-Bigge (Oxford: Oxford University Press, 1888).

Isaac, J. C. (1987a): *Power and Marxist Theory: A Realist View* (Ithaca: Cornell University Press).

Isaac, J. C. (1987b): 'Beyond the three faces of power: a realist critique', *Polity* 20: pp. 4–31.

Jessop, B. (1976): 'On the commensurability of power and structural constraint', revised version of a paper first presented to the EGOS Symposium on 'power'.

Johnston, R. J. (1995a): 'The conflict over qualified majority voting in the European Union Council of Ministers: an analysis of the UK negotiating stance using power indices', *British Journal of Political Science* 25: 245–54.

Johnston, R. J. (1995b): 'Can power be reduced to a quantitative index – and if so, which one? A response to Garrett, McLean and Machover', *British Journal of Political Science* 25: pp. 568–72.

Johnston, R. J. (1996): 'On keeping touch with reality and failing to be befuddled by mathematics', *British Journal of Political Science* 26: pp. 598–9.

Kenkel, W. F. (1957): 'Influence differentiation in family decision making', *Sociology and Social Research* 42: pp. 18–25.

Kenny, A. (1975): *Will, Freedom and Power* (Oxford: Blackwell).

Kuhn, A. (1966): *The Study of Society* (London: Tavistock).

Kuhn, A. (1974): *The Logic of Social Systems* (San Francisco: Jossey-Bass).

LaRossa, R. (1977): *Conflict and Power in Marriage: Expecting the First Child* (Beverly Hills: Sage).

Lasswell, H. D. (1936): *Politics: Who Gets What, When, and How?* (New York: Whittlesey House).

Ledyaev, V. G. (1997): *Power: A Conceptual Analysis* (Commack, NY: Nova Science Publishers).

Lewis, D. (1973): *Counterfactuals* (Oxford: Blackwell).

Lewis, D. (1976): 'The paradoxes of time travel', *American Philosophical Quarterly* 13: pp. 145–52.

Lewis, D. (1997): 'Finkish dispositions', *Philosophical Quarterly* 47: pp. 143–58.

Lewis, O. (1959): *Five Families* (New York: Mentor Books).

Lewis, O. (1962): *The Children of Sanchez* (London: Secker & Warburg).

Lewis, O. (1970): *A Death in the Sanchez Family* (London: Secker & Warburg).

Lipsky, M. (1968): 'Protest as a political resource', *American Political Science Review* 62: pp. 1144–58.

Lipsky, M. (1970): *Protest in City Politics: Rent Strikes, Housing, and the Power of the Poor* (Chicago: Rand McNally).

Locke, J. (1689): *An Essay Concerning Human Understanding*, ed. M. Cranston (New York: Macmillan, 1965).

Locke, J. (1690): *The Second Treatise of Government*, in J. Locke, *Two Treatises of Government*, ed. P. Laslett (New York: Mentor Books, 1965).

Lucas, J. R. (1970): *The Freedom of the Will* (Oxford: Oxford University Press).

Luce, R. D. and Raiffa, H. (1957): *Games and Decisions* (New York: Wiley).

Lukes, S. (1974): *Power: A Radical View* (London: Macmillan).

Lukes, S. (1979): 'Power and authority', in T. Bottomore and R. Nisbet, eds, *A History of Sociological Analysis* (London: Heinemann) pp. 633–76.

Lukes, S., ed. (1986a): *Power* (Oxford: Blackwell).

Lukes, S. (1986b): 'Introduction', in Lukes (1986a).

McClelland, D. C. (1975): *Power: The Inner Experience* (New York: Irvington).

McDonald, G. W. (1980): 'Family power: the assessment of a decade of theory and research, 1970–1979', *Journal of Marriage and the Family* 42: pp. 841–54.

MacIntyre, A. (1971): 'Is a science of comparative politics possible?', in A. MacIntyre, *Against the Self-Images of the Age* (London: Duckworth).

McLachlan, H. V. (1981): 'Is "power" an evaluative concept?', *British Journal of Sociology* 32: pp. 392–410.

Mackie, J. L. (1973): *Truth, Probability and Paradox: Studies in Philosophical Logic* (Oxford: Oxford University Press).

Macpherson, C. B. (1973): *Democratic Theory: Essays in Retrieval* (Oxford: Oxford University Press).

Manley, J. F. (1970): *The Politics of Finance: The House Committee on Ways and Means* (Boston: Little Brown).

Mann, I. and Shapley, L. S. (1964): 'The a priori voting strength of the electoral college', in M. Shubik, ed., *Game Theory and Related Approaches to Social Behavior* (New York: Wiley).

March, J. G. (1966): 'The power of power', in D. Easton, ed., *Varieties of Political Theory* (Englewood Cliffs, New Jersey: Prentice Hall).

Martin, C. B. (1994): 'Dispositions and conditionals', *Philosophical Quarterly* 44: pp. 1–8.

Martin, C. B. (1996): 'Final replies to Place and Armstrong', in D. M. Armstrong, C. B. Martin and U. T. Place, *Dispositions: A Debate* (London: Routledge).

Martines, L. (1980): *Power and Imagination: City States in Renaissance Italy* (London: Allen Lane).

Marx, K. (1845): 'Theses on Feuerbach', in K. Marx and F. Engels, *Selected Works in One Volume* (London: Lawrence and Wishart, 1970).

Marx, K. (1867): *Capital*, Volume I (London: Lawrence and Wishart, 1974).

Mattern, R. M. (1980): 'Locke on active power and the obscure idea of active power from bodies', *Studies in History and Philosophy of Science* 11: pp. 39–77.

Miller, D. (1983): 'Constraints on freedom', *Ethics* 94: pp. 66–86.

Mills, C. W. (1956): *The Power Elite* (New York: Oxford University Press).

Mills, C. W. (1959): *The Sociological Imagination* (London: Oxford University Press).

Morriss, P. (1975): 'The pluralist case not proven: Hewitt on Britain', *British Journal of Political Science* 5: pp. 385–9.

Morriss, P. (1986): 'Being discriminating about discrimination', *Politics* 6 (no. 1): pp. 23–30.

Morriss, P. (1995): 'Review of K. Dowding, *Rational Choice and Political Power*', *Utilitas* 7: pp. 181–4.

Morriss, P. (1996): 'Qualified majority voting and power indices: a further response to Johnston', *British Journal of Political Science* 26: pp. 595–7.

Nagel, J. H. (1988): 'The marriage of normative values and empirical concepts: mutual integrity or reciprocal distortion?' in Shapiro and Reeher (1988).

Nozick, R. (1969): 'Newcomb's problem and two principles of choice', in N. Rescher, ed., *Essays in Honor of Carl Hempel* (Dordrecht: D. Reidel).

Nozick, R. (1974): *Anarchy, State and Utopia* (Oxford: Blackwell).

Ollman, B. (1976): *Alienation* (second edition; Cambridge: Cambridge University Press).

Olson, M. (1965): *The Logic of Collective Action* (Cambridge, Mass.: Harvard University Press).

Oppenheim, F. (1981): *Political Concepts: A Reconstruction* (Oxford: Blackwell).

Owen, G. (1982): *Game Theory* (second edition; New York: Academic Press).

Parent, W. A. (1974a): 'Freedom as the non-restriction of options', *Mind* 83: pp. 432–4.

Parent, W. A. (1974b): 'Some recent work on the concept of liberty', *American Philosophical Quarterly* 11: pp. 149–67.

Parry, G. and Morriss, P. (1974): 'When is a decision not a decision?', in *British Political Sociology Yearbook* Volume 1: *Elites in Western Democracy*, ed. I. Crewe (London: Croom Helm).

Partridge, P. H. (1963): 'Some notes on the concept of power', *Political Studies* 11: pp. 107–25.

Payne, J. L. (1968): 'The oligarchy muddle', *World Politics* 20: pp. 439–53.

Penrose, L. S. (1946): 'The elementary statistics of majority voting', *Journal of the Royal Statistical Society* 109: pp. 53–7.

Penrose, L. S. (1952): *On the Objective Study of Crowd Behaviour* (London: H. K. Lewis).

Peters, R. S. (1956): *Hobbes* (Harmondsworth: Penguin, 1967).

Pettit, P. (1997): *Republicanism: A Theory of Government and Freedom* (Oxford: Oxford University Press)

Pitkin, H. F. (1972): *Wittgenstein and Justice* (Berkeley: University of California Press).

Pollock, J. L. (1975): 'Four kinds of conditionals', *American Philosophical Quarterly* 12: pp. 51–9.

Polsby, N. W. (1963/1980): *Community Power and Political Theory* (New Haven: Yale University Press).

Poulantzas, N. (1969): 'The problem of the capitalist state', *New Left Review* 58: pp. 67–78. Reprinted in J. Urry and J. Wakeford, eds, *Power in Britain* (London: Heinemann, 1973) pp. 291–305.

Prior, E. (1985): *Dispositions* (Aberdeen: Aberdeen University Press).

Quine, W. V. O. (1952): *Methods of Logic* (London: Routledge & Kegan Paul, 1966).

Quine, W. V. O. (1953): *From a Logical Point of View* (Cambridge, Mass.: Harvard University Press).

Quine, W. V. O. (1960): *Word and Object* (New York: Wiley).

Rae, D. W. (1969): 'Decision rules and individual values in constitutional choice', *American Political Science Review* 63: pp. 40–56.

Rae, D. W. (1971): 'An estimate for the decisiveness of election outcomes', in B. Lieberman, ed., *Social Choice* (New York: Gordon & Breach) pp. 379–92.

Rae, D. W. (1981): *Equalities* (Cambridge, Mass.: Harvard University Press).

Rae, D. W. (1988): 'Knowing power: a working paper', in Shapiro and Reeher (1988).

Rawls, J. (1971): *A Theory of Justice* (Cambridge, Mass.: Harvard University Press).

Reeve, A. (1982): 'Power without responsibility', *Political Studies* 30: pp. 77–86.

Rescher, N. (1961): 'Belief-contravening suppositions and the problem of contrary-to-fact conditionals', *Philosophical Review* 70: pp. 176–96. Reprinted in Sosa (1975).

Rescher, N. (1964): *Hypothetical Reasoning* (Amsterdam: North-Holland).

Rescher, N. (1973a): *The Coherence Theory of Truth* (Oxford: Oxford University Press).

Rescher, N. (1973b): *Conceptual Idealism* (Oxford: Blackwell).

Rescher, N. (1975): *A Theory of Possibility* (Oxford: Blackwell).

Riker, W. H. (1964): 'Some ambiguities in the notion of power', *American Political Science Review* 58: pp. 341–9. Reprinted in Bell (1969).

Riker, W. H. and Shapley, L. S. (1968): 'Weighted voting: a mathematical analysis for instrumental judgements', in NOMOS X: *Representation*, ed. J. R. Pennock and J. W. Chapman (New York: Atherton) pp. 199–216.

Russell, B. (1938): *Power: A New Social Analysis* (London: George Allen & Unwin, 1975).

Ryan, A. (1965): 'Freedom', *Philosophy* 40: pp. 93–112.

Ryle, G. (1949): *The Concept of Mind* (London: Hutchinson).

Safilios-Rothschild, C. (1970): 'The study of family power structure: a review, 1960–1969', *Journal of Marriage and the Family* 32: pp. 539–52.

Safilios-Rothschild, C. (1972): 'Answer to Stephen J. Bahr's "Comment on 'The Study of Family Power Structure: A Review, 1960–1969'"', *Journal of Marriage and the Family* 34: pp. 245–6.

Said, E. W. (1986): 'Foucault and the imagination of power', in Hoy (1986).

Sen, A. K. (1987): *The Standard of Living*, ed. G. Hawthorn (Cambridge: Cambridge University Press).

Sen, A. K. (1990): 'Justice: means versus freedoms', *Philosophy and Public Affairs* 19: pp. 111–21.

Sen, A. K. (1993): 'Capability and well-being', in M. Nussbaum and A. K. Sen, eds, *The Quality of Life* (Oxford: Oxford University Press).

Shapiro, I. and Reeher, G., eds (1988): *Power, Inequality, and Democratic Politics: Essays in Honor of Robert A. Dahl* (Boulder, Colorado: Westview Press).

Shapley, L. S. (1953): 'A value for N-person games', *Annals of Mathematics*, Study No. 28, pp. 307–17.

Shapley, L. S. and Shubik, M. (1954): 'A method for evaluating the distribution of power in a committee system', *American Political Science Review* 48: pp. 787–92. Reprinted in Bell (1969).

Sheleff, L. (1978): *The Bystander* (Lexington, Mass.: Lexington Books).

Simon, H. A. (1953): 'Notes on the observation and measurement of political power', *Journal of Politics* 15: pp. 500–16. Reprinted in Bell (1969).

Simon, H. A. (1957): *Models of Man* (New York: Wiley).

Skinner, B. F. (1972): *Beyond Freedom and Dignity* (Harmondsworth: Penguin).

Sosa, E., ed. (1975): *Causation and Conditionals* (Oxford: Oxford University Press).

Spivak, G. C. (1992): 'More on Power/Knowledge', in T. E. Wartenberg, ed., *Rethinking Power* (New York: SUNY Press). Reprinted in D. Landry and G. MacLean, *The Spivak Reader: Selected Works of Gayatri Chakravorty Spivak* (London: Routledge, 1996).

Stalnaker, R. C. (1968): 'A theory of conditionals', in *Studies in Logical Theory*, ed. N. Rescher (*American Philosophical Quarterly* Monograph No. 2) pp. 98–112. Reprinted in Sosa (1975).

Steiner, H. (1974): 'Individual liberty', *Proceedings of the Aristotelian Society* 75: pp. 33–50.

Stevenson, C. L. (1944): *Ethics and Language* (New Haven: Yale University Press).

Straffin, P. (1977): 'Homogeneity, independence, and power indices', *Public Choice* 30: pp. 107–18.

Strodtbeck, F. L. (1951): 'Husband–wife interaction over revealed differences', *American Sociological Review* 16: pp. 468–73.

Tawney, R. H. (1931): *Equality* (London: George Allen & Unwin, 1952).

Taylor, C. (1984): 'Foucault on freedom and truth', *Political Theory* 12: pp. 152–83. Reprinted in Hoy (1986).

Taylor, R. (1966): *Action and Purpose* (Englewood Cliffs, New Jersey: Prentice Hall).

Titmuss, R. (1970): *The Gift Relationship* (Harmondsworth: Penguin).

Tooley, M. (1972): 'Abortion and infanticide', *Philosophy and Public Affairs* 2: pp. 37–65. Reprinted in J. Feinberg, ed., *The Problem of Abortion* (first edition; Belmont, California: Wadsworth Publishing, 1973).

Tooley, M. (1983): *Abortion and Infanticide* (Oxford: Oxford University Press).

TUC (1983): *Report of 115th Annual Trades Union Congress* (London: TUC).

Walters, R. S. (1967): 'Contrary-to-fact conditionals', in *The Encyclopaedia of Philosophy*, ed. P. Edwards (New York: Macmillan) vol. 2: pp. 212–16.

Walzer, M. (1983): *Spheres of Justice* (Oxford: Martin Robertson).

Ward, H. (1987): 'Structural power – a contradiction in terms?', *Political Studies* 35: pp. 593–610.

Wartenberg, T. E. (1988): 'The concept of power in feminist theory', *Praxis International* 8: pp. 301–16.

Wartenberg, T. E. (1990): *The Forms of Power: From Domination to Transformation* (Philadelphia: Temple University Press).

Weber, M. (1920): *The Theory of Social and Economic Organization* (New York: Free Press, 1947).

Westergaard, J. and Resler, H. (1976): *Class in a Capitalist Society: A Study of Contemporary Britain* (Harmondsworth: Penguin).

White, A. R. (1975): *Modal Thinking* (Oxford: Blackwell).

White, D. M. (1971): 'Power and intention', *American Political Science Review* 65: pp. 749–59.

Willinsky, J. (1994): *Empire of Words: The Reign of the OED* (Princeton: Princeton University Press).

Wolin, S. (1960): *Politics and Vision: Continuity and Innovation in Western Political Thought* (Boston: Little Brown).

Wormuth, F. D. (1967): 'Matched-dependent behavioralism: the cargo cult in political science', *Western Political Quarterly* 20: pp. 809–40.

von Wright, G. H. (1963): *Norm and Action: A Logical Enquiry* (London: Routledge & Kegan Paul).

von Wright, G. H. (1971): *Explanation and Understanding* (London: Routledge & Kegan Paul).

Wrong, D. H. (1979): *Power: Its Forms, Bases and Uses* (Oxford: Blackwell).

Young, R. A. (1978): 'Steven Lukes's radical view of power', *Canadian Journal of Political Science* 11: pp. 639–49.

Index